"There has never been a more complex and confusing idea in theology or biblical studies than justification by faith. And there has never been a scholar who has been more consistently helpful in thinking through this cardinal doctrine than Douglas Campbell. Campbell and DePue courageously intervene in troubled readings of Paul's thought which means they intervene in troubled readings of Christian life. This text rescues and restores a Christianity born in the freedom of God. I hope more people will see this beacon."

—WILLIE JAMES JENNINGS, ASSOCIATE PROFESSOR OF SYSTEMATIC THEOLOGY AND AFRICANA STUDIES, YALE DIVINITY SCHOOL

"Every time I read a Douglas Campbell work on the apostle Paul's gospel, I wonder if I have Paul wrong. Campbell's apocalyptic gospel challenges not only the standard views, and the new perspective, and the Paul within Judaism perspectives, but it challenges even lines in Paul's own writings. Whatever one thinks of the apocalyptic gospel as framed by Campbell and DePue, it is pastoral, it is filled with hope, and it is grounded entirely in a God who liberates humans utterly in Jesus Christ. You can disagree with them, but you cannot ignore them. If you ignore them, you will miss the glory of the gospel."

—SCOT McKNIGHT, PROFESSOR OF NEW TESTAMENT, NORTHERN SEMINARY

"A powerful argument for hearing Paul's gospel apart from the theory of justification. It is exciting to engage with the authors' fervor for a gospel about Spirit-enabled participation in Jesus's death and resurrection, resulting in transformative, life-giving liberation from sin and death. Deep concern for Jewish people and the condition of the church, combined with scholarly skill executed with graciousness, make this essential reading. The book offers challenge and refreshment to both scholars and church communities."

—L. ANN JERVIS, PROFESSOR EMERITA OF NEW TESTAMENT, WYCLIFFE COLLEGE, UNIVERSITY OF TORONTO

"The apostle Paul is a complex figure, whose writings are open to (mis)inter-pretations that can be enormously harmful. Not only do Douglas Campbell and Jon DePue offer a bulwark against hazardous uses of Paul, but they also provide a pastorally powerful message that will be an enormous source of hope, encouragement, and joy for so many. Moreover, they do so with a book that is beautifully crafted and highly engaging, while never ceasing to be sophisticated and profound."

—ANDREW TORRANCE, SENIOR LECTURER IN THEOLOGY, UNIVERSITY OF ST. ANDREWS

"The misrepresentation of Paul's account of justification has damaged our understanding of God's grace and the outreach of the church. The rigorous exegetical corrective of Campbell and DePue establishes that Paul's interpreta-tion of God and our transformation in Christ reflects a radically inclusive vi-sion—one with immense relevance for the Christian church and its witness to contemporary society. Throughout this outstanding monograph, the authors' argumentation manifests scholarship of the highest order but also a concep-tual clarity and coherence that reflect the profound logic of Paul's vision."

—ALAN J. TORRANCE, PROFESSOR EMERITUS OF SYSTEMATIC THEOLOGY, UNIVERSITY OF ST. ANDREWS

"This. THIS. If you want to have any hope of navigating the sludge, both subtle and obvious, in academic and popular books on Paul, THIS. You'll be given the keys for a beautiful, historically sensitive, and exegetically robust reading of Paul more clearly than perhaps anywhere else. Seriously, if you read that last sentence and don't get this book, then you've got trust issues as this book could literally change your life."

—CHRIS TILLING, HEAD OF RESEARCH AND SENIOR LECTURER IN NEW TESTAMENT, ST. MELLITUS COLLEGE

Beyond Justification

Beyond Justification

Liberating Paul's Gospel

DOUGLAS A. CAMPBELL
& JON DePUE

Foreword by Brian Zahnd

CASCADE *Books* · Eugene, Oregon

BEYOND JUSTIFICATION
Liberating Paul's Gospel

Cascade Books
An Imprint of Wipf and Stock Publishers
199 W. 8th Ave., Suite 3
Eugene, OR 97401

www.wipfandstock.com

PAPERBACK ISBN: 978-1-5326-7898-1
HARDCOVER ISBN: 978-1-5326-7899-8
EBOOK ISBN: 978-1-5326-7900-1

Cataloguing-in-Publication data:

Names: Campbell, Douglas A. (Douglas Atchison), 1961– [author]. | DePue, Jon [author]. | Zahnd, Brian [foreword writer]

Title: Beyond justification : liberating Paul's gospel / Douglas A. Campbell and Jon DePue ; foreword by Brian Zahnd

Description: Eugene, OR: Cascade Books, 2024 | Includes bibliographical references and index.

Identifiers: ISBN 978-1-5326-7898-1 (paperback) | ISBN 978-1-5326-7899-8 (hardcover) | ISBN 978-1-5326-7900-1 (ebook)

Subjects: LCSH: Bible.—Epistles of Paul—Theology. | Bible.—Epistles of Paul—Criticism, interpretation, etc. | Justification (Christian theology)—Biblical teaching. | Justification (Christian theology)—History of doctrines. | Faith—Biblical teaching.

Classification: BS2650.52 C367 2024 (paperback) | BS2650.52 (ebook)

01/02/24

From Jon

For my brother, Michael

I have imitated you (however annoyingly) because you imitate
Christ.

From Douglas

As always, for Rachel

". . . (anywhere
i go you go,my dear;and whatever is done
by only me is your doing,my darling) . . ."

e. e. cummings, "[i carry your heart with me(i carry it in]"

Contents

Foreword

Ever since the Reformation it has been fashionable in certain Protestant circles to speak blithely of the perspicuity of Scripture. A desire to democratize the Bible led to the wishful thinking that the proper interpretation of all Scripture is self-evident. But if anything is self-evident about the Bible, it is the glaring fact that a myriad of possible interpretations set forth by well-meaning exegetes compete for our allegiance. And this is never more the case than when we consider the Pauline epistles. The New Testament itself admits that when it comes to Paul's letters, "there are some things in them hard to understand" (2 Pet 3:16). So the notion that one can just open the Bible to Romans and easily grasp Paul's often dense arguments is wildly over-optimistic. Though it may offend our individualist and egalitarian aspirations, the truth of the matter is that we often need some scholarly assistance if we are to properly interpret our sacred text. Thankfully, the church has such scholars, among them Douglas Campbell and Jon DePue.

I am of the opinion that, other than the book of Revelation, no portion of the New Testament has been subjected to more misinterpretation than the Pauline corpus. There are several reasons for this. First of all, even when writing to contemporaries, Paul's sophisticated theology wasn't always easily grasped. But we are saddled with the additional disadvantage of reading from a distance of two thousand years. Between the composition of Paul's epistles and the modern reader there lies a chasm of linguistic, cultural, theological, and rhetorical distance. To bridge this gap we need assistance in translation of language, assistance in understanding Jewish thought in late antiquity, and, importantly, assistance in recognizing the rhetorical devices that Paul often employed when making his arguments.

Beyond Justification is the assistance we need to liberate Paul's gospel from a very long captivity to a fundamental misreading—a misreading that came about in large part from trying to read Paul's first-century letters through sixteenth-century lenses. This inherited misreading of Paul has become so pervasive that it is essentially considered *the* gospel—except that it is no such thing! This theological misreading of Paul, known as justification theory (JT), distorts the image of God into that of a severe sovereign whose glory is founded upon retributive justice. This is an egregious departure from the image of God as a loving Father—the image that is actually given to us by Jesus and Paul. The JT misreading of Paul has been the source of a host of theological errors that has both diminished the glory of God's unconditional love and vilified the Jewish people. It is high time that this abuse of Paul's theology come to an end. Or as Campbell and DePue say, "it is time for the JT tail to stop wagging the Pauline dog."

Beyond Justification sets forth a major breakthrough in Pauline interpretation—a breakthrough that really does liberate Paul's gospel from so much that has been confusing and misleading. Campbell and DePue convincingly show that the 10 percent of Paul's texts that are the source of JT should not be read as Paul's theology of salvation, but as Paul using a Socratic rhetorical device to set forth the arguments of his theological opponents—arguments that Paul then goes on to refute. Paul's theological opponents (known as "the teachers" in *Beyond Justification*) were legalistic Jewish believers who were harassing Paul's gentile converts, teaching that salvation for gentiles required Torah observance. The teachers seem to have had little or no understanding of the salvific accomplishment of Jesus' death and resurrection—they appear to have regarded the resurrection of Jesus as God's vindication of a righteous Torah teacher. For Paul, the resurrection of Jesus is not merely vindication, but the raising of the human race from our sinful, fleshly condition.

Paul's so-called JT texts are found primarily in his letters to Galatia and Philippi, where the teachers have already arrived and troubled Paul's converts, and in his letter to Rome, where Paul anticipates the soon arrival of these missionary teachers. In these letters, Paul employs the rhetorical devise of Socratic debate in reproducing and refuting the legalistic "gospel" of the meddlesome teachers. The catastrophic mistake in Pauline interpretation has been the failure to recognize these Socratic debates, and thus to conflate and confuse Paul's reproduction of the teachers' legalism with Paul's gospel of liberation. It is little wonder that read through the lens of JT, Paul's letters so often lack coherence. For if we fail to recognize the Socratic debates as such, we literally end up with Paul arguing with himself (and making no sense), instead of Paul arguing with the legalists (and making perfect sense).

I am forever grateful to Campbell and DePue for showing me this groundbreaking discovery. It's the sort of thing that once you see it, you cannot unsee it. And once you see it, it changes everything! Instead of a thin JT gospel—which is not Paul's gospel at all, but Paul's lampoon of a false gospel—we discover Paul's robust gospel, one that Campbell and DePue describe as a participatory, resurrectional, transformational gospel. At last we come to see that salvation is not achieved by retributive justice, but by participating in the death and resurrection of Jesus. Salvation is literally found "in Christ," as Paul says over and over. With Paul's gospel liberated from a conflation with the false gospel of the teachers, it becomes much bigger, bolder, better, and ultimately, far more universal—it is a gospel proclaiming salvation for Jews as Jews, and for gentiles as gentiles.

But alas I have run too far ahead. In my enthusiasm for Paul's participatory gospel as set forth in *Beyond Justification*, I have leapt all the way to the end of the journey, yet this is merely a foreword. So let me now step aside and entrust you to Douglas Campbell and Jon DePue as eminently capable guides to the exhilarating terrain of Paul's revelation of Jesus Christ. It's often been observed that it's not the learning that is hard, as much as the *un*learning. And for most of us, there's much to unlearn regarding what we have wrongly imagined as Paul's gospel. But if you will stick with Campbell's and DePue's patient unpacking of the problem and their careful setting forth of the solution, you will be richly rewarded with a clear vision of Paul's beautiful gospel of liberation.

BRIAN ZAHND

Acknowledgments

I (Jon) owe an incredible debt to the folks who have walked with me along my journey in both the academy and in the church. I first want to thank Douglas Campbell for giving me this opportunity to co-author a book. You may be a world-renowned Pauline scholar, but to me you are first and foremost a damn good Christian, mentor, and friend.

To my amazing religion and philosophy professors at Simpson College in Indianola, Iowa—Mark Gammon, Jan Everhart, Maeve Callan, and John Pauley: thank you for your commitment to me as a religion major with philosophical interests at that little liberal arts college. You helped me gain the confidence to pursue further theological education and to cultivate a passion for thinking and writing about God.

I also want to thank Brett Roes for being my best friend and embodying the unconditional love of Jesus that this book is really all about. Thanks to Ethan Taylor for being a wonderful friend and conversation partner on all things Paul and Barth; additionally, being a part of your band Beket has been a gift to me, both musically and spiritually. Joshua Musser-Gritter and Kollin Absher-Baer, both of you have helped me think theologically and pastorally about Paul in ways that you will probably never really know. To my parents, Jim and Josie, who let me bother them for years with late-night conversation about what I was learning in college and divinity school. Thank you to my former community of faith at Good Shepherd United Church of Christ in Cary, North Carolina—especially Rev. Carla Gregg-Kearns and Linda Velto. You all believed in me and embraced my ministerial strengths, and for that I will be forever grateful.

Most of all, I want to thank my incredible wife, and favorite New Testament scholar, Laura Robinson. Thank you for your constant support, for your love, for your brilliant insights, and for your undivided companionship.

And I (Douglas) want to thank, first of all, my co-author, Jon. If there is a Platonic form in heaven of the perfect co-writer, then that form looks like Jon DePue. He has been a model of patience, clarity, and insight, and I will always be grateful to him for his collaboration on this project, which I think has really brought out the best in me. I also thank, as always, my spouse, Rachel. Pretty much all the good ideas in my life have come from her, and this was just one more. I trust that she really is a channel of the Spirit, and it is just as well that at least one of us is listening properly. Michael Thomson was as welcoming and enthusiastic as he always is. I have greatly appreciated his support during a long literary gestation, along with the support of the entire team at Wipf & Stock. The beer-and-Barth boys are always important, and this project has been no exception—Jeff, Alan, Andrew, Chris, Ethan, Chris (Cheeto), and now Austin, along with Jon. And Andrew Rillera (ably supported by Heather Griffin), deserves special mention. His tracking within his Duke doctoral dissertation (defended July 2021) of the influence on Paul's opposition from Philo is critical to much that we ultimately suggest here. His dissertation is not yet published so we must simply, a little unfortunately, acknowledge his programmatic importance here. His insights inform much that follows. Thank you Andrew (and Heather). Jackson Shepard has kicked in with energy and help at several crucial moments. And I am grateful to my other students at Duke for their support, which is both increasingly important to me and greatly appreciated. I particularly remember an encouraging comment by Claire Shelnutt.

I once asked a group of students in a Pauline theology class which text a puzzled student would be best to consult to get a quick fix "on Campbell on justification." Claire, who had been in other Paul classes with me, blurted out instantly "*Beyond Justification!*" I knew at that moment that our labors were not in vain. Thank you, Claire.

Abbreviations

JT   Justification Theory
NPJ   "The new perspective on Judaism"
NPP   "The new perspective on Paul"

Introduction

We have written this book because, at bottom, we believe that God is at stake. We don't mean God *per se* obviously; it is a central thesis of this book that God takes care of God. But our *witness* to God is at stake, and a great deal rides on this. If our proclamation—in the original Greek *euangelion* or "gospel"—is off, then the church is off, and our influence on surrounding society is off, and it is increasingly apparent where we live, in the USA, that this is the case. The "gospel" frequently being proclaimed, which so many people hear and associate with God and with the work of Jesus on our behalf, is damaging, aggressive, and hurtful, and this is clearly a great tragedy on many levels. More than this: it is a crisis. And at the heart of this crisis is our understanding of Paul.

Paul is the key figure for Protestants, and Protestants are the key players in the current vicious spiral between the church and American culture. So where Paul goes, with his gospel, most American Protestants follow— veritable legions of well-organized followers both here and, increasingly, abroad. And there is something badly off about how Paul is being read and proclaimed for much of the time as these legions march. Indeed, our deepest conviction is that for much of the time the proclamation is just plain wrong. The wrong God is being announced, the wrong account of Jesus, and bound up with this is a distorted account of those on the outside of the church, with an especially damaging definition framing Jews. A great deal of damage is being done in the name of Christ as authorized by Paul.

Fortunately, we only know this because we already know the true gospel—which is not, we hasten to add, something we have discovered for ourselves; it is a gift from God. And in the light of this we can see that it is not so much that the wrong gospel is being proclaimed and that is the end of the matter (although it can be). The situation is more subtle, as one might expect, when evil is involved. The right gospel is still present in much Protestant teaching, but it has been cleverly reframed so that its key truths have been lost. It has been overlaid, obscured, and marginalized. Moreover, even as many scholars have grasped that something is wrong and have tried to fight their way back to the truth, the battle itself has been confused and frequently misdirected. We have often been boxing the air. So the crisis continues, while those who cannot cope with the damage quietly exit a church that they do not want to leave but can no longer endure.

We hold, however, that there is a clear path through the mayhem to the truth—to the recovery of Paul's authentic gospel in all its wondrous power, and to the ensuing renewal of church life and cultural engagement. We think that there are some basic underlying reasons that explain both the capture of Paul's gospel by a "gospel" unworthy of that name, and why so much subsequent discussion has been confused and ineffective. The problem has not yet been correctly identified. And when it is, the route to a solution becomes apparent.

This book tracks the pathway to clarity through a series of realizations. We will travel from a description of the problem that damages our reading of Paul on multiple levels, as well as the church that reads him so devotedly, to its solution, by way of the insights and difficulties of some of the most significant readers of Paul, and ultimately through Paul's texts themselves where the key problems lie—in the way many are reading his powerful letter to the Romans. But the journey begins, as it must, with the gift of the gospel by God to us.

We begin, that is, with revelation, and with a revelation focused on Jesus Christ. Everything begins here, and unfolds from here, and Paul himself attests clearly to this starting point with his famous encounter with Jesus as he was near Damascus. Since this gospel grounds everything that follows, we spend some time unpacking this Christ-centered revelation through the first three chapters. It is vital that we understand the mode in which truth is present here (so chapter 1), the God it attests to (so chapter 2), and the way it understands the work of Christ on our behalf (so chapter 3). Here, that is, we recall that Paul knows a God who is characterized fundamentally by revelation and by love. And he proclaims our salvation on the basis of what Jesus has done for us as he came to us as a person made of flesh, faithfully walked to the cross, died, was buried, was raised, and ascended. In other words, all of the Easter events are critical to the account Paul gives us of what salvation is, resulting in what we call a "participatory," "resurrectional," and "transformational" gospel. And the role of the Spirit is vital here as well, resulting in an implicitly trinitarian account of God's activity among us, from which it follows that the great ecumenical creeds affirm our developing description. Paul refers to this gospel in a very abbreviated way by using the short phrase "in Christ," or something very similar, and when we see this connection, we also see that this theology characterizes just over 90 percent of what he wrote.

With this foundation in place—a foundation not built by human hands—we turn to our besetting problem. Why is the proclamation of Paul by so many in the church so off? And it is here that our readers will require a little courage.

We introduce in chapter 4 our hypothesis that a particular model of the gospel that is very different to what we have just set out is nevertheless frequently present within much teaching on the basis of Paul. Indeed, it is often presented as *the* gospel according to Paul. But we hold that it is *not*, and for reasons that will become increasingly clear. We will trace the damaging consequences of this false gospel through several chapters that follow. But first we must know what it is. So here we use a famous, and beautifully clear, book by John Piper, *The Future of Justification*, to articulate the structure and details of the problematic gospel that we hold is distorting. Piper can be taken as a faithful representative of this widespread view of Paul.

This model of salvation has two characteristic phases or stages that track the journey of an anxious non-Christian (or Jew) to salvation, from "works of law" to "faith." It is often known as "justification" because the texts it relies on in Paul frequently use the Greek verb *dikaioō* to frame this journey, and translators usually translate this Greek word in that way. So we will refer to this model of salvation as "justification theory" or JT in what follows. It is often presented as the correct account of salvation in Paul—or at least as the place where any account of salvation in Paul should begin—on the basis of 10 percent of what he wrote (and in fact just under 10 percent: it is frequently held to be the right reading, counting at times rather generously, of 172 of the 1,791 verses written by Paul and appearing in our Bibles, JT material occurring principally in Romans and Galatians).[1]

With this alternative model of the gospel, JT, clearly in place, we turn to consider the various difficulties that its announcement causes.

First of all, in chapter 5, we lay out the deep contradictions that are present between the participatory, resurrectional gospel we began with, which we hold to be true, and an account of the gospel in terms of JT. These contradictions occur even as we simply read through Romans. Justification

1. We have excluded the Pastorals from consideration here (i.e., 1 and 2 Timothy and Titus). If they are included then the percentage of JT in Paul drops much further. It really only occurs, even arguably, in 1 Tim 3:16, where the verb is used. Note, many scholars would work with fewer letters than we do, excluding Ephesians, Colossians, and 2 Thessalonians from Paul's authentic letters. This judgment increases the prevalence of JT—and we suspect it is often partly because of their loyalty *to* JT that this judgment of exclusion is made.

theory dominates the interpretation of chapters 1 through 4 and then a participatory account kicks in from chapter 5. Justification theory only then makes a relatively brief reappearance in chapter 10, Paul utilizing participatory arguments and presuppositions on both sides of this shorter discussion. How do we resolve the tensions here? We consider Philip Melanchthon's famous solution in terms of a "justification-sanctification sequence," but find it wanting. And our problems are only just beginning.

In chapter 6 we highlight the fundamental level at which the tensions between our opening account of the gospel and JT play out. These tend to be glossed over but we need to face them squarely. Paul's theology is riven with the most profound fault-lines if both these theories of salvation stay in play. With these realizations in place, we then pivot to consider in several chapters the major problem that has captured the most attention of scholars, and this needs to be introduced in a brutally honest fashion.

For the last fifty years Paul's interpreters have been carefully reexamining how he characterizes Jews because—of course—we have witnessed the horrors of the Holocaust. But, as chapter 7 describes, it has become apparent that not only was this an unprecedented attack on the existence of the modern Jewish people by a fundamentally Christian nation; it was rooted in centuries of Christian teaching about the Jews in derogatory terms—the infamous "teaching of contempt." This terrible history, in which the church is so complicit, has mandated a careful reexamination of how Jews are handled in Paul's texts, and the results have been sobering.

We track this engagement through three of its key representatives in three subsequent chapters. In chapter 8 we describe the main contributions of E. P. Sanders. Sanders does not really offer solutions as much as describe and deepen this particular interpretative problem in a learned and unavoidable fashion in relation to Paul. Sanders shows us that when Paul is read in the usual way, his descriptions of Jews are both mean-spirited and unfair in light of what the Jewish sources from his day reveal about Jews. Examining those ancient Jewish sources is what Sanders does at length. In the writings of many Jews in Paul's day we find a very different and very reasonable view of the Jews and their approach to salvation—something Sanders calls "covenantal nomism." And this discovery leaves us with a nasty problem on our hands. What are we to do with Paul's arguments that seem to describe Jews so harshly and apparently unfairly and inaccurately? Is his gospel based on a combination of misrepresentation and sheer racism—and against his own people?!

Two key protagonists have stepped forward and dominated much debate in this relation with a so-called "new perspective" on Paul that ostensibly solves the problems caused by the "new perspective on Judaism" associated with Sanders and his post-Holocaust insights: J. D. G. Dunn and N. T. Wright. So we look carefully at their approach in subsequent chapters but, while finding several of their insights helpful, nevertheless conclude that their solutions to this painful problem fail to convince. We are left then, at the end of this sequence, with another, powerful, problem in place in relation to Paul's interpretation: his apparent utterly unfair characterization of Jews as mean-spirited legalists—and this problem plays directly into a mean-spirited characterization of non-Christians in general. The crisis of Pauline interpretation has deepened.

The tensions present in relation to how we read Paul seem pretty extreme by this point in our analysis—because they are—and the stakes are also clearly very high. The integrity of the gospel is at stake. But we do have a solution that we propose will resolve the situation, to which we turn.

It seems best to present this solution first in overview. So in chapter 11 we identify what we take to be the key culprit and then sketch out the basic contours of our solution. The spectrum of tensions resolved unsatisfactorily by Melanchthon, the further tensions modern theologians and scholars detect between two basic models of salvation operating in Paul alongside one another, and the appalling description of Jews that is so acutely painful and dangerous in a post-Holocaust age, are all, it turns out, generated by the presence of JT within Paul's description. It is JT that is *demonstrably* doing the damage at all these places. And so at this critical moment we simply have to ask if JT is really the *right* reading of Paul.

Justification theory does after all only lay claim to about 10 percent of what Paul wrote, and it is spelled out in full in parts of just one letter, Romans. So might it not be the expectation that JT is present in Paul that has led to it being found in his letters? If so, by removing that expectation—in the way that we might take off a pair of rose-tinted glasses—might we see that Paul is saying something a little different in these texts? We go on to argue that this is in fact the case.

If the texts that are usually held to speak of JT are really talking about something else then we eliminate JT from Paul and, hey presto, all our problems disappear; the tensions between JT and Paul's participatory and resurrectional gospel, along with Paul's ostensibly rather vicious description of Jews, vanish. But we clearly need to offer a responsible, close reading of Paul's JT texts to achieve this—one that does not activate JT—and so the rest of the book walks through how we do this.

In some respects, our suggested alternative is very close to the readings offered by advocates of JT, but this should not be surprising. Justification theory readers can be very attentive and accurate readers of Paul. We argue, however, that at a few critical moments they have overinterpreted Paul's arguments, and JT has snuck into the gaps in these ancient texts and flipped a few key commitments around, finding itself by doing so. When this process is detected and resisted, Paul's JT texts turn out to be talking about something that is very similar at a basic *textual* level to JT but very different at the *theological* level. A "justification" reading of Paul's texts parts way at this moment with JT. And if our solution holds up, then JT is no more and our problems are solved.

We sketch out this alternative reading rather programmatically in chapter 11 in relation to a very famous but abbreviated JT text: Galatians 2:15–16. So far so good. But we then turn to the decisive interpretative encounter. Justification theory is really only spelled out by Paul in full—if it is—in Romans. So we need to show how our alternative reading works in detail through all the key texts in Romans. If JT is eliminated from Romans then JT is really gone. But this is a fairly complicated interpretative journey so we break it down into manageable steps.

First we address, in chapter 12, Romans 1:18—3:20, which is really the key to the problem and to the solution. This is where JT launches, from an apparent failure by a Jew to be "justified through works of law." But we show how this approach badly misunderstands what Paul is trying to do, and we offer a different interpretation of Paul's argument that subtly but significantly reorients it. Several features of the text that JT struggles to account for are resolved by our new approach, so we are confident that it is the correct one.

We then turn to Paul's faith texts, which arrive in a very famous paragraph in Romans, 3:21–26 (although this was cryptically anticipated by 1:16–17). We begin to treat this paragraph in chapter 13, but the analysis of "faith" in Paul raises broader and very important questions, so we track two important debates within Pauline studies through two subsequent chapters. In chapter 14 we show how "faith" in Paul often refers to *Jesus's* faith: the faith he displayed as he steadfastly walked to the cross, obeying the hard command of his heavenly Father. In chapter 15 we then explore how Paul uses Scripture—for him the OT—to point repeatedly to Jesus and to what he has done for us. These two debates then join hands and open up Paul's JT texts still further, placing Jesus's faith in the center of his arguments, and so by chapter 16 we are ready to engage Paul's great treatment of faith in relation to Abraham, which really begins from 3:27, going on to dominate chapter 4.

Romans 4 is considered one of the great bastions of JT so we have to tread carefully. We analyze the first half of Romans 4 in chapter 16, showing how our reading seems to be more sensitive to the different argumentative steps Paul takes here. Then, in chapter 17, we turn to consider the description of Abraham's extraordinary faith that Paul undertakes in the second half of Romans 4. Scholars of all persuasions seldom know quite what to do with this part of the chapter, and it is a particular problem for JT advocates, but we are able to show how this material integrates smoothly with our developing alternative reading.

By this point, our reinterpretative journey will almost be complete. It will remain only to show in chapter 18 how our approach to Romans chapter 10 also integrates smoothly into what we have been saying—and how the curveballs that that chapter might be throwing at our approach can be handled without too much trouble. And with this done, our rereading journey is complete. All the JT texts in Romans will have been interpreted faithfully and accurately, but in a way that does not activate the *theory* of justification; when we are aware of the influence of JT on our reading, we can compensate for that and see that Paul is really talking in these texts about something else.

At this point then, our journey in search of a more coherent—and a kinder—Paul will be complete. We will be back where we began, affirming the participatory, resurrectional, and transformational gospel that we started our analysis with in the first three chapters, but able to do so without confusion and subversion. And our teaching from Paul will be simpler, clearer, and more powerful because of this. Paul's true gospel—a gospel that liberates—will itself have been liberated.

1

God's Truth

How do we know the truth about God?

Reading Paul in a constructive way will involve us constantly in claims about God. In fact, is there any point in reading Paul if we are *not* constantly involved in claims about God?! But we will never get anywhere with any important claims about God if we do not sort out some key questions up front, and these start with God's relationship with us right here and right now. We need to think hard about who God is, which means that in the same breath we must think hard about *how* we know about God. A little counterintuitively, how we learn about God determines who we think God is, because how we find God leads to *where* we find God, and that in turn tells us *who* God is. And the stakes are high as we try to answer these questions.

If we start off on the wrong foot, all our claims about God are likely to be compromised and possibly quite severely. We might think we know about God and are speaking accurately about his ways but in fact we aren't. Irreversible distortions and misrepresentation will ensue and this book will address several of those in due course. Conversely, if we grasp onto the correct way of learning and speaking about God, we need to hold on to that as if our lives depend on it (which, ultimately, they do). Many forces will try to draw us away into confusion and deception.

So what exactly are we supposed to be grasping on to? What is the right way of learning about God, and of speaking accurately and truthfully about him? Where do we find out what God is really like?

It is our strongest recommendation that we accept at the outset the humbling fact that we are not in charge of this process. We grasp the truth about God *only because God has first grasped us.*[1] The term theologians generally use to describe the disclosure of the truth about God by God himself is "revelation," which literally means "unveiling." God unveils himself to us and thereby shows us what he is like.

Paul attests clearly to this process at work in his life. At the beginning of his letter to the Galatians he tells his listeners,

> I did not receive [the gospel proclamation][2] from a human
> source,
> nor was I taught it,
> but I received it through a revelation of Jesus Christ.
> (Gal 1:12)[3]

Let us not move past what Paul says here too quickly. These are important words. He is suggesting at least two crucial things: first, he did not receive his gospel from other people around him; and, second, he received it, rather, by a direct revelation from God. And this might strike us initially as very odd.

When we want to learn about most questions, gaining some initial understanding through investigations done by others who know more than we do seems to be the obvious course of action. If I want to learn what a car engine is and how it functions I would do well to find a car manual, to talk to a mechanic, or to watch a YouTube video on the subject. But this is not the case for Paul and his knowledge of God. As much as we would like to think that we can know God through intense study, building on the insights of others—perhaps these days by a quick glance at a Wikipedia page or even an inquiry by way of AI—Paul is clear that he did not receive his insight by sitting at the feet of a learned teacher. As he puts it on one occasion, God's wisdom does not come by listening to a sage, an academic, or an intellectual.[4] Neither did he receive it by reading the best texts he could get his hands

---

1. Gal 4:9: "Now, however, that you have come to know God, or rather to be known by God, how can you turn back again to the weak and beggarly elemental principles? How can you want to be enslaved to them again?" Phil 3:12: "Not that I have already obtained this or have already reached the goal; but I press on to lay hold of that for which Christ has laid hold of me."

2. The word "gospel" in Greek, *euangelion*, really denotes an official proclamation or declaration made by diplomats or ambassadors. So, for example, in the history of the USA, an important place is occupied by the "*Declaration* of Independence," made in 1776, and, later on, by "the Emancipation *Proclamation*" made in 1863.

3. Unless otherwise noted, all translations are from the NRSVue.

4. 1 Cor 1:20: "Where is the one who is wise? Where is the scholar? Where is the debater of this age? Has not God made foolish the wisdom of the world?"

on, scriptural or otherwise. (He was deeply learned in the Scriptures when he was persecuting Jesus's body on earth, the church, and so clearly not learning the key things about God from the Scriptures that he needed to.) The truth about God came to him more directly, abruptly, and concretely, as a revelation *of* Jesus Christ and *by* Jesus Christ.[5] And what Christ reveals is not "*a* truth among other truths";[6] it is not one gospel proclamation alongside other equally valid and compelling gospels.[7] Christ's revelation is *the* proclamation, and there is no other.[8]

Someone might ask here how we can be so sure that a process of divine revelation was this central to Paul's understanding of the God. But there is plenty of good evidence that this was the case. On several occasions Paul appeals to the dramatic shift in the direction of his life that resulted from his encounter with Jesus. He was coursing in one way, wholeheartedly, and then suddenly he was heading in a very different direction as an apostle. It follows that some sort of dramatic intervention by God had taken place to effect this shift; a revelation had broken into his misguided activity and reoriented him completely. Certainly he did not generate this for himself, and

5. The Greek in Gal 1:12 can be read in both these ways, the rest of the letter suggesting that both meanings are ultimately in some sense appropriate.

6. This language comes from the great twentieth-century Swiss theologian Karl Barth's *The Epistle to the Romans*, 35.

7. Gal 1:6–7: "I am astonished that you are so quickly deserting the one who called you in the grace of Christ and are turning to a different gospel—not that there is another gospel, but there are some who are confusing you and want to pervert the gospel of Christ."

8. Paul emphasizes the divine agency operative in this revelation here in Galatians because he wants to set it so sharply over and above alternative accounts of the gospel that lay claim to human tradition and to transmission by way of the apostles. We will see in due course how this revelation can be mediated through human and textual channels, as Paul notes explicitly in texts like 1 Cor 15:1–7: "Now I want you to understand, brothers and sisters, the good news that I proclaimed to you, which you in turn received, in which also you stand, through which also you are being saved, if you hold firmly to the message that I proclaimed to you—unless you have come to believe in vain. For I handed on to you as of first importance what I in turn had received: that Christ died for our sins in accordance with the scriptures and that he was buried and that he was raised on the third day in accordance with the scriptures and that he appeared to Cephas, then to the twelve. Then he appeared to more than five hundred brothers and sisters at one time, most of whom are still alive, though some have died. Then he appeared to James, then to all the apostles."

However, even when the truth about God is received through either people or the things people are involved with creating, Paul is clear that any perception or reception of the truth still rests fundamentally in the hands of God. So, for example, in the same letter in which he notes a role for human transmission, he notes the importance of the work of the Spirit. 1 Cor 2:10: "God has revealed to us through the Spirit, for the Spirit searches everything, even the depths of God."

in fact this journey by Paul that was so dramatically interrupted by God's revelation is worth dwelling on a little longer.

In the same discussion in Galatians during which he speaks of God's revelation of his Son Paul also speaks of his "earlier life." He had moved quickly past his peers in his understanding of the ancient Jewish traditions and was zealously persecuting Jewish non-conformists. (This persecuting activity that we just noted was a disastrous mistake that we will talk more about shortly.) His letter to the Philippians provides further details about all this.

Paul was "circumcised on the eighth day, a member of the people of Israel, of the tribe of Benjamin, a Hebrew born of Hebrews; as to the Torah, a Pharisee; as to zeal, a persecutor of the church; as to righteousness under the Torah, blameless" (3:5–6 NRSVue modified).[9] It is worth emphasizing that Paul gives no indication here that he was plagued by a sense of guilt. There is nothing to suggest that he had a particular problem arising from his Jewish practices. On the contrary, he clearly thought that he was doing the will of God and doing it better than pretty much everyone else. As we just read, he thought he was "blameless." But the zealous advocate of Torah and its Jewish commentary suddenly became the ardent advocate of pagans joining the Jesus movement—an entirely different career trajectory. God had suddenly interrupted his work with this radical new vocation.

This intervention contains a further critical dynamic as well. God's unveiling of himself through Jesus frequently reveals something wrong with us that we did not know about at the time. This misguided sin may even be intertwined with our previous piety to a degree that we previously found impossible to distinguish. The very thing we were doing *for* God can turn out to be something that we are doing ourselves *against* God thereby *resisting* God and in the name of God! But only in the light of the revelation of Jesus Christ does this become evident, accentuating why it is so important both to begin with this revelation and to cleave to it through thick and thin. Our previous conceptions about God and God's will might need to be significantly corrected, as Paul's were.

So Paul states in Galatians not only that he was an educated advocate of Jewish tradition who turned in a sudden about-face to missionary work among the pagan nations, but that before this he was "violently persecuting the assembly of God's people [i.e., Jesus's followers in the early church] and trying to destroy it" (1:13, our translation). Now Paul's previously violent life as a Pharisee is certainly not meant to be read as a universal description

---

9. In certain settings the translation of the Greek *nomos* by "Torah" (literally "sacred teachings") rather than "law" as used by the NRSVue is preferable.

of all Jews, or even of all Pharisees. In the aftermath of the Holocaust, we need to be very careful not to construe Paul's account of his past involvement with a particular group of over-zealous Jews as an accurate account of Jews more broadly—an extremely dangerous generalization.[10] But it is clear nevertheless that Paul himself was part of what we would now consider to be a kind of terrorist group—a religiously motivated death squad—whose particular interpretation of its Scriptures and traditions led them to endorse violence against those whom they thought were unacceptably different. Paul and his colleagues presumed that God was a God who commissioned people to punish and to kill those who were interfering with God's righteous purposes.

Hence in Acts' developing story of the early church we meet Paul as he stands approving of the lynching of Stephen outside of the city of Jerusalem.[11] Then, at the beginning of chapter 8, Paul personally instigates "a severe persecution" against the Jerusalem church, "entering house after house," "dragging off both men and women . . ." to prison (vv. 1–3). After this Paul decides to head to Damascus to arrest even more people who "belonged to the Way," "breathing threats and murder against the disciples of the Lord" (9:2, 1).[12] And it is at this moment that God's purposes interrupt Paul's. Jesus is revealed—unveiled—from heaven.

> Now as [Paul] was going along and approaching Damascus,
> suddenly a light from heaven flashed around him.
> He fell to the ground and heard a voice saying to him, "Saul,
> Saul, why do you persecute me?"
> [Paul] asked, "Who are you, Lord?"
> The reply came, "I am Jesus, whom you are persecuting."
> (Acts 9:3–5)

This event is often called Paul's "conversion." However, the word conversion can be unhelpful because it is frequently used to refer to a moment in a person's life when they decide that Jesus is Lord and join the church, leaving a previous life of unbelief behind. In a related way, it can refer to dramatic changes between religions: "I heard that Frank went to college in

10. This concern will be addressed more directly in later chapters.

11. Acts 7:58—8:1: "Then they dragged him out of the city and began to stone him; and the witnesses laid their coats at the feet of a young man named Saul. While they were stoning Stephen, he prayed, 'Lord Jesus, receive my spirit.' Then he knelt down and cried out in a loud voice, 'Lord, do not hold this sin against them.' When he had said this, he died. And Saul approved of their killing him."

12. Paul's confirmations of this zealous persecuting activity render moot the strictly historical question whether this happened in Jerusalem and Damascus, or simply in the latter. See 1 Cor 15:8–9; Gal 1:13; Phil 3:6.

Florida and converted to Islam." But Paul does not use the ancient word for conversion to refer to this event in his life, and neither does he suggest that he switched religions and left his Jewish tradition behind. On the road to Damascus he was grasped instead by the *fulfillment* of the religion he was *already* a part of—a fulfillment, to be sure, that he wasn't expecting. So it is significant that Paul describes his experience of the risen Lord by using the language of "call," thereby echoing the prophetic call narratives in the Jewish Scriptures in general, and the call of Jeremiah, the prophet to the pagan nations, in particular.[13] This call language emphasizes God's sovereignty over the entire process.[14] The divine Lord made a claim on Paul's life as he reached out to commission him in the way that he also commissioned his prophets of old. However, this call was certainly an unexpected one that involved a massive reorientation.

It goes without saying that the fundamental direction of Paul's life changed markedly after this call. Indeed, it was not long before Paul was proselytizing on behalf of Jesus in synagogues where previously he had been hunting down Jesus's followers and trying to eradicate them (9:19b–22). In Paul's own words, he was now "proclaiming the loyalty that previously he was persecuting" (Gal 1:23, our translation). And this is all good evidence of the importance of revelation. The unveiling of Jesus to Paul on the road to Damascus was now *the* key truth, not to mention, the key relationship, from which all Paul's other activities would depart—and some of those departures involved the painful recognition that activities he previously considered pious and good were in fact misguided and destructive. His persecutions undertaken in the name of God turned out to be directed against God. It must have been a humbling realization.

But before we develop this last point, we need to press a little more deeply into the revelation that has just taken place and that lies at the heart of everything else. Paul learned something critical about God from this revelation. God had actively and dramatically altered his understanding of God by way of Jesus. But what did Paul learn exactly?

13. Jer 1:4–10: "Now the word of the LORD came to me saying, 'Before I formed you in the womb I knew you, and before you were born I consecrated you; I appointed you a prophet to the nations.' Then I said, 'Ah, LORD God! Truly I do not know how to speak, for I am only a boy.' But the LORD said to 'Do not say, I am only a boy; for you shall go to all to whom I send you, and you shall speak whatever I command you. Do not be afraid of them for I am with you to deliver you, says the LORD.' Then the LORD put out his hand and touched my mouth; and the LORD said to me, 'Now I have put my words in your mouth. See, today I appoint you over nations and over kingdoms, to pluck up and to pull down, to destroy and to overthrow, to build and to plant.'"

14. It also subtly suggests that Paul, like Jeremiah, would be sent to the pagan nations, and not just to the Jews.

We get an important clue from some statements that he makes in his first letter to the Corinthians, although, like all of Paul's theological insights, his claims are embedded within a discussion of practical matters.[15]

The Corinthians

In 1 Corinthians 8 Paul is responding to a particular point of tension arising at Corinth from the eating of meat that had been butchered by priests in a local temple and so dedicated to its pagan gods. Various members of Paul's congregation at Corinth viewed eating such meat as an act of idolatry; these would have been Jesus-followers more influenced by Jewish practices.[16] This issue might seem somewhat petty to us, but I am sure that if presented with the dilemma of whether or not we should eat a Big Mac that had first had its meat patty offered to Norse gods out the back of the outlet, many Christians today would probably have a lot to say. Paul goes on to offer a subtle set of instructions that is sensitive to both sides involved. But more important to us than the issue is the way that he begins his argument and what he bases it on.

Paul's advice begins with the quotation of an important Jewish confession drawn from the Bible. This confession was so treasured that many Jews, including Paul, would have recited it multiple times per day. We find it in full in Deuteronomy 6:4, which begins, "Hear, O Israel: The LORD is our God, the LORD alone. . . ." This confession, called the *Shema* after the Hebrew word for "hear," was widely held to be a key statement concerning Israel's God, and it continues in verse 5 of Deuteronomy with the famous

15. Strictly speaking, this was his second letter to the Corinthians, but the first has not been preserved in our Bibles. It is referenced and described a little in 1 Cor 5:9–13: "I wrote to you in my letter not to associate with sexually immoral persons—not at all meaning the immoral of this world, or the greedy and robbers, or idolaters, since you would then need to go out of the world. But now I am writing to you not to associate with anyone who bears the name of brother or sister who is sexually immoral or greedy, or is an idolater, reviler, drunkard, or robber. Do not even eat with such a one. For what have I to do with judging those outside? Is it not those who are inside that you are to judge? God will judge those outside. 'Drive out the wicked person from among you.'"

16. We use the phrase "Jesus-followers" to describe them here and elsewhere because they were not, strictly speaking, "Christians." Christians were converts to the Jesus movement from paganism. See Acts 11:26: "And when [Barnabas] had found [Saul], he brought him to Antioch. So it was that for an entire year they met with the church and taught a great many people, and it was in Antioch that the disciples were first called 'Christians.'" Jews who followed Jesus were not Christian converts. They were messianic Jews, and even more specifically, they were Jews who held Jesus of Nazareth to be the Messiah. The early church was composed of Jesus-followers, and included *both* Christian converts from paganism *and* messianic Jews.

words, "You shall love the Lord your God with all your heart, and with all your soul, and with all your might." But Paul does not quote this confession in 1 Corinthians from Deuteronomy verbatim. He inserts some interesting additional material—and perhaps we need to pause here for a moment to think about what it would be like if a pastor in our own church inserted some extra clauses into the Nicene Creed and then proceeded to address a local issue from the pulpit on that basis! Yet this is basically what Paul does with the *Shema* when he writes,

> Yet for us there is one God,
> the Father,
> from whom are all things
> and for whom we exist;
> and one Lord,
> Jesus Christ,
> through whom are all things
> and through whom we exist.
> (1 Cor 8:6)

A first reading of these statements suggests that Paul now thinks that there is one God known as "the Father" and another figure called "the Lord," who is Jesus, and these two beings are separate from one another.[17] But this is not quite right. Paul is not suggesting that the Father is simply God and Jesus is some lower-ranking sidekick so that the two gods now operate a bit like a celestial Batman and Robin. Rather, Paul has included Christ quite precisely *within* the wording of the *Shema*, distinguishing between the two figures of the Father and the Lord all the while subtly holding onto their unity *and* their divinity. Paul describes both the Father and Jesus as creating all things, which is an activity that the Jewish Scriptures generally attribute to God alone. Similarly, the title "lord" given to Jesus here is not in this setting the title merely for someone inhabiting a superior social or political position, equivalent in Paul's day to calling someone "sir." Jews used the word "Lord" in place of the sacred divine name for God in the Scriptures—YHWH—which was so holy that it was not even to be said aloud. So Paul's insertion of Jesus into the confession about Israel's one God who is referred to as "the Lord our God" by the words of Deuteronomy suggests that he is using the term "lord" to demonstrate Christ's *divine* identity. It is clear then that Paul's encounter with the risen Jesus has taught him in some deep way

17. Paul's use of "Father" (and, later, of "Son") is not meant to be read as gendered; that is, Paul does not actually think that God is male. Rather, he is drawing on explicitly familial language to drive home the fact that God is a *personal* and relational God—a divine family of persons in relationship. We will talk more about this important dimension in God shortly.

that Jesus is "*the* Lord," which is to say in our language, Jesus is God as well. God is not limited to the person of Jesus, because we see Paul speaking immediately of God the Father, but from now on for Paul and the Corinthians the truth about God must include Jesus.[18]

These new insights into God focused on Jesus will lie at the heart of everything that follows. They reoriented Paul's life around two thousand years ago and they still orient our lives today.

Most Christians around the world attend churches that follow a familiar order of worship on Sunday mornings, and it is common at some point to hear the words of one of the creeds echoing in unison through the sanctuary. So the Nicene Creed begins,

> We believe in God, the Father Almighty,
> maker of heaven and earth,
> of all things visible and invisible;
> and in one Lord Jesus Christ,
> the only Son of God,
> begotten from the Father before all ages,
> God from God,
> Light from Light,
> true God from true God,
> begotten, not made,
> of one being with the Father.

Such creeds provide precise summaries of what Jesus-followers over the centuries hold to be true and accurate about the nature of God as revealed by Jesus. They also show us that an accurate grasp of this truth is central to the very identity of the church. They clarify and repeat the basic truth about God that has been revealed to us. And they basically say that when we see Jesus we see God.

We really need to let this truth sink in. We now understand in the light of this that there is simply no "part" of God hiding behind Jesus waiting to be found; there is no divine nature that is more real or true than Jesus. Jesus *is* God and he reveals the very nature of God fully. So, as the Nicene Creed emphasizes, the Son is "God from God, Light from Light, true God from true God." If you want to see what God is like you look at Jesus. The answer to every question from now on about God is *Jesus* (with one or two qualifications that we will note shortly, but with no mitigations!). This is *where* we

---

18. A superb recent study of Paul's Christology and its implication for the nature of God is Chris Tilling's *Paul's Divine Christology* (2015). His work builds on two classic analyses: Richard Bauckham, *Jesus and the God of Israel* (2008); and Larry W. Hurtado, *One God, One Lord* (2nd ed., 1998).

know what God is like, and it is *what* we know God is like. (Where we find God dictates what sort of God we find, we might recall.)

An important question arises for us at this moment, however. If people have not had Damascus Road experiences like Paul, how do they know about the God revealed through Jesus because clearly not everyone has had this sort of dramatic, undeniable encounter?

The Spirit

Once again, the Corinthian situation provides us with some important answers. As far as we know, the Corinthians had not had a "Damascus Road" experience like Paul, but they still knew the God revealed through Jesus. How? Paul writes in chapter 2 about how the community at Corinth came to grasp the truths that he himself had learned so dramatically near the city of Damascus.

> Now we have received not the spirit of the world,
> but the Spirit that is from God,
> so that we may understand the gifts bestowed on us by God.
> And we speak of these things in words not taught by human
> wisdom but taught by the Spirit,
> interpreting spiritual things to those who are spiritual.
> (1 Cor 2:12–13)

The Corinthians did not simply figure out what God is like by drawing on their own intuitions, nor did they gain this information from a teacher's elegantly crafted instructions—by his own admission, Paul was anything but a compelling communicator.[19] Instead, God became present among the Corinthians *through the activity of the Holy Spirit*. This Spirit, who searches the "depths of God," *revealed* God's secrets to the Corinthians, disclosing "what no eye has seen, nor ear heard, nor human heart conceived" (2:9–10). In other words, a revelation took place, and the Holy Spirit thereby communicated to the Corinthians, in a profound and deep way, what God is like. The Spirit was revealing Jesus through Paul's teachings and other actions but the basic agent at work within this event, driving it and shaping it, was God's Spirit.

As a result of this dynamic, we can perhaps begin to see how the church's understanding of God as the Trinity began to take shape, which

---

19. 2 Cor 10:10b notes that Paul's speaking was judged "despicable" by the learned Corinthians, which is to say, they considered it uneducated, unrefined, and embarrassingly crude.

is something all the creeds go on to affirm. And three figures are now discernible bringing God near to us: God the Father, Jesus his Son and our Lord, and the Holy Spirit. Further, we can now grasp why Paul sums up his understanding of this God at the end of his second letter to the Corinthians in the following compact but profoundly insightful blessing:

> The gift of the Lord Jesus Christ,
> the love of God,
> and the partnership of the Holy Spirit
> be with you all.
> (2 Cor 13:13, our translation)

It is a fairly common phenomenon in some Christian circles to describe our relationship to God as a process of "searching" for God, perhaps as a journey at the end of which someone eventually finds God. And, of course, journeys make sense to us. Our brains enjoy compelling stories of discovery. What would J. R. R. Tolkien's perennial favorite *The Lord of the Rings* be without its fellowship of motley companions embarking on an epic journey to Mount Doom? However, this way of framing things presumes that people are basically in control of their own salvation. We formulate our goals and set out on our expeditions and adventures. We can see at this point, however, that Paul understood humanity's relationship with God the other way around. It may be construed as a journey of sorts but it is a story of God journeying all the way down to us. In the person of Jesus, God comes to humanity, coming still further through the Holy Spirit, gathering people into his family. In this journey God finds us and discloses to us what he is really like, so a Trinity of divine persons is working together to draw us back to God.[20]

But someone might still be asking: "Is it really enough to learn that Paul and his Corinthian community were convinced that God had revealed himself definitively in the person of the Lord Jesus and by the power of something they called the Holy Spirit? How does this matter for *us* in our communities of discipleship roughly two thousand years after Paul wrote his letters and the Corinthians listened to them? Putting things bluntly, thus far we have only really discovered that Paul and his communities were convinced of Jesus's Lordship—*Paul* and *his communities*. And this does not help us all that much in *our* contemporary locations other than giving us historical insight into how one first-century Jew and his converts thought

---

20. Karl Barth uses the parable of the prodigal son as an image to say that Christ travels into the far country of our humanity to draw us back to God. See his famous subsection "The Way of the Son of God into the Far Country," in *Church Dogmatics, vol. IV, pt. 1*, ch. 18, § 59, s. 1, pp. 157–210.

God had acted in the world. How do *we* know without a shadow of a doubt that Paul's claims about God being revealed through Jesus are accurate?"

And we would reply, like Paul, "Because the same process of revelation still holds—because the same God actively reveals himself to us in just these terms, in just this way, right here and right now."

In Jon's tradition, the United Church of Christ, we like to say that "God is still speaking; don't put a period where God put a comma." This is as profound as it is catchy. The only way we grasp the truth about God is for God to grasp us by telling it to us again and again and again. Why? Because God is in charge of the truth, and neither Paul nor any of the other authors of the New Testament can inhabit his position of revealer. As broken and fractured beings, we have no capacity in and of ourselves to measure or to validate the truth about God. God alone shares it with us and validates it for us.

Fortunately, those of us in the church have most likely experienced God telling us in one way or another that he is fully and completely present for us through Christ and the Spirit. Some may have experienced Christ's revelation directly in such a way that they are able to point to a specific moment when Jesus took hold of their lives; we have heard or perhaps even shared our own testimonies about suddenly being overwhelmed by God's presence. For others, God's arrival is experienced progressively, perhaps through significant relationships with other people, and over quite long periods of time. In these cases, it is much more difficult to identify a specific time when Christ revealed himself. But this doesn't matter. There are many different ways in which Christ's revelation can be mediated to us and it is wise for us not to limit God's freedom to reveal the things of God through avenues that seem best to us. God will reveal himself through Christ wherever and however the Spirit delights to do so.[21] The important thing is the conviction that God has in fact done this.

But if we are still a little unsure about all this it might be worth noting that further markers of the rightness of this way of thinking about the truth of God are the centrality of *witness* and *confession* to our lives. In the light of revelation, we voice our conviction that God is present with and for us in Christ. Hence we affirm the truth in response to its revelation by *confessing* it and *witnessing* to it—by attesting to its truth. (And this is of course what we are doing right now.)

God *is* alive, God *is* still speaking, and God *is* present here as the Father and his Son Jesus Christ through the power and the partnership of the Holy Spirit. As we realize and confess this together we can see that Paul, his

---

21. John's Gospel also knows this well, speaking of how "the wind blows where it chooses" (3:8).

communities, and we modern Christians, along with any messianic Jews who follow Jesus, are actually convinced of the same Lordship of Jesus and in much the same way. The same Lord rules us all. The same process of revelation and the same conviction of God's full presence in the person of Jesus through the power of the Spirit has extended through space and time, from century to century, to take hold of people within the one, eternal, and loving embrace of the triune God. We have joined our hands across the ages with Paul and the Corinthians confessing together that Jesus is Lord and that the Spirit has been present with us leading us into all truth.[22] Moreover, now that we have joined in this confession, we attest to the fact that the deepest truth about God is revealed by Jesus Christ and by the Spirit of Christ. All other claims about God will now be measured against Jesus; all our God-talk will be brought into subjection at his feet.[23]

But things do not stop with our confession of this truth, central as it is. To be sure, we have grasped the truth about God that is Jesus even as the truth that is this God has grasped us. But Jesus has grasped us for a very important reason and it is time to investigate this. God has revealed himself to us for the same reason that he has created us in the first place: he loves us and has a wonderful plan for our lives.

22. See John 16:13: "When the Spirit of truth comes, he will guide you into all the truth; for he will not speak on his own, but will speak whatever he hears, and he will declare to you the things that are to come."

23. 2 Cor 10:5b.

2

God's Love

Does God really love us?

The saying is true and worthy of full acceptance that God loves us and
has a wonderful plan for our lives.[1] But it is tragic that so many people
struggle so hard to believe this, when to do so allows us to live lives of joyful
partnership with a loving God. It is not as if the question of God's love for us
is either uninteresting or unasked.

Now it is obviously possible for someone to ask this question out of
mere curiosity, but there are often important existential reasons for asking
it as well. Maybe we have made some kind of a mistake and feel so ashamed
that we cannot really believe that there is a God who chooses to remain
committed to us. Perhaps this feeling has led us to think that we are unworthy of being in God's presence. Maybe deep down we believe that we
need to earn our way into God's heart first, or perhaps we think that we
continually mess up and so squander the chance that we will ever be loved
by God. Maybe the preaching and teaching that we have heard in the church
has even underscored this way of thinking about God. Or perhaps we have
been deeply hurt and broken down by a parent, a partner, a friend, or even a
church community, which has left us feeling dirtied and unlovable. It seems

---

1. The is the first of the well-known "Four Spiritual Laws," formulated by Bill Bright
for Campus Crusade. Bright based his four laws on "the Roman Road," but added this
first law to the progression because he felt that the other laws began in too negative a
way, quoting Rom 3:23, and other scriptural texts to suggest that all humanity is sinful
and under God's wrathful judgment. He based this first, more positive law on John 3:16
and 10:10.

that so much is at stake for so many people at this moment that the question of God's love needs to be answered with absolute clarity. Fortunately for us, Paul is quite sure that God does love us and he has his usual rock-solid reasons for this confidence.

We began to lay the basis for this confidence in the preceding chapter when we observed how both Jesus and the Spirit are at work actively gifting to people "the knowledge of God's mystery, that is, Christ" (Col 2:2). This was the dynamic at the heart of Paul's experience with the risen Lord, and it was how Paul's converts in Corinth became convinced of the truth. We saw in those two places how three distinct actors were working together as one God to reveal themselves: the Spirit, the Lord Jesus (whom Paul also calls "the Son"), and the Father. But we need to ask now what this God who has so fully disclosed himself to us through Jesus and the Spirit is really like and what his resulting purposes for us are.

The answer to the first critical question here begins to emerge as we reflect on the fact that this God is composed of persons, specifically, of the three persons of the Trinity. Paul is quite clear that God the Father sent his Son Jesus so that through him humanity would be drawn back to him, a journey that involved the Son's rejection, suffering, and death, followed by his resurrection, enthronement, and heavenly acclamation.[2] Complementing the journey of the Son, the Spirit indwells, affirms, and suffers with humanity as we wait for Jesus's return.[3] And all this divine activity reveals, among other things, that God is intrinsically *personal*. God is so personal that he is *constituted* by his persons. There is one God comprising three persons, and this has important implications for us since we are persons created in the image of the personal God.

---

2. Phil 2:5–11: "Let the same mind be in you that was in Christ Jesus, who, though he existed in the form of God, did not regard equality with God as something to be grasped, but emptied himself, taking the form of a slave, assuming human likeness. And being found in appearance as a human, he humbled himself and became obedient to the point of death—even death on a cross. Therefore God exalted him even more highly and gave him the name that is above every other name, so that at the name given to Jesus every knee should bend, in heaven and on earth and under the earth, and every tongue should confess that Jesus Christ is Lord, to the glory of God the Father."

3. Rom 8:9–11: "But you are not in the flesh; you are in the Spirit, since the Spirit of God dwells in you. Anyone who does not have the Spirit of Christ does not belong to him. But if Christ is in you, then the body is dead because of sin, but the Spirit is life because of righteousness. If the Spirit of him who raised Jesus from the dead dwells in you, he who raised Christ Jesus from the dead will give life to your mortal bodies also through his Spirit that dwells in you." Rom 8:16: "[I]t is that very Spirit bearing witness with our spirit that we are children of God. . . ." Rom 8:23: "And not only the creation, but we ourselves, who have the first fruits of the Spirit, groan inwardly while we wait for adoption, the redemption of our bodies."

God the Father is who he is, the divine parent, *because he has a Son*, which means that his relationship with his Son *establishes who he is*. Without his Son he is not the Father. A father is only a father because he has a child. So the Father needs the Son to be who is, namely, the Father. And the same dynamic applies in reverse to the Son. Jesus is the Son *because* he has a Father who has sent him to us. The Father enables him to be the Son and so the same relationship thereby determines his identity as the Son. In just the same way we infer that the Spirit is the Spirit *of* the Father and *of* the Son. In terms of ancient thinking about the composition of persons (although not, to be sure, trinitarian thinking), a spirit is a critical part of a person so this language is telling us that the Spirit is inconceivable without those of whose Spirit it is. Without the Father and the Son then the Spirit is not the Spirit either.

These realizations generate a critical insight into the nature of personhood. The divine persons are tightly bound up with one another—so much so that we cannot think of one person apart from another. Their relationships with one another make them who they are as persons. But it follows from this that all persons, made in God's image—which we are—are defined in the same way: by their relationships with one another. Human persons too are relational to the point that being relational is what makes them persons.

We can think about this in terms of healthy families where we can now see that the identities of parents and children are primarily constituted by their relationships with one another,[4] although deep friendships deliver the same definitional impact as well. Our own parents are who they are in relation to one another and then as they relate to us and to our siblings. And we are who we are in relation to our parents and our siblings. Without them we, Jon and Douglas, would not be who we are at our deepest levels—sons and brothers—while without us our brothers and sister and parents would not be who they are, namely, our brothers, our sister, and our parents. These things define who they and we actually are. We constitute one another because our identities are inextricably bound up with one another. These relationships are what make us who we are as people.

If, led by the Trinity, we have grasped the deeply relational nature of persons then we are ready to take a further important step. The relationships intertwining people together, whether perfectly in God or imperfectly

4. Sadly, many families do not deliver healthy personhood, visiting various forms of brokenness and harm on their members. Indeed, perhaps because of their very importance delivering relational identity, they can also deliver some of the most painful and tragic distortions of this truth. Fortunately, it seems that a single committed relationship can still go a long way—a grandparent, aunt or uncle, sibling, cousin, friend.

within human families and friendships, are relationships of a certain specific type. They are relationships of *love*. Certainly God is a set of persons constituted by relationships of perfect love.

In a section of near incomparable importance Paul tells his listeners in Rome that "God proves his own love for us in that while we still were sinners Christ died for us" (Rom 5:8). The very nature of God is made clear here as the Father offers up his beloved Son to die for humanity even as humanity faces God in hostility and hatred. Before people even responded to God appropriately the Father undertook this supremely costly act on their behalf, and so with no guarantee of a response, and the Son obediently endured his fate. This is another critical truth then that we need to let sink down into our bones, although it is also deeply shocking. God died for his enemies while they were still his enemies and with no guarantees that they would ever leave that posture. And the only explanation for this can be God's extraordinary love for humanity. *God loves his enemies enough to die for them.* Mind blowing. It is no surprise then to find Paul praying in Ephesians for help from God to even begin to grasp the dimensions of this love.

> For this reason I bow my knees before the Father,
> from whom every family in heaven and on earth takes its name.
> I pray that, according to the riches of his glory,
> he may grant that you may be strengthened in your inner being
> with power through his Spirit,
> and that Christ may dwell in your hearts through faith,
> as you are being rooted and grounded in love.
> I pray that you may have the power to comprehend, with all the
> saints, what is the breadth and length and height and depth
> and to know the love of Christ that surpasses knowledge,
> so that you may be filled with all the fullness of God.
> (Eph 3:14–19)

This God of three persons is a God of love—a love so deep and vast that we lack the capacity to imagine or to understand it. And we can see now that God has taken us here still deeper into the revelation of himself. He has revealed through Jesus's death on our behalf that his nature is a limitless ocean of love between the Father, the Son, and the Spirit, an ocean that overflows to encompass humanity even when that humanity has turned against him.

It is also worth emphasizing here in passing that the information we have just received concerning God's loving nature is not something we derive from our own conceptions of love, which might be influenced a little too much by the latest pop song or rom-com. It is not simply a cultural construct.

Rather, it is a love that we can only see clearly when we pay close attention to how God has evidenced it through the activity of his Son and his Spirit. Paul is saying that Jesus reveals what God is like, specifically in his supremely costly death, and he has revealed that God is love. So here and only here can we be confident that we know what love looks like—by gazing on the cross—and we can now begin to grasp that this is what God is really like.[5]

But it follows from this that God has *always* been like this, from "before" the foundation of the world ("before" being in scare quotes because we cannot speak literally of something happening in a temporal way before time itself was created). This is an important development in our understanding of God that we should pause to explore a bit more.

God's electing love

There is a common narrative in the church today that says that the God witnessed to by the Hebrew Bible was a God of wrath and fury, but the New Testament shows that Jesus is a new, and presumably better, God of love. There was an angry God back then, but later on in history a different God showed up and revealed his true nature. But we need to say quite strongly here that God did not change to become more loving when Jesus arrived. Rather, the one who is both human and divine, Jesus, provides us with the clearest picture of what God has been like *all along*—a communion of love that has existed prior to the creation of the cosmos. Indeed, it is this loving communion that *explains* the creation of the cosmos.

It is almost obvious to suppose that this loving God would create people outside of the divine communion and go on to invite them into a relationship of love with it. Love shares itself with others. Paul articulates this programmatic cosmic insight compactly in Romans chapter 8 when he writes,

> For those whom [God] foreknew he also predestined
> to be conformed to the image of his Son,
> in order that he might be the firstborn
> within a large family.
> (Rom 8:29)

This verse says nothing less than that our communion with God, bearing the image of the resurrected Son, is the point of the cosmos. It is the goal of all history. Given its importance then it might be worth expanding on

---

5. Note also that, according to Paul, the cross reveals God's love for us. We will talk in more detail about just how it does this in the next chapter.

the larger story alluded to by this verse, which Paul does at the beginning of Ephesians.

Douglas has argued elsewhere that the letter we know by the name Ephesians was probably the letter written by Paul to a community in Laodicea that he had yet to meet. Colossians, which was written at the same time, speaks of this companion letter and this destination in 4:16.[6] (Laodicea and Colossae were just half a day's walk apart, and were situated in the same river valley in what is now western Turkey.) More important than its destination, however, was the letter's place of origin.

Paul penned "Ephesians" from jail. (He was probably locked up, Douglas suggests, somewhere to the east of Colossae, possibly in the important town of Apamea. This town lies between Colossae and the region of Galatia, in what is today central Turkey.) Paul's incarceration meant that he had ample time in the forced downtime of the jail to craft a letter carefully. However, being in this location also meant that he was in a serious situation. Being detained before trial in a Roman jail always meant the possibility of being executed. So Paul was aware that this might be his last chance to introduce an unknown group of converts to all of the good news about Jesus. Moreover, this community in Laodicea did not know Paul personally and so he had not taught them directly. Fortunately for us then Paul had to write things out in full—and this is the only letter in which he really did this. "Ephesians" is consequently the closest thing we have to a systematic

---

6. "And when this letter has been read among you, have it read also in the church of the Laodiceans, and see that you read also the letter from Laodicea." This meant making copies of the letters. For the detailed arguments see Douglas's *Framing Paul: An Epistolary Biography*, 309–38; and *Paul: An Apostle's Journey*, 83–89. The name "Ephesians" was a much later guess made by scribes copying out full editions of the Bible. Our earliest manuscripts of the Bible have a blank space where the place name should be. Possibly earlier scribes omitted the name Laodicea from their editions of the New Testament because they were shocked that a church written to so eloquently by Paul could end up in the mess described by Revelation 3:14–22: "And to the angel of the church in Laodicea write: The words of the Amen, the faithful and true witness, the origin of God's creation: I know your works; you are neither cold nor hot. I wish that you were either cold or hot. So, because you are lukewarm, and neither cold nor hot, I am about to spit you out of my mouth. For you say, 'I am rich, I have prospered, and I need nothing.' You do not realize that you are wretched, pitiable, poor, blind, and naked. Therefore I advise you to buy from me gold refined by fire so that you may be rich; and white robes to clothe yourself and to keep the shame of your nakedness from being seen; and salve to anoint your eyes so that you may see. I reprove and discipline those whom I love. Be earnest, therefore, and repent. Listen! I am standing at the door, knocking; if you hear my voice and open the door, I will come in and eat with you, and you with me. To the one who conquers I will give a place with me on my throne, just as I myself conquered and sat down with my Father on his throne. Let anyone who has an ear listen to what the Spirit is saying to the churches."

theology from Paul. It answers the question, "What does it mean to be a group of Christians?"

In view of all this it is inordinately important that Paul begins his account with God's love, expanding its reach through time and space. He freights this theology in the Jewish form of a blessing in which God's love evokes an act of praise. In a single sentence which stretches from verse 3 in chapter 1 all the way to verse 14—in what seems like a single breath—Paul describes God's loving plan for us as Jesus has revealed this, blessing God for doing so throughout. He begins,

> Blessed be the God and Father of our Lord Jesus Christ,
> who has blessed us in Christ
> with every spiritual blessing
> in the heavenly places,
> just as he chose us
> in Christ
> before the foundation of the world
> to be holy and blameless before him. . . .
> (Eph 1:3–4)

The first two verses of the blessing reveal when God's plan actually began. Contrary to what we might expect, Paul does not begin narrating this story with creation. Rather, he suggests that God's purposes have been set in place, and irrevocably so, from *before* the foundation of the cosmos. God's decision for us, to choose us, took place at that "time," in Christ. We know then that God's love for us preceded creation. But what was the purpose of this election, as theologians call it (drawing literally on the Greek word for "choice," *eklegomai*), that God effected before the creation of the world, and before God's Spirit swept over the face of the waters of the formless earth?[7]

Through Jesus Christ, God

> . . . destined us for *adoption* . . .
> according to the good pleasure of his will,
> to the praise of his glorious grace
> that he freely bestowed on us
> in the Beloved.
> (Eph 1:5–6, emphasis added)

"Adoption" was a common occurrence in Paul's day so his audience in Laodicea would have understood exactly what he was trying to say. Given high infant mortality in the ancient world, people often adopted youths into

---

7. Gen 1:2: "[T]he earth was complete chaos, and darkness covered the face of the deep, while a wind from God swept over the face of the waters."

their families and sometimes made them heirs to their households, and this was an especially common practice among the Romans. (It is a crucial plot device, some of us might recall, in *Ben Hur*.) But Paul's point at the outset of Ephesians is that God has done just this for us. The purpose of God for humanity, which was set in place from before the foundation of the world, was to adopt us into a family with God and with one another. So we are now destined for a heavenly fellowship together as a family, and for this inheritance, along with all that goes with it. God does this, moreover, out of his own freedom and generosity, which is to say that he freely does so and delights in drawing us all together in this way.

There is something enduringly enchanting about stories of integration into a family. To be sure, not all fostering and adoption scenarios are healthy. Some can end up being tragically destructive and abusive, and most of our human acts of adoption have their troubling side, which is often overlooked.[8] But in the very act of recognizing this harm we affirm that this process can, rightly done, and at least in part, speak about something profoundly important and restorative. It is no surprise then that our culture is fascinated with heartwarming adoption stories. From movies like *Instant Family* to books such as *Wonderful You* we are captivated by stories of children being welcomed into a new, loving family. And Paul thinks that this kind of positive, familial metaphor is crucial for grasping the divine plan that lies at the heart of all reality. God has freely and joyfully chosen us to join *his* family through his own Son, Jesus. We don't belong there naturally; we were not born children of God. God only has one Son. But God wants to adopt us. Remarkable.

However, God's care for us is not exhausted by his original decision that we should be adopted and join his family, ultimately going on to receive a great inheritance. We will explore the following dynamics in more detail in the next chapter. For now it suffices to note that God also lovingly *saves* us and rescues us when his plan goes off track.

Clearly, we are not yet completely holy, happy, and blameless, nor are we actually living together in perfection and fellowship. We are not *obviously* a part of God's family. Something has gone wrong—something that at times can be quite horrific. But our loving God rescues us.

Paul does not get into the details of God's rescue operation at this early point in his letter to the Laodiceans, but he does quickly note the way this too speaks of God's great love. Not only are we chosen to be adopted into God's family from before the foundation of the world, but, Paul continues, through Jesus

8. See MacFarquhar, "Living in Adoption's Emotional Aftermath."

. . . we have redemption,
by means of his blood,
release from our sinful debts,
according to the riches of [God's] gift,
which he lavishes upon us.
(Eph 1:7–8a)[9]

The Bible calls the basic problem here "sin" (or "sins"), and this clearly interferes with our ability to live in full fellowship with God and with one another. And like many Jews in his day, Paul is probably conceptualizing sin/s here in terms of financial debts. As we will see shortly, this problem of debt is only one part of the human plight. But it is an indicative one. There is a sense in which we have harmed God and taken something from him—we have loaned from him without repaying, or have even just robbed him outright—and now we need to pay him back. In order for this debt to be dealt with appropriately it needs to be wiped away or cancelled. And Paul states here that God himself does this. He cancels our debts, which is to say, he simply releases us from them, and he does so for free, without conditions. Hence it is almost as if there is a vast sum of divine cash pouring down from heaven until, finally, the total is complete and our negative balance paid off—something that those who have accumulated real debt here and now can only fantasize about. The important point for our current discussion is that God does this for us to save us, and he saves us because he loves us and wants to pull his original plan back onto its positive trajectory.[10]

But clearly, even with our debts released, we still have to wait for the great moment when God's rescue plan reaches its fulfillment, when we receive our inheritance, and when the entire cosmos is reconciled. And our loving God does not leave us alone during this fraught period either.

Using another financial metaphor, Paul tells us that the Spirit is the "down payment" (Gk. *arrabōn*) or "the *guarantee* of our inheritance, until [God's] final redemption of his possession, [which will result in] the praise of his glory" (Eph 1:14).[11] There is a moment in every Roman adoption when a person receives the gift and promise of the parent's future inheritance. People are adopted often primarily in order to inherit. But in the

---

9. Our translation.

10. We noted earlier that a copy of Paul's letter to the Colossians would have been read out to the Laodiceans as well (see Col 4:16: "And when this letter has been read among you, have it read also in the church of the Laodiceans; and see that you read also the letter from Laodicea"), and it adds another dimension to this story when it speaks of how God liberates us from underneath the crushing weight of our massive debt to "the rulers and authorities," who are evil powers currently ruling and oppressing us.

11. Our translation.

divine economy of adoption, our access to these promised future funds is not dependent on how qualified we may be as adoption prospects or how much we deserve to have our debts released. Technically, we do not (and cannot) do anything to be adopted by God. Instead, the Spirit takes us by the hand and gently welcomes us into this new, divine family out of God's sheer generosity, and so establishes our status as God's children who will eventually receive our inheritance in full. (And the Spirit comforts us and strengthens us as we wait for this.) Moreover, our inheritance is, as Paul goes on to say, amazing. It is nothing less than resurrection, transformation, and eternal life in God's glorious presence.

Paul, like any good theologian, emphasizes in passing that we have learned all this because God has told us about it through revelation. God has gifted us with "all wisdom and insight" as

> . . . he has made known to us the mystery of his will,
> according to his good pleasure that he has set forth in Christ,
> as a plan for the fullness of time,
> to gather up all things in him,
> things in heaven and things on earth. . . .
> (Eph 1:9–10)

Paul uses the word "mystery" here (Gk. *mystērion*), which denotes a divine secret that has been kept hidden until the arrival of Jesus, from which moment his appointed emissaries can reveal it. In other words, people were not able to simply figure this plan out by looking at the world around them and attempting to discern what God had in store for them. God's plan was a secret that had to be revealed, and prior to this point it was locked up in the counsels of God.

And at this moment it is interesting to reflect on how Paul's language throughout his articulation of God's cosmic plan in Ephesians 1 is both familial and financial. Paul's Laodicean recipients, shaped by their Greco-Roman context, would have resonated strongly with this sort of imagery. It would have been concrete and accessible to them. We can see here then that Paul has been *contextualizing* his message, using his listeners' own culture—the language of the streets, of the marketplace, and of their families—to communicate the good news about God's purposes. God wants to adopt us into a happy and blameless family, he makes a gift of debt-release to us after we had gone astray, and the Spirit's down payment guarantees our full inheritance on Jesus's return, strengthening us and comforting us as we wait. *And it's all free.*

What could have possessed God to draw us into a new family, to pour out vast riches, to wipe away our debts, and to give us the down payment of the Spirit as we wait for our glorious eternal inheritance? The answer lies back in the second verse of the blessing. Paul tells us that God has done all of this "in love" (1:4). God loves the Laodiceans and has a wonderful plan for their lives, namely, *this* gracious plan of electing or appointing them for adoption, fellowship, and inheritance, along with, if necessary, redemption—a plan, as Jesus Christ has disclosed, that has been in place since before the foundation of the world.

But God in no way limits the scope of this plan to a certain group of people, whether to the Laodiceans or to anyone else. God loves *us* and has a wonderful plan for *our* lives. God loves everyone without exception. And there is no other God behind this God, or alongside of him, or around him. God is love and that is all there is to it. *This is the God whom Jesus Christ and his Spirit reveal and there is no other.*

Of course an important question now arises. What happens if we throw God's loving plan off course (this being a question we have already touched on)? How does a God of love act when those he loves have turned their backs on him?

He will rescue us—the story of the next chapter.

3

God's Salvation

We have learned that God has chosen to draw humanity into fellowship with himself "in love."[1] This is the plan that God formulated from before the foundation of the world, and it is fundamentally positive and caring from the get-go. We need to remember that this is where Paul's story about God's relationship with us begins because it will continue in this vein and it will end there. God speaks a "Yes" to us without reservation, as the great theologian Karl Barth used to say.[2] But clearly something has gone wrong that is preventing us from living in perfect fellowship with God and one another; things are not the way they have been planned. We can sense this immediately as we look at all the broken relationships, violence, and decay in our world. So we need to learn from Paul what exactly is wrong, and how God is at work pulling his original plan for humanity back on track. God must speak a "No" here to something, Barth would add. God's "Yes" to us comes first and is always more important, but the "No" is spoken as well and must always be heard. So we need to grasp the story that Paul supplies concerning the basic problem that grips humanity and the corresponding solution that God has provided for that problem through Christ and the Spirit.[3] What has God saved us from and how?

---

1. Eph 1:4: ". . . just as he chose us in Christ before the foundation of the world to be holy and blameless before him in love."

2. See especially Barth's discussion of God's "yes" and "no" in *Church Dogmatics, vol. II, pt. 2*, although this phraseology is threaded through the entirety of his *Church Dogmatics*.

3. Because it is oriented toward salvation, theologians refer to this story as "soteriology" from the Greek word for "salvation," *sōteria*.

We suggest that chapters 5 through 8 in Romans are a good place to base our answers. We have already been dipping into key statements in this stretch of text, but we will now work through it a little more thoroughly. Romans chapters 5 to 8 provide the apostle's most extensive and detailed account of the problem that people face as they try to act in a good way—although it is a rather depressing one, expressed through the anguished struggles of an incapacitated sinner in chapter 7. Fortunately, some of the most insightful accounts of salvation that Paul ever penned are wrapped around these reflections. The solution, he affirms, is in glorious counterpart to the story of Adam (the story of much of Romans 5); we reach it by being baptized or immersed into the dying and rising Christ (so Romans 6); and we are comforted as we wait for its final victory by the Holy Spirit (so much of Romans 8).[4]

A story of Adam: flesh and sin

Paul's initial explanation of the problem facing humanity occurs in Romans 5:12–21, where the story of Adam from Genesis chapter 3 is cited; this story appears again in Romans chapter 6; it is intensified in chapter 7,[5] where echoes of Adam return; and it is contrasted with life in God's Spirit in the first thirteen verses of chapter 8. In all these passages Paul develops a detailed description of the problem intrinsic to the human condition, although we find short summaries of this description in other letters.[6] But we also need

4. This is a useful place to begin a brief description of Paul's soteriology, but it is emphatically not where we would derive his soteriology from. In fact, the account of the problem is illuminated by the solution. Paul "thinks backwards," reflectively and retrospectively, about the plight from which God has rescued us in the light of the rescue that has taken place. But this is not the place to describe these dynamics. See elsewhere "Resurrection and Death" (chapter 5), and "Resurrection and Sin" (chapter 6), in Campbell, *Pauline Dogmatics*, 92–136.

5. It is anticipated in verses 5 to 6 and dramatized in verses 7 to 25.

6. See Gal 2:19: "For through the law I died to the law, so that I might live to God. I have been crucified with Christ . . ."; 3:21–22: "Is the law then opposed to the promises of God? Certainly not! For if a law had been given that could make alive, then righteousness would indeed come through the law. But the scripture has imprisoned all things under the power of sin, so that what was promised through the faith of Jesus Christ might be given to those who believe"; and Gal 5:17–25: "For what the flesh desires is opposed to the Spirit, and what the Spirit desires is opposed to the flesh, for these are opposed to each other, to prevent you from doing what you want. But if you are led by the Spirit, you are not subject to the law. Now the works of the flesh are obvious: sexual immorality, impurity, debauchery, idolatry, sorcery, enmities, strife, jealousy, anger, quarrels, dissensions, factions, envy, drunkenness, carousing, and things like these. I am warning you, as I warned you before: those who do such things will not inherit the kingdom of God. By contrast, the fruit of the Spirit is love, joy, peace, patience, kindness, generosity,

to bear in mind that Paul's position here in Romans is articulated in deliberate contrast to the sunnier views of certain opponents he was anticipating arriving in Rome whom the apostle thought were dangerously naïve about the challenges people face.

When these opponents, whom we will talk about in more detail in later chapters, described the problem confronting humanity, they tended to be quite optimistic. People were basically good and certainly Jews were supposed to be. (These opponents were probably a certain sort of early, messianic Jew.) People just needed a little guidance to walk on the right path toward God and with one another. We can infer this optimism from the way that these "teachers," as some scholars refer to them,[7] held that God's written instructions in the Scriptures could help everyone out. "Read, obey—get circumcised if you are male—and be saved." On one level, it was as simple as that. Hence, while these teachers viewed humanity's existence in Adam as problematic, it was far from hopeless. Attention to God's instructions in the Scripture would fix everything.

Paul is not so confident. He observes—arguably rather more realistically—that while part of the human mind might joyfully recognize God's instructions given in the Bible, people will not always carry them out. Indeed, the presence of these instructions *creates new opportunities for people to*

---

faithfulness, gentleness, and self-control. There is no law against such things. And those who belong to Christ have crucified the flesh with its passions and desires. If we live by the Spirit, let us also be guided by the Spirit." Also 1 Cor 7:21–23: "Were you a slave when called? Do not be concerned about it. Even if you can gain your freedom, make the most of it. For whoever was called in the Lord as a slave is a freed person belonging to the Lord, just as whoever was free when called is a slave belonging to Christ. You were bought with a price; do not become slaves of humans"; 15:20–23: "But in fact Christ has been raised from the dead, the first fruits of those who have died. For since death came through a human, the resurrection of the dead has also come through a human, for as all die in Adam, so all will be made alive in Christ. But each in its own order: Christ the first fruits, then at his coming those who belong to Christ"; 15:45–49: "Thus it is written, 'The first man, Adam, became a living being'; the last Adam became a life-giving spirit. But it is not the spiritual that is first but the physical and then the spiritual. The first man was from the earth, made of dust; the second man is from heaven. As one of dust, so are those who are of the dust, and as one of heaven, so are those who are of heaven. Just as we have borne the image of the one of dust, we will also bear the image of the one of heaven"; and Eph 2:1–3: "You were dead through the trespasses and sins in which you once walked, following the course of this world, following the ruler of the power of the air, the spirit that is now at work among those who are disobedient. All of us once lived among them in the passions of our flesh, doing the will of flesh and senses, and we were by nature children of wrath, like everyone else."

7. See especially J. Louis Martyn's classic discussion of these figures in his *Galatians* commentary (1997), especially 117–27. We will talk about these teachers in much more detail later on in this book, leaning again on Martyn's analysis.

transgress: "For sin, seizing an opportunity in the commandment, deceived me and through it killed me" (Rom 7:11).

It may be helpful to think about this for a moment in terms of the way that children behave. Parents, schoolteachers, Sunday school volunteers, and those of us who remember our childhoods, can doubtless relate to the following scenario. When a child is instructed specifically *not* to do something, it is pretty common to discover that they will do exactly what they have just been told not to do—and it may have been something that they had not even thought about doing before it was prohibited. "Don't steal the brownies I just made that are in the jar on the kitchen counter; don't touch it or open it." "Don't pull the cat's tail." "Don't pull my irises out of the ground and use them as toy swords." Similarly, humanity's attempts to faithfully respond to God's instructions in the Bible, Paul observes in Romans chapter 7, tend to lead to the multiplication of wrongdoing, attempts that thereby repeat the transgression of Adam in the garden. An instruction not to do something creates the opportunity for that very thing to be done.

We learn from this, Paul explains, that people are in the grip of sinful desires that frustrate their ability to do good things, pulling them away from living with God and one another in a loving fashion.[8] These desires, perhaps more accurately called "lusts," manipulate rules and instructions, turning them into opportunities to do wrong. Paul summarizes this situation by using the term "flesh" (Gk. *sarx*) to describe human beings. This term denotes how our human nature is in the grip of sinful lusts that oppose any desire to do the right thing. So Paul goes on to say in Galatians, "For what the flesh desires is opposed to the Spirit, and what the Spirit desires is opposed to the flesh" (Gal 5:17a). Moreover, humanity does not seem to have any ability in and of itself to resist or to break away from these negative desires: "For I know that the good does not dwell within me, that is, in my flesh. For the desire to do the good lies close at hand, but not the ability" (Rom 7:18). The problem that a humanity made of flesh faces then is some irresistible urge to harm that interferes with any attempt to obediently respond to God's will. Indeed, so deep-seated and deceptive are these desires that they even manipulate God's expressed will in the Scriptures to generate more damage.

We began this discussion with some references to childhood transgressions which were fairly mild and even faintly charming. But the underlying situation is far from trivial. One is reminded here ultimately more of

---

8. Having said this, "desire" is not always a bad thing for Paul (it is *sinful* desires that are bad). Phil 1:23: "I am hard pressed between the two: my desire is to depart and be with Christ, for that is far better"; 1 Thess 2:17: "As for us, brothers and sisters, when for a short time we were made orphans by being separated from you—in person, not in heart—we longed with great eagerness to see you face to face."

the painful battles fought by substance abusers. Chronic substance abusers are technically accountable for their actions, that is, they have agency. But any sense that they are quite free simply to choose one course of action over another is horribly unaware of the struggles they face from their own desires. Urgent needs to find and to take mind-altering substances can dominate their thinking to the point that they feel utterly exhausted and overwhelmed, sunk in distorted thinking, self-deception, and relational collapse. Moreover, the resulting behavior is often deeply destructive, both to themselves and to all those around them; the damage done by substance abusers ripples outward through spouses and children, friends, and on through subsequent generations. So there is nothing trivial about the destructive urges that inhabit constitutions of flesh. They oppress, damage, and destroy. But on some deep level Paul grasps and points out that we are *all* substance abusers, trapped and "imprisoned" by our flesh.[9]

Hence in chapter 7 of Romans Paul famously dramatizes sin not just as a small lapse in judgment or a mistake but as a dominating force or *power*—"Sin" we might say with a capital "S." Sin "deceives" through the commandment(s) and then goes on to wage war on us, to enslave us, and to imprison us: "For we know that the law is spiritual; but I am of the flesh, sold into slavery under Sin. . . . But I see in my members another law at war with the law of my mind, making me captive to the law of Sin that dwells in my members" (Rom 7:14–23, caps added). For Paul, Sin is not primarily an individual transgression then—a misstep, a bad decision, or a violation of some kind of rule. We could speak of all these things as *a* sin and we might be left with the feeling that we are still in control and will not make the same mistake again, or at least, not very much. For Paul, Sin is vastly more serious. It is an evil force that has captured humanity and occupied its very constitution, constantly assaulting any desire to do the right thing with compelling alternative suggestions. In this situation, we are not free in any full or ultimately meaningful sense. Our willing and acting are contested domains, caught up in a great struggle. But Paul detects a further significant problem facing humanity (although are things already not bad enough?).

Paul frequently refers to "the rulers of this age" (1 Cor 2:6), "cosmic powers of this present darkness" (Eph 6:12), and "elemental principles of the world" (Gal 4:3), and calls their leader "Satan."[10] These powers occupy "the

9. Gal 3:22–23: "But the scripture has imprisoned all things under the power of sin, so that what was promised through the faith of Jesus Christ might be given to those who believe. Now before faith came, we were imprisoned and guarded under the law until faith would be revealed."

10. Rom 16:20: "The God of peace will shortly crush Satan under your feet. The grace of our Lord Jesus Christ be with you." 1 Cor 5:5: "[Y]ou are to hand this man

air," which is to say that in Paul's mind they roam the zone that lies above the earth but below where God, his angels, and other celestial beings live in the heavens.[11] And the powers are indeed powerful. They are also evil, warring against God and God's good purposes. Their attacks are so severe Paul even charges them with crucifying Jesus (1 Cor 2:8).[12]

It is easy for Paul's modern readers to ignore or to redefine these apparitions of evil that seem to belong to an ancient mythological past, but it would be unwise to do so. While some subtle redefinition is ultimately

---

over to Satan for the destruction of the flesh, so that the spirit may be saved in the day of the Lord"; 7:5: "Do not deprive one another except perhaps by agreement for a set time, to devote yourselves to prayer, and then come together again, so that Satan may not tempt you because of your lack of self-control"; 2 Cor 2:11: "And we do this so that we may not be outwitted by Satan; for we are not ignorant of his designs"; 11:14b: "Even Satan disguises himself as an angel of light"; 12:7: ". . . even considering the exceptional character of the revelations. Therefore, to keep me from being too elated, a thorn was given me in the flesh, a messenger of Satan to torment me, to keep me from being too elated"; 1 Thess 2:18: "For we wanted to come to you—certainly I, Paul, wanted to again and again—but Satan blocked our way;" 2 Thess 2:9: "The coming of the lawless one is apparent in the working of Satan, who uses all power, signs, lying wonders. . . ."

11. Eph 2:1–2: "You were dead through the trespasses and sins in which you once walked, following the course of this world, following the ruler of the power of the air, the spirit that is now at work among those who are disobedient."

12. 1 Cor 2:8: ". . . which none of the rulers of this age understood, for if they had, they would not have crucified the Lord of glory." An obvious question arises here that we can only address briefly, that is, why does evil seem to exist when we know we are involved with a benevolent God who has a wonderful plan for our lives? This conundrum is sometimes referred to as "the problem of evil." Some thinkers attempt to solve this problem by emphasizing the "free will" of the individual who makes bad choices and thereby introduces evil into the world, while others emphasize the sovereignty of God in creating some people to do the good and others to do evil. Unfortunately, both these explanations unwittingly commit to the origin of evil being God himself, either by creating a world so fragile that sin was next to inevitable, or by choosing a select group of beings to enact evil in the world. Neither of these options will do. Instead of attributing a precise origin to evil, we should speak of it as a kind of *absence*. God never intended it. It is, as Barth writes in §50 in *Church Dogmatics, vol. III, pt. 3*, "not-ness" or "no-ness" (German *das Nichtige*, arguably translated unhelpfully as "nothingness"; 289–368). This might be difficult to wrap our minds around, and that is partly the point. The categories we use to describe created things—which are good, rational, and ordered—simply do not work when trying to talk about something non-created, chaotic, irrational, and disordered. The moment we try to apply words and phrases to evil that should be reserved for God's good creation, we are giving it more power and reality than it deserves. So it will benefit us not to be too concerned about "where it came from." A solution does not come from "solving" what is often reduced to a philosophical problem but in the reality of God's activity in Jesus Christ—a solution that we will unpack throughout the rest of this chapter. Note, Barth's insightful account of evil in terms of sheer negation or "not-ness" joins hands with an ancient explanation of evil in terms of privation, or, of the absence of good. An excellent account of this is Stanley Hauerwas's essay "Seeing Darkness, Hearing Silence: Augustine's Account of Evil" in his *Working with Words*, 8–32.

necessary, Paul's constant emphasis on oppressive powers speaks to the sense in which individual people are caught up in a cosmos that is itself disordered and harmful. Our world both sustains us and assaults us. Our environments give us life but only at great cost, with ingenuity and hard work, and their unpredictable disorders can still catch us up in vast dislocations that harm and even kill us—floods, earthquakes, plagues. And we are caught up in the grip of vast historical forces beyond our control that manipulate and frequently coerce us. Systems and states and classes carry us to and fro; we cannot free ourselves from their strictures and diktats. Moreover, at bottom these forces can be malevolent. Deep tendencies can be at work seeking only to damage and to destroy.

There is a sense then in which humanity has been enslaved by evil forces both from within and without. Our flesh is in the grip of evil desires and our cosmos is in the grip of evil powers. What is the solution?

Initially, the only possible solution is *death*.

Sin must die

It is easy enough for us simply to observe that all living things decay and ultimately die, and that we ourselves are constantly declining toward this end at various speeds. But Paul gives a very Jewish explanation for this phenomenon. Utilizing the story of Adam in the garden of Eden he notes in Romans chapter 5 that "death spread to all" (verse 12) and so "reigned" over all (verse 14) because of Adam's transgression and the consequent "infection" of human nature by sinful desires. There are explicit connections between our existence as flesh, our deaths, and sin: "[t]o set the mind on the flesh is death" (8:6a) so "if you live according to the flesh, you will die" (verse 13a). Indeed, Paul's account of death articulates a critical insight for us at this moment. It shows us how, from God's point of view, sin and all that it contaminates does not and must not have a future. It must be terminated, which is to say, it must die. It must end. And this makes sense.

There is nothing good about evil desires and oppressive powers. They deal in suffering and pain. They delight in inflicting harm on people, ranging from the trivial to the megalomaniacal. From the barbed nickname or bullying shove in school to the systematic collection and murder of entire classes and races, the wrong that evil does *must cease*. It has no place in the new heaven and the new earth that God is planning for his people in the future. Evil must not be allowed to continue indefinitely. Instead, it must end, which is to say, it must die. And this termination must apply to everything. The entire cosmos, as Romans chapter 8 tells us further, has been "subjected to futility" (verse 20) and is in "enslavement to decay" (verse 21). This fallen world must end one day. That is, our contamination is too deep and comprehensive to allow of some simple separation of the good from the bad; we are shot through with evil to the point that everything is polluted and must be shut down. The entire rotten mass must be eliminated.

But what will happen to *us* in the midst of this deserved termination? The good will perish along with the bad, the personal with the impersonal. The wheat will be burned with the tares. Will not the entirety of God's plan to gather us into communion thereby come to nothing as he closes the door rightly on our evil? Will the death of everyone and everything frustrate God's cosmic purposes?

Not necessarily.

Even if death has the first word in God's response to evil it will not have the last. As many Jews in Paul's day knew well, God is not a God of death; the God of Israel is a God of life.

The solution: a story of Jesus

God is faced with quite a conundrum at this moment. The evil with which we are entangled must be terminated. It cannot be allowed to continue to contaminate our perfect future together and everything it has infiltrated must be terminated as well, and this means humanity too. We must die. But we must also live if God is to gather us ultimately into a communion with him. Only our ongoing life will fulfill God's original plan to live in a joyful family with us. So for God to live in a beautiful world with happy people, that world and those people must exist. But they must exist in a beautiful and happy form. We must therefore live somehow in a cleansed, perfected way. We cannot bring our evil and twisted lives into the presence of God and one another for eternity.

It follows from all this that God must let us die and then *resurrect* us (although "must" here is arguably a little too strong; God is under no obligation to resurrect us but is free to do so if he wants to—and he does). We must go through death, but we must then be recreated after our deaths so that we rise and live in a new, perfected way that is free from the contaminations of sin and evil. We must be terminated, then raised and transformed. And in fact, many Jews in Paul's generation believed that God would one day create a new heaven and a new earth, miraculously raising his people from the dust of death, in a new, glorious form, to live in it. But Paul will take this Jewish rescue plan some important steps further.

Technically there is no need for God to do anything more than to resurrect his chosen people at the end of the age to make his original plan work—although this is quite a gesture—and this is what many Jews in Paul's day thought would happen. The old world would be extinguished and the new world would be created with all its new, happy inhabitants who would feast together.[13] Such Jews lived in hope of inheriting "the age to come," and there was much discussion about who would actually get in (while there were the usual skeptics who thought that the entire idea was utterly foolish).[14] But the coming of Jesus revealed to Paul various still more profound dimensions within this general plan, and thereby within God.

Jesus's death

Paul articulates Jesus's long journey to wrench God's plan back on track with particular precision in a song that he inserts into chapter 2 of his letter to the Philippians (2:6–11). The first half of the song speaks of Jesus's descent into our humanity with all its struggles, struggles that culminate in his endurance of a violent and shameful death:

> Christ Jesus . . .
> . . . though he existed in the form of God
> did not regard equality with God as something to be grasped,
> but emptied himself,
> taking the form of a slave,
> assuming human likeness.
> And being found in appearance as a human,
> he humbled himself
> and became obedient to the point of death—
> even death on a cross.
> (Phil 2:5b–8)

13. Isa 25:6–10: "On this mountain the Lord of hosts will make for all peoples a feast of rich food, a feast of well-aged wines, of rich food filled with marrow, of well-aged wines strained clear. And he will destroy on this mountain the shroud that is cast over all peoples, the covering that is spread over all nations; he will swallow up death forever. Then the Lord God will wipe away the tears from all faces, and the disgrace of his people he will take away from all the earth, for the Lord has spoken. It will be said on that day, 'See, this is our God; we have waited for him, so that he might save us. This is the Lord for whom we have waited; let us be glad and rejoice in his salvation.' For the hand of the Lord will rest on this mountain."

14. Apparently, the Sadducees: see Luke 20:27: "Some Sadducees, those who say there is no resurrection, came to him."

Paul's song notes first that the Son became a human being and so became one of us and one with us. And we see here first of all and very clearly that "emptying himself"[15] was an act of incomparable humility. The God revealed through Jesus—our loving God—is a humble God.

In the church we refer to this event of the Son's arrival with us, as a human being, as the incarnation, which we anticipate every year during the season of Advent and celebrate during Christmas. But Christmas is not simply a time of remembering Jesus's birth, complete with shepherds (a humble birth), and wise men. It joyfully acknowledges God's arrival in our midst alongside us as a flesh-and-blood human being. And Paul is not shy about making explicit just how close and intimate this relationship actually was. As he tells us in Romans 8:3, God the Father accomplished this by "sending his own Son *in the exact likeness* of sinful flesh . . ." (our translation). Hence Christ did not just assume special, non-corrupt humanity but our *fleshly* humanity—*a humanity enslaved to evil desires and oppressed by the evil powers*. As Paul clarifies further in 2 Corinthians, "For our sake [God] made the one who knew no sin to be sin . . ." (5:21a).[16]

We tend to underplay the extent of Jesus's commitment here because we view the human condition as reasonably impressive. Despite its problems, it is a great thing to be a person. We are, after all, the self-proclaimed rulers of the animal kingdom, and we have done impressive things like creating the semiconductor chip, mapping the human genome, and flying spacecraft to the moon. But Jesus was *God*. For him to enter into our condition in all its fullness, including into its corruption and contamination, was an extraordinary act of humility. He had to come a very long way down and become something vastly inferior to what he was. C. S. Lewis captures the point nicely when he asks us to contemplate becoming a crab or a slug to share life alongside those species in their respective habitats, to bear their burdens, and ultimately to save them.[17]

However, as the Philippian song goes on to say, Christ's descent into our corrupt humanity did not end with its mere adoption. It ended when his flesh was destroyed in his execution, a death that we in the church remember on Good Friday. It is a fairly simple point so it is easily missed but we need to appreciate it fully. The Son of God, fully present in the person of

15. A probable echo of Isa 53:12: "Therefore I will allot him a portion with the great, and he shall divide the spoil with the strong; because he poured out himself to death, and was numbered with the transgressors; yet he bore the sin of many, and made intercession for the transgressors."

16. This is a possible echo of Isa 53 as well, perhaps especially of verses 9–10, or simply of the thought of the chapter as a whole.

17. Lewis, *Mere Christianity*, 146.

Jesus, was dead and buried and so his flesh was also dead and buried. The evil desires within him thereby perished, and the vulnerability of the fleshly body to the suggestions of the evil powers living in the cosmos inhabited by flesh thereby ended as well. The Jesus who has died has had all his assumed and problematic existence as fleshly terminated. The first critical step has consequently been taken as God creates a way out of our current situation. But with this death in view—the necessary completion of the great downward arc that began with Jesus's incarnation and assumption of our sinful flesh, flesh that had to die—we perhaps need to pause to emphasize that God did not *need* to do this. But he did it *because he loves us.*

We have not been left alone in our struggles. God is with us. God cares about us. He does not abandon us to battle away by ourselves through our contaminated and corrupted existence. He cares so much about us that he became one of us. He walked alongside of us through the valley of the shadow of death. He did not have to do this, and it was in many respects a deeply horrific experience. Ultimately Jesus was tortured to death. But he chose to do this because he loves us. Our humble God is a loving God, as shown above all by the Son's death on a cross, at which moment we turn to a third dimension within this story.

Scope

It is clear that Paul views this fleshly extinction in much broader terms than just the death of Jesus's own body of flesh. He writes in 2 Corinthians 5:14 that "one has died for all; therefore all have died," meaning by this that Jesus's death creates a new existence beyond the flesh *for all of humanity*. Everyone in Adam can now move beyond their construction *as* Adam, which means as fleshly, thanks to Jesus. A doorway into a new, saved, and perfected condition has been opened. And we should be especially careful not to try to limit things when Paul says "all" here, however uncomfortable this might make us. This is, after all, what the text of the Bible says.

That is, we might be tempted to think, perhaps without even realizing it, "Paul probably means all *Christians* or all people *provided that they meet a certain set of criteria.* Surely Paul is not including in Jesus's death people that I don't particularly like." That is, we limit the significance of what Jesus does. But Paul says no such thing here, and giving in to this temptation actually prevents us from encountering the sheer expansiveness and magnanimity of God's activity in Christ, the one who created all things.[18] When Paul says

18. Col 1:16: "[F]or in him all things in heaven and on earth were created, things visible and invisible, whether thrones or dominions or rulers or powers—all things

"all" in 2 Corinthians chapter 5 verse 14 we can and should be confident that
he means it. We can see this especially clearly when we revisit the story Paul
tells of Adam in the light of Christ.

We know that for Paul part of the problem we face is that sin came
into the world through Adam and death thereby spread to all.[19] But when
Paul articulates this in Romans chapter 5, he makes a point of showing
just how superior the resulting scope of Christ's assumption of our fleshly
condition is to Adam's story. As a counterpart to the reach of Adam, Paul
views Christ's act of assuming humanity's sinful condition of flesh as universal—as humanity-wide. In fact, it is universal in a way that is clearly more
significant than the act of Adam:

> But the free gift is not like the trespass.
> For if the many died through the one man's trespass,
> much more surely have the grace of God
> and the gift in the grace of the one man, Jesus Christ,
> abounded for the many.
> (Rom 5:15)

We learn here then that our loving and humble God is also *a radically inclusive* God. He loves *all* that he has made.

Resurrection

For God's solution to our corrupt situation to be complete we need a second
act and, thankfully, there is definitely more to the story. The one who opens
a door for us into new life has passed through the necessary valley of death;
the flesh has been terminated. But there is as yet no new life. *However,* as
Paul says in the second half of his Philippian song:

> Therefore,
> God exalted him even more highly
> and gave him the name that is above every other name,
> so that at the name given to Jesus
> every knee should bend,
> in heaven and on earth and under the earth,
> and every tongue should confess
> that Jesus Christ is Lord,

have been created through him and for him."

19. This does not explain the presence of the evil powers, which are related for Paul
but seem to be roaming about the cosmos and so not tied to Adam specifically in the
way sin and death are.

to the glory of God the Father.
(Phil 2:9–11)

So the story does not end with death but continues through resurrection, as so
many Jews hoped and as the early church could now so emphatically affirm.

The Jewish hope was firm; indeed, it was now guaranteed. God had
resurrected Jesus and exalted him on high, enthroning him at his right hand
(Rom 8:34), from which position he rules until all his enemies have been
brought in subjection under his feet (1 Cor 15:24–28).[20] So the new age
has clearly begun to arrive even if it is not yet here in all its fullness. And
one day the risen Jesus will return, and we will all be resurrected, receiving
glorious new spiritual bodies that will not decay or die.[21] So one immediate
and happy result of this event is that we have a definitive guarantee of the
future arrival of the new age.

20. It is worth noting that we can see all three divine persons at work effecting this
Easter uplifting. The Father raises his Son, and the Spirit, the life-giving breath of all of
creation, gives life to the Son. So Rom 8:11: "If the Spirit of him who raised Jesus from
the dead dwells in you, he who raised Christ Jesus from the dead will give life to your
mortal bodies also through his Spirit that dwells in you." Jesus's identity is consequently
re-established by God in this act of resurrection beyond his death.

21. See 1 Cor 15:35–55: "But someone will ask, 'How are the dead raised? With
what kind of body do they come?' Fool! What you sow does not come to life unless it
dies. And as for what you sow, you do not sow the body that is to be but a bare seed,
perhaps of wheat or of some other grain. But God gives it a body as he has chosen
and to each kind of seed its own body. Not all flesh is alike, but there is one flesh for
humans, another for animals, another for birds, and another for fish. There are both
heavenly bodies and earthly bodies, but the glory of the heavenly is one thing, and that
of the earthly is another. There is one glory of the sun and another glory of the moon
and another glory of the stars; indeed, star differs from star in glory. So it is with the
resurrection of the dead. What is sown is perishable; what is raised is imperishable. It
is sown in dishonor; it is raised in glory. It is sown in weakness; it is raised in power. It
is sown a physical body; it is raised a spiritual body. If there is a physical body, there is
also a spiritual body. Thus it is written, 'The first man, Adam, became a living being';
the last Adam became a life-giving spirit. But it is not the spiritual that is first but the
physical and then the spiritual. The first man was from the earth, made of dust; the
second man is from heaven. As one of dust, so are those who are of the dust, and as
one of heaven, so are those who are of heaven. Just as we have borne the image of the
one of dust, we will also bear the image of the one of heaven. What I am saying, brothers and sisters, is this: flesh and blood cannot inherit the kingdom of God, nor does
the perishable inherit the imperishable. Look, I will tell you a mystery! We will not
all die, but we will all be changed, in a moment, in the twinkling of an eye, at the last
trumpet. For the trumpet will sound, and the dead will be raised imperishable, and we
will be changed. For this perishable body must put on imperishability, and this mortal
body must put on immortality. When this perishable body puts on imperishability and
this mortal body puts on immortality, then the saying that is written will be fulfilled:
'Death has been swallowed up in victory.' 'Where, O death, is your victory? Where, O
death, is your sting?'"

But Paul has yet another dimension within the story of Jesus's resurrection to speak of and it is here that we begin to see one of his key insights come into view. This was something that not even other leaders in the early church in his day always understood.

Paul writes in Ephesians chapter 2,

> But God, who is rich in mercy,
> out of the great love with which he loved us
> even when we were dead through our trespasses,
> made us alive together through Christ
> —by grace you have been saved—
> and raised us up with him
> and seated us with him in the heavenly places in Christ Jesus,
> so that in the ages to come
> he might show the immeasurable riches of his grace in kindness toward us
> in Christ Jesus.
> (Eph 2:4–7)

Paul is clearly not talking here about Christ's enthronement as taking place exclusively in the future. He envisions this as having taken place *already*, with Christ seated on high at this very moment. But the further twist is that *we* are somehow thereby resurrected and seated with the liberating King Jesus as well. We are "in him" *and therefore alive and raised up already as well.* Indeed, for Paul this resurrected and enthroned location is the key to our current life in community with one another in the church, where we live beyond the power of sin and are able to respond to God's will for us with a full and joyful obedience. This is one of the most crucial theological insights Paul ever gave us into God's work on our behalf through Jesus Christ and the Holy Spirit.

A new mind

A quick survey of some of Paul's most important summary texts indicates that he really did believe that we are presently resurrected in some way, on some level, within Jesus. In 2 Corinthians 5:17 he states,

> If someone is in Christ, he is a new creation.
> The old has departed. Behold, he has become quite new.[22]

And he concludes his letter to the Galatians with the same claim.

---

22. Our translation.

For neither circumcision nor uncircumcision is anything;
but a new creation is everything! (Gal 6:15)

(Note, to be in the new creation already is to presuppose that a resurrection and recreation have taken place.) Paul's most famous assertion of this situation, however, is probably Galatians 3:28, which is best read along with its two preceding verses:

All of you who are in Christ Jesus are,
by means of that fidelity,[23]
sons of God.
For you have been immersed into Christ;
you have been clothed with Christ.
There is no "Jew" or "pagan," no "slave" or "free," no "male and female."
All of you who are in Christ Jesus
are one and the same.
(Gal 3:26–28)[24]

To have left the old age behind definitively is the same thing as to claim that the new age has begun and is decisive. Race, class, and gender no longer determine our lives.[25] Being a "son of God" (that is, a "child of God") is what counts. And so, in Colossians 3 Paul makes the same basic claim in relation to ethnicity and class:

Do not lie to one another,
seeing that you have stripped off the old self with its practices
and have clothed yourselves with the new self,
which is being renewed in knowledge according to the image of its creator.
In that renewal there is no longer Greek and Jew, circumcised and uncircumcised, barbarian, Scythian, slave and free;
but Christ is all and in all!
Therefore, as God's chosen ones, holy and beloved,
clothe yourselves with compassion, kindness, humility, meekness, and patience.
(Col 3:9–12)

23. As we will see later, this is best read as a reference primarily to Jesus's faithful walk to the cross.

24. Our translation.

25. It should be noted that what we are not saying is that these things are unimportant in any way. But they can no longer be understood as defining who we are in a way that is equal or superior to Jesus's definition of who we are.

The point does not need to be labored further. Paul is clearly committed to the resurrection of Christ doing real work within the lives of his
followers, changing them in some invisible but fundamental way. (The work
of the Holy Spirit is clearly crucial here too.) They (we!) are living now out
of the age to come and not on the basis of the present age, which is characterized by various temporary "ordering structures," and by sin and death.[26]
To live beyond the present age, and in the coming age, is to live beyond a
mind gripped by evil lusts and oppressed by evil powers. It is to have taken
the impress of a new image who has died and left the flesh behind, being
raised in new, pure state. Hence, it is to be able to act like that image, Christ
himself, obediently, lovingly, and wholeheartedly, and to do so now. It is to
have been liberated and set free from the age of Adam even as we still walk
through it. (Hallelujah!)

It should be clear then as we draw this overview of our salvation to a
close that resurrection is doing a lot of *saving* work for Paul. Jesus's death
on our behalf is clearly crucial. There is no way out of our current cosmos
except through death because sin and all that it contaminates must die. But
in equal measure there is no future without our resurrection and recreation.
It is this act that brings God's great cosmic plan fully back on track. Moreover, even as Jesus's resurrection guarantees the completion of God's plan at
the end of the age, the Spirit introduces that "future" into our "present" now,
claims Paul, by way of our transformed minds. We think like Jesus already.

And with this account of the good news as grasped and proclaimed
by Paul clearly in mind, we are ready to turn and to consider how some
interpretations of Paul have lost sight of it. This, needless to say, is a tragic
outcome for how Paul is read, and ultimately, for the church.

---

26. See T. F. Torrance, *Space, Time, and Resurrection*, 185. While Torrance is really talking about the fields of space and time as ordering our present reality, we can
also think of these other dimensions—race, ethnicity, et cetera—as temporary ordering
structures as well that are, in some ways, quite helpful but not a part of God's original
or new creation.

4

Justification Theory

A Brief Description

A Great Conundrum

We have just spent a chapter describing a particular soteriology in Paul, that is to say, a particular theory of how we are saved, rooting that account principally in Romans chapters 5 through 8. And it will not be unfair if from this point onward we call this Paul's "gospel." This theory "proclaims the good news"—as the Greek word for "gospel," *euangelion*, suggests—that God has resurrected us in Jesus Christ, so it is really a very Jewish story of salvation with this heavy investment in eschatology. The new twist is the proclamation that *Jesus's* glorious resurrection and ascension guarantee *our* resurrected transformation in the future, in the new age, after our deaths—or at the second coming, Paul would remind us; whichever comes first. And, in equally good news, Paul tells us that this resurrection impinges already on our thinking and acting so that we are empowered to live now in a godly fashion, despite the constant pressures from the lusts in our flesh and the seductive operations of evil powers on us from without.[1] This account of salvation, which holds that we have been gifted with a saved mind now while we wait for the salvation of the cosmos, addresses our wrongdoing and our

1. Rom 12:1–2.

current locations in our conflicted and troubled world. But it also fits into a broader plan by a loving God to create us and ultimately to draw us into perfect communion with him. This is what we were destined for from before the foundation of the world; *and this is what we are still destined for now that God has intervened at great personal cost to rescue us and to drag his overarching plan back on course.* Overall, then, we can see Paul articulating here a captivating panorama of God's purposes effected through Jesus and his Spirit, and they reveal a God of very great love, generosity, and humility.

As scholarly greats of past Pauline interpretation like Albert Schweitzer have long suggested, this cosmic panorama that pivots around the resurrection of the Son and our involvement with him by way of the Spirit—something scholars usually explain in terms of "participation"—explains most if not all of the other things that Paul has to say in the letters that we have preserved for us in our Bibles, although this can sometimes be a little hard to see initially because his letters are so practical.

Paul's letters address various, quite specific problems. Local gatherings of Jesus-followers in places like Corinth, Thessalonica, or Colossae, are confused—or simply outright defiant—about sexual ethics, the second coming, the right posture toward ascetic practices in relation to diet, and so on. Paul's letters were written to address these practical local problems that we have long lost sight of. Consequently, his own most important theological insights are seldom if ever directly described. They *inform* what he is saying, but he never lays out his theology systematically or overtly. We have to ferret his deepest theological convictions out from his practical pronouncements and advice. But scholars like Schweitzer point out that after all this careful investigative work has been completed we can nevertheless see that when Paul addresses localized problems he almost always applies or develops the foregoing theological insights grounded in participation, often summarizing them with the phrase "(you are) in Christ" or a close equivalent. Underneath Paul's arguments, driving them, is his resurrectional gospel, with our partial resurrection through Jesus being referenced by Paul in terms of our ongoing life "in Christ." This phrase denotes our partially resurrected state as we participate in Jesus, and especially our new minds that can act obediently beyond the grip of sin. It no surprise then to see that this expression "in Christ" or its close equivalent is found through all his letters, occurring upward of 160 times, and in all of the important places.[2] And it is equally unsurprising to see it placed centrally in all the key summaries quoted in the previous

---

2. The realization in the early 1900s by the great German scholar of Paul G. Adolf Deissmann.

chapter about our present resurrected transformation.[3] At this moment then we arrive at the great conundrum that this book is ultimately addressing.

The vast majority of what Paul teaches is explained with reference to being in Christ, which is simply the brief evocation of the resurrectional and participational gospel we have just described. But a smaller, minority set of passages seems to speak differently—at least as they are usually explained to us. Of the many verses we have from Paul's authentic letters,[4] approaching 1,800, this distinctive, countervailing cluster of words and arguments appears in around 172, which is just under 10 percent of what he wrote.[5] We will refer to this distinctive language in what follows as "justification," since this is how it is usually referred to.[6] And many scholars, especially Protestants, think that *this* is the most important material that Paul ever wrote. They suggest that this is where his gospel is located—or certainly where our explanation of his gospel must begin. But what do we do now with the other *90 percent* of material in Paul that we have just spent three chapters describing, which speaks of a gospel of participation, transformation, and resurrection?

It turns out that coordinating the interpretation of Paul's justification material with what he wrote in the other 90 percent of his texts is one of the central puzzles of modern Pauline scholarship. But before we press into some of the complex ins and outs of this discussion, and ultimately offer what we take to be the best solution, we need to understand very clearly what the distinctive material in question is. Only when we have grasped justification tightly can we work out how to coordinate it with his other participatory material, as well as evaluate where previous claims to have coordinated it successfully are premature and even somewhat dubious. We must know the 10 percent like the backs of our hands if we are ever to resolve the question of its integration with the 90 percent. So we will begin the next stage in our argument by providing a brief description of justification, and we will again focus this description on how justification functions soteriologically, as a theory of salvation, because this is how it is usually understood.[7] Consequently we will speak in what follows of justification

3. 2 Cor 5:17; Gal 3:26–28; 6:15; and Col 3:9–12.

4. Excluding 1 and 2 Timothy, and Titus, as pseudonymous. Douglas makes a detailed case for these decisions in *Framing Paul.*

5. Rom 1:16—5:1; 6:7–8; 9:30—10:17; Gal 2:15—3:26; 5:5; Eph 2:8–10; Phil 3:2–11. We estimate that this is about 172 verses within a total from Paul of around 1,791.

6. Later we will suggest that this translation of one of this cluster's prominent verbs is not very helpful. See further on this question in note 7 following.

7. It really does not matter what we call it—we could call this reading by a number of other names—so long as we understand how the theory actually operates. But we

theory—JT for short—meaning by this an account of *salvation* in terms of something called "justification."

Justification theory as a "pre-understanding"

But perhaps at this moment we are thinking that it is unnecessary or even inappropriate that we are going to work our way into this problem by describing justification *theory*. Can't I just read the Bible and worry about the theory later? Isn't justification in the first instance a reading or interpretation of what Paul wrote in the Bible, with any theory and/or theology just rising out of that? Isn't this how the reading of our Scriptures works all the time?

As much as we wish it were this simple, we need to realize that we all come to texts with certain presuppositions that affect how we read them.[8] Having these theories in place first—what the great German scholar of interpretation Hans-Georg Gadamer called a *Vorverständnisse* or "prior understanding"[9]—is an unavoidable part of being a thinking human being. In fact, we take our experiences, social locations, cultural influences, emotional programing, and ideological commitments with us wherever we go to process the cacophony of data that confronts us. If this was not the case—if we lacked these theoretical pre-understandings—we would lack the basic mental tools that allow us to interpret reality at all; we would simply be overwhelmed by a great mass of uninterpreted data flooding in upon us. But reading is just an especially specialized instance of data interpretation. Hence, with respect to the Bible in general, and Paul in particular, we already have certain expectations in place about what we are reading well before we start reading him for ourselves. We all stand within "traditions" of interpretation that help us to read, just as we have been tested and then taught to wear spectacles to help those of us with challenged eyesight to grasp the words on a page or a screen with clarity. Once we are reading

---

have chosen to proceed here by referring to it as "justification theory" (abbreviated to "JT"), partly because this links up with earlier research we have done on this subject. In particular, Douglas demonstrates in full in *The Deliverance of God* how JT has dominated the interpretation of Paul for many years, at both an academic and a popular level, and how it is structured. These discussions are introduced more briefly in *Quest*, and summarized and debated by other scholars in Tilling (ed.), *Beyond*. Justification theory is treated in relation to Paul's life in *Framing* (because related biographical questions always come up), and everything is drawn together more briefly and accessibly in *Journey*. *Pauline Dogmatics* also repositions this material more helpfully, principally in chapter 27, "Beyond Colonialism" (pp. 652–87).

8. And these texts are being read in an especially "theory-laden" fashion.

9. Gadamer, *Hermeneutik*, vol. 1, 272–312. For an introduction to Gadamer's thinking in English, see Grondin, *The Philosophy of Gadamer*.

with the help of our glasses, we don't notice the adjustments our brains have already made to their lenses (and so on), although we certainly noticed that process when we first put on a new set. Just so, we have often been taught that Jesus's death on the cross, faith, justice, the law, and salvation all mean something very specific—and important!—and when we find these words in Paul's texts we tend to assume we already know what they mean and how they cohere together, and our reading tends to confirm this prior viewpoint. The construal of the words on the page before us seems natural and obvious, although in reality it is anything but. It is the presence of our "prior understanding" that makes our interpretations *seem* natural and obvious.

We emphasize this point because long experience has taught us that Paul's justification material—the 10 percent of his texts that we are now concerned with—is read with an especially powerful prior understanding in place. These often-unnoticed spectacles are actually doing a great deal of work to bring Paul's texts into focus. In short, what we call justification theory—hereafter JT—is a particular combination of received expectations concerning what certain words and phrases that occur in around 10 percent of Paul's texts mean, along with how they fit together into an extended account of salvation, and it has dominated much of Paul's interpretation since the Reformation.[10] It is time now to press into just how this theory works so that we recognize the work it is doing, often unnoticed, when we process the textual data in Paul.

The mechanics of justification theory

One of the most well-known advocates of JT is pastor, author, and founder of DesiringGod.org, John Piper, who argues for a certain sort of Reformed reading of Paul (and of Christian theology in general). Piper has written and preached extensively on the subject of justification and this version of Paul's gospel, and his works and theological influence have made their way into countless church contexts. His most well-known work on the subject of justification in Paul was written in 2007, which was, a little ironically, just after Douglas had submitted the manuscript of *Deliverance* for publication.[11]

10. Justification theory so pervades our modern western contexts—especially if we are Protestants—that we will have a hard time grasping its nature and influence until we reach a certain vantage point. Our hope nevertheless is that we can get there.

11. It is in fact interesting to note that Piper's analysis bears many of the key claims of *Deliverance* out. *Deliverance* begins with an account of JT, describing its internal workings in detail, rather as we are about to do here. And all of its claims are confirmed *exactly* by Piper's slightly later book.

Piper's rather shorter book, *The Future of Justification*,[12] was a response to the position of another vastly influential Christian figure and scholar then serving as the bishop of Durham, N. T. Wright.[13] Wright is one of the most well-known proponents of the "new perspective" on justification in Paul, and we will talk about his suggestions in more detail later on, in chapter 10. For now we need only note that Piper was deeply concerned by Wright's perceived innovations, and crafted a beautifully lucid account of JT in its classic form in response to him. (Wright then responded quickly to Piper with another book simply entitled *Justification*,[14] and we see here immediately just how contested this material in Paul has been in recent times.) The account of justification that Piper advances in his book against Wright is an especially cogent example of how JT works and of how it reads certain key texts in Paul. His treatment also makes the point nicely that justification is a *theory*. So when people speak of "justification" in Paul, even though they are, strictly speaking, referencing just a word that Paul uses in a variety of ways (i.e., the nominalized form of the Greek verb *dikaioō*), they generally mean that this word, read in a certain way, evokes arguments in certain key texts that are best read ultimately as a theory about how we get saved—in terms of something called justification. But what exactly does this mean?

Justification theory according to Piper: 9 steps

1. Everyone, without exception, knows God accurately

Much of JT is dominated by Paul's supposed description of "the situation of the world," to quote Piper, which is based almost entirely on a particular reading of Romans 1:18—3:20.[15] There Paul seems to begin his argument specifically by saying that all individual human beings have an accurate and enduring knowledge of God's expectations for them either by analyzing the cosmos or by looking inward. Romans 1:20–21 states this clearly,[16] *and this*

---

12. Piper, *The Future of Justification: A Response to N. T. Wright* (2007).

13. Wright is an important representative of one modern attempted solution to the challenges of JT usually referred to as "the new perspective" on Paul. We will argue in due course that this solution creates more problems than it solves.

14. *Justification: God's Plan and Paul's Vision* (2009).

15. Piper, *The Future of Justification*, 67.

16. See, e.g., Piper, *The Future of Justification*, 108: ". . .every human being is truly and justly guilty before God because everyone has access to the truth but suppresses it. . . . All are accountable to God."

is the theory's foundation—the thing upon which everything else rests. (Note, this looks initially like a rather different starting point for the gospel and its truth claims from the account supplied in the previous three chapters, where information about God came through Jesus and the Spirit by revelation.) In order for the rest of JT to unfold, however, we need more information from Piper about the God who is known simply by reflecting on the cosmos as in chapter 1:19–20 and/or our consciences as Romans 2:15 suggest. What is this foundational, self-evident knowledge?

2. The righteousness of God is God's commitment to his glory

God is *righteous*, although what Piper means by "the righteousness of God" (in Greek, *dikaiosynē theou*) is quite specific. He suggests at first that "God's righteousness consists in his unswerving commitment to do what is right" (p. 63). But there is not much to argue with in this rather general initial definition. Indeed, it risks being tautologous or empty—"God is characterized by righteousness because He is right." Piper's criticism of Wright's specific construal of the righteousness of God (that is, of the Greek phrase that Paul uses, *dikaiosynē theou*) in terms of "covenant faithfulness," however, begins to reveal just what he thinks the content of this important noun phrase in Paul actually is.[17] He writes:

> Not in the least do I want to question that God's righteousness impels him to be faithful to his covenant promises, to judge without partiality, to deal with sin "properly," and to stand up for those who are unjustly oppressed. . . . [But] the question is: What is it about God's righteousness that compels him to act in these ways? *Behind* each of those actions is the assumption that there is something about God's righteousness that explains why he acts as he does. (pp. 62–63, emphasis added)

Piper states here that we need to press "behind" God's specific activities of faithfulness, liberation, and so on, to understand what his righteousness *really* consists of, underneath it all, deep down. If we just observe how God is acting, we are only viewing "some of the things righteousness *does*" (p. 62). For Piper, God's particular attribute of righteousness cannot be the same thing as God's acts of rightness, just as (presumably) God's being is

---

17. The phrase occurs in Rom 1:17; 3:21 and 22, implicitly in 25 and 26; 2x in 10:3; probably, in a slightly different form, in 1 Cor 1:30; in 2 Cor 5:21; and in another probable variation in Phil 3:9. The expression might also be implicit in Gal 2:21; 3:21; and 5:5.

necessarily distinguishable from his activity.[18] What, then, is this righteousness that lies behind God's activity?

Piper states now that God is righteous in the specific sense that he is committed in an utterly unwavering fashion "to uphold[ing] the glory of his name" (p. 64). Any act of God comes from "this deepest allegiance" (p. 65) to "preserve the honor of his name and display his glory" (p. 66). How does Piper know this?

He holds that this is, as step one just suggested, simply self-evident:

> The reasoning goes like this: The ultimate value in the universe is God—the whole panorama of his perfections. Another name for this is God's holiness (viewed as the intrinsic and infinite worth of his perfect beauty) or God's glory (viewed as the outstreaming manifestation of that beauty). Therefore, "right" must be ultimately defined in relation to this ultimate value, the holiness or the glory of God—this is the highest standard for "right" in the universe. (p. 64)

Having said this, for Piper, this understanding of God's righteousness is also witnessed to by "dozens of Old Testament texts" (p. 64), although if it is self-evident, then its truth is technically accessible to anyone without direct appeal to the Bible.

In fact, Piper is revealing here his specifically Calvinist leanings—although the language of Ephesians 1 is also not far from view—and we might still suspect this definition of being a little empty. It is certainly fair to suggest that God's righteousness and rightness will be closely related to his holiness and his glory. But we need to know now just how that holiness and glory are defined. We see, that is, that further vital pieces of information still need to be supplied, and Piper is well aware of this. They begin to emerge as he turns to address God's righteous demands of *us*.

3. Both the Jewish law and personal conscience reveal God's righteous expectations

Piper goes on to argue quite fairly that God's righteousness defines true human righteousness as its standard: "Therefore, what is right is what upholds in proper proportion the value of what is infinitely valuable, namely, God. 'Right' actions are those that flow from a proper esteem for God's glory and

18. There is a potential problem here for Piper and those who think like him if we pay close attention to the way God has *acted* through Jesus, coming among us as this person, thereby revealing who exactly he (God) *is*. God's activity and his being must here be identical. But this is not the right moment to develop this insight.

that uphold his glory as the most valuable reality there is" (p. 64). But this esteem and upholding turn out to mean a due attentiveness to God's *demands*, and this is a crucial further step.

God's demands are made clear in just the same way that the knowledge of his existence and nature are—to gentiles through their consciences, while Jews possess written information in their Scriptures which Piper refers to in the usual way for this model as "law" (Gk. *nomos*). This arrangement ensures that "God is impartial" (p. 106), preventing God from being unjust or unrighteous, since someone might object that a particular constituency does not "have equal access to what they will be held accountable for!" (p. 106). So, while Jews have the written Torah, "the deeds required in the moral law of God . . . are on [gentiles'] hearts" (p. 107). Consequently "Gentiles *do* have the law" and, like Jews, know God's expectations for them (p. 107, emphasis original).

As a result of this arrangement, all of humanity is asked to act in accord with God's righteous demands, which are well known: "the moral behavior of all kinds of people all over the world shows that they have a sense of many true, God-given, moral obligations and their conscience confirms this with the conflicting self-defenses and self-accusations that it constantly brings up" (p. 107).[19]

This is a critical step in Piper's articulation of JT that must be noted carefully. He has ended up by this point in his account arguing that God's rightness is defined in terms of *moral demands* made of humanity that function like rules or laws, which means that God himself is functioning here above all like a *judge*. God is a judge—and a certain sort of judge—and the basic relationship between God and humanity is consequently *legal*. That is, God relates to us primarily through *laws* which he oversees, adjudicates, and enforces. The definition of just what is right by these laws is, moreover, according to Piper, self-evident. Everything else in JT will build from this set of assumptions.

4. Reward or punishment result from fulfilling God's demands (or not)

It follows directly from what we have just learned that a conditional logic lies at the heart of JT. It is not enough for Jews and gentiles to have access to God's demands; they must fulfill them, and this means all of God's expectations. If

19. This arrangement also presupposes with the giving of this demand that the ability to act rightly is also present—what philosophers tend to refer to as capacity. We all know God's righteous demands, and can act in accordance with them; if we can't then the entire arrangement is not very fair. But if we do know and we can act and yet fail to do so, then we are "without excuse" (Rom 1:20).

they do so, then they will uphold God's glory and be rewarded. But if they fail to do so flawlessly and therefore turn away from God's glory, they will be punished: "Jews and Gentiles will receive or not receive eternal life on the same terms," that is, "'according to . . . works,' not according to their ethnic or religious advantage" (p. 105).[20] God is clearly relating to humanity, whether Jew or pagan, in terms of rules and laws, which specify conditions that must be fulfilled if the judging God is to stay in relationship with them.

We should note here as well, most importantly, that God's rightness is now further defined as *retributive* in the sense that actions must elicit the appropriate payment or recompense from God in response; the Latin verb *retribuere* from which the English word retribution comes means "to pay." As Piper makes clear then, "having access to the moral law of Moses and hearing it is not an advantage at the final judgment. At the judgment, the question will not be: How much of the law did you hear? The question will be: Did you do it?" (p. 106). Depending on our answer, the appropriate retribution will follow—the "payment" of eternal life for the good, and the "payment" of pain, exclusion, and hell, for those who have acted wickedly. The righteousness of God, or his rightness, is now clearly interchangeable with his justice, defining that justice in retributive terms. And this last qualification needs to be born in mind because "justice" can be defined in so many different ways.[21] God's retributive justice is now going to be the key aspect of his character. It will drive the rest of the salvific progression, although, as most of us probably know well, this initial arrangement is not going to work out very well.

5. *The problem: humans, in their sinfulness, fail to follow God's commands*

A significant problem now emerges into view for humanity because, as Piper goes on to observe, "everyone has access to the truth *but suppresses it* (Rom 1:18)" (p. 108). People apparently *resist* God's righteous expectations intentionally, which renders them guilty before God: "[E]very human being is truly and justly guilty before God *because everyone has access to the truth but suppresses it* (Rom 1:18). None lives up to this truth, *nor even up to the*

20. This reference to ethnic advantage is a specific rejoinder to some of Wright's suggested reorientations of JT.

21. See, for example, Michael Sandel's well-known introduction to nine different accounts of doing the right thing or acting justly, none of which is retributive, in *Justice: What's the Right Thing to Do?* A deeper engagement with the difficulties of defining "justice" is supplied by Alasdair MacIntyre in his *Whose Justice? Which Rationality?*

demands of his own conscience" (p. 108, emphases added). Hence everyone "will be without excuse" and will be "guilty before [God]" (p. 108). Indeed, it turns out that this is "the point of it all" (p. 108) with respect to humanity's knowledge of God's expectations: we cannot actually fulfill them (or, strictly speaking, we do not), whether Jew or pagan, *and are consequently destined for punishment.* Quoting Stephen Westerholm, another prolific advocate of JT, Piper claims that human beings in fact have a "'massive, unremitting sense of answerability to their Maker.'"[22] But this sense of answerability must mean, at least in part, that people *expect* a coming condemnation because of their sinful inability to do the necessary righteous actions. Referencing Paul's calling in Acts, Piper writes:

> I do not think it would be wild speculation to suggest that when Saul, who hated Jesus and his followers, fell to the ground under the absolute, sovereign authority of the irresistible brightness of the living Jesus, his first thoughts would not be about his concepts, *but about his survival.* His first thoughts would not have been about a new worldview and a new vocation, *but whether he would at that moment be destroyed.* (p. 87, emphasis added)

The assumption here is that Paul would have expected to be punished by God, knowing full well his own sinfulness, guilt, and answerability to God because of his failure to live up to God's expectations.[23] And this depiction of Paul's own basic introspection is extended to the rest of humanity. As people attempt yet fail to do God's commands there is a sense in which they are confronted with the knowledge of their own sinfulness and inability to please God, and with what that entails (see especially Rom 3:20)—death! *God* will basically execute them for their wrongdoing at the end of the age, pronouncing and carrying out this verdict on the day of judgment.

6. All humans deserve retributive punishment for their sins

As JT has already suggested, a right and holy God who is committed to upholding his own glory in the sense of his own retributive justice must

22. Piper, *Future of Justification*, 87; quoting Stephen Westerholm, "The 'New Perspective' at Twenty-Five," 38.

23. We should note in passing that this example doesn't prove Piper's point very well because Paul did not apparently have the sense prior to this moment, or even right as his experience was taking place, that he was doing something wrong when he was persecuting Jesus's followers. In fact, the Acts data suggests that his first thought was simply, "Who are you, Lord?" (Acts 9:5), which is what he says. Jesus's revelation *itself* would eventually disclose the error of Paul's ways, as we noted at length in chapter 1.

necessarily respond to any human failure to do the good with *wrath*, and wrath of a specifically retributive sort. If this is not the case then "how would God judge the world?" (Rom 3:6). Moreover, as Piper makes clear, the pending reality of God's wrath and the need for escape from it is not a "subplot." Rather, it is what Piper calls "the bad news" entailed by the gospel itself—the "absolutely terrifying message to a sinner who has spent all his life ignoring or blaspheming God the Father of the Lord Jesus Christ and is therefore guilty of treason and *liable to execution*" (p. 86, emphasis added). Harm must be visited on any wrongdoers for the wrong that they have done at the end of the age. Moreover, this clearly applies to *everyone*. We are *all* "on trial in God's law court" (p. 165), because "we all have failed" (p. 164). And God's wrath will consequently be revealed against all humanity in its entirety because of its unrighteousness, as God "cannot deny himself" (2 Tim 2:13). In God's law court, our sentence will inevitably be that we all "deserve to die," as Romans 1:32 also affirms.

Piper neatly summarizes the situation thus far by saying, "Paul operates with the Old Testament understanding that the deepest meaning of God's righteousness is his unwavering commitment to act for the sake of his glory. The belittling of his glory by all humanity is the problem Paul sets up in Romans chapters 1 to 3" (p. 68), although we have also learned from Romans chapters 1 to 3 that this belittling has a quite specific legal content. (Romans 1–3 never actually says that we belittle God's glory.)[24] Disobedience to God's law is "belittling," and retribution is the appropriate form of justice by way of response. When your glory is belittled you respond with punishment. Hence there is a very real sense in which, according to this gospel, the restoration of God's glory can only be achieved through the universal application to humanity of the death penalty.

Where do we go from here? We seem to be trapped!

7. The solution: Christ's satisfaction of God's wrath

Thankfully, there is finally some good news—at least for some—namely, "God's solution," which Paul articulates in Romans 3:22 and following (p. 68). And we move at this moment into a second broad phase within JT.

---

24. The closest the text comes to this idea is possibly in 3:23 when it speaks of "lacking" or "falling short" of the *doxa tēs theou*, which might mean lacking/falling short of God's glory, but might also mean that we lack the glory that comes *from* God, that is, we lack the original, glorious image of Adam, because we have sinned and been expelled as a race from the garden of Eden. Certainly this is where Paul seems to be going later in the letter; see 5:12 and 8:18–21. In 1:23 God's glory is "exchanged" which might be what Piper is getting at.

We have laid out the contours of the non-Christian situation, and they are closing in on the people occupying that state. But the non-Christian can step out of this parlous situation into the saved Christian state thanks to the work of Christ. God has graciously redirected the punishment he should inflict on unrighteous and ungodly humanity onto Christ. God the Father "puts forward Christ to vindicate his righteousness, that is, to show that he does not take lightly the scorning of his glory. When he justifies 'the ungodly' (who have treated his glory with contempt, Rom 1:18, 23; and 4:5), he is not unrighteous, because *the death of Christ exhibits God's wrath against God-belittling sin*" (p. 67, emphasis added). God has thereby "removed his judicial wrath from us" (p. 185) and offers Christ specifically as a "propitiation" (p. 67). As some theologians put this, God's wrath is *satisfied* in Christ's crucifixion. Someone still gets punished as they should; the unleashing of divine harm necessitated by human wrongdoing and its absorption is a price that still gets paid; the death penalty is still exacted. And this is clearly one of the crucial moments at the heart of JT. Without this appeasement of God's wrath on the cross there is no hope in the offer made by the gospel and all would be lost. However, in Christ's death, the gospel according to JT declares, he receives what we deserve and in so doing satisfies the Father's righteous need to respond with retribution to anything that fails to "uphold the worth of his glory" (p. 164). A way out of our predicament has been created. Our wrongdoing need not result in our eternal death.

8. Imputation of Christ's perfect righteousness

Piper goes on to remind us that God still requires the moral righteousness from us that he has in himself: "His demand is [our] unwavering and complete allegiance of heart, soul, mind, and strength" (p. 164). As we have seen, however, we cannot actually achieve this unwavering allegiance; we fall far short of it in a downfall exposed by the law. But through Christ this aspect of our situation is dealt with as well. Through Christ "we are *counted* as perfectly honoring and displaying the glory of God, which is the essence of God's righteousness, and which is also the perfect fulfilling of the law" (p. 165, emphasis added; note, Piper is drawing here especially on language that Paul uses in Romans 4). This is what JT refers to as "imputation." God also imputes or "credits" or "reckons" Christ's perfect righteousness to us "because we are in Christ *who perfectly honored God in his sinless life*" (p. 165, emphasis added). This is a slightly odd notion but it basically means that God looks at us *as if* we were Christ. God *views* us, in effect, as righteous. It is as if we are "clothed" in Christ's righteousness, which covers up our shortcomings. Hence, the solution to our predicament offered by the gospel has two complementary halves: the death penalty we should justly experience for our wrongdoing is redirected onto Christ on the cross, and the righteousness we need positively in order to be judged righteous on that fearful final day is "credited" or "imputed" to us from Christ's perfect life.

9. *Appropriation of Christ's righteousness through faith alone*

It might be asked why God does not simply gift a generous combination of forgiveness and imputed righteousness to all of humanity. All the people who do receive it are fundamentally undeserving. So why doesn't God just save everybody now "justly" through Christ? But God does not do this for reasons that lie deeply embedded in the opening assumptions of the theory. First, such a gift would erase the church, and this theory is in part an explanation of why the church exists in distinction from the rest of humanity. (In fact, it also exists in distinction from any "religious" parts of humanity that purport to belong to God's people and try to observe the law but have not understood their sinful state properly—unbelieving Jews, misguided Christians, and so on.) Second, this move would erase the basic give-and-take that lies at the heart of the model—the notion that we are asked to respond to God and God's demands in some way, and that God's response to us is then justly calibrated to how we have responded. Only a model incorporating such an arrangement, followed by accountability for how we respond to that arrangement, is just. Deep down—or perhaps not so deep down—there are obligations from God that we must accept and obey. So it seems entirely reasonable to suggest that while Christ allows us to escape the consequences of our wrongdoing in phase one, we will still be asked to do *something* in order to access that escape. We still need to act in fulfillment of our side of a certain sort of saving contract to be judged forgiven and saved.

Piper explains that we have access to this forgiveness and this righteousness "through faith." For JT then there is a clear criterion or condition for receiving the benefits of both God's gracious redirection of his wrath and his imputation to us of Christ's righteousness. "The ground of justification is the sacrifice and obedience of Christ alone, *appropriated through faith alone* before any other acts are performed" (p. 217), and we see here a new, alternative arrangement by which we can be saved. The gospel proper, according to Piper, announces this new, easier, more generous contract—one accessed by faith.

Exercising the all-important criterion of faith leads to us being "justified," so "justification," we now learn, names the situation we are in when we have had our punishment redirected onto Christ and his righteousness redirected to us after grasping onto those gifts through faith. So we are not, strictly speaking, *made* righteous, but merely *viewed* as righteous and so *pronounced* innocent or righteous, as well as acquitted of wrongdoing. We should consequently not be spoken of as righteous, because we aren't; hence, there is a sense in which we could perhaps speak more accurately at this point of "acquittal theory." But justification is the word that has passed into popular parlance to describe this situation, probably because it allows us to speak of the closely related justice of God. The just God justifies us in spite of our unjustness—and our remaining unjust—through the work of Christ, a process summed up by speaking of our "justification" and explained in terms of JT. And it is our faith that provides us with access to "all that God requires of us" (p. 184), something Christ has accomplished for us.

"Through faith alone, God establishes our union with Christ" (p. 184), "at the point of our justification when God removed his judicial wrath from us, and imputed the obedience of his Son to us, and counted us as righteous in Christ, and forgave all our sins because he had punished them in the death of Jesus" (p. 185). Piper emphasizes this key point a lot, so, for example, we can see that in the statement we just quoted he is essentially just repeating what he has already written: "God counts us as having his righteousness in Christ because we are united to him through faith alone" (p. 165). Moreover, because it is Christ's righteousness that is reckoned to us, and not our own attempted righteousness, we are guaranteed that God's future act of judgment will confirm our salvation, and this is the heart of our present justification, which consequently includes *assurance*. We are secure in "the fact that God is for us forever" (p. 186). Christians will therefore receive a positive evaluation from God in the end. And in view of this it is understandable why the imputation of Christ's righteousness to us by faith alone is nonnegotiable for Piper (and this is one of his key disagreements with Wright, who denies the cogency of imputation): "It is not nonsense [as Wright suggests]. It [i.e., our imputed righteousness] is true and precious beyond words" (p. 165).[25]

But someone might ask why Piper places such a strong emphasis on justification by faith *alone*. There are several probable reasons for this that are worth noting as we close out this description of JT.

First, this is clearly what he thinks the Bible just says. Opposite all the texts in Paul that speak of our failed attempts to achieve justification by works of law are statements that speak of justification "through faith" or a

---

25. Piper is repudiating here Wright's suggestion that the imputation to believers of Christ's righteousness is exegetically suspect and theologically a little silly.

close equivalent (although we will subject this phrase to careful analysis later and find something just a little different). Moreover, this stipulated action also seems to fit the bill. We ought to believe in the good news concerning Christ that is proclaimed by Christian preachers, evangelists, and missionaries (and we certainly agree with this). We should respond to the proclamation of the gospel with faith. But, equally importantly, having faith looks to be much more manageable than trying to be justified by doing perfect good works. Faith feels like a "work," so to speak, that we can actually undertake consistently to uphold our side of the saving bargain. Faith looks possible.

But someone might ask, "why faith *alone*?"

This emphasis is a warning not to slip back into the misguided efforts of phase one. Some people—in Paul's text, Jewish figures—seem to capriciously refuse to accept that the attempt to be justified perfectly by doing works prescribed by the law will fail; they stubbornly persevere in that arrangement, showing thereby only that they are resisting the true lesson that that arrangement is trying to teach them. They are supposed to realize from all these efforts that they are sinful and so need instead to reach out to the merciful and much easier arrangement extended through Christ! The act that complements this realization is a reliance for salvation on faith by itself, alone, without making any other claim to righteousness through some other human effort. We must accept that we are sinful, and saved therefore just by faith and not by performing extensive good works. And although Piper does not spell out these considerations in detail, he clearly endorses this dimension within JT with his repeated emphasis on justification by faith alone. This is noteworthy, moreover, because Paul never actually uses this phrase. (It appears just once in the NT, in Jas 2:24.)[26] But the phrase fits into the logic of JT very well—to the point that Luther added it to his translation of the Bible in Romans 3:28.

And with this last element in place, we have completed our journey through JT. We have relied throughout on the presentation of this model by John Piper, whose exposition of it we consider to be especially clear and also especially widely known. Admittedly, it contains some distinctive emphases because of his Reformed convictions; Piper's constant emphasis on God's glory is "Calvinist." Having said this, Piper departs from other dimensions in Calvin's own thinking—along with the theology of some of Calvin's most careful interpreters—aligning in the end very closely with contemporary Evangelical positions. But much more important than any specific slants is the basic theory he articulates so well. And we need now to appreciate

26. "You see that a person is justified by works and not by faith alone." The letter from James introduces faith in context in 2:1 and then makes the claims that so upset Luther in 2:14–26.

that the distribution and influence of the basic model of salvation that he endorses—of JT—is hard to overestimate.

It is *everywhere*.

We can find the theory and all its key propositions—albeit stated a little more allusively at times than by Piper—stretching back through shoals of academic commentaries, and in the majority of modern New Testament theologies.[27] We see the model's domination in important scholarly commentaries on Romans from both the United Kingdom[28] and the United States, and in accounts written by scholars ranging from Evangelical to Roman Catholic.[29] Popular introductions to the New Testament mirror this situation as well.[30] Academic treatments incorporating or defending JT in Paul are legion.[31] The theory appears in recent scholarly and ecclesial journals,[32] in confessional statements and declarations,[33] and in evangelistic

27. Wilkens, *Der Brief an die Römer*, vol. 1, *Römer 1–5*; Bultmann, *Theology of the New Testament*; Käsemann, *Commentary on Romans*; Schlatter, *Romans*.

28 Cranfield, *A Critical and Exegetical Commentary on the Epistle to the Romans*, vol. 1 (ICC; see also his *Romans: A Shorter Commentary*). The conventional model is, for him, "the centre and heart of the whole of Romans 1:16b–15:13" (*Shorter*, 68); Sanday and Headlam, *A Critical and Exegetical Commentary on the Epistle to the Roman* (ICC).

29. Moo, *The Epistle to the Romans* (NICNT); Schreiner, *Romans* (BECNT); Fitzmyer, *Romans* (AB); Esler, *Conflict and Identity in Romans*; Witherington, *Paul's Letter to the Romans*; Keener, *Romans* (NCC); Byrne, *Romans* (SP). Robert Jewett's approach is slightly different, and much more attuned to the original circumstances of Romans than most commentaries, but it is debatable to what extent he breaks with JT; see Jewett, with Kotansky, *Romans* (Hermeneia).

30. Ehrman, *The New Testament*, especially 407–8, 410–13; Carson and Moo, *An Introduction to the New Testament*; Powell, *Introducing the New Testament*; Holladay, *A Critical Introduction to the New Testament*.

31. Ridderbos, *Paul: An Outline of His Theology*; Seifrid, *Christ, Our Righteousness*; Westerholm, *Justification Reconsidered*; Gathercole, *Defending Substitution*; Schreiner, "Paul: A Reformed Reading"; see also Schreiner's "Penal Substitution View."

32. Williams, "Violent Atonement in Romans"; Matson, "Divine Forgiveness in Paul?"; Witt, "Anglican Reflections on Justification by Faith"; Westerholm, "Justification by Faith Is the Answer: What Is the Question?"; Seifrid, "Paul's Turn to Christ in Romans."

33. See, i.a., the Evangelical Free Church of America Statement of Faith adopted in 2019, https://www.efca.org/resources/document/efca-statement-faith; The World Evangelical Alliance Statement of Faith, https://worldea.org/en/who-we-are/statement-of-faith/; the Cru Statement of Faith, https://www.cru.org/us/en/about/statement-of-faith.html; Joint Declaration on the Doctrine of Justification (The Lutheran World Federation and the Roman Catholic Church), https://episcopalchurch.org/files/documents/jddj2019.pdf.

tracts.[34] So when it comes to the interpretation of Paul, JT is a bit like the God it discerns in the cosmos—omnipresent if not also omnipotent.

Surely then, turning to the next obvious question, there must be some simple solution to the question of how to coordinate JT with the other 90 percent of things that Paul wrote which emphasize participation—the emphases, in other words, of the gospel we articulated here in chapters 1, 2, and 3? Justification theory only occurs, after all—and counting generously—in just under 10 percent of what Paul actually wrote. So there must be some plausible and obvious solution that explains how we should coordinate the 10 percent of this data, explained in terms of JT, with the other 90 percent of Paul's material that appears in our Scriptures—and certainly many of the foregoing scholars who endorse JT in Paul seem confident of this. Unfortunately, we will see in our next chapter that things are not nearly as straightforward here as we have often been led to think.

34. See especially "Have You Heard of the Four Spiritual Laws?," https://crustore. org/media/Four_Spiritual_Laws_English_.pdf.

5

Melanchthon's Solution, and
Its Central Dilemma

Justification and Sanctification

We need now to appreciate very clearly, if we do not already, that the 10 percent of Paul's texts involving justification exert an influence out of all proportion to their size because of their perceived importance for key Reformers. Luther, along with many of his colleagues and followers, are often remembered as viewing justification as foundational to any account of the gospel, and the two things were even identified by him on occasion.[1] This claim is recognizable immediately as hyperbole, however—something Luther was famous for—because justification material focuses on the journey of the individual Christian rather than on Christ himself, and Luther at his best is relentlessly focused on Christ. But the equation is nevertheless frequently reiterated, often in contradistinction to some notion of Catholicism. Catholics may even have their approach to salvation equated with the approach that JT attributes to the Jews in Paul's texts—a foolish ongoing attempt in phase one of the model to be justified by works. Hence, many Protestant and post-Protestant traditions, and especially those that root themselves directly in the turbulent events of the sixteenth century, view JT as their key denominational identifier or distinctive. The very identity of Protestantism as an authentic recovery of the heart of the gospel and hence

---

1. Perhaps most famously in *The Schmalkald Articles*.

59

as a legitimate divergence from Catholicism is held by many scholars and preachers to rest on an account of the gospel in terms of JT.[2]

But advocates of this viewpoint still need to deal with the question that our last section ended with. How does the 10 percent of material in Paul that, read in a certain way, delivers JT, relate coherently to the 90 percent that he wrote everywhere else, which emphasizes a highly transformational and participatory approach to salvation based on being resurrected in Christ? (And we should note that the Reformers emphasized this participatory material in Paul a great deal as well.)

The usual answer was provided most clearly by Melanchthon, who, although not generally regarded quite as highly as Luther and Calvin, was certainly an eminent leader and scholar of the Reformation in his own right.[3]

Melanchthon's solution involves a number of key assumptions. First, like many Bible scholars in his day, he assumed that in his letters Paul was writing systematic theology for the church. Paul's thinking about the gospel could be read straight off the page and did not need to pass through any reconstruction of the circumstances that gave rise to his arguments, although the latter would be the approach that a modern scholar trained in historical methods of inquiry would take. The longest letter Paul ever wrote, moreover, was Romans, which was the first of Paul's letters to appear in the New Testament canon precisely because it was the longest. (The Pauline letters are basically arranged in order of length.)[4] So reading Paul's letters as systematic theology, and reading Romans first, due to its length, Melanchthon found that although justification material only occurred in 10 percent of what Paul wrote, its largest concentration (Romans 1:16—5:1) occurred in what Paul wrote first; this material occurred *first of all in the first great Pauline letter*. As a result of this Melanchthon felt that it was reasonable to treat this material as Paul's gospel of salvation and then sequence all Paul's other material after it as a second phase within salvation, which is what

2. One reason we use JT rather than "the Lutheran reading of Paul" or something similar is to allow the appropriate nuancing of these relationships in due course. Justification theory is present in Luther, Calvin, and so on, but it by no means dominates their work. Scholars of Luther and Calvin continue to debate the real center of gravity in their thinking, and *not* usually in terms of JT. Moreover, much that Luther said about Paul that was very important has nothing to do with JT. Similarly, Lutheranism and Calvinism should not be reduced to the influence of JT—an absurd oversimplification of the histories of these respective traditions—and that oversimplification should definitely not be extended to the entirety of the Reformation.

3. Biographical details about him can be found in Steinmetz, *Reformers in the Wings*, 49–57.

4. The letters were probably arranged in this way, after the Gospels and the book of Acts in the emerging canon, at the end of the second century CE, so in the late 100s.

seems to happen as we read on in Romans (reading this letter, to reiterate, as a treatise on systematic theology). Romans chapters 5 to 8 does follow Romans chapters 1 to 4, and everything else that Paul wrote does follow Romans chapters 1 to 4 in the Bible. It seems reasonable then, given these assumptions, to begin here. If Paul in Romans is writing systematic theology for the church in Romans—and if the Bible has put Romans first in line for a reason—then JT is where Paul begins.

But what do we do with the material that follows Romans chapters 1 to 4, and that ultimately undergirds 90 percent of what Paul wrote?

Melanchthon has a reasonable answer.

The material in the second phase is usually designated "sanctification," and it tells us, Melanchthon suggests, how to act as disciples—how to go on in the church—*after* we have *entered* the church by way of justification and faith. Hence for readers of Paul like Melanchthon this participatory material is not Paul's soteriology or even his gospel and it is certainly not where theology begins. Paul begins with JT. But after we have been justified then we need to get on with being sanctified—and justification does not involve that much for us, apart from faith—and participation describes the dynamics of this new situation and its implications. It is as if we enter a new delightful but strongly-walled garden by way of justification; our faith and our faith alone is the key that unlocks the gate. Once we are inside we nevertheless need to learn about the garden and how to tend it and this is where we press into Paul's teaching about sanctification. So the 10 percent is the wall around the 90 percent specifying its all-important gate; we enter the 90 percent through the gateway of the 10 percent, and hence *only* by going through the 10 percent can we get to the other 90 percent!

But a simple question now lies before us. Can these two types of material be integrated together smoothly within Paul's thinking or not? Can we fit the 10 percent and the 90 percent neatly together with justification and the 10 percent explaining how people get saved and then sanctification following in the other 90 percent detailing how life as a Christian should then be lived? Certainly a large number of scholars, teachers, and preachers endorse Melanchthon's arrangement without detecting any major difficulties here. But it might be that their loyalty to JT is overriding some subtle signals that this explanation does not work as well as it really needs to. And shortly we will suggest that some major problems are present here. It is as if the wall does not really fence off *this* garden; it presupposes a very different sort of garden inside its boundaries. Moreover, the garden we do find in Paul, once we begin to explore it carefully, asks us to set up a very different sort of boundary, with different entrances and different ways of getting in. Arguably it is even a garden without walls, surrounded by inviting fields and paths. Any wall erected by JT is consequently the wrong sort of construction altogether for this sort of garden.

This is, admittedly, a difficult inquiry to enter in to. Many of the defenders of the classic Protestant reading of justification contend that JT is the gospel and that denying or modifying JT in any way undermines the gospel. It must be defended! John Piper certainly thinks this, as we saw in the previous chapter. The very gospel is supposedly at stake.

We contend, however, that the opposite is the case.

Maintaining that JT is the gospel and advocating in turn the subordination of everything else Paul says to JT—subordinating the 90 percent to the 10 percent—*obscures and undermines the real Pauline gospel, which is actually found in the 90 percent.* It will become apparent, that is, as we press deeper, that Paul's real gospel—in something of an irony—has been held in "a Babylonian captivity" for at least five hundred years, imprisoned by a false account of his gospel inherited from certain descendants of Luther (although arguably not from Luther himself) that has prefaced and over-ridden it—JT. It is long past time then for the captives to be released from their quasi-Protestant exile. Put a little more colloquially: it is time for the JT tail to stop wagging the Pauline dog.[5] And it is time for the JT tail to stop wagging the Protestant dog, insofar as it ever did.

The groundwork for this critical realization has already been laid by previous chapters. In chapters 1 through 3 we laid out a brief account of God's cosmic plan and of his specific plan of salvation within this which pulled us back on track after we had foolishly strayed into sin, a plan that pivoted dramatically around Jesus's death and resurrection. In chapter 4, we then laid out an account of salvation in Paul in terms of JT as one of its leading representatives, John Piper, describes it. With these two accounts from our earlier discussions in place we are now in a position to compare them and to ask if they fit together in a neat sequence or not, as Melanchthon suggested.

And the answer is "no."

Careful consideration suggests that these two models of salvation contradict each other at the most fundamental level. In particular, their accounts of the nature of God are different, and not just a little different; *they are utterly divergent.* Piper's gospel of JT is based on a God of retributive justice whereas the gospel of resurrectional participation is based on a God of love, and these are different Gods. Having said this, the full gravity of this difference is sometimes not appreciated so we will spend some time here

---

5. Again, it needs to be appreciated that not all Lutherans or Protestants in general are committed to JT as the definitive account of Paul's gospel. Many are, but many are not.

reflecting on just how different these two accounts of God are.[6] Furthermore, other deep differences will become obvious as we do so, and it is the presence of these differences that renders Melanchthon's solution unworkable.[7] His suggested arrangement of this material in a simple sequence of salvation followed by discipleship—of salvation by justification followed by discipleship by sanctification—is just going to come apart. It is an attempt to hitch a trailer to a fish. These two things are just different. They don't fit together and they were never meant to. But in order to appreciate the full scale of our difficulties we need to identify some basic insights that have been implicit in everything that we have said up to this point that now need to be brought to full clarity.

Contractual relationships

Modern human societies, especially those in the western world, are primarily structured in their public realms—what some philosophers refer to as "civil society"—in legal and hence in conditional terms. The United States in particular has a special fondness for doing things this way, which is to say, for organizing society in terms of rules that must be enforced if broken. US politics rests on laws and consequently it is conditional in this legal sense from top to bottom. "If you observe X and Y then you will be safe and unbothered, but if you break X and Y then you will be apprehended and appropriately punished." Vast numbers of tax dollars go into maintaining and equipping the huge institutions that make all this happen—the Department of Public Safety, the Department of Justice, and the Department of Corrections. But complementing all this somewhat negative conditionality in terms of law enforcement and public order is a mass of positive commercial conditionality. The way that we exchange goods and services in almost all of our economic and cultural domains is based on contracts. Indeed, capitalism is unthinkable without them. So most of us have signed important

6. No one lays out the differences here more clearly than James B. Torrance. In two articles he describes the battle between these two accounts of salvation through the eighteenth and nineteenth centuries for the soul of Scottish Presbyterianism: see his "Covenant or Contract: A Study of the Theological Background of Worship in Seventeenth-Century Scotland" (1970); and "The Contribution of Mcleod Campbell to Scottish Theology" (1973). Although these essays present as somewhat technical, they are extremely lucid. They can be found as "Appendix A" and "Appendix B" in Tilling (ed.), *Beyond Old and New Perspectives on Paul*, 261–301.

7. And certain unhelpful psychological and institutional dynamics will often become apparent here as well. Advocates of JT, and of a smooth, untroubled justification-sanctification sequence, have a vested interest in *not* seeing any problems in this arrangement!

contracts—maybe for a job, or perhaps a book deal—and those of us in-volved with the direct provision of goods and services are signing them all the time.[8] Every purchase that we make is a contract. And every time that we do this we are committing to a *conditional* relationship.

That is, we are saying when we sign a contract, or even tacitly in-voke one, that we will fulfill certain conditions in order to receive certain promised rewards. If we fulfill the stipulated conditions then we will re-ceive what we contracted for, and if we don't then we won't: no provision of what we promised to do and no provision from our contracted partners of what they promised to do is forthcoming, and penalties might even be activated. Hence, in our case here, no manuscript, no book publication, and no royalties, assuming, that is, that we will sell enough books to get any. . . . But provided that we do eventually provide a manuscript, the publisher, as contractually obligated, will publish it and eventually send us a check for the amount of remuneration agreed upon. Hence, our entire relationship is framed legally and conditionally.

In a slightly less obvious sense, every time we swipe our credit card and reach out to take a cup of coffee from our charming Starbucks host we invoke a contract; we contract with Starbucks by providing a certain sum of money in exchange for which we expect a cup of coffee made to order and of reasonable quality—and if it isn't, we ask for our money back! Again, our relationship is contractual.

This sort of arrangement between parties feels quite natural to us even though it is, in fact, culturally constructed from top to bottom. Capitalism is, we should remind ourselves, a relatively recent entrant onto the human historical stage, gathering steam, both metaphorically and literally, from the eighteenth century onward.[9] It is understandable, nevertheless, in view of the vast influence of contracts and their legal conditions on our politics, so-ciety, and commerce, that in the first quarter of the twenty-first century we would be tempted to think that God operates in this fashion too. Christians growing up in highly productive societies of which they are quite proud find this a very "natural" way to think about God, and so many do. (Note the powerful influence of a "prior understanding" here.) But what happens if we suppose that God constructs his relationships with us in this way—that he has made the cosmos rest on the rule of law and the enforcement of legal and contractual relationships and their conditions?

The consequences are theologically disastrous.

8. It should be obvious at this point that we do not think marriage is reducible to a legal contract.

9. See Briggs, *The Age of Improvement, 1783–1867*.

If God enters into a contractual relationship with us, complete with legal sorts of conditions, then it is hard to see how it can be the case that God really loves us, which means in turn that the sort of God we would be talking about would not be the God that we saw in Paul's gospel as it was described in the opening chapters of this book. A God of contract would not be the God definitively revealed in the person of Jesus Christ. Why? Because Jesus revealed to us a God characterized by limitless love, and love is fundamentally *un*conditional, not conditional in a contractual sense, and we all know this once we sit down and think about it.

We have already determined that God's loving nature is best described by the healthiest relationships among us, which are especially found in, although not limited to, family relationships. And family relationships in their best and healthiest instances *never let go*.[10] Their love is *irrevocable* and never abandons its object. Parents will always be the parents of their children, and should always be committed to them in spite of what they do. So our children will always be our children and we will never let go of them, even as our spouses are always supposed to be our spouses. (We are speaking in ideal, perfect terms here obviously, but God is perfect.) Put slightly more prosaically: a quick examination of our own lives suggests that kinship relations are not constructed in contractual terms, which terminate if certain conditions are not met. Indeed, the very moment we introduce a legal type of condition into kinship relationships we completely undermine what it means to be in a loving relationship. Kinship relations are utterly different from contractual relationships *and it is critical that they remain so.* They are in fact vastly more important than contractual relationships. Our kin matter to us in ways that our contractual partners never will. It is kinship relationships that bring us into being, shape us, surround us (or not . . .), and that we tend to foster in turn, noting that close friendships can and should function in the same way as well. And God relates to us as kin, which means that he loves us extravagantly, unconditionally, and irrevocably—again, supposing that kinship is working at its best, not its worst. Our families and friends are meant to love us and God *does* love us.

In a contractual construction of kinship, however—to entertain this bizarre arrangement just for a moment—any love would be something that could only occur if the people involved had fulfilled certain conditions, so, strictly speaking, if people break the agreement that brought them together then the love and the kinship ceases to exist.[11] But what sort of parent or

10. We note again the important caveats that no human family is perfect, and that some human families have been horribly destructive. But we hold that this damage is parasitic upon a set of relationships that are supposed to be fundamentally healthy and good.

11. The existence of prenuptial agreements is therefore a blatant theological error; it

spouse or sibling or child or even close lifelong friend thinks like this?! We are not parents *because* our children fulfill certain conditions that make them our children.[12] We do not cease to be their parents if they fail to do what we expect them to do and thereby break a parent-child contract. There are no criteria that our children can violate that will abrogate our parenthood of them. We are stuck with them and they with us. We will always be their parents and they will always be our children, just as our parents will always be our parents and we will always be their children. In like manner, our closest friends are not our closest friends because they fulfill certain conditions in the absence of which we could casually unfriend them as we would reject some irritating connection on Facebook. They are our friends because they love us and are there for us even when we aren't our best selves. Instinctively then we know, deep down, that there are no conditions of this nature on love. (Expectations yes, but conditions, no.) Love is what it is in large measure because it holds *in spite of* conditions. It *defies* conditions. "I will love you for better, for worse, for richer, for poorer, in sickness and in health, until death do us part." So to construe our relationship with God in terms of conditions like a contract is to fundamentally alter and to undermine it. Indeed, it is to fundamentally alter our picture of God. If God does not relate to us in an unconditional way as in the best sort of family relationship then he is no longer a God of love. The God of contractual relations and the God of kinship relations are just not the same thing; they are not the same God. So the fence that justification wants to place around the garden of sanctification *destroys that garden*. For those who open the gate, nothing but a scorched and blighted terrain awaits within.

However, someone might object at this moment that God is retributive toward humanity in general but then loving to those people who have entered into an obedient relationship with him by fulfilling the relevant conditions, for example, by having faith. He is loving to his own—and only to his own, and this is enough. Once we have gotten through the gate there is love on the inside.

---

denies that a relationship *is* ultimately beginning from a place of unconditional and—at least attempted—irrevocable commitment. It is then a classic instance of the subversion of a proper, covenantal account of marriage into a false, contractual account.

12. It is worth emphasizing here in passing that covenantal relationships possess very strong expectations of good and right behavior, and ultimately place stronger pressures on their participants to act well than contractual arrangements do. Does the strongest influence on our good behavior come from a local politician or law-enforcement official, or from our spouse or parent or close friend? *Because* we are covenanted to certain people, we have strong and specific expectations of right behavior in those relationships.

But this is a flawed solution that actually returns us to the problem we just noted. Careful reflection suggests that God does not *really* love even a privileged, special group who gain entrance if they gain entrance in this conditional way. God is *generous* to this group but this is not the same thing as love.

If God only loves us after we fulfill certain conditions and enter the church then God has to be conditioned into loving us in the first place. So even if God does treat us with affection for a time, it is not really proper love. It began from another place after a two-way deal was made. God did not reach out to us and engage with us *because he loved us.* Moreover, he *only* loves us *while we do certain things,* and if we stop or falter *then he stops loving us.* This "love" will be withdrawn the moment that we slip up and break the conditions of our relationship. So we might enjoy a time of warm affection and benevolence with God, but we know that if we make a bad mistake and break the terms of our agreement God's affection will disappear to be replaced by a pending death penalty. How is this loving or even fundamentally parental then?[13]

It isn't.

What parent says, "I am your father and you are my daughter as long as you do X and Y; if you stop then our father-daughter relationship will be dissolved and our relationship will shift into a law-enforcement mode; indeed, if necessary, when you do A and B, which are wrong, I will arrest you, try you, sentence you and then, if it is appropriate, execute you." A God of love reaches out to us before we reach out to him, and holds onto us even when we cannot hold on back. He is committed to us with unwavering grace even when we struggle, resist, or fail. He lives and acts beyond contracts and if necessary against them. His love never fails. Love that has to be conditioned into existence is not love at all, and "love" that begins this way can never be true love.

Theologians who structure God's relationship with us contractually basically admit all this when they characterize God's deepest nature in terms other than love. So Piper states that God is characterized fundamentally by rightness, glory, and holiness, which he goes on to define in terms of retributive justice. But this is a very different thing from unconditional love. Indeed, it is quite fascinating to note that in his account of JT he mentions the love of God very seldom, and never in a fundamental position. Did we *ever* have to speak of a God of love as we set out his account of the gospel in terms of JT? We did not.

---

13. Strictly speaking, hard-line Calvinism would not frame things this way (though it has problems of its own). Piper himself, however, is in fact deeply inconsistent here; what he gives with one hand in terms of a loving God he immediately takes back with the other hand, by way of the contractual God.

Now justice—and this particular type of justice—is a good thing in its place. But if it is not controlled by Jesus Christ it can be brutally harsh and it can never be called love in any meaningful sense. And in view of this it is unsurprising that all of our most important human relationships—the relationships that form us and that we in turn form others through—are *not* based on retribution. Indeed, it is fairly obvious that our key relationships are not contractual or based on some vague notion of "justice" at all. We do not deal with our children retributively, as we just saw, and hopefully our parents did not deal with us that way either. Neither do our spouses or best friends treat us in that way. These critical, formative relationships are *covenantal*, which is to say, they are loving in the senses that they are strong, secure, and ultimately unbreakable.[14]

What we learn at this moment then is that love enters into *covenantal* not contractual relationships, and since we know that God loves us, he must be in a covenantal relationship with us. It is then precisely *non*-contractual and *un*conditional. God offered up his only beloved Son for us *while we were still hostile sinners*—when we were completely resistant to and alienated from his loving purposes, and hence refusing to fulfill any conditions, possibly never to do so (Rom 5:6–11). Nevertheless he *still* loved us extravagantly and unconditionally—enough to die for us—which is what love does. God loves us deeply and permanently in spite of ourselves.

In view of all this we can hopefully see that the very idea that God must be conditioned into loving us, as JT suggests, undermines the central revelation that he does love us, along with any gospel that understands and proclaims this. A gospel that proclaims God's deep love for us only after the fulfillment of key conditions would not be a gospel based on Paul's deepest insights into God as revealed by Jesus, and it is not the gospel that we Christians should be proclaiming to the world. It would be a gospel unworthy of that name and we should really identify and resist its proclamation (see Gal 1:6–7).[15] And yet how many of us have heard conditional and contractual preaching in churches today that purports to be the gospel?

- *You have to be baptized, and freely choose to do so as an adult, or you're not saved.*

14. We are defining this important concept and word in this particular, specific sense, in the light of the disclosure of God's nature in these terms through Jesus and the Spirit.

15. "I am astonished that you are so quickly deserting the one who called you in the grace of Christ and are turning to a different gospel—not that there is another gospel, but there are some who are confusing you and want to pervert the gospel of Christ."

- *You need to accept Christ by saying a particular prayer, or you're not saved.*

- *You need to speak in tongues, or you're not saved.*

- *You need to believe in a particular doctrine of Scripture, or you're not saved.*

- *You need to refrain from drinking alcohol, or you're not saved.*

- *You need to believe that the earth is X number of years old, or you're not saved.*

- *You need to care for the earth in a particular way, or you're not saved.*

- *You need to work for social justice, or you're not saved.*

In all these "gospel proclamations" a person is either "in," provided they fulfill the required conditions of belief and activity and so become a part of God's people, or a person is "out" and destined for eternal damnation. Hence these proclamations are actually all contracts as betrayed by their specifications of certain conditions for salvation, and the final result is that they all proclaim a God of retribution and not a God of love, at which moment we reach our crucial realization, if we have not already.

Justification theory is conditional and contractual from front to back. It specifies conditions for any relationship with God, whether works of law or faith. So it is in fact a contractual approach to salvation and it proclaims a God of retribution. As a result of this, it necessarily *resists* the suggestion that God is, at bottom, a God of love, and so, as we have just seen, it must fundamentally redefine love so that it ends up not being love at all. In terms of its very structure then *it denies a God of love.* And it follows from this that it thereby obscures and undermines the real gospel in Paul because Paul clearly does think, after encountering Jesus, that God loves us and is in a covenantal relationship with us. After all, God refused to let him go even when he was zealously executing God's devoted followers. It follows from this, perhaps shockingly but nevertheless critically and inexorably, that JT is a false gospel—or it is a *very* bad moment on Paul's part if he admits this model into 10 percent of his instructions that undercuts what he is trying to say for the other 90 percent of the time! But before exploring the interpretative options moving forward, one of which is to suppose that Paul is just having a bad moment in these texts (although we do not view this solution as either ideal or necessary), we should concentrate our attention on the key judgment we need for this moment in our discussion. (Rest assured that we are going to suggest a helpful solution to this nasty quandary in due course.)

Key conclusion

When it comes to the relationship between the 10 percent of Paul's material that freights JT and the 90 percent that delivers a gospel of resurrectional participation we can now see with absolute clarity that the theological differences between them are irreconcilable. And this is important. It simply will not do in light of this cleavage to claim that they can just be sequenced together like some sort of theological train. The wagons of sanctification that JT advocates want to hitch on to the back of the JT engine *are really another train altogether on a different set of tracks pulling in a different direction.* Different Gods are being proclaimed in each type of material. There is a major problem here.

Now JT advocates do not make their synthetic suggestions maliciously. This model of the gospel is proclaimed with the very best of intentions. However, careful reflection—which is what scholars of the gospel must ultimately undertake—reveals that JT is incompatible with the gospel of resurrectional participation. These two theories of salvation simply cannot be connected together coherently at all. The differences between them are too deep and too profound. These gospels are different all the way down, and Melanchthon's solution to the problem of coordinating these two types of material within Paul *does not work.* So we have a big problem now in front of us.

If we are beginning to grasp the depth of our difficulties it will nevertheless be useful to add some of the other main contradictions that can be detected between the two models of salvation—between a reading of JT in 10 percent of Paul's texts and the gospel of resurrectional participation in the other 90 percent. These additional problems will reinforce our growing realization that something in the way Paul is frequently being taught is not right and that some radical exegetical surgery might be necessary to rescue him. Equally importantly, as we press into these difficulties, not only will we begin to grasp the full extent of the problem we face when we hear or even proclaim JT; we will also begin to grasp a little more clearly than perhaps we did before just what is doing the damage. And at *this* moment, a potential solution will begin to emerge into view.

6

Three Further Problems

The knowledge of God

In chapter 4 we began to see how JT works and is structured, in two broad phases. It begins with individuals trying to be justified by doing works informed by law, and when that process fails, it continues to another phase if an individual accepts the offer of salvation by faith alone. The preceding chapter demonstrated how this whole process clashes with the basic theological assumptions about God underlying almost everything else that Paul wrote—two different Gods are in view. But we need now to press a little deeper into the model's difficulties, focusing here on the way in which the knowledge of God available in phase one is both obvious and universal.

In phase one of JT, the God lying behind JT is known clearly by reasoning in relation to the things he has created and this is supposedly where all good theology begins. His nature and character are self-evident being detectable from his creation (Rom 1:19–20).[1] Hence the knowledge of God is primarily *information*. We know things *about* God rather than knowing him directly and personally. Moreover, the entire thrust of the theory clearly pushes from *our* own capacity for understanding things, including God, to certain inferences and conclusions about his nature and expectations for humanity. We work out all the key things about God for ourselves—and we detect an omnipotent, omniscient, and omnipresent God of retribution. Theologians

1. This is immediately somewhat awkward because in the same breath the model asserts, following Paul's text, that God is the creator and not created and hence transcends what has been created. He is invisible. So we have to infer from the visible and created to the invisible and uncreated. Philosophers have placed pressure on this process.

denote this type of theology "general revelation" or "natural theology," and it is doing foundational work here. Indeed, this last point is worth emphasizing.

Because we learn about God in the pre-Christian state, we do not yet know God through the gospel—through "special revelation." Our journey begins in the non-Christian state and progresses forward, we might say, to the church and its special truths that are focused on Jesus, to prepare us for those. We reason then from our plight to its solution precisely so that we will grasp the solution, the solution that is Jesus Christ. So clearly, in terms of the model, we cannot understand that solution before we have generated the problem that leads to us grasping for the solution in the first place. So we only learn about Jesus *after* we have learned a lot of critical things about God and how God relates to us. And there is a very basic sense in which JT works forwards as a model. Natural theology grounds and leads to special revelation.

A useful way to think about this is in terms of a progression by a some-what philosophical individual from an unsaved state that we can designate Box A to a saved state that we can designate Box B. The saving process starts in Box A with the individual's realizations there; these reflections, which grasp key pieces of information about God and the cosmos as we just saw, basically *propel* the individual to grasp the conditions by which s/he can be saved, and so make the jump across the great divide between the unsaved and the saved to the church.

Justification Theory

(JT) Box A: Unsaved   **Box B: Saved**

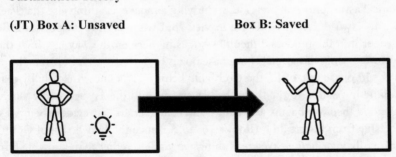

The gospel we described in the first three chapters of this book, how-ever, which begins with a relationship with God established *by* God through Jesus, progresses in a very different mode: namely, *revelationally*.

We know God *because God has first known us.*[2] Hence the knowledge of God is "special" from the get-go. It focuses on Jesus and is disclosed by

---

2. See Paul's telling correction in Gal 4:9: "Now, however, that you have come to know God, or rather to be known by God. . . ." See also 1 Cor 8:2–3: "Anyone who

Jesus and the Spirit, both of whom often choose to work through designated followers—people like Paul, along with other preachers in the church. As a result of this, the entire thrust of the model is different, and really runs exactly the other way around, from God to us rather than from us to God. God gifts correct thoughts about God to us rather than us generating correct thoughts about God. The struggle to think clearly about God—as here in this book—should still happen, but only in dependence on what we got and continue to get from God as that is focused and clarified by Jesus; it responds to a relationship that has been established rather than initiating that relationship. Moreover, this Jesus-centered information about God that is given to us is disclosed as one dimension within a larger saving process that draws us into relationship with God and with one another; this model is corporate and communal, not individual. People enslaved by sinful passions, evil powers, and ultimately by death, are released, healed, and transformed by participating in the loving communion of the Father, Son, and Holy Spirit. And these realities are mediated most clearly—at least ideally—by the church. So the process is fundamentally interpersonal and relational, and ultimately communal, as against purely individual and informational.

The Participatory Gospel

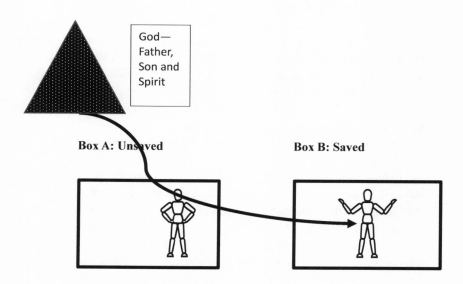

claims to know something does not yet have the necessary knowledge, but anyone who loves God is known by him."

If, in the light of God's revelation of himself in and through Christ and the Spirit, we grasp what God is all about (including perhaps the fact that we have a creator) then another important dynamic comes into view—what we might call, the directionality of the model's understanding *of* Box A, which is to say, of the past.

In the participatory gospel, it is only after the event of revelation and salvation and in complete dependence on it that we begin to understand with real clarity our own situation, including our sinful pasts. Box B gives us real clarity into the nature of Box A, and not the other way around. We may have had intimations of wrongdoing before we became Christians—or perhaps we did not—but the definitive insight into our sin is generated retrospectively, in the light of Christ. Christ's light illuminates our darkness because only in the light is that darkness fully apparent (to slip for a moment into Johannine idiom). Only as the good is fully revealed do we see clearly—or at least more clearly than we did before—what the wrong really is. So the model "thinks backwards," understanding the plight of Box A in the light of the solution provided within Box B. The solution, which has been gifted to us, reveals with true clarity our plight. Like substance abusers who are working through a re-hab program, the full horrors of addiction and its harmful impact on our lives in the past come slowly into view only as we are on the path to recovery and as part of that path to recovery. In essence, the past is understood in the light of the clarifying mind of the present, which is the opposite of what happens in JT and we need to press into the implications of this directionality for a moment.

In JT, the knowledge of sin arrives as part of the entire package of infor-mation about God that is inferred from reflecting on the cosmos and on the workings of our consciences, a package that begins the process of salvation within Box A. And obviously it is very important that these reflections are true. After all, they will constitute the truth-basis of the entire model. Everything that follows, including the knowledge of God revealed by Jesus, will build on this basis (and in chapter 4 we saw Piper doing just this). Box B, which talks about Jesus, builds directly on Box A and confirms it; hence in no way does it modify the first critical layer of truth claims generated by Box A (and again, this was very obvious in Piper's account of JT). So the model's directionality is different from the participatory gospel. Justification theory works *forwards* or *prospectively*. And sin is known *immediately*, in a *foundational* position, hence independently of any knowledge of God's will as that might be revealed by Jesus. It is known from the laws of God inferred from the cosmos and the conscience. The direction, as we noted earlier, is from plight to solution.

It is apparent at this moment then that the two soteriological systems in Paul that we are comparing in this part of our discussion do not clash merely in relation to their definitions of the basic nature of God. They clash fundamentally in terms of their accounts of the nature of the truth about God—and not just *what* we learn but *where* we learn and *how*. A universal, individual-centered, informational account of divine knowledge simply collides here with a relational, revealed account of the knowledge of God. These two different modalities are diametrically opposed in terms of directionality, moving in opposite trajectories in their journey of understanding about sin and the unsaved state (Box A), JT moving from plight to solution, forward, and the transformational gospel moving in the other direction, on analogy to a recovering addict, from solution to plight, backward.[3] Once more then the contradictions run deep.

A comparison:

where the definitive knowledge of sin is found; and the resulting view of Box A

For Justification Theory (JT), definitive knowledge is found in Box A; and the direction of the journey is prospective (forwards), building from Box A, which is primary

A: Unsaved   B: Saved

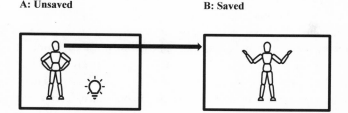

For the Transformational Gospel, definitive knowledge is found in Box B; and the understanding of Box A is retrospective (backwards)

A: Unsaved   B: Saved

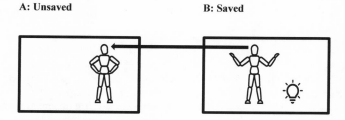

3. The revelational way of knowing also enjoys significantly more support from Paul's own texts than the merely informational; it dominates 90 percent as against only 10 percent of his texts. In fact, strictly speaking, the informational mode only dominates around two chapters of material within Paul—Rom 1:18—3:9a—because even JT switches to a revelational model quite quickly. So it dominates about 2.9 percent of what Paul wrote.

We turn now to the conceptions of salvation that the two models offer, bearing in the mind that the two models are all about salvation so if major differences are detectable here then they are especially serious (although it is only fair to say that some pretty serious differences have been noted already).

The atonement

The word "atonement" focuses our attention on Jesus's saving work undertaken on our behalf, and particularly as that is affected by the events of Easter.[4] And again our two models understand the exact mechanics of atonement in Paul very differently.

At bottom JT holds that harm must be visited retributively and proportionately upon those who do harm—something generally achieved by inflicting pain on a body. But in JT the harm due to us is of course visited instead upon Jesus. This is the way that retributive justice supposes that wrongs are righted, and the peculiar way it gets around the problem of our wrongdoing in relation to Jesus to save us. But we can detect here the model's fundamentally legal and political sensibilities—legal and political sensibilities of a certain sort we hasten to add. So Jesus endures a great weight of pain, harm, and judgment as he is tortured by his captors and then dies on the cross, thereby experiencing the punishment that should be falling on sinful humanity. This event technically allows the removal of God's wrath from sinful humanity, because it has been exhausted by falling on Jesus, although this benefit still needs to be appropriated by faith. Christ died in our place, receiving what we actually deserved. This selfless act sets those who accept this offer free from having to face God's future punitive penalty. And this is the great saving moment in JT, rescuing us from the model's crucial problem, which is actually God's own retributive action toward an erring humanity. (God then, perhaps a little curiously, is our principal problem.) According to JT, the solution is effected by the cross and the cross fully effects the solution.[5] And it is our fear

---

4. The word was coined by William Tyndale (d. 1536) from the phrase "at-one-ment," so it is not drawn directly from the Bible's own language and we should consequently be cautious about letting it dictate the terms of our investigation too strongly. (He was himself influenced by John Wycliffe's use of "at onement.") In broad terms it points toward the repair and restoration of a healthy relationship between God and humanity, leaving the terms of that repair and restoration open to further detailed definition. And these details, as we have just seen, will almost certainly differ depending on whether we are thinking prospectively, in terms of JT, or retrospectively, in terms of the participatory gospel.

5 For a powerful biblical critique of penal substitutionary theory's interpretation of the cross, see now Andrew Rillera's study of Jesus's death as a sacrifice in *Lamb of the Free*.

of God's future wrath that propels us toward an acceptance through faith of the offer made by the gospel of salvation and its good news about the cross.

The alternative, participatory account of atonement we outlined earlier in special dependence on Philippians 2:6–11 emphasizes, by way of contrast, *two* overarching movements within Jesus that effect our salvation, and we should recall that this reflects at least 90 percent of what Paul wrote. Christ's atoning work encompasses both a downward trajectory through his incarnation, faithful life, and obedient death on the cross, and an upward trajectory running through his resurrection and ascension. *Both* of these trajectories, along with their climactic events, play a critical role in God's solution to sin and death as this gospel understands it.

Jesus's death is certainly important in the participatory account. His execution terminates our sinful, fleshly condition, which he assumed in his incarnation. In this assumption and termination, as the Spirit joins us to these events, our sinful flesh is thereby rendered extinct; it is dead and buried. The ravages of sin are thereby contained. Few things are as important as this termination then.

But Christ's resurrection and ascension are *equally* critical *as the basis of our reconstitution and new life*. Without the resurrection we just stay dead. But the good news is that we rise from the dead, leaving our flesh behind, bearing Jesus's new resurrected image—a process that has begun miraculously to impinge on our own lives already. Hence without participating in the resurrection we are not saved, even from our sins, as Paul points out quite directly to the Corinthians on one occasion.[6] For him it is two steps or none.

It is clear then that the atonement is handled very differently by the two models. For the participatory gospel Christ's death is a single part of a bigger story of divine lowering, bearing, terminating, and then re-creating through resurrection; all of these acts together comprise Paul's understanding of the atonement. And, in particular, both cross and resurrection work together to save us by transforming us as we participate in them. However, JT struggles to ascribe any kind of atoning value to most of these events in Jesus's life. Everything is effected by the cross. For JT Jesus does need to maintain his innocence through his life so that he can die in a pure, uncontaminated form, and in Piper's Reformed version, offer the clothes to us of perfect righteousness, but it is difficult to supply a soteriological rationale for his life beyond this. As a result of its focus then, JT struggles to provide a strong justification for either the incarnation or the resurrection. Moreover, nothing is *transformed* by this theory, except, in a sense, God's attitude

---

6. 1 Cor 15:17: "If Christ has not been raised, your faith is futile, and you are still in your sins."

toward us.[7] We are left very much as God found us, although relieved of fear and hopefully motivated by gratitude. Still, we are essentially the same.

In sum: for the transformational gospel, Jesus must certainly die, although for different reasons from those suggested by JT; Jesus's death is all about termination, not punishment. But "to atone" fully for our problems he *must* also be resurrected, and it is this act that is so important for the changes it delivers for us. For JT, however, Jesus must simply die, and then explanations for the resurrection, which will not involve salvation (at least, this sense), must be found somewhere else.

When one theory of salvation focuses almost entirely on Jesus's death, and the other model combines that death with the resurrection in order to save humanity in a dramatically reconstituted way, we are really talking about two fundamentally different models *of* salvation. One model, we might say, just needs Good Friday. The other, needs Friday, Saturday, and Sunday. One, moreover, needs Easter only (and here Good Friday only), and the other needs Easter *and Christmas* (not to mention, Pentecost as well). And these are just not the same thing. These differences show up clearly when we think again about how the resurrection maps onto our Box A–Box B sequence.

The location of resurrection

For Justification Theory (JT), the resurrection is future to Box A *and* Box B.

A: Waiting   B: Still Waiting

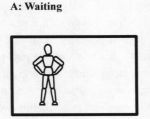
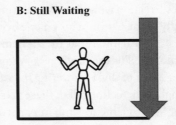

For the Transformational Gospel, Box B *is* the arrival of the resurrection, to some significant degree.

A: Waiting   B: Inaugurated

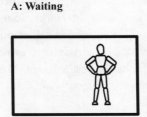
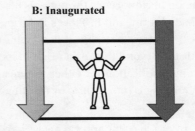

7. And his attitude toward us is not so much changed as redirected.

A final point of contrast is worth noting before we move on. How do the two models "preach," which is to say, how do they actually make their offer of salvation to the unsaved and seek to convert them? What warrants do they use and what appeals do they make? Equally importantly, what method of evangelism corresponds to their mode of proclamation?

Preaching and evangelism

Justification theory begins with natural revelation and the realizations that every thinking person ought to reach as s/he reflects on "the starry sky without and the moral law within."[8] We are in trouble! It is the realization that we are sinners who have violated the divine decrees and so will shortly be in the hands of an angry God that supposedly motivates us to grasp the offer of salvation by faith in Jesus. There is a sense then that the gospel must begin with bad news and with the preaching of the law. Only once the bad news has been processed will the good news be accepted. (We once heard this put memorably as "the gospel is offered at gunpoint.") It follows then that the bad news about our relationship with God is proclaimed first and the good news second—although because the bad news is first and is so basic, the good news is fairly heavily qualified. The great Swiss theologian Karl Barth had a nice way of putting this, which we have already used once: he would observe that in this version of the gospel God's "No" to us precedes and frames his "Yes." He would then generally add words to the effect that God's "No" is more fundamental than his "Yes"; the "Yes" is only heard through the "No" and is qualified by the "No." God's "No" is spoken "in a very loud voice" and dominates his "Yes."

Implicit in this model of address, with its essentially rational pressure and its focus on information, the heavy lifting in any evangelism can be done by straightforward proclamation, although proclamation of a certain sort. Evangelists essentially make a speech about all this to anyone who will listen, and at least some listeners—those who are, strictly speaking, appropriately rational and moral—can draw the appropriate conclusions and choose faith and salvation.[9] But in fact they are told about their perilous situation, and the preacher's framework names that situation irrespective

8. A famous comment by one of the parents of modern philosophy, Immanuel Kant, who was a deist. In a slightly fuller form: "Two things fill the mind with ever new and increasing admiration and awe, the more often and steadily we reflect upon them: the starry heavens above me and the moral law within me" (originally found in his famous *Critique of Practical Reason*, and later written on his tombstone in Kaliningrad).

9. There is in fact an important assumption here of competence. This model struggles mightily to include those with intellectual disabilities.

of what they are actually thinking and otherwise doing. Hence, all of the preacher's listeners *should* go on to choose faith because it is both irrational and immoral not to. Experience suggests that as the net of JT is cast out a number of fishes will be drawn in (although sociological and conversion studies suggest that some of the fishes drawn in may have made this decision a number of times, and others might be swimming into the net for different reasons than those they give).

The resurrectional and participatory gospel begins its proclamation in a very different way from JT because it begins with Jesus. The assumption is that as the story of God's love for us is declared as that love is disclosed by Jesus's death and resurrection on our behalf (see Gal 3:1), the Spirit convicts us that this is true. Furthermore, preachers invite us to join them on their journey. We then begin a journey of discipleship that is oriented toward and motivated by God's great and unbreakable relationship of love with us. And in the light of this journey we begin to see and to address our sinful habits and practices. So the good news comes first and the bad news second, at which moment we are tempted to suggest that this really is good news. In Barthian idiom, God's "Yes" precedes and frames his "No." His "Yes" is consequently more fundamental and important than his "No," and his "No" is qualified and framed by his "Yes." The "Yes" is spoken in a loud voice—although the "No" remains and must still be heard and taken seriously; indeed, the "No" is all the clearer and more striking now that it is being heard within the ambit of the "Yes."

This might seem a little counterintuitive at first: did we not all sin and lose our glorious image that Adam and Eve possessed in the garden so that the story of our relationship with God begins with a "No." Actually no! Christ reveals God's created purposes for us that were in place *before* the creation of the world and they were a "Yes." Long "before" there was any earth or Edenic state, or any fall into sin, God intended to fold us into his Son and to adopt us into his family (Rom 8:28–30; Col 1:15–17).[10] This was God's plan and nothing gets permanently in the way of this. God's purposes for us revealed through Christ and the Spirit have always been loving, covenantal, and inclusive; the story begins with an unqualified divine "Yes." And since

10. Rom 8:28–30: "We know that all things work together for good for those who love God, who are called according to his purpose. For those whom he foreknew he also predestined to be conformed to the image of his Son, in order that he might be the first-born within a large family. And those whom he predestined he also called, and those whom he called he also justified, and those whom he justified he also glorified. . . ." Col 1:15–17: "He is the image of the invisible God, the firstborn of all creation, for in him all things in heaven and on earth were created, things visible and invisible, whether thrones or dominions or rulers or powers—all things have been created through him and for him. He himself is before all things, and in him all things hold together."

they were established in and by our creator, these purposes precede and ground anything that we might do to disrupt our relationship—disruptions that God does say "No" to, although in the right way and at the right time.

It follows from this that the current order of our boxes isn't the best reflection of the underlying theological realities articulated by a revelational and Jesus-centered approach. Strictly speaking, the first box, namely, Box A, derives from Christ and is a fundamentally positive state—a Yes!—and denotes the state we were both created from and are destined for and will one day occupy. It is the state that matters. Box B is then the aberration from this principal state into which we have fallen where we experience God's "No," and from which God rescues us, thereby ensuring that the divine "Yes" remains on course.

For Justification Theory (JT), the divine NO precedes and frames the YES.

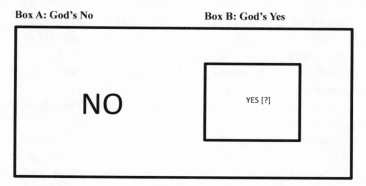

For the Resurrectional Gospel, the divine YES precedes and frames the NO.

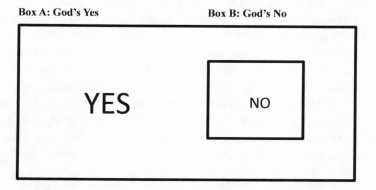

A final useful observation: because the resurrectional model presupposes a relational God drawing us into a deeper relationship with both himself and one another, the emphasis within evangelism is less upon correct information and reasoning about God—although these will play their part—and more upon correct relating. In particular, the friendships that operate through and around the church will be critical, and talking will be—or can be—more informal and conversational than in the more rationalistic, structured, informational preaching of JT. Indeed, communication by evangelists may involve listening as much as it involves declaring. It follows from this, moreover, that there might not be a single important moment of conversion as much as a slow, gradual process, or a zigzag journey with many important moments, although it doesn't really matter. In terms of content—of what to say when asked if an important or even pivotal moment arrives—we just need to ask ourselves how we would introduce someone to one of our other very great and faithful but somewhat controversial friends? How would we draw them into this new relationship? This would probably take place through numerous informal get-togethers, some short, some long, and probably over a period of time. And we would just talk about that important friend accurately and informally, as invited. This is how the transformational and resurrectional model thinks about evangelism, so "friendship evangelism" can get quite close to this approach. We answer questions about the God revealed through Jesus as and when we are asked them, speaking about Jesus as someone we know (which, hopefully, we do).

Intriguingly, this is also how we see Paul evangelizing people as we read his letters carefully. He is certainly not averse to a bit of public preaching and proclaiming when he gets the opportunity, but he seems to have made a lot of his converts by befriending them, whether this was as he worked alongside them in a craft shop or met them in a jail.[11]

This last comparison, in terms of evangelism, completes our quick survey of some of the key differences between the two soteriologies we have previously detected in Paul. And it should be fairly clear by now that these are really two different systems. So we will speak, moving forward, as we have from time to time in what has preceded, of two gospels in Paul (see Gal 1:6–7). In the previous chapter we identified how JT is based on a God of retributive justice and not, like the resurrectional and participatory gospel, on a God of love. Another way of talking about this is in terms of the contrast between a God who acts in terms of contracts as against a God who is

---

11. The story of Paul that the book of Acts tells emphasizes his public preaching because it has a particular focus on the public progress of the gospel through the Roman empire. Paul's letters reveal a rather different emphasis in his actual missionary work: see especially 1 Thess 2:9; 2 Thess 3:8; Philemon, *pass.*

covenantal in his dealings with us. And in this chapter we have identified three further differences:

1. The first difference is the place where the decisive knowledge of God is revealed along with the means by which it is revealed. In JT the individual finds God through a process of rational reflection that happens before they meet Jesus; in the participatory gospel, God reveals himself to the person—who is not viewed or treated as an individual— through Jesus and the work of the divine Spirit.

2. The directionality of the two models is diametrically opposed as well. The progression of understanding in JT works from the plight to the solution, so "forwards" from Box A to Box B. In the participatory model the understanding of the non-Christian situation is generated in the light of Christ, who illuminates its contours clearly, and who clarifies our minds; we look "backwards." Like a recovering alcoholic, we understand our past more clearly in the light of our present location in Christ.

3. The two models also understand the saving work of Christ in different ways. The emphasis in JT falls almost entirely on Good Friday and the cross, although in some variations of JT, like Piper's, there is an emphasis on Jesus's sinless life as well. The participatory gospel also emphasizes Good Friday, but the incarnation that precedes Easter is critical, along with Jesus's faithful life leading to the cross. And Easter *Sunday*, in terms of both resurrection and ascension, is vitally important in saving terms as well.

But perhaps, someone might say, we are overcooking all these differences. Can we not just live with the various contrasts between the 10 percent and the 90 percent? It is not that difficult, after all, to glide around 10 percent of what Paul wrote—to soft pedal those texts—and to concentrate on the God of love, repentance, and covenant in the other 90 percent.

Unfortunately, allowing the 10 percent to remain—allowing JT to retain its foothold within Paul—is far too dangerous a matter for this easygoing solution. We must, that is, turn our attention now to some of the truly dreadful consequences that JT can unleash (while we also note in a brief appendix below, in a slightly more technical discussion, how this sort of interpretative decision allows JT to colonize Paul's participatory gospel, overriding many of its basal insights; basically, this decision will lead to Paul being read in perpetuity in terms of JT everywhere). These harmful consequences are, we hasten to add, unintentional. No one preaching JT wants to unleash evil. But it has to be said, with equal firmness, that this is what has happened. History is very clear about it. And JT must be held accountable for the harm it has unleashed. Furthermore, when we realize what has happened—the damage that has been done—and face up to it honestly, we will see that we have no other option than to courageously and determinedly learn to read Paul in a way that moves beyond its parameters. It is time to turn, that is, to a particular grievous problem set up by JT—the fifth major issue we are identifying at this stage in our description—and to face its awful reality with candor and humility. Justification theory, as part of its permanent preamble, *necessarily crushes Jews*, and the historical legacy of this particular emphasis within the theory has come, quite simply, from the gates of hell.

EXCURSUS
The Tacit Colonization Effected by a Justification-
Sanctification Sequence

Justification theory answers a lot of key theological questions, and this is unsurprising; any soteriology will provide answers to a lot of the important questions. So JT provides answers to the question of the fundamental nature of God (retributive), to God's key way of relating to humanity (legal and rule-governed), to the structure of the good and of ethics (legal), and thereby to politics (retributive and rule-governed), and to eschatology (legal and retributive again). It also gives an account of human nature, i.e., anthropology (rational individualist and not too deeply corrupted or incapacitated), and of humanity, providing a strong othering dynamic (a view of "the other" as immoral and irrational). Needless to say, it also provides an account of the church (contractual and voluntarist). And it provides a basic account of sin (law-breaking criminality), and hence of the atonement (punitive and satisfactory). It generates critical leverage by specifying content to the laws of the cosmos which are supposed to be perceived innately and/or philosophically, but are principally developed in the modern world in terms of the story of Adam and Eve (i.e., heteronormativity). (Unvarnished "idolatry" is not a strong feature of the modern world, except arguably in Hinduism.) And none of the different answers to these questions offered by Paul's participatory material—by 90 percent of what he wrote—can or will now be admitted or allowed—answers that would be informed primarily by the God revealed through Jesus Christ.

In other words, no answers to these questions can now be admitted *that are informed by Jesus and/or the Trinity.*

This is pretty extraordinary once one sits down to think about it. As we have spent some time in our opening chapters noting, the God-talk controlled by the revelation of Jesus through the Spirit, and articulated by Paul most clearly in texts like Romans chapters 5 to 8, has dynamic and important answers to all the questions we just noted concerning the fundamental nature of God (loving), God's relationship with us (covenantal), the structure of the good and hence of our politics and our eschatology (restorative); our account of human nature (relational), of "the other" (inclusive), of the church (interpersonal), of sin (addiction and oppression), and of the atonement (transformational). Hence a complete theological system emerges from these answers too, and it is quite different from JT. But these answers, grounded in Jesus, must all now be ignored in favor of the answers generated by JT if that is what we begin our analysis of Paul with, a model that presupposes rational individuals reflecting on their cosmos before they have received any information about God from the gospel, or even from Israel. Extraordinary.

It is as if a palace has been built for a long-awaited monarch who is soon to arrive. The gardens are planted and tended, the rooms built, furnished, and decorated. The feasts are prepared. The monarch then duly arrives and is crowned. They are shown to their fabulous bedroom *and they are then locked in it and never allowed out.* The systems set up in their honor continue unabated, ungoverned and uninformed by their wisdom and guidance. Hence, although they are honored in theory—by the beautifully-decorated palace and exotic gardens, by the repeated feasts and celebrations, and they are being looked after sumptuously in their bedroom—they have no practical, concrete input into anything that was set up prior to their arrival. They do not govern anything, or arrange anything, or affect anything. They have been captured in the most subtle of fashions—and obviously they are not really being treated like a monarch at all.

In just this way, if we endorse a justification-sanctification sequence, we allow JT to frame and to control everything that follows, and this means that we allow JT to frame and to control what Jesus would reveal to us about God and all his ways. Jesus is imprisoned in a palace set up for him that he did not design and does not want to live in. (Our monarch does not want to live in a palace surrounded by and waited on by servants; he wants to leave the palace *as* a servant and to show everyone else just how to *be* a servant, both of God and of others.)

We suspect that the justification-sanctification sequence only works as a supposed solution to the problem of coordinating the 10 percent with the 90 percent in Paul because its advocates have become accustomed to the ongoing silencing of so many of the key contributions of Paul's participatory material to his theology. Or they have become comfortable living with the tensions that result from endorsing both systems simultaneously (although when push comes to shove, JT's answers tend to be privileged). If we are told that we must silence our doubts about Paul's coherence for the sake of the gospel we will strive to do this, and might even succeed. The human brain can do this if it really wants to. But this is hardly satisfactory. Moreover, what if in our zeal we have ended up silencing the gospel itself?

7

The Teaching of Contempt

The Holocaust

Some of Paul's letters talk a great deal about Jews, and much of that material can be found in the texts that are usually read in terms of JT.[1] Box A is an account of the attempt to be justified by doing the works prescribed by "the law," meaning the law(s) of Moses, an attempt that fails and that needs to fail, and it even speaks from time to time of a Jewish figure.[2] So these texts are read by JT as focused on Jews, who were the people who actually possessed the laws of Moses. It follows that JT is *very* concerned with what Jews are like, what they think about God and God's expectations, and what the consequences of this are—negative!

But it is now incumbent upon all modern readers like us to rethink our readings that speak about Jews in these terms. We must revisit these texts and at the least ask certain disturbing questions of them. Pressing upon us is the horrific phenomenon of the Holocaust and this must never be forgotten. What is the relationship between this model of salvation, its reading of the texts in relation to Box A and the picture of the Jew created there, and the genocide effected by Germany during World War 2? And this last event *must* challenge us. We cannot sweep this question blithely aside and carry on as if a nation-state at the heart of the greatest concentration of Christian

---

1. Justification theory occurs primarily (and ostensibly!) in Rom 1:16—5:1; and Rom 10; and in Gal 2:15—3:26; with possible short summaries elsewhere, for example in Gal 5:5–6; Eph 2:8–10; and Phil 3:6 and 9.

2. See, e.g., Rom 2:17: ". . . you call yourself a Jew and rely on the law and boast of your relation to God."

nation-states in history did not systematically target the Jewish people for removal and, failing that, incineration, while in preparation for its meticulous genocide it characterized the Jews in vicious sub-human terms—as deformed and verminous.

Perhaps, someone might say, this was simply a Nazi thing and hence cannot be laid at the feet of the church, and there is some truth to this objection. But only some. Research has shown that the Christian populations of countries like France and Poland, not to mention of Germany itself, in the main cooperated enthusiastically with the Nazis' anti-Jewish program.[3] Certainly there was no widespread rejection of and obstruction to the final solution, only tiny acts of resistance that, by their size, cast the collaboration and complicity of the vast majority into even sharper relief.[4] The final solution only succeeded as well as it did because many Europeans wanted it to. Furthermore, complementing the appallingly efficient executions and disposals of the death squads and the camps was the complete indifference of nations further afield to the plight of the Jews. Had countries like the UK and the USA simply accepted mass Jewish emigration before World War 2 as Germany requested then the Holocaust itself would have been unnecessary. The Nazi state only turned to the solution of the death camps in 1942—to the *final* solution—because an earlier expulsion of the Jews from Germany proved impossible and this was the only way they saw remaining to cleanse their land from a Jewish presence.[5] Hence the countries that many of us live in are also complicit in the Holocaust to this degree.

Moreover, the church and its members cannot escape responsibility even this lightly. The Nazi vilification of the Jews intensified centuries of European exclusion and derision, building directly on pre-existing stereotypes and hatreds; it was this fertile soil, prepared by centuries of Christianity, that allowed the Nazi program to take hold so effectively and to be supported by the majority of the population so widely. Anti-Semitism presupposed anti-Judaism, and the final solution presupposed what is now widely recognized as the teaching of contempt, and *this* must be laid squarely at the feet of the church.

3. See also especially the populations of Estonia, Latvia, and Czechoslovakia.

4. Oskar Schindler, made famous by the Oscar-winning film *Schindler's List* (dir. Steven Spielberg, 1993), saved around 1,200 Jews.

5. The final solution was debated formally at the Wannsee Conference, January 20, 1942. The minutes from this meeting are extant and have been extended into a German-language film: see *The Wannsee Conference* (dir. Heinz Schirk, 1984). Some remaining transcripts were then used verbatim in the English-language film *Conspiracy* (dir. Frank Pierson, 2001). This is especially sobering viewing.

The teaching of contempt

We need to realize, if we do not already, that much of the church has long fostered what has become known as a "teaching of contempt" concerning Jews. Centuries of anti-Jewish characterizations can be catalogued from the sermons, exegesis, papal bulls, lectures, pamphlets, and books of church leaders. The Jews are charged there, alone of all people, with "deicide," namely, with the execution of God. They are "Christ-killers," with the blood of Jesus on their heads (and Matt 27:25 has been enlisted in service of this charge). Supposedly they practiced barbaric rites involving reprehensible and disgusting deeds like the sacrifice of children—the infamous "blood-libel." This othering had a practical bent, however. Jews were forbidden in many Christian states from owning property, and from living anywhere other than in certain urban quarters. They were permitted to engage in financial practices that Christians felt themselves ethically prohibited from engaging in but nevertheless needed (especially after the Cluniac reforms), namely, banking. This then led, however, to the association of the Jews with usury and other mercantile stereotypes. They are miserly and greedy—lovers of money. Unsurprisingly, there were periodic outbreaks of mob violence against their easily identified and much-vilified communities. Indeed, these were so frequent that the Slavic name for them, "pogrom," has entered the English language as the standard term for this type of event. The awful fate of Jewish communities in what is now the Ukraine at the hands of Orthodox Cossacks even generated a universal proverb for suffering that exceeds all bounds; such suffering is now known as "beyond the Pale" because this is the name of the area where the local Jews lived, who were hunted down, and massacred.

Perhaps especially noteworthy, however, was the role of the Inquisition. The impact of the Inquisition should not be exaggerated or contrasted too triumphantly with the parallel actions of many Protestant states against perceived deviants like witches and Anabaptists. But neither should its public burnings of Jews and purported Jews (in Spain known as *Marranos*) alongside other heretics be overlooked. The symbolism of the *auto-da-fé* (the great public ritual of penance, shame, and punishment carried out after the Inquisition's work in an area was done) tells us everything we need to know. Those who were proved to be unrepentant Jews—and they were guilty until proven innocent—would process in public in costume wearing cartoonish tokens of their sin to a place outside the city where their sentences would be pronounced. (These sentences were generated in secret and were previously unknown to the accused.) Vast crowds, who may have heard the masses being said through the night or, more likely, eaten the free celebratory breakfast banquet, would then see those deemed guilty be whipped, with many subsequently being tortured and burned to death. These carefully orchestrated events took place periodically in territories controlled by the Inquisition for many hundreds of years.

But someone might object that this antipathy toward Jews is a universal human phenomenon caught up in the awful undulations of racism that various ethnic groups have visited upon one another through the centuries. Unfortunately, however, the hatred directed toward the Jews has been especially sustained, detailed, and noteworthy, in large measure because it has so frequently been fostered and perpetrated by the church. Christianity is an enormously powerful tradition stretching through time and space, and its direct influence on the contemptuous posture of so many toward the Jews is historically obvious. Jews living in the Islamic empire generally received no such vilification or exclusion.[6] The fate of these "Sephardic" Jews, as they were known, was very different from the fate of the "Ashkenazic" Jews living in central and eastern Europe which were under Christian control. Pogroms were *not* a widespread phenomenon in Islamic territories, whereas in Christian Eastern Europe, as we saw earlier, they were so common that their own special Slavic nomenclature passed into common usage. Similarly, the richly cultured Sephardic community that generally flourished in the Iberian peninsular under Muslim rule was largely eliminated after the Christian reconquest. Small wonder then that the Nazi vilification, persecution, and final extermination of the Jews encountered such widespread indifference and even cooperation from other Europeans, who had been subject to centuries of anti-Jewish teaching.[7] These were Christian areas, which had been, *for millennia*, influenced, and often effectively ruled, by the church.

The key point for us, in the midst of this rather overwhelming story of cruelty, is the prompt to reconsider the way we might be interpreting Paul, and especially when his supremely influential texts talk about Jews. Do Paul's writings contribute directly to this vast program of vilification and punishment of what the Bible in the majority of its texts calls God's people?[8] Or have Christians who stand within a long tradition of Jewish vilification unwittingly projected their anti-Jewish hostility onto Paul's texts, assuming

6. Toleration was not universal. For example, the twelfth-century Almohad era in Spain was oppressive to Jews and Christians.

7. To be fair, Franco's Spain refused to surrender its small Jewish population to the German state.

8. It is often forgotten that the OT makes up 80 percent of the Bible and that God's people in that 80 percent are the Jews.

that Paul thought like they do but subtly misreading him in the process? (Paul was after all a Jew himself and not a Christian.)[9]

We will continue to focus here on the texts that underlie JT. The other texts in Paul that address Jews and Jewish questions can be read much more constructively once JT has been accounted for (and Douglas has done this in other places);[10] but our principal concern here is JT. And it is one of our key contentions that JT has been caught up in this deeply problematic tradition of anti-Jewish interpretation and, furthermore, that this has distorted what Paul was really trying to say. Realizing this, and re-engaging JT's underlying texts in a way that is alert to this distortion, will open up some surprisingly helpful ways forward for understanding these texts specifically and Paul more broadly.

So just where is JT tangled up with the anti-Jewish dynamics that we have just briefly documented? This involvement is almost certainly unintentional. But it is still real and so it must be faced honestly and addressed. What does JT say about Jews now that we are learning to ask this question in the light of the Holocaust?

The complicity of JT—strong othering

We already know well that the occupants of Box A in JT are non-Christians who understand certain things about God and about themselves.[11] They know that God is legal and retributive, placing certain obvious moral demands on them. However, those same non-Christians ideally also admit that they do not fulfill these demands and so they are sinners; they are basically cosmic felons who are liable to God's righteous punishment on the day of judgment. Possibly they strive to meet these demands for a time, attempting to observe God's moral demands perfectly. But they should realize that they fail to do so and that they have thereby only become still the more deeply liable to God's future retribution. It is this set of realizations that should fill them with a sense of dreadful urgency and motivate them powerfully to grasp the offer of salvation made through faith alone and thereby to be saved, a realization that walks hand-in-hand with their realization that

9. This might seem counterintuitive, but it is in fact anachronistic to suppose that "Christianity," in the sense of a distinguishable religion with adherents universally called "Christians," actually existed in Paul's day. This issue will be discussed more shortly.

10. See chapter 12, "Israel Past and Present," in *Paul, An Apostle's Journey* (2018), 151–61; and chapter 28, "Beyond Supersessionism," in *Pauline Dogmatics* (2020), 688–719; along with the further readings listed there on pp. 716–19.

11. See chapter 4 for our most extensive description of Box A in this book.

they are demonstrable sinners. And they should go on to stick to salvation through faith alone because this continues to acknowledge their initial sinfulness and their repeated failures to be pronounced righteous by doing enough works.

It needs to be emphasized now, however, especially in view of our immediately preceding discussion, that this description applies above all to Jews. The texts freighting JT in Paul, which are read in terms of "Box A," speak frequently of the attempt by certain people to be pronounced righteous through "works *of law*," obviously meaning by "works informed by the laws of Moses." So these figures are Jewish. They possess copies of what we now call the Old Testament, and they have been seeking salvation by trying to keep its rules and regulations perfectly. In terms of the broader model, along with some of the textual moves that Paul ostensibly makes in Romans 1–2, these specifically Jewish figures represent humanity in general in the non-Christian state. But everyone who is a non-Christian is really operating like a Jew; it is just that they do not possess written instructions exactly like Jews (as Romans 2 is well aware). Non-Jews infer God's demands by reflecting with their minds on the cosmos without and with their consciences on the moral law within. Nevertheless, the basic structure of their situation is exactly the same. Hence in JT, the Jew is the quintessential occupant of Box A. More than this: Jews *define* the occupant of Box A, so Box A, in turn, *necessarily defines the Jew.* And this clarification brings us face-to-face with some rather uncomfortable implications in JT that we might not have noticed before. We will build through these implications step by step to their final tragic conclusion.

First, the basic construction of Judaism must correspond to the basic structure of non-Christian humanity, and this means that there is something very generic about its account of people—technically, about its anthropology. It is the same at all times and in all places. It follows, furthermore, that the Jewish people is composed of *individuals*, who are fundamentally *rational* although they also possess a degree of *morality*. These individuals will probably try to respond rightly to God's righteous demands, but they will do so out of *self-interest*; they are trying to gain future positive rewards, notably heaven and eternal life, and to avoid future negative punishments, namely, annihilation and exclusion from heaven (or worse). Hence, the relationship between God and the Jews is constructed *legally* with a corresponding *politics.* The entire situation is characterized rather strongly by "law and order." Wrongdoing is defined by law-breaking and responded to by punishment, which is to say, by the infliction of harm on any law-breakers by some official figure or figures. It follows in addition that this anthropology and the legally-informed cosmos that frames it will be *universal*; it can be found everywhere, at all times and in all places. There might be local variations but there will be a basic underlying uniformity. Box A is an account of all of human history apart from Christ—of all people not in the church. But the typical representative figure of unsaved humanity is, as we have just said, a Jew. And with these basic parameters clarified we can emphasize a second cluster of implications.

As occupants of Box A, Jews are clearly meant to be *transcended*. The entire situation is supposed to be temporary. Box A is a preparatory condition that is designed to unfold into the saved state of Box B. To grasp the parameters of Box A, which means here to understand fully what it means to be a Jew, is to learn that this situation *should cease to exist*. To grasp it clearly—to understand God's purposes here completely—is to grasp that it should be left behind. The *point* of Box A is to propel its occupants *into Box B*, and Box B is *Christian*. We are not supposed to stay in Box A!

Moreover, Box B is entered through faith in Jesus, and accompanying this dependence on faith alone is a continued repudiation of any attempt to be saved through works. As we saw earlier, this emphasis is critical because any alternative emphasis—any addition to faith—is, in terms of JT, automatically to lapse back into Box A and its futile attempts to be justified by works. It is to deny one's own sinfulness. It seems to follow inexorably then—and certainly many proponents of JT do emphasize this—that works of law should cease after salvation, from which emphasis it seems to follow that any Jews who understand fully what their Judaism involves should step out of that structure and into the Christian church, *leaving their Judaism behind*. Jewish practices are to be abandoned as a failed attempt to be saved; once saved by faith alone, these must not be revived. To be a Jew and to understand that identity completely then is to know that this identity is deeply and fundamentally inadequate in and of itself and must be abandoned for Christianity. In short, to be a Jew is to occupy a state that is both temporary and inadequate.

As we well know by now, however, many Jews through history have resisted this abandonment and have remained identifiably Jewish. And we need now to press into the implications of this posture in our third set of implications. How does JT characterize people who continue to live in Box A in defiance of its ostensible lessons, and what fate does it pronounce for them?

These are critical realizations.

People who consciously resist the lessons of Box A fall into the category of being recalcitrant and hence deserve the designation of being especially appalling sinners. They are necessarily *irrational* and/or *immoral*, because by resisting the obvious rational and moral lessons of the situation—which lead to Box B—they demonstrate that they are one or both of these undesirable things. Moreover, if they persist in teaching others to remain in Box A they are *hypocritical*, because they are urging those around them to strive to be righteous, as they themselves seem to strive, but ignoring all the while that they are in reality terrible sinners. So they are either deeply lacking in self-knowledge to the point of ethical obtuseness or they are knowing teachers of righteousness who cover up their hypocrisy deliberately—an especially odious category. In addition, by continuing to insist on the futile saving system in Box A, they show that they are deeply committed *legalists*. They insist that God relates to us positively *only as we fulfill our part of a saving contract*, and we can and ought to *earn* our way to heaven, so a spillover into mercantile imagery for salvation is usually detectable here. Salvation must be earned or merited or paid for (and it can't be). In short then, those who resist salvation and who continue to live in Box A, but who are nevertheless religious—or at least contend that they are—are appropriately described as immoral, irrational, hypocritical, legalistic, and mercantile. But it follows that these negative descriptors apply above all to unconverted Jews. Recalcitrant Jews who resist conversion to Christianity by way of faith alone are, of all people, immoral, irrational, hypocritical, legalistic, and mercantile. And we are surely in touch here with at least one poisonous source for the teaching of contempt.

But we need now to take a further step—our fourth—and to confront the implications of this set of designations. What does JT *prescribe* for recalcitrant sinners?

Again, we know well by now that JT threatens ongoing recalcitrant occupants of Box A with the appropriate retribution on the day of judgment. They will be executed by God as the appropriate punishment for their sins, since these have not had their punishment transferred onto the shoulders of Christ on the cross. (Strictly speaking, the punishment has been transferred but they have not accessed this transfer by grasping its offer of forgiveness through faith.) Moreover, in versions of JT like Piper's, the recalcitrant will stand guilty and condemned for their own personal unrighteousness as God does not view them as clothed in Christ's perfect righteousness. And clearly any unconverted Jews will suffer just the same fate. But we now need to appreciate that any infliction of this type of punishment on Jews, as on any other recalcitrant sinners, in the *present* cosmos *is also not unreasonable*. This is, after all, the right way to respond to wrongdoing.

The cosmos in Box A is constructed primarily in terms of law and order, and transgressors are appropriately punished even there by God's appointed representatives (and Rom 13:1–7 might be invoked here).[12] Moreover, resistance to the offer of forgiveness and righteousness through Christ is a transgression—it is *the* transgression—since it signifies the presence of all the other sinful qualities just enumerated. Immoral, irrational, and hypocritical people deserve to be punished—to have harm inflicted on them in an appropriate response to their failings—and perhaps this might even shock them out of their foolish legalism and grasping mercantilism. At bottom then, when we are convinced that God will punish and execute recalcitrant Jews on the day of judgment, we have few qualms about seeing them punished and executed in advance of that date. The unsaved *deserve* punishment. A ghastly punishment for them is inevitable, so there are few reasons for protesting against some early occurrences of that future fate. And at this moment it is apparent that we are not just identifying a key factor within the teaching of contempt; we are probably also identifying a key factor within the Holocaust.

These are sobering realizations. But before pressing on to the next stage in our broader discussion it is worth pausing here for a moment to consider a complementary dimension within this situation.

Othering

We are possibly just beginning to realize that JT unleashes an extraordinary othering operation against Jews. Their identity, defined by Box A, consists essentially in the realization that their identity should be abandoned. Moreover, if they resist this dynamic, then harsh retributive powers are unleashed against them. The identity in question, moreover, is the set of "righteous demands," as Piper put it, that JT specifies are self-evident within the cosmos and within our consciences. God holds us to account when we fail to observe these.

---

12. 13:1 Let every person be subject to the governing authorities, for there is no authority except from God, and those authorities that exist have been instituted by God. 2 Therefore whoever resists authority resists what God has appointed, and those who resist will incur judgment. 3 For rulers are not a terror to good conduct but to bad. Do you wish to have no fear of the authority? Then do what is good, and you will receive its approval, 4 for it is God's agent for your good. But if you do what is wrong, you should be afraid, for the authority does not bear the sword in vain! It is the agent of God to execute wrath on the wrongdoer. 5 Therefore one must be subject, not only because of wrath but also because of conscience. 6 For the same reason you also pay taxes, for the authorities are God's agents, busy with this very thing. 7 Pay to all what is due them: taxes to whom taxes are due, revenue to whom revenue is due, respect to whom respect is due, honor to whom honor is due.

It would be instructive to explore more deeply at this moment just what the content of these righteous demands is, but this would take us too far away from our present concern. Suffice it to say that the detailed content of these demands, although theoretically self-evident both in the cosmos and in our consciences, is likely to be supplied by the people preaching the gospel in terms of JT; it is likely that the demands will reflect what *they* take to be self-evidently righteous, and this content is likely, in turn, to reflect their particular cultural location. Every culture, rooted in a certain history and set of traditions, as well as in key narratives, has deeply embedded notions about what is right and good, and about what is therefore wrong and bad. And one sure way of avoiding scrutinizing these too closely is to claim that they are just obvious to thinking upright people who contemplate the cosmos and also consult their own inner moral voice. But let us now take these self-evident sets of cultural assumptions about the right and the good and locate them within JT in a missionary situation and see what happens.

Suppose a group of JT advocates have traveled zealously to a distant land that the church has yet to reach. There they encounter various tribes, so they diligently learn their languages and begin to present the gospel to the fortunate locals in terms of JT. They begin of course with Box A, asking the indigenous people to whom they are preaching to accept its self-evident parameters. Everyone they are talking to needs to realize that they are self-evidently sinners in the hands of an angry law-abiding God; they have tried to work their way to heaven, and to a state of future blessedness with the one God; they have failed; they have turned their backs on God's righteous demands; and if they do not repent and turn to Christ in faith alone they are destined for retribution on the day of judgment. They will, that is, if they fail to convert, suffer the same fate as the Jews. But we can see at this point that JT has now *framed* these indigenous non-Christian people in a certain, rather sinister, fashion.

First of all, they have had their *own* accounts of righteousness and goodness overridden by the missionaries who have framed them in terms of JT. It is the missionaries' accounts of the right and the good that must be accepted, not the indigenous accounts. There is no need in this model to hear what the indigenous people have to say for themselves. Their accounts of their own situation must necessarily be in error. Now, they are probably not entirely correct in everything that they assert about God or the cosmos, but they are probably not entirely incorrect about everything either, and presumably not everything that they do needs to be judged as irrelevant or idolatrous. Nevertheless, JT insists that their accounts of the right and the good are irrelevant and, where different, necessarily inferior. Second, if the indigenous potential converts go on to resist the conclusions of Box A like recalcitrant Jews, they are also framed in retributive terms, by a structure of law and order, and destined for punishment. The non-converting indigenous are *criminalized* on account of their resistant behavior. But what has just happened? Their conquest is now merited, or, at the least, is unobjectionable, perhaps even if it is accompanied by their enslavement.

We see here then, by shifting the terms of our discussion slightly—that is, by shifting JT's target audience from Jews to indigenous non-Christians—that JT has a nasty *colonizing* tendency, and an integrated set of unhealthy dynamics is operative here. Justification theory frames outsiders irrespective of their own circumstances and narratives; it frames them in terms of assumptions about rightness that are obvious to the advocates of the model. Moreover, those assumptions are not subject to any strong theological control; they are derived by thinking about the cosmos and consulting the inner voice of conscience. A recipe for cultural capture is harder to imagine. Hence, at bottom, JT advocates tell outsiders what to think. Moreover, if outsiders resist that instruction, they will be categorized by that very act of resistance as *inferior*. They are operating with some debased notion of rightness and hence are immoral; and/or they are resisting the obvious logic of the situation, so they are stupid. As if this was not enough, the appropriate response to this foolishness is *coercive*. These inadequate responses to the overtures of JT are transgressions, which is to say, offences and felonies, and the appropriate response to felonies prescribed by JT is *retribution*.

It simply has to be said that this is a nasty set of interpretative dynamics to set in place for the analysis of non-Christians by Christians. Christians operating in terms of JT are basically trained to strongly other non-Christians, viewing them as morally inferior, and happily subjecting them to coercive actions if they resist. It is difficult to conceive of a missionary program more distant from the God who loved humanity so much that he became one of them, walking alongside them and dying for them even as they resisted this loving overture. But it is very easy to see the way that JT could both generate and reinforce Christian colonialism and authoritarianism (and an especially toxic dynamic will be unleashed when these tendencies intersect with racial, gender, and/or class differences).[13] Just think for a moment how these dynamics play out if the missionaries arriving in a distant land are white and come from an industrial society, but the locals are colored black and are still living in terms of tribal customs and norms. How will JT handle this situation if the locals do not convert? Inferior, stupid,

---

13. Groups who are experiencing various types of marginalization will be defined by JT in meritorious terms, hence as guilty of their own misfortune and so justly liable to any existing inequalities and to any coercive consequences. Moreover, opposing authority in protest will be framed negatively as well.

black people will be justly coerced and chastised for their recalcitrance by their superior, wise, white European preachers.

Some scholars of race have argued perceptively that the mistreatment of Jews is intrinsically connected to the mistreatment by many Christians of other minority populations like Black or Indigenous American groups; anti-Jewishness they suggest is a litmus test for the presence of a sinister othering program that is operating with theological cover, as the will of God.[14] And they are right. Moreover, we can see now that JT is directly implicated in this situation.

Justification theory strongly others the Jews, framing them ultimately in inferior and criminalized terms. And, as if this was not bad enough, this framing applies necessarily to every other non-Christian group as well, not to mention, to Christian groups who are regarded as misguided or deviant. The problems we are detecting in JT run deep.

It is time to draw the strands of our discussion here together.

Summary

It should be clear by now that JT launches what anthropologists would call a strong othering operation. The Jews, along with other non-Christians, are defined very much as "other" to Christians by JT, over against them, and we have just seen that this strong othering will be extended to other non-Christians, along with Christians perceived to be deviant. Moreover, this definition is decidedly negative. The negativity is key part of the operation, achieving certain important goals. The parameters of Box A teach people about sin, explain the cross, undergird the construction of the cosmos in terms of law and order and, most importantly of all, propel non-Christians to reach out with a real sense of urgency and dread to become Christians, saved by faith alone. But this pressure is achieved by defining non-Christians essentially as cosmic felons—by criminalizing them. *And this characterization applies above all to recalcitrant Jews.* Stubbornly resistant Jews are defined necessarily by JT in comprehensively awful terms—as immoral, irrational, hypocritical, legalistic, and mercantile. They are destined for punishment on the day of judgment, and of the most stringent sort. God will execute them (if they are not cast permanently into a lake of fire, but Paul does not talk about this). Moreover, this judgment is self-evident. Everybody can figure out that this is what non-Christians, and most especially Jews, are, simply by reflecting on the world and their consciences. It is

14. The most eloquent explanation of this that we know of is Willie James Jennings's *The Christian Imagination: Theology and the Origins of Race.*

obvious that this is the case. And Jewish resistance to these definitions—to the conclusions that they are religious felons who should leave their Jewishness behind—only confirms the "truth" of these conclusions more strongly.

It now simply has to be said that it is hard to imagine a more negative construction of the Christian "other" than the version supplied by JT. However, we must now also mark well both that this negative construction applies in the first instance and hence above-all to Jews, *and* that the entirety of Christian salvation rests upon it, so it is not negotiable, and this last realization is absolutely critical.

This is the definition supplied by Box A, and the entire account of salvation offered by JT—of God, Jesus, the atonement, salvation, etcetera—rests on the presuppositions of Box A. The model works forwards. Box A is the foundation upon which Box B is built. And it follows from this that the definitions supplied by Box A are nonnegotiable. The identity of *the Christian* when it is defined in terms of JT—and this is really the nub of the issue—*rests on* this powerful, initial, negative, othering operation. The nature of Box B is delivered by Box A. Put slightly differently, the account of the gospel offered by JT—of its Christian claims and truths—is based completely and directly *on* this prior negative account of outsiders in terms of Jews. Buried in this model of salvation then is the derivative nature of Christian identity—and of the gospel understood in these terms—and its sinister basis. The Christian, in order to remain a Christian in these terms, *must* define the Jew as a cosmic felon destined for divine execution. So JT only works, we might say, if the Jews remain on death row.

This might all sound a little shocking, but it is inexorable. It is built into the presuppositions and dynamics of the model. Advocates of JT understandably tend to shrink from full disclosure at this point. But the God revealed in Jesus is a truth-telling God and his followers must strive to follow that path, difficult though it is at times. And that path has led us to a confessional moment.

Justification theory is deeply involved in the teaching of contempt (and hence, albeit indirectly, at many removes, but nevertheless indelibly, in the final solution). And the right response to these realizations is *repentance*, so here, as we read Paul, to *interpretative* repentance. We need to turn away from a model that has caused this much harm and damage in the name of the gospel, and to endorse another way if that is possible. But before we offer our own solution to this complex and painful dynamic, we need to quickly dispel some of the confusion that has arisen over the scholarly discussion of Jewish questions in relation to Paul. Many scholars have tried to respond to these Jewish questions as their sinister dimensions have emerged in the last half-century, but often the result has generated more of the proverbial heat than light. So we will need, as we move forward, to locate our own position in relation to this broader scholarly terrain: to show where we have learned from these new proposals—or, at the least, can endorse them—as well as where we think they fall short. And that conversation must begin by considering one of the most important books on Paul ever written.[15]

---

15. Having said this, those wishing simply "to cut to the chase" can jump to chapter 11, where the detailed account of our solution begins.

8

A New Perspective on Jews—
from E. P. Sanders

The contribution of Sanders

Our steps forward from this point will be guided by one of the great scholarly contributors to this entire discussion, E. P. Sanders. His book *Paul and Palestinian Judaism*, published in 1977, caused an earthquake in the study of Paul—a quake whose tremors are still being felt almost fifty years later. Hence, it is important that we grasp his key contributions to our unfolding engagement here, and as precisely as we can. Sanders set up an entire angle of approach to the challenge of interpreting Paul in relation to Judaism that can be helpful when it is utilized appropriately. But it can also mislead subsequent scholarly conversations into overlooking key dynamics that his angle of view misses. We need to know then just what lesson to learn from Sanders's epochal book, and what we need still to address.

Sanders's main focus is on the description of Jews in Paul's day *as they described themselves*, as seen in the Jewish sources preserved from around the New Testament period. He then sets this self-description over against what he sees going on principally in Paul—the 90 percent of the apostle's texts that speak of what we have tended to call "participatory" and "resurrectional." Sanders helpfully dubbed this material "participationist eschatology." But we will focus here on his description of the Jews in Paul's day as they wrote about themselves, which is what most of his book describes.[1]

---

1. Sanders did not try to resolve the tensions evident within his 1977 book, although

Sanders's account of the Jews

Sanders did his homework. He analyzed carefully a vast archive of Jewish texts preserved from the centuries surrounding Paul that scholars tend to refer to as "late Second Temple Judaism": the noncanonical works collected together generally known as the Apocrypha and Pseudepigrapha, the Dead Sea Scrolls, and the Rabbinic writings, which were ultimately collected together into the sixty-three volumes of the Talmud. (He also knew the work of Josephus and Philo well, although this did not figure so centrally in his 1977 work.) Sanders searched through these texts to find their underlying narrative of salvation—their soteriology. And his conclusions were very instructive. Sanders judged that all the texts, with just one or two exceptions,[2] articulated the same basic underlying story of God's relationship with the Jews. Moreover, and most importantly, this story was *not* a mercantile, legalistic story—a story of repeated attempts to be proved righteous by doing the works prescribed by the law thereby somehow earning salvation from God. It was a very different story, which he named "covenantal nomism."

"Covenantal" names the fact that the vast majority of these Jewish texts ascribe the relationship of the Jews with God *to God's initiative*. God called them and summoned them into being just as he called creation into existence in the first place, as explained by Genesis 1. In theological terms, God "elected" Israel, and thereby pledged to be their God, just as they were called to be his special people. This privileged arrangement of creation and commitment was named "covenantal" by Sanders (drawing here on a notion often used by scholars to describe God's relationship with Israel in the OT that overlaps closely with how we have been using this concept earlier on). The relationship between God and the Jews is a covenant, like a marriage, and is consequently constructed more in terms of kinship than in terms of legality. God loves Israel and protects it as mothers and fathers brood over their children and partners love and covenant with their spouses. (Marginally less intimately, God also acts here like a benevolent monarch who loves his people deeply and so nurtures, sustains, and, if necessary, delivers them.)

---

he pushed his analysis in a number of brilliantly insightful directions. He simply stated that the Jews in Paul's day, and Paul himself, were articulating fundamentally different soteriologies. He also attempted to resolve the conundrum that we spend a lot of time articulating here, which is to say, the coordination of the 10 percent of justification material usually construed in terms of JT with the 90 percent of material that speaks of a participatory, resurrectional gospel, in a later book—*Paul, the Law, and the Jewish People*, published in 1985. We do not find his solution satisfactory, although, again, it contains a number of brilliant insights.

2. The position of the angel Uriel in 4 Ezra was a particular problem for his monolithic description.

This covenantal arrangement comes with expectations, however—as all parental and spousal relationships do! So God gifted Israel with various instructions about the right way to live. In particular, Moses was given divinely endorsed teachings that are embodied in the Scriptures that Jews are supposed to study and to follow. And these are a very great gift. That God has given these precious teachings to Israel alone is something that marks them out as special above all the other nations of the earth, who do not know God as God really is or what God wants (and these things are closely related).

Because this point is often misunderstood, we should possibly think at this point—if we are identifying members of the church—of the way many of us treasure the Bible because God's teachings can be found there. We do not ever carry out its instructions perfectly but we are devoted to it, learn much from it and venerate it. Similarly, what Christians call the OT and Jews the Tanakh *was* the Bible of Paul's day—the Scripture—and so Jews like Paul were devoted to it, learned from it, treasured it, and venerated it. It is consequently best not referred to as "law" but rather as "sacred teachings," "Scripture," or something similar.

Noting the importance of their sacred teachings—their Scripture—and its centrality to their lives and actions before God—to their ethics—Sanders described the expected response God prescribed in those teachings for Israel as "nomism." The Greek word often translated "law" in Paul is *nomos*. So Sanders is deliberately nuancing the translation of this word here in a different direction from JT to denote the response informed by Scripture that God expects from his people, the Jews. They are to live their lives *guided by the instructions found in their nomos.* Hence, they participate in a nomism, *not* in a legalism. They are operating within a nomistic or Torah-guided response, and this response is located within a secure and loving covenantal arrangement. They are not engaged in a legalistic relationship based on a reading of the Scripture as a law with certain stipulated conditions that must be fulfilled lest an essentially retributive God turn away and abandon them, having punished them as they deserved.

It is worth noting at this point that by describing the Jews' self-understanding—which they would ascribe to divine revelation!—in terms of "covenantal nomism," Sanders was also pressing the analysis of Jews in several further important and highly realistic directions. Whereas JT, by way of contrast, defines Jews rationalistically, individually, and very generically—the same across time and space—Sanders saw a *corporate* identity that travelled *through history.* Moreover, the Jews were whole people, so to speak, who responded to God with study (i.e., rationality) but also with devotion and piety (i.e., with prayer), with fidelity, and with emotion and commitment.

Sanders himself summarizes his position as follows:

> The "pattern" or "structure" of covenantal nomism is this: (1) God has chosen Israel and (2) given the law. The law implies both (3) God's promise to maintain the election and (4) the requirement to obey. (5) God rewards obedience and punishes transgression. (6) The law provides for means of atonement, and atonements results in (7) maintenance or re-establishment of the covenantal relationship. (8) All those who are maintained in the covenant by obedience, atonement and God's mercy belong to the group which will be saved. An important interpretation of the first and last points is that election and ultimately salvation are considered to be by God's mercy rather than human achievement.[3]

Sanders now turned his attention to various important secondary features of this story.

Did the Jews sin? Of course! Did they know it? Of course! *And so did God.* So the sacred teachings provide numerous ways of having a relationship with God restored. In particular, much of the teaching of Moses concerns the tabernacle, which directly informed the temple that Paul himself would have worshipped in regularly.

The temple was a place where God could dwell with his people, the Jews, in large measure because of all the detailed instructions set forth in Scripture that made this possible. Numerous regulations for its construction and its rituals were laid out, all of which point toward the creation and maintenance of a holy space where a holy God could dwell with his people—and many Jews were *very* devoted to the details in these instructions. One reason why we know of a sect of Jews living a deeply disciplined, ascetic life near the Dead Sea is because they had felt the need to leave Jerusalem and to dissociate from the temple cult there *because it was operating on the wrong calendar.* The days on which its feasts and sacred events were being observed were subtly off, following a lunar calendar, whereas the Qumran sect endorsed a sort of solar calendar. How many of us would emigrate into the desert and live there in our own isolated community, enduring all the hardships of that life, because the liturgy in our local church and its denomination was following the church year on a lunar rather than a solar cycle and so locating the events of Easter on the wrong weekend? The Jews were

---

3. Sanders, *Paul and Palestinian Judaism*, 42.

dedicated to their teachings—far more, we suspect, than most Christians are to theirs.

In addition to the way that the temple carefully prescribed numerous rituals that enabled a holy God to dwell with his people, the Jews were aware that God accepted various practices that dealt with sin, beyond the temple's specific removal of unintentional sin with the sin and guilt offerings, and the offering of appropriate compensation[4] (and some of these received further emphasis after the destruction of the temple by the Romans in 70 CE).

Suffering could be accepted by God as a way of dealing with sin. Moreover, some Jewish texts argued that *vicarious* suffering by Jewish heroes or martyrs could function to cleanse the sins of other people.[5] The story recounted by Genesis 22 of Abraham's (near) sacrifice of Isaac rose to special prominence in this relation, being viewed by many Jews as a definitive event that locked the Jews into relationship with God in perpetuity. (The utterly remarkable faithfulness and devotion to God shown by Abraham during this story, and the Jewish embellishment of this story in terms of the complementary devotion and obedience of Isaac, heavily informed later Christian understandings of Jesus as well.)

In like manner, alms-giving could be accepted by God as an appropriate response that maintained the covenant. The great generosity encouraged among Jews is exemplified in the charming story of Tobit, who gives money freely to his Jewish kin, although especially to the poor, and who even stops unbidden to bury a Jew who has died on the street—presumably no mean effort in the baked earth of the Mesopotamian plain. "Alms deliver from death," the book sagely observes (Tob 12:9). The point is that God responds to pious Jews in just the manner that they respond to the less fortunate around them—with forgiveness springing from an overwhelming generosity, compassion, and mercy.

However, perhaps most importantly Sanders noted the constant refrain in the Jewish texts that pointed simply to deep repentance and/or to accompanying requests to God for forgiveness as means of dealing with sin and maintaining the covenant relationship. A parent will usually forgive an erring but repentant and begging child. So Psalm 51 is traditionally read as speaking poignantly of David's journey to forgiveness after committing the horrendous sins of adultery and (proxy) murder—and God did not withhold his release from David. As Paul says in Romans 4:5–8, quoting Psalm 32:1–2, David was blessed with God's forgiveness.

---

4. See Lev 4:1–6:7.

5. See, for example, 2 Macc 7, or the entirety of 4 Maccabees.

The view that God was loving and committed to his people and hence willing to forgive them like a parent persisted deep into Paul's day. The pseudepigraphic Prayer of Manasseh speaks eloquently of God's compassion and forgiveness as this infamous sinner throws himself onto God's mercy (citing here the shortened version used in the *Book of Common Prayer*):[6]

> O Lord and Ruler of the hosts of heaven,
> God of Abraham, Isaac, and Jacob,
>   and of all their righteous offspring:
> You made the heavens and the earth,
>   with all their vast array.
> All things quake with fear at your presence;
>   they tremble because of your power.
> But your merciful promise is beyond all measure;
>   it surpasses all that our minds can fathom.
> O Lord, you are full of compassion,
>   long-suffering, and abounding in mercy.
> You hold back your hand;
>   you do not punish as we deserve.
> In your great goodness you have promised forgiveness to
> sinners,
>   that they may repent of their sin and be saved.
> And now, O Lord, I bend the knee of my heart,
>   and make my appeal, sure of your gracious goodness.
> I have sinned, O Lord, I have sinned,
>   and I know my wickedness only too well.
> Therefore I make this prayer to you:
>   Forgive me, Lord, forgive me.
> Do not let me perish in my sin,
>   nor condemn me to the depths of the earth.
> For you, O Lord, are the God of those who repent,
>   and in me you will show forth your goodness.
> Unworthy as I am, you will save me,
>   in accordance with your great mercy,
>   and I will praise you without ceasing all the days of my life.
> For all the powers of heaven sing your praises,
>   and yours is the glory to ages of ages. Amen.

Christians pray this prayer with good reason; it captures exactly their view of God as revealed by Jesus: a God of limitless compassion and hence also of forgiveness. Yet it is (most probably) a Jewish text,[7] and it integrates

---

6. This version cites verses 1–2, 4, 6–7, and 11–15.

7. It is difficult to determine the time of composition and the author with precision,

smoothly with Sanders's broader version of the Jewish story. If Jews sinned they could repent and appeal to God for forgiveness, comforted by the fact that the God of "Abraham, Isaac, and Jacob" had called Israel into being in the first place and so loved them with an undying love. The covenant would hold and the Jews, in spite of any sin, would be forgiven—after which they would redouble their efforts to live *as* God's people informed by their precious Scriptures. Did God "judge" the Jews? Of course! But this was a *parental* judgment, the sources attest—harsh, potentially yes, like many acts of discipline in ancient societies, but ultimately *restorative*. It was an exercise in discipline and not an utter repudiation or destruction that could be visited by God on sinful outsiders. (Jews could other outsiders just as well as the next ethnic group in ancient times.) The Wisdom of Solomon expresses this dynamic with famous precision. In 11:9, it says, "For when they [i.e., the Jews] were tried, though they were being disciplined in mercy, they learned how the ungodly were tormented when judged in wrath." And then in verse 10: "For you tested them [the Jews] as a father does in warning, but you examined them [the ungodly] as a stern king does in condemnation."

But someone might ask at this moment: Could some Jews actually be thrown out of the covenant? This understandable question was debated and various answers were given by different Jews in relation to various special cases, and Sanders notes many of them. It seems that there were usually exceptions, just as Jews debated if occasional righteous pagans could be admitted to the blessings of the age to come. But could the Jews as a whole, as a people, be thrown out of the covenant? Put differently, could the covenant *itself* be annulled? This was a much more important question and the answer was, "Emphatically not!" If this were to happen, the implications for *God* were simply unthinkable, whether in terms of his power or his commitments. The covenant could never bend to the point that it was broken so that the God of Abraham, Isaac, and Jacob ceased to be the God of their children and of their more distant descendants. God's loving choice and election of Abraham, Isaac, and Jacob—and of Sarah, Rebekah, Leah, and Rachel—could *never* be undone. And this is what Paul himself, a Jew, states quite clearly in Romans 9:6–13, and 11:28–29. The God who ceased to love and to be in relationship with the children of Abraham and Sarah was a God who had abandoned Abraham and Sarah and his commitments to them, and this was impossible.

With this capsule summary of Sanders's analysis of the Jews in Paul's day in place—although there is a sense in which many devout Jewish

---

although Jewish composition seems most likely.

covenantal nomists are present around us today as well—we need to consider quickly some of the immediate responses to his analysis.

Immediate responses to Sanders

Some scholars have reacted against the rather monolithic nature of Sanders's proposal (although few dared to challenge this immensely learned scholar to his face!). Sanders set himself a massive challenge—to reverse centuries of false definition (by Christian scholars) of Jews as legalists. In his zeal, he argued much the converse: *all* Jews, with very minor exceptions, only attest to a warm-hearted covenantal nomism. Legalism is *nowhere* in sight. He also backed up his claims made in 1977 with another massive analysis of textual and material evidence arguing for the existence of something he dubbed "common Judaism."[8] But blanket theses like these are always vulnerable to the complexities of history.

It is as unlikely that all Jews in Paul's day, with one or two exceptions, were compassionate covenantal nomists, as that they were all mercantile, narrow-minded legalists. They were probably, like any religion or ethnic group—not to mention, like the church—a mixed bag. Some were probably narrow-minded, some were probably deeply compassionate and inclusive toward their pagan neighbors, and some were probably utterly focused on responding to God's instructions in the Torah as devout covenantal nomists. Moreover, some were living in the desert because they were upset that the temple was being run on the wrong calendar; some, presumably, did not care much either way; and some wanted the house of Herod in power in Judea instead of direct Roman rule. The Jewish people as they existed in Paul's day were a complex, variegated entity.

Having said this, it is important to note, however, that they did not lack coherent definition altogether. They were recognizable as an ethnic group. Many outsiders would speak of them in typically racist but recognizable ways suggesting that Romans and Greeks had a fair idea about the existence of a people called the Jews, as well as of some of their key practices. ("Avoiding pork?!" "Resting on Saturdays?!" "Males cutting off their foreskins!?!") It is fair to suggest then that Jews, despite their differences, possessed a "family resemblance." Moreover, that resemblance undoubtedly had a relationship with a key underlying family of narratives; all ethnicities do. And so we think that it is entirely fair to affirm that "covenantal nomism" describes, at the very least, *a significant proportion of Jews in Paul's day*. This is how they understood God, the world, and their special relationship with God, and

---

8. Sanders, *Judaism: Practice and Belief 63 BCE–66 CE* (1992).

that story interwove with various other key practices—prayer, almsgiving, support for the temple, dietary and calendrical observances, endogamy, and so on.[9] These powerful sociological practices then fostered in turn a recognizable people. And we should grant, as we say this, that the way in which narrative, interpretative practices by scribal elites, different historical and cultural locations, and various other practices like endogamy, not to mention additional factors still as yet not entirely understood, interact to generate an ethnic identity is complex. Nevertheless, even if we allow due nuance and diversity to qualify Sanders's key thesis we are nevertheless still left with his core challenge, and in our view in the main it holds good. A significant proportion of Jews in Paul's day were *not* "legalists" (although some were); they were covenantal nomists of one sort or another. And this *must* have an impact on how we read Paul's arguments that discuss Jews, and especially when JT is in play. But before pressing into this difficulty further we should pause to note that some scholars have made another criticism of Sanders's thesis that functions a little differently from the foregoing methodological and historical concerns about descriptive homogenization.

Is there not a lurking value judgment informing Sanders's binary analysis concerning the best sort of God and resulting saving arrangement—compassionate and merciful as against just and retributive?, which is to say, covenantal and unconditional as against contractual and somewhat conditional? What's so wrong with the construal of the cosmos in legal terms, someone might ask, and hence with the construction of Judaism in essentially contractual and legal terms as well? Why is it *better* to be a covenantal nomist than a legalist?

To this we reply that there *is* a value judgment operating here and it is important to acknowledge this. Many Christian scholars are operating within this discussion ultimately informed by this judgment although being coy about its basis, and we view this last manoeuvre as unwise. The judgment's ground for us lies ultimately in the God revealed by Jesus Christ who *is* compassionate, unconditional, and covenantal. Furthermore, in the light of this covenant we also frequently learn that we are deeply fallible and broken agents, and so need a saving arrangement that rescues, liberates, and transforms us, rather than asking us to bring a lot to that arrangement in and of ourselves (and note the order of education in this sequence carefully; in the light of God's gracious action we learn about our sinfulness, and not vice versa). It is better to have a compassionate God in view: this is what God is really like; and this way of relating ultimately resonates with and operates through our most important human relationships, which are

---

9. Sanders's *Judaism: Practice and Belief* documents these masterfully.

familial relationships, working at their best, or friendships that work in the same way. It is good and right that these relationships too function as covenants, not contracts. So we endorse the value judgment operative in Sanders's characterizations, and will continue to raise questions concerning the legitimacy and constructiveness of a God understood in legal, retributive, and conditional terms. It is better that God is a loving heavenly parent than a harshly punitive politician. But we would also affirm the explicitly theological ground for this judgment: the God revealed by Paul's gospel of participation in the dying and resurrected Christ, complemented by the gift of the Spirit. Only in the light of this gospel do we know these truths about God, and it is important to be clear about this. And with these qualifications and clarifications in place, we can reaffirm Sanders's key contributions to our unfolding discussion here. But what exactly *are* Sanders's precise contributions in this regard?

There are actually two critical insights for us that unfold from the two parts of his epochal 1977 book.

The first and most widely-known derives from his comprehensive redescription of Judaism in Paul's day in terms of covenantal nomism and not in terms of legalism. Even granting that Sanders's definition of the Jews in terms of covenantal nomism was too monolithic and somewhat overstated, we can see quite quickly that this thesis poses an enormous challenge to any reading of material in Paul's letters in terms of JT. Justification theory begins, as we know well by now, with Box A; and its further moves—into Box B, acceptance of Jesus, and the church—are based on the claims of Box A. Box A propels us forward intelligibly into Box B. Moreover, as we also know well by now, Box A is based on a particular characterization of "the Jew." This description is *typical*, *self-evident*, and *universal*, so it applies to non-Christian pagans as well. But Jews are the quintessential occupants of Box A who strive to be pronounced before God on the basis of doing works informed by the law. And they are also meant to realize that they fail, and in that anxious state, to grasp for the offer of salvation in much easier terms by faith and faith alone, so becoming Christians. And we can see at this moment just why Sanders poses such a difficult problem for JT. It is just supposed to be obvious that all Jews are legalists and, as such, that they thereby represent Everyman, and the further unfolding of the gospel progression depends on this starting point along with its eventual failure. And Sanders asserted with overpowering documentation and clarity that this description is *not true*. Jews were *not* legalists. They were, in the main, something quite different, namely, covenantal nomists. They related to God in covenantal, not contractual, terms; God offered the Scriptures as a teaching, not a law; and the entire arrangement was well aware that the Jews would struggle to respond faithfully, and supplied numerous systems for dealing with that, including a temple system that much of the "law" was taken up with describing! It is as if Sanders drives a great spike here through the side of the wooden ship that is JT, and the ocean now begins to gush in through the gash. The opening definition of this model—the key claims that get the whole theory going, which are focused on a particular definition of Jews—are *false*, at least for much of the time. Justification theory is based on a lie.

Now, there are only so many ways in which one can deal with this sort of problem. And an obvious initial response would be to conclude that Paul's theory of salvation as set out by JT is just plain wrong. It begins with a universal definition of the Jew that is false. So it is a bit like a situation when someone says that they have worked out the key to human happiness with a beautiful mathematical model, but to make the equations work they just need to begin with the assumption that human beings are perfect mathematical spheres. We will need to dump this theory. But no one is going to just dump 10 percent of what Paul wrote, and especially when they think that the gospel is at stake. Having said that, surely there cannot just be a catastrophic descriptive mistake in the first chapters of Romans and in all the other places where "justification through works of law" is attacked by Paul. So other solutions have been much explored. Before turning to these, however, we should note quickly the second challenge that Sanders set in play in 1977.

This challenge was thrown down to other Pauline scholars by the final section of his book—about 20 percent—where Sanders turns to address Paul. And here Sanders basically reaffirmed the famous thesis of Albert Schweitzer which had been asserted many years earlier in 1930 when that immensely famous scholar published *his* epochal book on Paul, *The Mysticism of Paul the Apostle*. Schweitzer was an early—and remains a singularly insightful—proponent of the view that the 90 percent of material in Paul that we have described here in chapters 1 through 3 (the participatory and resurrectional gospel) is the heart of Paul's thinking about God. Schweitzer wanted to begin, to continue, and to finish his account of Paul's theology with this material—although he had some distinctive interpretative flourishes—and so essentially did Sanders. Moreover, both of these powerful intellects nipped and worried at the reading of the 10 percent of material in Paul that many scholars want to arrange in terms of JT. They marginalized this material in multiple subtle ways even as they lifted up the importance of participation and eschatology in Paul's thinking.

But while they managed to cast doubt on the central importance of the JT data, we think it is fair to say that they never quite knew what to do with it. Certainly they never landed a knockout punch. The data persisted, vastly less centrally to Paul's interpretation than the other participatory 90 percent that he wrote, but it persisted, and this entailed certain ongoing dynamics that are with us to this day.

If we have registered the support for our view of the centrality of participation and resurrection in Paul's gospel from these two earlier giants of Pauline scholarship, Schweitzer and Sanders (this being Sanders's second contribution—to recall the earlier views of Schweitzer), we are ready to recall Sanders's particular contribution to the debate to mind, in terms of Jewish description, and to move on to explore the reactions to it from other scholars in more detail, because his work was seismic in its effect. Reverberations from its impact spread through Pauline scholarship in all directions and it is worth recalling just why, before turning to explore some of the key fault-lines.

Although Sanders was not the first to point to the unfairness of a legalistic characterization of Jews, he made the case for their kinder, gentler definition in especially powerful terms and at an especially propitious moment.[10] The 1970s was a great decade to be championing the cause of a previously-voiceless and marginalized minority, and to be doing so, moreover, as the full horrors of the Holocaust were emerging steadily into view. Hence, many scholars had to step up and to try to respond to the challenge Sanders posed to the interpretation of Paul, especially in terms of JT. Numerous questions were raised *and they could no longer be ignored.*

"What is Paul doing when he describes Jews as legalists?" "What was Paul's problem with Judaism?" "What did he really think was going on in relation to the law?" And so on. And one response in particular was important.

A particular network of important scholars went on to offer "a new perspective on Paul" in response to Sanders's articulation of "a new perspective on Judaism," and their position has become very widely known—sometimes to the point that it has dominated subsequent discussion. Indeed, when Sanders's Jewish challenge is discussed, along with possible solutions in terms of how we should reinterpret Paul, it is sometimes hard to sense

---

10. See, for example, George Foot Moore's protests in his essay "Christian Writers on Judaism" (1921). A famous theological protest parallel in many of its concerns with Sanders's work is Rosemary Radford Ruether's *Faith and Fratricide: The Theological Roots of Anti-Semitism* (1974). It is worth noting too that Douglas's doctoral supervisor, Richard N. Longenecker, tutored by W. D. Davies, had published a book well before Sanders urging due sensitivity to the complexities of Judaism in Paul's day, and especially to its compassionate dimensions; see his *Paul, Apostle of Liberty* (1st ed., 1964). W. D. Davies was Sanders's teacher as well, and wrote a classic analysis of Paul that was deeply sensitive to the Jewish sources. This was first published in 1948: *Paul and Rabbinic Judaism: Some Rabbinic Elements in Pauline Theology.*

that there is any other alternative to the response offered by "the new perspective." And we regard this as unfortunate.

Although there is much to learn from scholars who articulate the new perspective on Paul (hereafter NPP)—and we certainly think that the challenges posed by Sanders in a post-Holocaust era are both crucial and unavoidable—we think that the solution offered *by* the NPP is inadequate. In particular, it has not grasped the underlying problem in Paul's texts and their legalistic interpretation with sufficient clarity and depth. There is a sense in which the NPP is deeply superficial. Nevertheless, a brief tour through the struggles of the view's main representatives, noting both the strengths and the weaknesses of their proposals, will serve to highlight the accuracy of the solution that we will ultimately offer here still more clearly. In the end of the day, we share the basic concerns of the leading representatives of the NPP—this cannot and should not be faulted—and we respect many of their suggestions, some of which our own suggested solution will overlap with directly. But we consider their overarching solution to the challenge of interpreting Paul's account of Jews and of Judaism constructively in a post-Holocaust era to be inadequate. And it is important that we understand why.

9

A New Perspective on Paul—
from J. D. G. Dunn

As we learned in the previous chapter, what is often called "the new per-spective on Judaism"—the NPJ—is generally associated with Sanders's classic study *Paul and Palestinian Judaism*, which was published in 1977. Prior to Sanders, various Christian and Jewish biblical scholars had periodi-cally suggested that the conventional way of reading Paul was profoundly unfair to Jews. But their voices were muted, whether through indifference or diffidence.[1] By 1977 though scholars were becoming more intentional about attending to the voices of marginalized groups—of women, of the poor in Latin America, of people of color in the United States, and so on. And so as the full horrors of the Holocaust were sinking in, and the liberational Zeitgeist of the 1970s was flowing through the universities, Sanders broke through with his crucial insights about how to understand Jews more ac-curately in the first century in terms of what they actually said about them-selves, which is to say, at least for much of the time, in terms of covenantal nomism.

Needless to say, this breakthrough caught the attention of other Pau-line scholars at the time, and a family of new readings developed in an im-mediate response to Sanders that became known as the "new perspective on Paul" (and we will abbreviate this often in what follows as the NPP). Although often attributed to J. D. G. Dunn or N. T. Wright—and these are the two leading scholars of the NPP whom we will concentrate on here—the designation was actually first made by Jack Kingsbury. More important than

1. One of the earliest protests, as just noted in n. 10, p. 112, was George Foot Moore's "Christian Writers on Judaism" (1921).

the origin of the name, however, is the ongoing realization that the NPP is a *response* to the NPJ; they are not the same thing. The NPP attempts to reinterpret Paul in a way that takes both the post-Holocaust concerns and the descriptive claims of the NPJ on board successfully. So it is a rereading project, and it ends up concentrating largely on the material in Paul that freights JT, since this is where the legalistic description of Jews largely lies. Consequently the NPP characteristically addresses Pauline motifs like "works of law," "justification," and "faith." Can Paul's descriptions of Jews in the texts usually read in terms of JT be read in a way that aligns him with covenantal nomism, not with legalism? The representatives of the NPP claim with their new perspective to have answered this challenge satisfactorily—they say "yes!"—and it is important for us here to see whether this is in fact the case. (We will ultimately, and somewhat sadly, say "no," but we will learn from this brave misadventure.)

We will begin our assessment with the first prominent respondent to Sanders in these revisionist terms, namely, the late James D. G. Dunn. Wright's response is the subject of the following chapter. The then Lightfoot Professor of Divinity at Durham University was characteristically fast out of the blocks.

Dunn's solution

Dunn made an early attempt to take up Sanders's challenge and to use the pressure from that scholar's important insights to reinterpret the Pauline data concerning Jews and Judaism. He introduced this pressure primarily in relation to the construal of Paul's key phrase "works of law" (Gk. *erga nomou*), which occurs in all the JT texts as part of the description of the Jew in Box A. Justification theory suggests that the inhabitants of Box A, who are prototypically Jewish, are attempting to be justified before God by doing works of law (Rom 2:6–10), a task that fails, opening up the way to faith. So the Jews as described there are supposed to be legalists. Dunn's central claim, in response to this challenge, was that the phrase "works of law" should *not* be read as referring to "legalism," but as referring to "sociological boundary markers," and that this solves our problems. And there is a certain logic to this suggestion.

The JT texts are widely assumed to be referring to Jews when they speak of "works of law" in Box A. But whereas previous generations of scholars thought that this entailed an underlying legalistic calculus, Sanders had revealed that Jews were in fact covenantal nomists. It followed then, for Dunn, that the Jews in Box A are not legalists; but because they are still Jews they must be, as Sanders said, covenantal and nomistic. However, the story cannot end here, with the redefinition of the Jews in Box A in these generous terms. The texts that underlie JT still critique and negate Jews in *some* way. It is after all Box A! The intense negative pressure generated by Box A is needed to launch questing individuals into Box B after a journey to faith. And Dunn was well aware of this. So he went on to develop a *covenantal* account of Jewish *sinfulness* over against the usual legalistic account. Hence, he opined, rather ingeniously, that the phrase "works of law" had something to do with Jewish *ethnicity* and went on to argue that the problem Paul detected in the Jews resulted from Israel's privileged position vis-à-vis God as covenantal nomists. Something went wrong in this arrangement. Paul was unhappy not with Jewish legalism then—a JT misreading—but with the exclusivism or the pride, the *ethnocentrism, which resulted from being a covenantal nomist!* Covenantal nomism had a dark side.

This set of inferences led Dunn to emphasize a sociological dimension in Judaism that the legalistic definition tends to erase and this allowed him to create in turn further connections with some of the pivotal events in Jewish history. The Jews of JT are rather like rationalistic, moralizing philosophers striding individually through the world thinking about God and God's demands, although failing to carry them out. There is no room here for either sociological dynamics or historical developments. They are the same legalists in all times and places. Dunn could suggest, however, that certain sociological features arose for God's people out of certain key historical events, and especially from the exile and from the Maccabean revolt.[2] These dramatic events placed the Jewish leaders in the case of the

2. The exile is central to the OT/Tanakh. Many of the major prophets wrote during and around this time—prophets like Jeremiah and Ezekiel. And it was a pivotal "learning experience" for the Jewish people (among other things). Jerusalem fell decisively to the Babylonians in 587 BCE, although leaders like Ezekiel had been taken into exile already, in 597 BCE. The exiles returned, miraculously, when the Babylonians were defeated by the Persians, in 538 BCE.

The Maccabean crisis is evident only in the Catholic, and similar, Bibles, which contain the Apocrypha, but is not as visible in the Protestant Bible, which has eliminated this material. The Apocrypha, sometimes referred to as the Intertestamental Literature, comprises Jewish texts written in Greek generally after the time when most of the OT/Tanakh's other texts were written (which were also composed in Hebrew or Aramaic), but before the time of the NT. (Malachi, traditionally the last Hebrew prophet, prophesied around 450 BCE.) So the intertestamental texts are dated (roughly) from the third through the first centuries BCE (200s to 0 BCE).

The Maccabean crisis erupted when Judea, then under the rule of the Hellenistic dynasty ruling Syria and Palestine after the conquests of Alexander the Great (the Seleucids), experienced a thoroughgoing paganizing program, including the robbery and desecration of its temple, and the suppression of circumcision. A revolt against this oppression in 167–60 BCE, recounted in 1 and 2 Maccabees, was miraculously

exile, and the population of Judea as a whole in the case of the Maccabean crisis, in situations of great pagan pressure. And what happened when the covenant people were placed under horrible pressure to abandon their precious practices of nomistic response to the covenant as set out in the Torah? They would respond as many people would—by emphasizing their ethnic identity and reinforcing it by way of several key practices prescribed by the Torah. And they would defend those practices and even police those who abandoned them within their beleaguered group.

The result was that these important "works of law" functioned sociologically as "boundary markers" (whereas JT views these works strictly individualistically and ethically). So Dunn speaks of "works of law" as "an identity factor, the social function of the law marking out the people of the law in their distinctiveness (circumcision, food laws, etc.)," creating the Jews' "religious and national peculiarities."[3] Dunn is referring here specifically to Jewish endogamy, Sabbath rest, the circumcision of male infants, and special dietary practices. For Dunn, these practices offset the Jewish people from the surrounding pagans, whether they were Babylonians, Persians, or Greeks, and marked out their special ethnic identity as God's people. When you marry only other Jews, mark the bodies of your male children, follow your own calendar, and eat only your own type of food together, you will be demarcated as a distinctive ethnic group. Observing these practices will set you apart. So "works" are defined here as a nomistic or law-guided response to the covenant. But because of the pressures of various key episodes of pagan pressure through Jewish history, they also became markers of distinctive ethnic identity.

It follows that such practices do still in *some* sense denote salvation, but in a responsive rather than a meritorious way, because they identify who belongs to God's own people. That people will eventually be saved. However, they simultaneously create key sociological distinctions between Jews and pagans, which is to say, between the covenant people and outsiders. And as a result of this process these boundary markers signified a privileged status for the people who practiced them, setting them apart in a special way—precisely as the people of the covenant.

---

successful, establishing a new dynasty of kings—and eventually, much less piously, of priest-kings—the Hasmoneans, who ruled Judea basically until the rise of Herod the Great from 37 BCE.

It is now worth noting, however, that the book of Daniel, found in all versions of the OT/Tanakh—although in different forms—is somewhat anomalous, being written in Hebrew and Aramaic, with additions in Greek, but dating from the 160s BCE, during the Maccabean crisis.

3. Dunn, *Romans 1–8*, 159.

But even granting the accuracy of this description of the Jews and their "works of law," Dunn still has to identify the reason for Paul's strong criticisms of this position. The JT texts are hostile to "works of law" in Box A. These must fail, however we define them. And unfortunately Dunn is a little unclear at this point in his suggested reconstruction.

Sometimes Dunn seems to be suggesting that the problem Paul has in view is that the Jews *hoarded* their special distinctive practices and refused to share them with the surrounding pagan nations. The Jewish people were supposed to be a missionary movement, but it is as if they sat on their hands and stubbornly refused to reach out to embrace their pagan neighbors, and Paul thought that this was a big problem. He himself had, after all, been called to reach out to his pagan neighbors. We can call this Issue I.

Another way of reading Dunn suggests, however, that there was just something too particular and narrow about this entire construction of the people of God, which needed to be broadened out considerably. Boundary markers, whatever they were, just had to go *as* boundary markers, so that everyone, from every ethnicity, could enter the church and be saved. Israel needed to be replaced by something less particular and more universal. We could call this Issue II.

Whatever the exact problem, whether in terms of Issue I or II, hoarding or distinctiveness, the Jews had begun to treat their special identifying practices in some deeply inappropriate way that othered the pagans too much for Paul's tastes, and he is ostensibly attacking them for doing this in Box A, from which difficult realization the journey away from works to faith in Box B should still take place.

So what should we make of this important early version of the NPP? Has Sanders's challenge been met? Does the NPP answer satisfactorily the NPJ? Sadly—but instructively—the answer is "no."

We will look at the difficulties Dunn runs into exegetically, at the level of the texts in Paul that speak of "works of law"; and then we will look at his struggles as he tries to supply a coherent account of Paul's unfolding argumentative progression within his modified version of JT. And we will learn a lot as we see here how the NPP as Dunn develops it fails.

The NPP's exegetical problem

As we have just seen, Dunn's suggested modification of the Greek phrase *erga nomou* in Paul that is usually translated "works of law" comes from a logical journey. We know already that the phrase summarizes a broader description of the Jew in the JT texts; but the Jew in Box A is incorrectly described as legalistic; the Jew is correctly described, as Sanders suggests, as a "covenantal nomist"; so the phrase "works of law" *means* something in relation to a covenantal nomist. And Dunn went on to reason that it referred to the practices that defined the boundaries of God's people as they resisted pagan pressure to apostasize and to lose their identity as Jews. Hence, they had a sociological function, thereby fitting neatly into a more historical and covenantal definition, and this went wrong, resulting in Paul's critique.

But Paul still needs to say this at some point. Dunn's moves are logical, and make sense in broad terms in relation to the history of the Jews as an ethnic group. But the phrase "works of law" operates within arguments that take place in about 10 percent of what Paul wrote, occurring in letters sent by the apostle to Rome, Galatia, and to Philippi. What does Paul actually say that "works of law" are there?

A little curiously, Paul only elaborates on "works of law" once, in the opening chapters of Romans. Elsewhere the phrase occurs largely undefined and undeveloped. So his audiences clearly knew what it was already and just needed to supply that definition when they were reading his abbreviated instructions. However, in Rome, apparently, his audience did not have this prior information. So how does Paul explain the phrase "works of law" there?

The answer, in a word, is "legalism." The phrase refers to a process whereby a person works their way to salvation. These works are informed by the Jewish Torah, which is indeed therefore functioning in this passage like a law. If the Torah's instructions are followed, then salvation will be granted by God on a future day of judgment on the basis of the doer's innocence and righteousness; if they are not followed with the appropriate deeds, a verdict of condemnation will result. And this is legalism. The system is in the text as plain as day; see Romans 2:6–10.

> 6 He will repay according to each one's deeds (. . . "on the day
> of wrath, when God's righteous judgment will be revealed"; see
> v. 5):
> 7 to those who by patiently doing good seek for glory and
> honor and immortality,
> he will give eternal life,
> 8 while for those who are self-seeking and who obey not the
> truth but injustice,
> there will be wrath and fury.
> 9 There will be affliction and distress for everyone who does evil,
> both the Jew first and the Greek,
> 10 but glory and honor and peace for everyone who does good,
> both the Jew first and the Greek.

The centrality of a system of "works of law" to this section is clear from the presence of the word "works" in the quotation from Scripture in verse 6 followed by the use of the phrase "good work" in verse 7, and then the presence of the cognate participles of "working" present in verses 9 and 10. So Paul speaks of "works" here four times. It is the most concentrated instance of this language in all of his writings. Moreover, that this is some sort of legalistic setup, which is individualistic, meritorious, and scrupulously fair (at least in these terms) is confirmed when Paul states in verse 11 that "God shows no partiality." If God judges strictly in accordance with works, as suggested here, then he does not! He truly has no favorites. Jews and gentile are all pursuing salvation here on an essentially level playing field.

The entire argumentative progression in which this paragraph appears in Romans then finishes with a set of short summarizing statements in 3:19–20 which emphasize the difficult side of this legalism: verse 20 states, again quoting Scripture (Ps 143:2), that "all flesh will *not* be declared innocent before him through works of law" (our translation). But the same basic legalistic scenario is plainly in view.

This then is where we learn what Paul means when he uses the phrase "works of law." And it clearly denotes some sort of legalism—the very caricature of Jews that Sanders so objected to because they so seldom speak of themselves in these terms. Hence, this textual data shows—and fairly unequivocally—that Dunn's solution, along with any solution like Dunn's, must fail. The text of Romans 2 will directly falsify their contentions. The phrase "works of law" will resist any redefinition away from legalism by later re-interpreters because when Paul explains what he means with this phrase, in Romans 2, he clearly means something legalistic.

But Dunn's problems are not over with this exegetical misfortune.

The NPP's failure as an argument

We have already had cause to note that Paul's JT *texts* are understood by many precisely in terms of JT as a *theory*, our name here being quite deliberate; we are concerned above all with the theory that justification unfolds. And we mean to signal by this that this reading is a coherent, unfolding argument that plots the journey of an individual from an unsaved to a saved state. It is a cogent theory, and a theory about how something very important takes place, namely, salvation. That journey begins, as we well know, in Box A, with the attempt to be saved or judged righteous by doing works of law, and under pressures generated by that initial state, which are self-evident, the individual should make the rational and moral choice and embrace the gospel by faith thereby entering Box B. And this all makes excellent sense both as a theory and as an argument, however many problems we might have with its assumptions. It fits together neatly, as we saw in Piper's lucid account. So when Dunn wants to reinterpret "works of law" in Paul's JT texts, thereby hoping to deal with the Jewish protest articulated by Sanders, he faces an additional challenge. Any alternative reading of any element within these texts must not only be plausible as a reading of the texts—a challenge we just saw that his suggestion fails in relation to Romans 2. It must also function within a smooth overarching *argument*. The argument *itself*—its progressions—must continue to make sense. Now we don't necessarily have to follow the argumentative progression suggested by JT; but we do have to at least equal the coherence of that reading. And this is where Dunn encounters his second major problem.

Earlier we emphasized how the logic within Dunn's reformulated critique of the Jews was a little unclear. He redefined "works of law" as sociological boundary markers defended by over-zealous covenantal nomists. It is this inappropriate defense that led to Paul's purported critique, which then unpacks into salvation by faith, as the broader argument in the JT texts expects. But we need now to ask if Dunn's redefinition succeeds in generating a coherent broader progression in these terms.

Justification theory it should be recalled, makes perfect sense as it understands things, with an individual journeying from the failure of legalism to salvation by faith alone.

We are repeating ourselves here, for which we apologize; but the logic supplied by JT needs to be crystal-clear at this moment. An individual in Box A, quintessentially a Jew (although not necessarily a Jew), strives to fulfill God's righteous demands as instructed by the law, but fails. She thereby becomes liable to the justly retributive anger of God on the day of judgment; she knows this is coming! So . . . fearing this prospect, she eagerly grasps the offer of salvation by faith alone, which seems to be a much easier, doable basis for salvation, when that offer is made by an evangelist or preacher. In this way, the individual progresses from an unsaved state in Box A to a saved state in Box B and does so by way of faith *alone*. This last qualification is a continual acknowledgement of the futility of any attempt to be saved by works, in terms of a full ethical perfection, along with God's generous provision of an easier route to salvation. It shows that the individual has learned and continues to learn the humble lessons of Box A concerning her own sinfulness.

JT—the progression from failed legalism to salvation by faith alone

A: Unsaved   B: Saved

Attempt to do works of law fails   Salvation by faith

And everything here makes excellent sense as an argument, although Jews would complain that this is not *fair*; for this is just not how they relate to God in the first place, as Sanders and others have noted at some length. But setting this problem aside for now, we should recall at this moment that the entire validity of salvation by faith alone rests on the prior failure of salvation attempted by the doing of works. Only *because* that process has failed does the reasonableness of salvation by faith alone become apparent. We learn that we need something much easier than perfect righteousness in order to be saved; we tried that and failed! And so salvation by faith alone seems to fit the bill, and does so nicely.

In short, the basic logic of JT is impeccable. Its argument makes sense. It all fits together, running, as it does, forwards from Box A to Box B. But it only makes sense *as* it runs from Box A to Box B—the issue of directionality. It is the prior set of assumptions operating in Box A, and its resulting collapse, that justifies the existence and rationale of Box B, which revolve around faith, as we all know. And at this moment a crucial additional problem for Dunn's alternative proposal emerges clearly into view.

If he changes the definition of "works of law" in Box A from righteous deeds performed as instructed by the Torah ultimately to be saved by merit to a sociological meaning—to practices of circumcision, food purity, Sabbath-observance, and so on, which mark off the Jews as a distinct ethnicity—then how is the broader argument impacted? Does it still work? And the short answer is that it does not. The journey of an individual from a state characterized by sociological boundary markers that collapses in on itself in some inappropriate way no longer unpacks coherently into salvation through faith alone. Box B has lost the all-important logic that precedes it, grounds it, and creates it. Paul's broader argument about salvation that culminates in faith no longer makes sense. But we probably need to spend just a little longer tracing these difficulties through, because they will affect all the subsequent representatives of the NPP in due course as well. Having said this, when we turn specifically to Dunn to trace the new logic he finds in Paul in detail we run into the problem we have already noted. He himself was a little unclear on how all this works (although perhaps now we know why). However, we will give him the benefit of the doubt, and trace quickly through both main variations of his suggestion, in terms of Issue I and Issue II. The key questions here are, after all, the same: do Box A and Box B still fit together as a coherent rational journey after Dunn has redefined "works of law"? And does this journey end up with salvation by faith alone?

What then is the overall logic in Paul's argument when the problem facing the performer of "works of law" in terms of Jewish boundary markers is defined in terms of Issue I?

Here the Jews in Box A "hoard" their precious practices and refuse to share them, resisting a missionary movement into the surrounding nations, thereby becoming guilty to charges of ethnocentric pride, arrogance, and selfishness. We might say—cautiously—that they have been miserly with their Jewishness, at which moment we see immediately that we are still on very dangerous ground. But addressing the logical issue, we can also see fairly quickly that Dunn has just run into a major problem.

The appropriate *response* to a charge of inappropriate hoarding of Jewish practices would be an open-handed and generous *sharing* of those practices with anyone who wanted to adopt them. The answer to hoarding is Jewish missionary work *qua* Jews. "Convert to Judaism and be saved!" This is the journey that now unfolds from this account of the problem in Box A. Hence, we have clearly *not* arrived at salvation by faith alone *and neither can we*. Box A has been sundered logically from Box B. These cannot be connected in any way that actually makes sense. (They only made sense when they were connected together in terms of the logic of JT.)

NPP attempt 1: a progression in terms of Issue I in Box A

A: Hoarded boundary markers   B: Shared boundary markers

(NOT faith!)

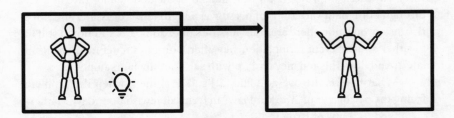

Any account of Paul's argument in his JT texts that can't make sense of Box B in terms of some account of faith is disqualified. It cannot be right. But perhaps a logic generated by Issue II in Box A will work better.

Dunn, perhaps aware of the limitations of an account of "works of law" in terms of Issue I, frequently speaks of the challenge facing the Jews in terms of Issue II, namely, in terms of ethnicity itself. The Jews were just too particular, and God needed a more universal body for people to join, namely, the church, which exists at some level of detachment from a particular nation and its distinctive practices (which is true). God wanted to move beyond ethnicity we might say. Ethnicity is too restrictive and narrow—and Dunn is drawing here, at least in part, on a particular philosophical and theological tradition that emphasizes the superiority of the universal over the particular.[4]

What are we to make of this suggestion?

Arguably it does succeed in making better sense of salvation by faith alone, which looks at first glance to be a fairly generic, universalizable action. Anyone can have faith. And if someone gets saved by faith alone, then *any* ethnicity (Jewish or non-Jewish) can be coupled with that, at least to some degree. So the church seems to be filled with all sorts of different peoples who live quite distinct lives in people groups with different languages, countries, customs, and so on. The church is more universal than any one of these groups, saved by faith alone. So Dunn seems to be on to something here.

---

4. One of its most influential proponents, who greatly influenced the earliest phase of NT interpretation, in Germany, in the 1800s, was the famous German-speaking philosopher G. W. F. Hegel.

NPP attempt 2: a progression from ethnicity to universalism

A: Ethnic (and unsaved)   **B: Universal, non-ethnic (saved)**

Ethnic practices   **By faith alone**

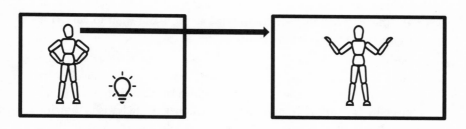

But as we press into this explanation, serious problems again begin to emerge. Unlike the logic generated by an account of Box A's problems in terms of Issue I, where a major fissure could be detected straightaway, a reading of Paul's argument in terms of Issue II generates problem after problem until the entire position eventually collapses into implausibility.

1. The focus shifts subtly in this version of Paul's logic from an emphasis on "works of law" in terms of boundary markers to a problem with any distinctive Jewish practices at all. *Anything* that a Jew does that is distinctively Jewish is wrong, because anything that contributes to a Jew's ethnicity is wrong. We know already that there is an immediate exegetical difficulty here because Paul does not say this in Romans 2. But for the moment we want to think about the logical problems. And it suffices to get us started to note that the terms of Dunn's argument—and presumably of his account of Paul's texts—have moved in a very important way. It is just wrong to be a Jew because that is ethnic and God wants the church to be universal.

2. But it seems odd for ethnicity *per se* to be accused by Paul of being deeply wrong. No one can exist except within an ethnic group. Humanity is simply constructed in this way, with variations in terms of language, dress, food, calender, flora and fauna, aesthetics, domestic architecture, humor, entertainment practices, sport, rituals, and so on. Is all this wrong simply because it exists with all these variations? It is not obvious why this should be the case. Accusing someone of being ethnic seems to be like accusing someone of breathing or eating or

wearing clothes. What else are we going to do? It would seem to be an indelible part of being human.

3. And it is certainly not obvious that this is *self-evidently* the case. By reflecting on our ethnicity, how can we draw the conclusion that it is wrong to be ethnic. There might be nasty aspects to our ethnicity and its defense, but that is a different matter. We do not generally conclude from an examination of our ethnicity that it is ethnicity *itself* that must go. The very fact that we are worried about it and want to correct it shows that it remains important.

4. But there is an acute theological problem present here as well. The ethnicity of the Jews is a *sacred* ethnicity that has been established by God's direct intervention and ongoing revelation. It is the teachings given by God, most dramatically at Sinai, that create Jewish ethnicity. And this reading of Paul turns the entire calling of the Jews in these terms into question (which in turn calls all of God's actions through the Jewish Scriptures into question). They just seem like a big mistake. And is it really plausible to suggest that what 80 percent of the Bible talks about (the OT/Tanakh) is just a big mistake?, and that we worship a God who makes these sorts of mistakes? Were the Jews a big mistake *qua* Jews? This seems highly implausible.

5. There is also a worrying dishonesty present within any program that supposes that Christians live in a universal church that lies beyond ethnicity. No Christian lives in a non-ethnic way either. No Christian is asked to repent of their ethnicity *per se*. They might need to reform its sinful aspects, and to accord it less value than they do; it is not sacred. But nowhere is anyone asked to abandoned ethnicity itself as sinful, and for the reasons we just noted, we can't.[5]

6. Similarly, if we nevertheless think that we do live beyond ethnicity, we have just created a recipe for the cultural erasure of other less powerful people groups and for the imposition of our own ethnicity, unseen, upon them. Christians who *think* they are living in a universal church, beyond ethnicity, have not abandoned theirs; but that ethnicity is now the universal church that others must adopt. We have turned Christianity into a colonizing program. It will begin by erasing Jewish ethnicity, and then continue by erasing all other ethnicities that it encounters. And this cannot be good.

---

5. The concern of Daniel Boyarin in his important book, *A Radical Jew: Paul and the Politics of Identity* (1994).

There are many grounds then for grave concerns if we pursue Dunn's reinterpretative program for Paul's JT texts by assuming that Paul is attacking Jewish ethnicity *per se* in Box A in the name of a Christian universalism created by salvation in terms of faith alone in Box B. Dunn is really drawing on philosophers like Hegel here—and a Hegel appropriated, moreover, in a rather sinister fashion by subsequent nationalists—and Paul was not Hegel. While we may grant there is an insight present in the claim that the church is universal and exists in some way beyond ethnicities, *that truth does not rest on the self-evident erasure of any ethnicity at all, beginning with the Jews!* And so we must judge the suggestion of Dunn in terms of Issue II a failure—and also strongly oppose its adoption by any who fail to detect its sinister entailments.

And with the failure of this account of Box A in terms of Issue II, we can now see that Dunn's entire reinterpretative program has collapsed. The NPP as he advocates it is not a coherent answer to the NPJ, and this means in turn that the challenges of the NPJ to JT remain intact. But we have learned some important things from Dunn's difficulties as we begin to think about our own response to these complex challenges.

The take-homes

There are five critical "take-homes" from our brief analysis of Dunn.

1. Perhaps the single most important realization we should carry on with us from a consideration of Dunn's difficulties is that Paul's texts that describe "works of law" *do* describe legalism. This is plain and there is no getting around this. Any solution to all the problems generated by JT, we might say, needs to journey through the prose of Romans 2. We will have to find some sort of space in our rereading for the legalism that that chapter speaks of, hopefully while still managing to address the challenge offered by Sanders and the NPJ about the nature of Jews in general as covenantal nomists.

2. Dunn's attempt to respond to Sanders's challenge led to his foregrounding of some of the sociological and historical dimensions within Judaism that scholars used to reading Paul's texts in terms of JT had lost sight of. And this, a little ironically, really has the effect of deepening Sanders's challenge.

    After being tutored by Dunn, and thinking about how the Jews are organized sociologically and impacted historically—and his broader claims here about the Jews can certainly be granted—it is even easier to see than it was before that JT's construction of the Jew is odd. Justification theory's account of the Jew in Box A creates a generic individual figure who operates in terms of strict rationality and philosophically driven morality. So he does not change through time and space. And this is simply not what the Jews were like. They were a *people*, with a distinctive sociological profile that waxed and waned under the pressure of historical forces, especially from aggressive paganism. They did change. And these are just not the same things at all. Dunn helps us to see this very clearly. (Given more time, we could even see from other things that Dunn wrote that he helps us to see that Paul himself in many of his texts that touch on Jews outside of the JT discussions tends to talk in historical terms as well, beginning with Romans 9–11.)

3. Dunn also helps us to see that the debate in response to Sanders's important challenge tends to run in a very narrow channel. The discussion focuses largely on the definition of "the Jew" and of Jews in Paul's JT texts. The underlying assumption then is that this is what Paul is talking about in his JT texts—thereby showing the influence *of* JT, which makes this assumption! Justification theory posits that a *generic* Jew is in view in Box A, and Sanders and Dunn—who are not alone—never really question that this *is* what Paul is talking about in these parts of his letters. But this is not necessarily the case.

4. In close relation to the foregoing, Dunn shows how the failure to recognize the broader influence of JT on the structure of the scholarly conversation as a whole leaves a lot of the other key challenges generated by that model unaddressed. Justification theory does not just generate problems for Jewish definition, although it certainly does this. We noted in our earlier chapters how it also offers a different basic understanding of God, of the location and nature of the knowledge of God, and of the work of Christ, from most of what Paul wrote elsewhere. And it thinks in a fundamentally different direction from that material—forward rather than backward. Hence a major interpretative challenge emerges into view whenever we try to pass from Paul's JT texts to the other 90 percent of what he wrote.

   If scholars are preoccupied with the Jewish challenge alone—important as that is—and allow JT to dictate the broader terms of the discussion, they are unlikely to come up with a solution to all of these challenges. Certainly they must struggle to come up with an appropriate solution. Moreover, their attempted solutions to this situation will be characterized by superficiality, when the challenges offered by JT seem to ask rather for a radical solution. A lot is wrong so a lot will need to shift around if we are ever to grasp a compelling solution to all our difficulties.

5. Dunn also shows us how formidable an opponent JT is for the Pauline interpreter. We might be troubled by its implications, and many modern scholars, alerted by Sanders, are very troubled by its description of Jews. But JT has a formidable exegetical base in Romans 2, along with an impeccable unfolding logic. And this poses a multi-level challenge for its critics. If they want to meet its challenges and to defuse its more toxic elements they must come up with a responsible exegetical solution that reads what Paul wrote accurately and fairly (and hence in a way that finds some space for legalism), *and* they must equal the unfolding argumentative logic of JT as a theory. Moreover, they must do so in a way that actually meets the spectrum of challenges that the theory offers, including a smooth integration with the rest of what Paul wrote. It is as if Dunn attempts to scale a cliff, but after an impressive and energetic start, he slips and falls back to the ground. Yet as we step back and survey his attempt we see that behind the cliff he was scaling a mountain towered out of view, with cliff after cliff still to conquer beyond it. To get to the top of this cliff then, would not suffice. Enough ropes, plans, and equipment would need to be in place to go much, much further.

10

A New Perspective on Paul—
from N. T. Wright

It is likely that those with an interest in studying the apostle have come across at least one of Wright's many works on Paul's epistles and theology—and he has written many.[1] Wright has been an especially important teacher for those who have noticed some of the problems with JT that we have already remarked on. Indeed, Wright's work has often provided the all-important gateway out of the restrictions of JT and its associated reading of the Bible into the exciting but slightly forbidding territory of modern historical scholarship in general. Consequently, he is a key re-interpreter for much of the justification material that we find in Paul.

Wright himself is clearly aware of JT's problematic presence in scholarly and ecclesial contexts. As he writes in the opening chapter of his book *Justification*, "The theological equivalent of supposing that the sun goes round the earth is the belief that the whole of Christian truth *is all about me*

---

1. Here is a list of the principal works by Wright that we have consulted on this subject; in order of publication: "The Messiah and the People of God: A Study in Pauline Theology with Particular Reference to the Argument of the Epistle to the Romans" (DPhil, Oxford, 1980); *The Climax of the Covenant: Christ and the Law in Pauline Theology* (1991); *The New Testament and the People of God* (1992), especially pp. 403–9; "The Law in Romans 2" (1996); "The Letter to the Romans. Introduction, Commentary, and Reflections" (2002); *The Resurrection of the Son of God* (2003), especially pp. 207–398; *Paul: In Fresh Perspective* (2005); "4QMMT and Paul: Justification, 'Works,' and Eschatology" (2006); *Justification: God's Plan and Paul's Vision* (2009); *Pauline Perspectives: Essays on Paul, 1978–2013* (2013); *Paul and the Faithfulness of God*: (2 vols., 2013); *Paul and His Recent Interpreters: Some Contemporary Debates* (2015); and *Galatians* (2021). In what follows we will concentrate especially on his position in *Justification* and in *Paul and the Faithfulness of God*.

and my salvation."[2] (Wright is directly criticizing Piper's account of JT with this comment.) He continues:

> I am suggesting that the theology of St. Paul, the whole of St. Paul rather than the truncated and *self-centered* readings which have become endemic in Western thought, the towering and majestic theology of St. Paul which, when you glimpse it, dazzles you like the morning sun rising over the sea, is urgently needed as the church faces the tasks of mission in tomorrow's dangerous world, and is not well served by the *inward-looking soteriologies* that tangle themselves up in a web of detached texts and secondary theories.[3]

Wright is clearly putting his finger here on one of the problems with JT that we have had cause to note fairly frequently earlier: it is strangely focused on the journey of an individual. The individual in question, moreover, tends to be a highly rational, moral, and self-interested figure who is both universal and yet also specifically Jewish. Wright just knows in his bones that there is something off here. The categories the Bible uses are corporate, historical, and encompass the whole person, and the Jewish people are distinctive from the surrounding pagan nations precisely *as* God's people. And these two things—the Jew of JT and the Jews of the Bible—are clearly not the same thing. But if we need to move away from an individualist, introspective account of salvation that seems to have lost contact with the larger sweep of the Bible what should we do?

Wright is not reticent in supplying bold answers to this question. Essentially, he solves it *by reversing all the key parameters in Box A that are problematic*, thereby generating a new, *panoramic* account of its data. As we just saw, JT produces a strangely ahistorical, individual Jew who does not vary through time and space. So Wright reinterprets this depiction in historical and corporate terms. Paul speaks of all Jews, hence of *Israel*, and not of a generic, individual Jew. In tandem with this, instead of the rather philosophical progression of an individual from an unsaved situation toward faith, Box A is now the great journey of Israel that runs right through the Old Testament, from Abraham—and in fact, from the garden of Eden—to the coming of Jesus. Moreover, since we are now following an entire people journeying through history, Wright can incorporate sociological dimensions into his analysis as well—the impact on the shape and identity of God's people imparted by their distinctive ethnic practices like circumcision, endogamy, a special diet and calendar, a special temple in a special city, and so on. (How Wright joins hands with a re-interpreter like Dunn is especially

2. Wright, *Justification*, 23, emphasis original.
3. Wright, *Justification*, 25, emphases added.

clear at this moment.) The result is a stunningly ambitious rereading of the Pauline data in Box A, followed by a corresponding recharacterization of Box B. But we need now to ask, obviously, if Wright—so to speak—is right. Does his ambitious agenda succeed? Or, does its frequently dazzling presentation obscure underlying shoals and rocks on which the struggling vessel of Pauline interpretation will founder and be wrecked?

In order to assess this question, we will need to press a little more deeply into his sweeping reinterpretation. And we will begin by summarizing the story that Wright wants to tell about Israel's journey that he sees unfolding through Box A.

Wright's re-narration of Box A

For Wright, although Box A presupposes a grand narrative focused on Israel, the story actually begins as the Bible suggests, before this people's inception, with creation, and with divine Wisdom. Through Wisdom, God created the cosmos, which is how God leaves a stamp of his existence on the cosmos.[4] So, citing the first major section in Romans, chapters 1–3 (specifically 1:18–32), Wright introduces an account of the created order in which human beings, collectively, can and should know who God is; and the appropriate human response to this plainly-known God is gratitude. Having said this, we all know well that right away something goes wrong.

The primeval humans, Adam and Eve, repudiating a grateful and obedient response, fall into sin.[5] A problem characterized by human disobedience is present almost immediately then within the grand narrative of Box A (485). Contrary to God's intended purpose for human beings—that people should be stewards of creation and "enable it to flourish"—they failed disastrously, thereby spiraling into sin, leaving themselves and the rest of creation in disarray (485). Sin entered the cosmos through humanity's refusal of God's love and its failure to reflect God's image in the world, generating the first of several plights that humanity will subsequently sink into. But the story's focus now narrows, following a plain reading of the Bible, to the origins of Israel.

Through Abraham God first chose Israel and gave it the vocation of being "a light to people in darkness" (496). God's people is supposed to be

4 Wright, *Paul and the Faithfulness of God*, 475. Note, the remaining citations from *Paul and the Faithfulness of God* will be in-text.

5. There is arguably a tension evident here between Wright's assertion of humanity's accurate knowledge of God in general through the contemplation of a cosmos created by Wisdom, leaning on Rom 1:19–20, and a particular incident that set the cosmos into a dreadful downward spiral that was associated especially with Adam and Eve, as spoken of in texts like Rom 5:12.

God's solution within Box A, from their inception. But, despite God's intention that Israel should be obedient, trustworthy, and bear the oracles to the nations, like Adam, the nation "as a whole . . . failed in this commission" (497). So Israel collectively falls under a curse, leaving Abraham and his descendants spiraling into their own particular failures (503).

But God does not leave the Israel of the patriarchs alone and bereft. The nation is given a "helper," the Torah, to assist it as it tries to faithfully live out the goal of being a light to the nations. However, the Torah paradoxically functions mainly to highlight the curse that Israel is already under, as the Jews are unable to obey it sufficiently themselves. It therefore brings "wrath on God's people" (507). This negative function is apparently part of the Torah's design (510), and self-evidently so (520), but it places Israel in an even more serious plight. God now condemns Israel because of its failed Torah-observance and so the Torah magnifies the sin within which Israel is now steeped. The now rather depressing story of Box A runs from the exodus through the monarchy, demonstrating how Israel has, in effect, been cast away "precisely through Torah" (509; and Wright cites Romans 9–11 here). God's single divine purpose for the world happens through Israel's corporate rejection (500).

The final stage of the Torah-induced plight within Box A is Israel's experience of the anguish of exile under God's wrath, where it waits for its Savior and Messiah (525). Someone could object at this moment that the Jewish leadership did return from exile, rather miraculously, establishing a small but long-lasting state back in Judea—"Second Temple Judaism."[6] But Wright integrates this epoch into his broader schema by arguing that the exile never really ended.[7] God's absence from the temple continued to be felt by the Jews in Judea, he suggests, right up to Jesus's day.[8] Only at *this* point, finally, with the coming of Jesus, did God return to his people in person, and

---

6. To reiterate (and expand) from our earlier notation: this is the scholarly designation for variegated Jewish traditions that existed between the Babylonian exile and the rebuilding of the temple ca. 520–516 BCE, through the destruction of the temple in 70 CE. Key Jewish literature during this time would have been the Dead Sea Scrolls, Josephus, Philo, the Pseudepigrapha, as well as certain archeological remains. For further study, see the very helpful essays under the "Literature" section in Brettler and Levine (eds.), *The Jewish Annotated New Testament*, 695–727.

7. Arguably a significant tension is apparent in Wright's overarching narrative at this moment. On the one hand, he argues that the exile never really ends, as we just noted, and that after it Israel remain under God's wrath because of their repeated failures. On the other hand, Wright traces the origins of the all-important notion of resurrection in Israel to the return from exile, thereby freighting it with positive ultimate significance.

8. This position is certainly apparent in the Dead Sea Scrolls.

to his temple.[9] So this moment clearly inaugurates God's response to Israel's recurrent problem. The great story of Box A draws to a close.

Wright's re-narration of Box B

Wright has deliberately set up the story of a problem in Box A with a primary focus on Israel, so his solution is couched in specifically Jewish terms as well. Jesus arrives on the scene as YHWH himself returning to Zion to deliver his people from slavery.[10] Additionally, Jesus is Israel's Messiah. Wright consistently translates the Greek honorific *Christos*, which is usually simply transliterated in our Bibles as "Christ," with the word "Messiah," to emphasize this critical Jewish dimension within Paul's thinking. But the Messiah comes to fulfill a particular task, namely, to save Israel. That is, he must respond to the problem that Box A has articulated at length.

In order to do so, Israel's Messiah bears Israel's sin, condemnation, and the "juridical punishment" previously directed at Israel because of its disobedience. God, in turn, declares "those 'in the Messiah', with his death and resurrection 'reckoned' to them, [as] the single forgiven family promised by the covenant God to Abraham" (964). Consequently, atonement has several dimensions suggests Wright, from representation to substitution to divine victory, all of which operate to remove those "in the Messiah" from exile and God's wrath. "Justification" denotes *both* a "forensic verdict" of acquittal from previous transgressions *and* a "covenantal declaration" of inclusion in the last Israel that Jesus has realized for Christians. And this last event fulfills God's original promise to Abraham that he would be the father "of many nations" (937).[11]

Wright proceeds to argue that in Paul's theology we can find a large-scale retelling of the exodus narrative as the apostle elaborates on this salvation—what Wright calls "the new-exodus" (658). This event functions as the typically panoramic transition of a people from Box A to Box B. But Wright does not stop here. After referencing the post-exilic hope represented in

9. Significantly, all of the preceding material that basically sketches out the "problem" is, Wright asserts, writ large in Romans from 1:18 all the way through chapter 2. In other words, Romans 2 read in this expansive way dominates Wright's construction of "'the problem' to which 'the gospel' is the solution," at least in *Paul and the Faithfulness of God* (764, and extending through 771).

10. Jesus is "what it looked like when YHWH returned to Zion. The God who refused to share his glory with another has shared it with Jesus" (*Paul and the Faithfulness of God*, 683).

11. Wright's full explanation of the meaning of Paul's justification words extends from 925–1032.

Isaiah, Zechariah, and Malachi (to name just a few of the key texts), which conceive of YHWH eventually returning to the temple, Wright even goes so far as to suggest that Paul views Jesus as the one who brings together the narratives of exodus, redemption, tabernacle, divine presence, God's return, wisdom, and kingship, in a new-exodus as foretold by the prophets (655). In particular, through Jesus the divine glory, which previously left the temple and essentially abandoned Israel in exile, has returned, although this also happens through the Spirit. Both figures now lead the Messiah-people through the waters of baptism, which Wright reads as a reference to the parting of the Red Sea (sic), to their inheritance, thereby justifying all who believe.

The main Pauline text for the presence of the new-exodus movement from Box A to Box B in Paul's thought is, according to Wright, Romans 6–8, which is the third major section of Romans he employs:[12] "It [i.e., this three-chapter-long section of Romans] takes us on the journey through the water by which the slaves are set free (chapter 6), up to the mountain where Torah is given, with its attendant paradox . . . [i.e., chapter 7] and then on the homeward march to the 'inheritance' [i.e., chapter 8]" (659).[13] So here we see, Wright argues, how the Messiah-people, who are now an eschatological Israel,[14] are set free through baptism (1335) and enter a new community of Jews and pagans where God's people emerge from the waters wearing the "badge of faith" (931).

This point of transition is of course critical. Previously, for "most Jews" the Torah and its associated practices were understood to be the key signs of being involved with God, hence they functioned as "boundary-marker[s] between Jews and non-Jews" (and the parallel with Dunn's position here is obvious). But this view led to boasting on the part of Israel, along with an egregious failure to take the law to the pagans (91, Wright developing what we identified as Issue I in Dunn). So Wright claims that now "*Pistis* [i.e., the Greek for *faith*] is . . . the Israel-characteristic which, according to Romans 3.2 and 3.22, was lacking in Israel itself and provided by the Messiah. *Pistis* is the appropriate sign that a human being is a Messiah-person, 'in the Messiah', 'belonging to the Messiah' . . ." (931). But Wright provides an additional rationale that Dunn resisted for the view that the new people of God is characterized by

12. While Gal 4:1–11 and 1 Cor 8–10 are also in play here, Rom 6–8 is where Wright detects the grand retelling of the new-exodus most clearly in Paul and is therefore where he plants his flag, so to speak.

13. Wright suggests that the textual support for the echoes and allusions forming Paul's retelling of the exodus narrative is cumulative, and the narrative is simply ubiquitous in so much Second Temple literature that it could be drawn on in various ways.

14. Wright deliberately and wisely refrains from ever referring to the church as "the second Israel."

the badge of faith. Jesus *himself* is spoken of several times by Paul as being the faithful One, says Wright, and he thereby reveals the covenant faithfulness of God. So it is appropriate that the followers of the preeminently faithful Jesus, joining the covenant people of God, would be characterized by faithfulness as well. (We will return to this insight at the end of this chapter.)

Wright is clear that once God's solution arrives in the Messiah those who become a part of this people through faith are shorn of "the symbolic praxis either of Judaism or of paganism" (729; see also 400, 444–45). Its practices are left behind, resulting in a unified community with a new corporate identity and a new worldview. A Spirit-circumcised community now awaits Christ's return (1258), its bodily resurrection (1093f.), and its final judgment (840).[15] In the meantime, having been justified, Christians work out their sanctification so that they will receive some reward for their virtue on the great final day—at which moment Wright's analysis is clearly visited by the shade of Melanchthon (see 957; 978).[16]

At the end then, viewing his position as a whole, we can begin to grasp some of the key reasons for Wright's popularity.

By way of a panoramic account of Boxes A and B he appears to have addressed any anxieties that might have been nagging the consciences of his Bible-believing audiences in *canonical* and/or *salvation-historical* terms if they were raised to understand salvation and their Scriptures in terms of JT. When Wright boldly narrates Paul's gospel on a broad narrative canvas, instead of in terms that are individualistic, rationalistic, and timeless, he gives his reader a way of speaking about the Bible as a whole by demonstrating its integrated history in relation to the Jewish people—and most of the time the Bible does talk about the Jews as they worked their way through history. Those teachers and preachers long constrained by JT are liberated to think in new ways about their texts. This richer narrative can then be pulled through into a thicker account of the Jewish Paul as the apostle speaks of his Messiah leading his people through the waters of baptism, leaving behind all that constrained them in Box A into a life of inheritance in Box B. And the New Testament seems now to fit neatly onto the concerns and dynamics of the Old, snapping in place like the final pieces of Lego needed to complete a model. Small wonder then that Wright's viewpoint—ably complemented

---

15. Wright references Rom 2:25–29 here, which turns out to be an important text for his project.

16. In fact, we can already detect the voices within Wright's project of all three of our significant precursors, Melanchthon, Sanders, and Dunn, along with great stretches of more unique claims. This provides some sense of the synthetic creativity and reach of Wright's work.

by his eloquence—has gathered such a following, and there is much to applaud in this impact. But we need now to turn to some harder questions.

The underlying logic

Our concerns are not just with incipient Marcionism, although this does concern us;[17] like Wright, we want the Bible to hang together *and* the Jews to have a key role within God's purposes within history. But we are also concerned by the sort of God Paul is thought to be proclaiming within all this scriptural material, along with the dynamics whereby we know this God, and what God's work accomplished through Jesus and through his Spirit exactly does. Hence, we are concerned in addition by the ongoing marginalization of most of what Paul has to say about these all-important questions in his participatory and resurrectional material by the punitive and limited mechanics of JT and its minority data-set. And we are also deeply concerned about how our construction of Paul describes *Jews*, and not just how the Jews traveled through history when the Bible speaks of them, back in the OT. For us the Jews are not primarily an interpretative cipher preparing the way in the Scriptures for Christianity. They are a people living in relation to Christians whom we must think carefully about relating to today. And at this moment a fundamental dynamic within Wright's ambitious reinterpretation of Paul emerges in to view that raises disquieting questions.

Wright's intricate canonical and historical work *still looks a lot like JT*, and if this is true, we will need to ask in due course if any of the deep, structural problems of JT that so worry us have been solved. In the first instance, however, we just need to grasp that this is what Wright has done.

17. Marcion was the first great heretic—and, to complicate matters, a great devotee of Paul's theology, as he understood that. Marcion had no time for the Jews or the God of the Jews as spoken of by the OT/Tanakh. He thought that the Jewish God was an inferior Demiurge characterized by rage, and the God of Jesus, a superior God—*the* God—who was characterized by benevolence. So to resolve this problem he simply discarded the Jewish Scriptures, and rejected the Jews, focusing instead on a new Scripture comprising just ten letters of Paul and the Gospel of Luke, Paul's companion, all suitably edited. The church was rightly hostile to this set of moves, intelligible as they are on some level, and insisted on retaining the OT/Tanakh, and many other NT writings besides Paul's.

Wright frequently identifies Marcionism as a problem, and finds it at work in the views of those he opposes (that is, both within the position we are calling JT and in the apocalyptic network of Pauline scholars, to which we belong). And he has himself clearly been accused of it: see 754, 806, 62, 1017, 1206, 20–21, 1453, 81. Suffice it here to say that if our concerns about Wright's rereading are correct, and both our and his concerns about JT are correct, then he risks being hoist by his own petard.

Certainly JT has been greatly expanded—extended and projected onto a huge biblical screen. The problem that JT sees facing the generic individual in Box A is now the problem that faces the Jewish people as a whole. The generic struggle to observe the demands of the law, which elicits God's wrath after its inevitable failure, is now the struggle of the Jewish people through its history to be obedient to God. But this broader story basically still elicits repeated episodes of disobedience and punishment culminating in exile. *And this is all still basically Box A.* It is just Box A writ large, after which we realize that Box B in Wright, which describes the new community, is just Box B in JT writ large as well. Basically, everything has just gotten a lot bigger.

JT: the journey to salvation of the generic, ahistorical individual

A: Unsaved individual   **B: Saved individual**

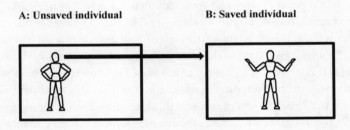

Wright: the journey to salvation from Israel to the Church

A: Unsaved Israel   **B: Saved Church members**

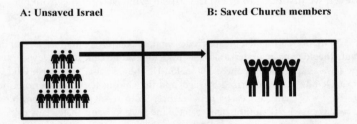

Moreover, it is clear that the entire story for Wright still works forward. Hence Box A is the start of the story and sets up the problem—the story of Israel, certainly, but still the story of a problem. And Box B offers the solution to this problem generated by a God who has already been defined by Box A—in essentially legal, conditional and, if necessary, punitive terms. The panoramic corporate and historical setting does not really change any of this.

In like manner, Israel's Messiah in Wright's telling of the story comes to do exactly what Jesus does in JT—to absorb the punishment justly due to the sinners disclosed by Box A. Certainly it is Israel's Messiah who dies for our sins, and that death solves our problem. But nothing has changed here apart from Jesus's title. Wright's dramatic reinterpretation of Box B in terms of a new exodus still offers the solution to the conundrums of Box A that JT prescribes by way of Jesus's work on the cross, and still prescribes its reception through the badge of faith. But someone might say that faith in Wright's account of Paul denotes community membership, and this is different.

But is it?

The traditional version of JT prescribed faith as the condition for membership in the church. And so very little here has changed as well. Moreover—and most significantly—since the community's "badge" is faith, the church is a community that acts *beyond Jewish practices*. Hence, Judaism and its practices are again erased, just like in JT.

All of this bespeaks of the continuing grip on Wright's thinking *of* JT. It seems, when all is said and done, that Wright's new perspective is really just JT rearranged in broader corporate and historical terms. The key might have changed but the tune has remained the same—although this is underselling Wright's interpretative virtuosity. More appositely, it is as if a local folk melody, traditionally played by a bluegrass band, has been utilized and reworked by a gifted composer so that it is now the leitmotif of a symphony, performed by a full orchestra, to stunning dramatic effect. But it is still the same tune, in a magnificent new arrangement. And if this is the case, it follows that the problems intrinsic to that tune have not been resolved, which is what we will find.

We will begin tracking these with the exegetical questions that we asked at first of Dunn as well.

Wright's exegetical problem

Wright's account is clearly dependent on a reading of Paul's justification material that finds a great scriptural narrative there concerning God and Israel. But this reading does not exactly jump off the pages of the epistles, which is to say that Paul never really *says* this directly. And Wright knows this. So he claims frequently that Paul *presupposes* a narrative about Israel, which we learn about by reading all the background texts written by Jews during late Second Temple Judaism. We should *assume* the operation of this Jewish narrative within Paul even when it is not explicitly stated because (supposedly) all Jews just thought this way, and Paul was a good Jew.

Wright also appeals here in a way that Dunn does not to intertextuality. When scholars speak about intertextuality they are referring to a relationship between different texts. Basically, all texts constantly quote from, reshape, and/or allude to other texts, and the authors of the Bible do this a great deal. Indeed, they are generally reworking Scripture, showing their respect for these earlier texts by including them, but including them—and subtly adapting them—precisely because of the new circumstances and insights that have inspired them to write something else. Texts always presuppose other texts. But for Wright, intertextuality is in play pretty much everywhere in Paul in a maximal sense. A mere verbal gesture on Paul's part allows an entire intertextual locomotive to steam into his thinking. So, for example, the use simply of the word "redemption" triggers the complete story of the exodus, which can be read into Paul's argument at that moment. Moreover, since the great story of Israel is the narrative that Paul presupposes, according to Wright wherever Paul speaks about a human plight to do with the law in any sense, or of the pressure of God's wrath on human disobedience, and/or about a solution arising through faith and the Messiah, Israel's journey with God is in play. Hence the *locus classicus* for JT in Paul, Romans 1–4, where most scholars hold Paul to be speaking of the contours of Box A and Box B and an individual's journey to salvation, devolves quickly for Wright into a panoramic discussion of the Jewish people's journey from wrath to salvation (which is then spoken of again in chapters 6–8, and then again in chapters 9–11, although there the text is more explicit).

Classic JT advocates, along with other scholars, have resisted Wright's readings at these points, and not unfairly. Figures like Piper have frequently pointed out that Paul's justification texts simply do not say what Wright wants them to say. The early chapters in Romans are not a panoramic story about the historical journey of Israel. Romans 1–3 is an ahistorical stretch of text that begins with rational individuals knowing God by searching the cosmos, who then look inward in some sense and realize that because of their disobedience to God's expectations his retributive wrath is upon them. This is clearly what the text is talking about, at least in some sense. Wright is, in short, not always the most compelling exegete. We hasten to add that he can be a very accurate reader when he wants to be, but when he reads Paul's JT material he tends not to do much close textual work, and this is significant.[18]

---

18. One of the finest examples of his analytical acumen would be the influential essay "Jesus Christ is Lord: Philippians 2.5–11," ch. 4 in *Climax of the Covenant*, 56–98. But this sort of scholarship within his oeuvre is rare. His commentaries on Romans and Galatians are very paraphrastic and loose—eloquent, enjoyable, and frequently true in their own terms, but frequently also a very long way from Paul's texts.

Re-interpreters like Wright who want to escape JT because of some of its obvious problems often struggle to defuse the direct implications of what the JT texts *mean* at the exegetical level. And although it is all very well to suggest that underneath the texts Paul is telling the story of Israel, after a while this has the effect of ignoring what the texts themselves say. Paul's prose is marginalized. And this effectively leaves what they do seem to say—which in Romans 2 is clearly something legalistic—in the hands of the advocates of JT. And any reinterpretative program, like the NPP offered by figures like Wright, must clearly falter at this moment. You cannot offer a new view of what Paul meant while leaving the old view in charge of what he wrote.

But Wright's difficulties do not subside as we turn from the textual details to consider how his version of the NPP describes Paul's argument. Here, Wright either falls into the same difficulties as Dunn or, in an effort to avoid them, he returns to JT. So he ends up caught between a rock and a hard place.

Wright's argumentative problem

Characteristically, Wright runs several different accounts of the plight. First, he sometimes depicts works of law in Israel up to Paul's own time much like Dunn, as referring to ethnic "boundary-markers" that separated Jews from surrounding pagans.[19] But he also argues, again like Dunn, although often rather more emphatically, that Israel failed in its commission to take its teachings to the world, thereby heaping the sins of humanity on themselves. But then, third, he states quite clearly on occasion that Israel also failed to be obedient and loyal to God; it could not observe the demands of the law as it was supposed to. And this is redolent of JT. In sum, prior to the arrival of the Messiah, Israel journeyed through a multi-dimensional plight that ultimately left it in exile, languishing under God's retributive judgment.

Having said this, the solution to this complicated conundrum that Wright finds in Paul is both surprisingly uncomplicated and rather familiar. When Jesus arrived he led his people out of their exile through the new exodus, at which moment the true Messiah-people emerged from the waters of baptism wearing the "badge of faith," and this indicates their acquittal in justification and their right standing before God, along with their membership of the covenant people. Moreover, Christians left behind in the waters of baptism—which were the new exodus, the symbolic praxis of

19. Dunn learned this sociological reading from Wright, although he was the first to publish on it extensively.

Judaism—those previous markers that kept them separated from the rest of the world.

So Wright's account of the church at this moment basically recapitulates JT's emphases on salvation by faith alone and its tandem claim that law-observance must be abandoned. But he has added in the dramatic historical and corporate flourishes concerning Israel for which he is famous. And we simply need to ask at this moment how these two broad phases fit together logically once they have experienced this expanded, corporate exposition. Do the multiple problems articulated in Wright's account of Box A devolve logically into the solution of Box B?

Here, as we might already have had cause to suspect, Wright ends up in a cleft stick. Insofar as he parallels Dunn's revised account of the Jews' sin in terms of some notion of utilizing "works of law" as boundary markers he runs into exactly the same problems of coherence as Dunn did. No account of the Jewish problem in terms of boundary markers, whether as selfishly hoarded or simply as boundary markers *per se* ("Jewish praxis"), can unfold logically into salvation by faith. The solution to selfishly-hoarded boundary markers is to share them; the solution to the possession of boundary markers *per se* as a construction of ethnicity is the erasure of ethnicity, which seems unrealistic if not shocking, and is ultimately hypocritical.

But Wright strongly emphasizes a second main dimension within the problem of Israel, namely, its failure to reach out to the pagan nations missionally as instructed by God. Arguably this is a variation on the problem of hoarding as against sharing boundary markers (Dunn's Issue I), but framing the issue missiologically makes it a little different. Nevertheless, this account of the problem in Box A in terms of missional disobedience still remains logically problematic for any plausible reading of Paul's solution in terms of faith. The solution to the stated problem of missiological failure is that the Jews should reach out missionally. And again, there is absolutely no argumentative or logical indication that they should radically shift the terms of that mission. They should, as Jews, reach out to the pagan nations and urge them to become Jews, which is clearly some distance from how Paul, the great apostle to the pagans, operated missiologically. Where Paul speaks of faith, Wright speaks of "the badge of faith," but the argument logically suggests the adoption of Jewish ethnicity. Once again then we find the new reading suggestions offered by advocates of the NPP collapsing into incoherence. Wright's account of Box A, in whatever new variation we trace, does not lead *logically* to Box B in Paul since Paul himself describes Box B in terms of "faith" not "works." Wright's rereading of Paul's argument, like Dunn's, insofar as it is a new reading, falls apart as an argument.

But one suspects that Wright can sense this difficulty within his broader reconstruction so, unlike Dunn, he also frequently reasserts the claims of JT in quite a straightforward way and these are logical. Part of the problem facing Jews was that they could not fulfill the demands of the law and so fell under God's curse. Wright historicizes this problem, expanding it and focusing it in the exile. But it still seems to follow that the Jews now need to be saved by some simpler arrangement like faith. It seems reasonable, that is, that they should leave the harsh demands of the Torah behind for faith. *This* argument is logical—at least to some degree. *But* it is, again, just JT writ large. And JT is an awkward bedfellow for Wright, who positions himself as going beyond its many deficiencies. It seems that Wright relies on JT even as he simultaneously wants to undermine it.

Problems solved?

It should be clear by now that Wright's suggested reinterpretation of Paul is in trouble. His NPP struggles to provide a sufficiently accurate account of the texts that Paul wrote—of the specific words and sentences that the apostle composed—and it collapses logically in just the same ways that Dunn's proposal did. As if aware of these shortcomings, and here unlike Dunn, Wright frequently reintroduces JT to get him out of his difficulties. But at these moments we can see that some of the most toxic consequences generated by JT remain in place within Wright's new approach as well—a problem it is vital that we fully appreciate. Indeed, they have even, on occasion, been intensified.

Wright's description of the Jews preserves the sinister descriptive framing by Box A that JT undertakes. Read carefully it is apparent that "the Christian difference" emerges for Wright as the Jews are repeatedly shown to be a recalcitrant and disobedient people. The entirety of their sacred history is largely a history of *disobedience*. But Wright articulates a *multi-layered* plight. The Jews are guilty of the disobedience to the law identified by JT *and* they are guilty of ethnic pride *and* of missional resistance as convicted by the NPP. Hence, of all humanity, their sins are heaped up the most, and they are liable to God's wrath the most. So this is JT's sinister definition of "the Jew" *but expanded and reinscribed even more severely.*

The dire plight of the Jews within Wright's reading is partly disguised by his constant emphasis on the story of Israel. Few exegetes see as much reference to Israel's journey within Paul as he does. But what we can see now is that Wright's concern with "Israel" is not the same thing as an ongoing concern with "the Jews."

Wright places Israel centrally to a *story* about a people who no longer exist; they serve a historical reconstruction of the central subject of the Old Testament, generated to aid the exegesis of the New. It is not an orientation to the Jews themselves as they live and worship in Paul's day, as well as in ours. So the Jews in Wright's system function as a scriptural motif—and a negative one at that—and not primarily as the Jewish people themselves. They primarily serve a scriptural and canonical concern as against a concern with our appropriate relationship with a living people whom the church has horribly abused for much of its history. So Wright conspicuously fails to offer anything of real value in relation to the NPJ. If anything, that conundrum has deepened.

In tandem with this, we can note in closing that none of the conundrums present since Melanchthon have been resolved either. A panoramic restatement of JT does not solve the clash between that model's assumptions and the assumptions underlying Paul's participatory and resurrectional gospel. Insofar as Wright channels JT, he interprets Paul's God as just, punitive, and self-evident; Jesus dies to resolve the problems Israel encounters trying to obey this God's instructions, leaving the soteriological function of his resurrection conspicuously underdeveloped, and the direction of the story is emphatically and constantly forward. Hence, there are no coherent connections here to the way that Paul elsewhere speaks of a God of compassion and love, who rescues us by lifting us into the transforming death, burial, and resurrection of his beloved son, and who after this revelation invites us to reconceive our past, and the past of his chosen people, Israel, thinking backward or retrospectively. We are no further ahead then. After much ado it seems we are left with nothing.

The take-homes

Fortunately, Wright is too gifted a scholar to leave us utterly empty-handed. In his complex, multilayered readings there is still much that we can learn from and use, although these insights need to be salvaged from a broader structure that fails to deliver on its promises. We find four especially important "take-homes" in Wright's project that will assist us significantly as we try to meet the challenge of coherently interpreting Paul in a way that moves beyond JT:[20]

20. The recent work of Edwin Chr. van Driel would add a fifth—the suggestion that both Douglas and Wright share a resurrectional emphasis in their accounts of justification; see his *Rethinking Paul*. But although it is correct to suggest that Douglas reads justification in a strong relation to resurrection, we are not convinced by Van Driel's

1. Wright has long championed an understanding of Jesus Christ as "Jesus Messiah," and we view this advocacy as both correct and somewhat prophetic. Other scholars are only now beginning to recognize the data that confirms this judgment and its importance. Jesus *was* the Messiah for Paul, "Messiah" functioning as an honorific rather than either a title or a name. (Subtle but important differences charted by Matt Novenson are in play here.)[21] Hence we can now affirm confidently, with Wright, that this category really mattered for Paul—although just what it entailed is still a matter of debate. Nevertheless, in what follows, tutored by Wright and others, we will continue to recognize the importance of Jesus's messiahship by frequently speaking of "Jesus Messiah" or "Messiah Jesus," as he would have been known by his Jewish followers.

2. Much that we have said concerning the interpretation of justification in Paul up to this point in our argument has been charted in relation to a polite but very public and strong disagreement between John Piper and Wright. This elicited the clear statement by Piper that we centered the analysis of chapter 4 on, and summarized in terms of JT. The catalyst for this debate, and for this description by Piper, was Wright's rejection in several of his writings preceding Piper's book of the doctrine of imputed righteousness, which the tradition of JT that Piper stands within endorses strongly. Piper holds to the particular classical view of JT that not only is the punishment due to the sinner for their sins imputed or credited to Jesus on the cross, but Jesus's perfect righteousness is credited to the sinner. So imputation or crediting runs in two directions. But Wright, like most modern scholars, finds the exegetical basis for the second type of crediting spoken of here— of Christ's righteousness to the sinner—to be implausible. (Amongst other things, Romans 2 gives no suggestion that such a system is in play; the judgment there simply affirms or denies the actual ethical worth and activity of the person in view, whether righteous or evil. A legal fiction and crediting of Jesus's righteousness to a sinful person are simply not in sight.)

    It was Wright's rejection of this particular claim that led Piper to write his little book reaffirming JT. Wright then reiterated his

---

argument that Wright reads it in this way too. Wright's latest work, *Galatians*, defines justification as denoting the "righteous" status of being a present member of the church (see especially pp. 9–19). Having said this, Wright's account of justification is complex, and we certainly welcome any emphases elsewhere in resurrectional terms.

21. Novenson, *Christ among the Messiahs*; and *The Grammar of Messianism*.

opposition to this component of JT in his book-length rejoinder to Piper's book simply entitled *Justification*. And this detail within the debate is worth noting. As Wright states, "That scheme [imputation] . . . always was an attempt to say something which Paul was saying, but in language and concepts which had still not shaken off the old idea that the law was, after all, given as a ladder of good works up which one might climb to impress God with one's own moral accomplishments."[22]

We regard the exegesis and arguments underlying Wright's critique of the traditional, rather mechanical view of imputation language in Paul as correct.[23] Furthermore, this is another problem for JT that we will need to keep in mind moving forward. Its reliance on a notion of "imputed righteousness" is unsupportable. It must either work as a theory without this element or collapse.

3. Wright has long advocated the interpretation of several faith phrases in Paul that read literally in the Greek "faith of Christ" not as references to *our faith in Christ*, as JT claims, but as references to *the faith of Christ himself*.[24] The main scholarly impetus for this reading in recent times came from Richard Hays,[25] but Wright has been one of its most well-known subsequent proponents. Scholars usually refer to this option as the "subjective genitive" reading. This is because "Christ" is in the genitive case in the original Greek—the "of"—and this case in Greek is susceptible to different interpretations (and we will analyze this situation in some detail in a later chapter). Justification theory advocates read it not unfairly as denoting the one whom we have faith in, so "Christ" denotes the object of the faith, and they translate these phrases as faith in Christ (which is consequently known, arguably a little inaccurately, as the "objective genitive" reading).[26] However, Wright

22. Wright, *Justification*, 135.

23. Wright, *Justification*, 33, 46, 95, 105, 158, 206, 233; see also, *Paul and the Faithfulness of God*, 881–83, 914.

24. See especially Rom 3:22, 26; Gal 2:16 [2x]; 20; 3:22; Eph 3:12; Phil 3:9.

25. Hays's doctoral dissertation articulated this interpretation, prominently reintroducing the reading into scholarly discussion after its first publication in 1983; see now *The Faith of Jesus Christ: The Narrative Substructure of Galatians 3:1—4:11*.

26. It has been argued recently that this is an inaccurate way of stating the issue. Strictly speaking, the phrase could be construed as an adjectival genitive denoting the content of that which is believed; see Grasso, "A Linguistic Analysis of πίστις Χριστοῦ The Case for the Third View."

This may be true—and certainly often is when later church texts speak of believing, especially in a creedal context—but it does not alter the argument or theological dynamics in question. This way of putting things, in other words, does not alter the operation of faith here in strict relation to the individual, salvation, and JT.

endorses the view that in these phrases Christ denotes the *subject* of the faith, namely, Jesus himself, and he does so for reasons that are entirely consistent.

If in what he writes Paul is alluding to a more historical, sweeping, and corporate story of Israel than many suppose, then it is less likely that he has an individual in view at this moment, along with their journey to salvation. It is more likely that he is focused on the moment that salvation comes to Israel, which is when Jesus came to Israel. Moreover, at this moment, God, who called Israel into existence, and endured her long history of disobedience, shows himself to be fundamentally faithful and reliable by way of the figure representing him who has indeed come to the Jews and saved them. The faithfulness of Jesus consequently speaks of the faithfulness of God to his people, and of the answering faithfulness he expects from his followers in return. Hence, Jesus's fidelity, displayed above all in his obedient walk to death on a cross, fits neatly into Wright's panoramic, historical viewpoint, and he endorses this reading firmly.

We strongly affirm this judgment and will consider its implications carefully in what follows. But it is worth noting that the correctness of this conclusion is detachable from the reasoning adduced in its support. It is a grammatical option that Wright endorses because of his sweeping interpretative perspective. In our view, additional strong reasons for the correctness of this reading exist that stand irrespective of whether Wright's broader rereading project is sustained (and we have already had good cause to see that it does not). His particular judgment here, nevertheless, we view as entirely correct. Paul does speak in some very important passages of the faithfulness of Jesus Messiah and Wright's advocacy of this reading is both positive and significant.

4. And, at the end, we affirm Wright's deepest instincts that, on the one hand, there is something badly off about any account of "the Jew," like that proposed by JT, which supposes the Jews can be detached from their existence through history as a people. Wright is entirely correct to affirm that "the Jew" is not a single, rational individual who holds constant in his legalism, through time and space. This is not the Jew of the Bible! There we read only of the Jews, who journey with God through history as a people, complete with special practices, lands, disobedience, obedience, failure, success, triumph, and humiliation. Any reading of Paul that cannot account for this basic biblical viewpoint has to be wrong, even if Wright's account of how to introduce this set of realizations into Paul, and how to read the JT texts as a

result, collapses. It is certainly fair to see these broader parameters in operation in Romans 9–11, as he does, but that stretch of texts is not the primary locus for JT. We affirm Wright's basic claims here in the strongest possible terms.

Despite these four helpful insights, when all is said and done, we judge Wright's proffered reinterpretation of Paul to fail in general terms, and for the exegetical, logical, and structural reasons just adduced. In the end of the day, it seems then that Wright's suggested reinterpretation of Paul is rather like a famous cul-de-sac in an ancient city—one lined with boutiques and stalls. We are certainly able to purchase useful and fetching products as we stroll down its pleasantly cobbled lane, but in due course we will find ourselves facing an impassible wall and will be forced, if we are to get anywhere important, to turn around and to retrace our steps. The journey down the lane will not necessarily have proved unprofitable, and may even have had its charming moments. But the lane itself, in the grand scheme of things, will have proved to be a dead end.

It is time then to find the lane that *does* lead us through to the garden, overflowing with leafy avenues and blooming flower beds, that is Paul's participatory and resurrectional gospel. We have several critical clues in hand from our stroll down the lane recommended by Wright. And one of the things that we have learned is that the way to the garden lies in a rather different direction.

11

Our Solution Begins

The state of play

We have not found a solution to our tangle of problems as we have detoured through the scholarly debate between advocates of JT and those urging a new perspective on the way Paul describes Jews (this being the debate that has led some to refer to JT as "the old perspective"). But we have collected some precious nuggets of information along the way and these will contribute to our proposed solution. Before articulating this, however, we need to look back quickly and to see where we have ended up and why. Our solution will make better sense when it is introduced against this summary.

Our detour began with a brief recollection of the church's "teaching of contempt" in relation to Jews—the recollection that for centuries many Christians have described Jews in deeply prejudicial terms, intertwining that rhetoric with harshly exclusive and frequently violent actions against them. For millennia Christian cultures have forced Jews to live in their own quarters within their villages and cities, characterized them with disgust and shame, looted and vandalized their shops and homes, and periodically gone on to butcher their inhabitants. It was difficult but very important to appreciate further that without this long prior tradition of rejection, vilification, and assault by Christians, the Holocaust would not have been possible.

Reacting against this horrific tradition, E. P. Sanders argued that readers of the NT needed to listen less to what figures like Paul were (supposedly) saying about "the Jew," and more to what Jews in Paul's day were saying

about themselves. He went on to suggest that Jewish writers often characterized their relationship with God in much kinder, gentler terms than later
Christian scholars supposed. Jews were "covenantal nomists," *not* mercantile
and unattractive "legalists" resisting God who almost invited persecution
upon themselves. And this rediscovery posed an acute challenge to readers
of Paul. What are we to do now with the apostle's texts that seem to speak
about Jews trying to be justified legalistically before God by doing works of
law—the very stereotypes that fed in to the teaching of contempt?

Sanders himself did not offer any satisfactory solutions to the problem he posed, although, following in the footsteps of Albert Schweitzer,
he strongly endorsed what we have called Paul's transformational and
resurrectional gospel. Like us, he saw clearly that this participatory gospel
was definitely what mattered most for Paul. But he could not explain how
it connected to the legalistic discussions in the JT texts, or how all that
harsher material related to what other Jews were saying about themselves.[1]
Moreover, Sanders almost certainly overstated his case (although perhaps it
needed to be overstated). The Jews in Paul's day were more diverse than he
admitted, and their representatives included *some* texts and traditions that
do seem rather legalistic.[2] Rather like Christians then, who are a diverse
crowd, it seems that some Jews were legalistic and harsh, some were gentle
and kind, and some were probably something else again.

But the recognition of a diverse situation does not actually change the
basic challenge all that much. It must still be granted that Sanders was right
about a lot of Jewish writing. Covenantal nomism definitely characterized a
great deal of Jewish piety in Paul's day. And even this reduced position still
poses a powerful challenge to readers of Paul today. Why do Paul's texts
often seem to describe "the Jew" as monolithically legalistic? The Jews were
not all the same and yet Paul seems to suggest in Box A that they were. And
why describe Jews at their worst? Why not include some description of their
better representatives? Paul's approach seems both unfairly stereotyped and
negative and hence really rather racist, and this when Paul himself was a
Jew. We are still waiting for good answers from post-Sanders scholars to
these questions.

1. Sanders proposed a solution in *Paul, the Law, and the Jewish People* (1983), but
this did not make the same impact as *Paul and Palestinian Judaism*, which posed the
problem. We do not find his suggested solution plausible (i.e., someone has interpo-
lated Romans 1–3 into Romans), although it is, as we might expect, frequently deeply
insightful.

2. Richard Longenecker was well aware of this diversity, highlighting it some years
before Sanders's publications in his *Paul, Apostle of Liberty*, first published in 1964.

After this rehearsal of the Jewish challenge, we went on to describe how some scholars took it on board and offered a NPP as a solution thereby generating the conversation that has dominated much subsequent debate, although in our view, a little unfortunately. Important figures like Dunn and Wright offered different interpretations of what we have identified as Box A in Paul's JT texts. Although Wright's reinterpretations were more expansive than Dunn's, both scholars basically claimed that Paul's legalistic account of "the Jew" in Box A, which revolved around doing "works of law," should be nuanced in more sociological, corporate, and historical directions, and they went on to claim that this reorientation would eliminate the difficulties Sanders saw. The challenge of Sanders's NPJ could be met by a new perspective on what Paul was really saying about Jews in the first stage of his gospel.

But we, along with many others, have found that this suggestion has not delivered on its promises. However this proposal was developed in detail, it ran into more problems than the original JT reading of Paul. It failed to provide accurate readings of the key texts. In particular, the struggle to free Paul's interpretation from a legalistic construction of "the Jew" tended to founder on Romans 2, which addresses a Jew and yet is unavoidably legalistic. The defenders of JT won this particular debate, and it is a key piece of textual territory to hold. Legalism just cannot be defined out of this text, and it clearly has something to do with a Jew. Moreover, as Dunn and Wright tried to tweak Paul's argument in more sociological, corporate, and historical directions, its logic fell apart. They ended up unable to explain how Paul's account of Box B in terms of salvation by faith alone made any sense following along after their new definition of Jews in Box A. And they actually struggled, in like manner, to explain the abandonment of Jewish practices taking place as pagan converts entered the church, which JT advocates could confidently explain precisely in terms of JT; there was no reason for converts to the new movement to leave the Jewish law behind, which means that scholars of the NPP could not explain the existence of Christians! At bottom then, we learned that the NPP basically does not work. And we also learned, in tandem with this, that JT is a formidable opponent with a highly accurate reading of many of Paul's texts.

Having said this, the arguments of Dunn and Wright were clearly not without merit altogether. The instinct that when speaking of "the Jew/s" Paul sometimes speaks in sweeping corporate, historical terms, as he does in texts like Romans 9–11, seemed to be profoundly correct. And Wright went still further than Dunn, tweaking Paul's Box B texts in a more Christocentric direction. There he saw Paul speaking of Jesus as Israel's Messiah, not infrequently also mentioning Jesus's great faithfulness as he walked obediently to a shameful death on a cross as suggested by texts like Philippians

2:6–8. These moves seem to recover deeply important emphases within Paul's thought that JT advocates had missed. Something more historical, more corporate, and ultimately more messianic is going on in Paul than JT sees. So it is as if the advocates of the NPP gave us some new pieces to try out in different places within the great puzzle that is Pauline interpretation, although they couldn't themselves put the entire puzzle together correctly.

So where have we ended up?

To continue the analogy: we are still in a very problematic situation. Even if JT advocates seem to put many of the pieces of the Pauline puzzle together more successfully than the NPP can, the puzzle *itself*, as a whole, is still disordered *and* they don't know what to do with the new pieces that the NPP has given to them! The great challenge to read Paul constructively in a post-Holocaust era remains, along with the great challenge to coordinate his JT texts with the transformational and resurrectional material that he wrote about for 90 percent of the time when he is not writing in terms of JT. (Those debating JT versus the NPP seldom get as far as addressing this problem, and it is a big one.) And yet we *must* try to figure all this out. We must solve this set of conundrums, if for no other reason than that the legacy of misinterpreting Paul for Jews is so important, widespread, and dangerous. Having said that, reading the apostle so that a coherent account of the gospel results, without fundamental conceptual fault-lines, is also important, not to mention, an account that can directly speak to our personal transformation and resurrection.

It is time to turn to our solution. And we suggest that we *can* resolve all these challenges and questions, but the journey to a solution begins as we recognize the significance of the theological dynamics that we spent the first three chapters of this book describing—dynamics that throw the very different theological dynamics of JT into sharp relief. These insights link hands with the more localized concern with Jewish description that so preoccupies modern scholars and that we have been talking about for the last four chapters. When we connect these two lines of discussion together a clear answer to all our problems begins to emerge.

The theological dimension

The basic inability of scholars to solve the challenge caused by the legalistic definition of a Jew in Paul arises, we suggest, from their inability to grasp with sufficient clarity the source of their difficulties. Certain key theological and argumentative identifications need to take place if this source is to be identified. In fact, the structure doing the damage vis-à-vis the Jews, not to mention vis-à-vis much else, is something we have spent some time already setting up, especially in the first chapters of this book. It is of course JT. Paul's justification *texts* are being read in terms of justification *theory*. And it is the construal of Paul's JT texts in terms of this theory of salvation that *generates* the Jewish problem, as well as the broader problem of conceptual contradiction. The problem is bad theology from the get-go.

In a little more detail: we need now to recall the critical insight that JT works forward, from "Box A" to "Box B." Box B, which involves an individual's entry into the church through faith alone, only makes sense when the claims of Box A are already in place. And it makes sense because, and only because, the attempt to be justified by doing works of law perfectly in Box A has first failed. So salvation in Box B builds directly out of, and on top of, this prior analysis in Box A. To get the individual from the pre-Christian to the Christian state, working forward, the prior situation must collapse in on itself, generating the necessary pressure that propels individuals forward to grasp an offer of salvation, and to receive an offer, moreover, that is manageable, saving by faith alone. But that prior situation revolves around the law and its key representative in the texts is a Jew. So it simply follows from this that the basis of the Christian gospel in Box B is the self-evident collapse of Jewish legalism in on itself in Box A. *And here is the root of our Jewish problem.* And it is deeper and more poisonous than many have hitherto supposed.

This model of salvation—JT, foundationalist, and forward-working—is *permanently* and *irrevocably* committed to the initial definition of "the Jew" in terms that are self-evidently legalistic because only this harsh definition can launch the individual's journey to salvation by faith alone. Hence, the definition of the Christian in JT, in terms of faith, depends on the prior negative definition of the Jew. An initial attempt to be righteous *must* fail and must fail self-evidently, and it must do so in relation to Jews. If it does not then no pressure is generated and the individual never advances on to grasp the offer of the gospel in fear and trembling. The Christian is never defined as saved by faith alone. And the law-free ethic of the Christian is never generated either. For a JT advocate, then, the definition of the gospel, and of the church, *rests on* this prior, negative definition of the Jew. In essence, any account of the Christian gospel in terms of JT arises entirely out of a prior, self-evident definition of a Jew who is necessarily under violent judgment for his immoral and irrational recalcitrance, at which moment we are clearly in touch with one of the most deadly tributaries for the teaching of contempt. The definition of the Christian (in these terms) rests on the prior negative definition (in these terms) of the Jew.

But at least we know by this point that the factor generating the Jewish challenge in Paul is JT. And so we know what any solution will need to be as well, namely, *the elimination of JT*. That is, it follows from all this inexorably that as long as JT remains, the Jewish problem remains, and Paul's texts, and his gospel, *contain* the teaching of contempt. And there are no other options here. If JT is retained, which means that our account of Paul's gospel begins with Box A, then it necessarily begins with a negative account of the Jew, who needs to realize first that he is legalistic and then, second, that he is a sinful failure who needs to leave this all behind or else. Hopefully after this he will hear about the gospel and choose to accept it and to become a Christian. This is just how JT works, and without this progression it isn't JT. So there is no way forward in relation to the Jewish challenge in Paul if JT remains. But if this seems like a formidable challenge, at least it follows in equal measure that if JT can be eliminated, then our Jewish challenge in Paul will be largely resolved.[3] And another interesting moment of clarity emerges now as well—when the theological dimension is introduced and understood clearly.

It is clear that the solution to the Jewish problem in Paul is more radical than advocates of the NPP have supposed. A new *perspective* on JT won't work. There is too much of JT left behind by this approach. Tweaking Box A won't work. Box A needs to go entirely, which means that the entire model needs to go. We need a comprehensively new *reading* of this textual data that lies *beyond* JT itself.

Having said this, any new reading will still need to take account of the stubborn contours of what Paul actually wrote, which at times clearly involve legalism, at which moment the exegetical dimension of our challenge emerges into clear view as well. The text of Romans 2 is overtly committed to legalism, just as JT says. The Jewish figure in view here *is* tangled up with some attempt to be declared righteous by God after doing works of law assiduously (although Romans 2 is followed by Romans 3, which asserts from verse 10 onward that no one is righteous and can actually do this, which creates a further puzzle). So at this point, we will still need to take on board some of the key exegetical insights of JT. We must still read Paul's texts fairly and accurately, as so many of JT's advocates do.

Hopefully by now then we are aware of the full scale of our challenge, and perhaps also have some sense of the courage needed to deal with it. Moreover, it is our theological investigations that tell us exactly what the

---

3. Strictly speaking, all the texts speaking of a Jew in the legalistic terms JT uses would be taken off the table. Paul does talk about Jews, the Torah, and Israel, elsewhere, and we would still need to read those texts constructively. But we are confident that once the negative influence of JT is removed, this can be done.

problem is and what the scale of any solution will have to be if one exists. We will have to face the dark side of a model of salvation that many of us have been taught and have taught others is the gospel. We will have to contemplate the culpability of this model for some of the most grievous actions by the church through history, and the corresponding need for the model itself as a whole to be ejected somehow from Paul's interpretation if those grievous problems are to be dealt with. However, assuming we have summoned the requisite bravery, what are we to do? Can we actually solve this conundrum? Can JT be displaced from Paul's texts?

We think that it can be, although we now need to introduce the other main challenge we face as we seek the way forward. Somewhat paradoxically, however, recalling this additional set of challenges at this moment should give us hope.

Our solution to the Jewish challenge will involve the elimination of JT. But the elimination of JT will also solve the great set of contradictions generated in relation to Paul's transformational material as well. Two birds can now be killed with one stone.

We saw earlier that a massive conceptual fault-line runs through Paul's thinking between the 10 percent of material interpreted in terms of JT and the other 90 percent that proceeds in a very different direction, speaking of a transformational and resurrectional gospel. Different views of Christ and Christ's work are in view, to mention just one key difference. But if JT is eliminated, we will reduce Paul's understanding of salvation largely to one consistent line of thought. The raft of tensions here is automatically expunged because *it is the presence of JT that causes these tensions*, working in terms of rational and self-evident truth, individualism, and forward, when everywhere else Paul depends on revelation, community, and a retrospective account of the past. Moreover, it is clear that we will still have many important theological things to say, and arguably the most important things. We will not lose sight of Paul's *gospel* if we lose sight of JT. Indeed, his gospel, especially if that is simply the joyful announcement of our transformation through the risen Messiah, will be greatly clarified, and Paul will emerge witnessing to it even more clearly than he currently does.

Hence, there is less holding us back from exploring a radical exegetical solution to the Jewish challenge in JT at this moment than we might suppose. We have nothing to lose except our anti-Jewishness, arguably along with our theological incoherence, while to remove JT will be to resolve both our challenges. What are we waiting for? But any solution will obviously also have to be worked out "on the ground," so to speak, hand in hand with a close, responsible reading of Paul's texts, and some of those are both Jewish and legalistic. So we turn now to the important task of reading Paul's

JT texts without JT as a theory being necessarily in play, and here our prior theological analysis of the problem in terms of JT assists us once again.

We have had frequent cause in what precedes to consider not just the nature of JT but how important it is to its advocates. John Piper wrote an elegant description of the model in immediate public response to what he perceived to be an unacceptable alternative suggested by Tom Wright's NPP, and he took pains to distribute his work for free, to whoever would read it. Clearly many Christians are deeply committed to JT as *the* account of the gospel and defend it vigorously if they feel that they have to. In particular, the model's Protestant advocates often trace its church-historical roots back to key leaders in the Reformation and so to the very foundation and identity of their denominations, and they write and read accordingly.

But it follows from this commitment that the very zeal of JT's advocates might have led to the imposition of this set of expectations onto Paul's ancient texts inappropriately. Keep in mind that Paul's letters were, after all, written almost two thousand years ago, not to mention, one and a half thousand years before the Reformation. These powerful expectations on the part of modern Christian readers—this "pre-understanding" as Gadamer would have put it—might have overridden subtle but significant clues in Paul's texts that are trying to tell us that this was not in fact what he was originally writing about. Paul might have been arguing something very close to JT—and we will suggest shortly that this is indeed the case—but he might not have been committed to some key points that JT needs to launch itself as a full-blown model of salvation from Paul. The reading of the JT texts in terms of a theory by those who expect to find that theory there might be subtly off, and the very zeal of JT's advocates raises this possibility. Such scholars and preachers are hardly very open to subtle textual suggestions that they have gotten things wrong. Just look at the reaction to the relatively mild suggestions made by NPP scholars to see how suggestions about change are greeted.

But if this is a possibility in general terms—that JT has found itself within Paul in a way that overreads what he actually wrote, at least at certain key moments—then how do we move forward in more specific terms? Where *exactly* is this expectation off? Where do Paul's texts subtly deviate from JT as a theory? When we have been reading Paul's texts for so long from a particular point of view, it can be very difficult to pivot and to read them in another way.

In order to find these key points of exegetical pressure we will need to compensate for the positive influence flowing from JT into our interpretation and to read Paul's JT texts carefully again from a *very* new perspective, and really from a position within a new paradigm. But we can do this by again reintroducing the broad theological distinctions we described earlier on between a gospel defined in terms of JT and a gospel of transformation and resurrection. This distinction and its entailments will create very different expectations of what Paul's JT texts are saying. Basically, we no longer have to read the JT texts in terms of the standard approach to Box A, on the assumption that phase one of that model of salvation is in play. We can set JT to one side and read these texts as if *anything transformational and resurrectional that Paul says in them expresses his gospel*, and *anything else does not*. We can read the 10 percent in terms of the 90 percent, and not the other way around—and fascinating new understandings will open up as we do so.

Towards a solution

Paul's gospel, our earlier discussions suggested, is found clearly stated in 90 percent of what he wrote where he speaks of our transformation through the risen Christ. It is our participation in Jesus's death and resurrection by way of the divine Spirit that transforms us—in part now, and in full in the future. And this is Paul's gospel, which is to say, the good news that he proclaims. Its central truths are enacted in the ritual of baptism, which originally was a full immersion into cleansing water and so signifies nicely our death, burial, and rising, within Christ. Moreover, this is a covenantal gospel because at its heart is a God who offers up an only child on our behalf to be crucified while we were yet sinners, showing us thereby that he loves us in spite of all our foolishness and hostility. The God proclaimed by this gospel will reach out to us unfailingly and hold on to us irrevocably.

Against this theological position, we have also already seen how JT really offers another gospel, a contractual gospel, which has a different account of God nestling at its heart—a God not of love but of retributive justice. Indeed, it is really no "gospel" at all. And as we pressed deeper into this opposition some further basic differences between these two ways of talking about God in Paul became apparent. In particular, the work of Jesus is parsed very differently in both models. The emphasis in the transformational gospel was on the entirety of Easter—Friday, Saturday, and Sunday—and included important emphases before and after Easter on the incarnation and the ascension. The contractual gospel, by way of contrast, is tightly focused on Good Friday, when Jesus died on the cross, ostensibly to pay the penalty for our sins. So it struggled to generate a saving role for the resurrection and ascension, along with any real need for the other key moments in Jesus's life like the incarnation.

Two different models of salvation

Model A: Contractual	Model B: Covenantal
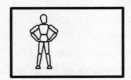	
Salvation is through a contract	Salvation is through a gift
God's relationship with us is conditional	God's relationship with us is irrevocable
God is retributively just	God is love
Focus on Good Friday	Focus on Good Friday *and* Easter Sunday
	(etc.)

If we have these fundamental dynamics and distinctions in mind, between these two ultimately very different accounts of salvation, then we can approach Paul's JT texts armed with new expectations. And it might be helpful at this point if we signal our solution in a brief way initially by engaging with a short text in Paul—Galatians 2:15–16. Here JT terminology enters Paul's letter for the first time in Galatians in a sentence Paul composed that ran through 2:15–16. (Intriguingly, the terminology then fades by the back end of chapter 3, "justification" occurring for the last time in this discussion in 3:24, and faith occurring for the last time in 3:26. There is then only one brief spot of JT material in the rest of the letter, in 5:4–6.) Galatians 2:15–16 is a useful text for us to focus on for the moment because it lays out all the critical words, moves, and issues, in brief. We can reconsider here its interpretation, self-consciously resisting any unnecessary influence from JT, at which moment a rather new understanding emerges. And after the basic moves within this possible solution are clear, we can then turn to a more detailed exposition of the other JT texts, especially in Romans, to see if it is sustainable through the main texts that undergird JT.[4]

4. As noted earlier, in chapter 4, JT occurs (ostensibly) in Rom 1:16—5:1; 6:7–8; 9:30—10:17; Gal 2:15—3:26; 5:5; Eph 2:8–10; and Phil 3:2–11. We estimate that this is about 172 verses within a total from Paul of around 1,791, or just under 10 percent of what we have from him.

Rereading Galatians 2:15–16

15 We who are Jews by birth and not sinful Gentiles
16 know that a person is not justified by the works of the law,
but by faith in Jesus Christ.
So we, too, have put our faith in Christ Jesus
that we may be justified by faith in Christ
and not by the works of the law,
because by the works of the law no one will be justified.
(NIV)[5]

Now it is clear when we view this text that we still have to orient ourselves in terms of Box A and Box B in some sense, because there is no question that there are two "boxes" in this text. There is a "works" box and a "faith" box. Justification theory is quite right about this. But we need now to consider a crucial assumption.

If we read these "boxes" in terms of a theory of how we get saved, as JT does, *then we assume that they should be joined together in a sequence.* They speak of an individual's journey to salvation, *from* an unsaved *to* a saved state. So Box A leads to Box B and grounds Box B. Consequently, both boxes *together* must lay out Paul's view of matters; they articulate his model of salvation, and quite systematically. So in this text Paul is speaking about his own theology all the way through and all the way down.[6]

We can see these expectations at work in the translation we just quoted, because the translators of the NIV are deeply convinced that JT is Paul's gospel and so this must be what he is talking about in Galatians 2:15–16. Note carefully how there is no real sense in this translation that Paul is doing

---

The individual terms can occur in other texts as well, for example, in Gal 5:4 and 5:6. But we need more than words to carry a theory. Justification theory needs Box A and Box B, so we have only counted texts that explicitly signal the presence of this antithesis. It is a serious mistake to suggest that a single word can evoke an entire theological system. This procedure tends to override the sentences that the words are appearing in, that is, what Paul actually wrote and was saying. See the classic exposé of this fallacy—"etymologism"—by James Barr in *The Semantics of Biblical Language*.

5. We will be working with the NIV for much of what follows because that translation is so heavily affected by JT. Tracing this influence will be instructive.

6. Moreover, as we know well by now, Box A is legalistic, although things are not meant to end here. At some point the person navigating through the challenges of Box A comes face to face with the fact of human sinfulness and the attempt to be saved there fails. Box B, which revolves around faith, then lays out something more positive and saving—something bound up with Christ, who makes no appearance in Box A. Under pressure from the realizations generated by Box A the individual grasps for salvation in Box B available to those who exercise faith.

anything other than laying out his own thinking about God, Christ, and salvation.

We want to emphasize that it is entirely understandable that translators influenced by JT would render Paul's text here in this way (i.e., as the apostle providing a compact summary of his account of salvation). But we know where all this goes ultimately and so we are unconvinced that this is necessarily the right way to understand what he is saying here. In particular, we think that Paul's gospel is participatory, with transformational and resurrectional dimensions. And we consider this participatory gospel to be in conflict with any account that explains the relationship between God and humanity conditionally and contractually. So where JT advocates see Paul's gospel unfolding we see something that is not Paul's gospel—unless he is having a very bad day. Paul's gospel is emphatically not contractual, and Box A is contractual. So *our* expectations lead us to explore the possibility that something else is going on in Box A that is not directly expressing Paul's own position.

If Box A, simply in conceptual terms, is not Paul's gospel because of its radically different, and ultimately rather sinister, transactional structure, which so derogates Jews, then what is it? It *is* legalistic, because Romans 2 develops the phrase "works of Torah" clearly in this way. And it is wrong. Paul clearly negates it in the text and does so repeatedly. The word "not" comes up a lot. "We are *not* declared righteous by doing works as prescribed by the Torah."

We have arrived at a critical moment for our entire discussion. And we are going to step forward into the first part of our solution in a remarkably unexceptional way—by introducing the historical circumstances that gave rise to the composition of the letter to the Galatians in the first place, which is something that every modern scholar of Paul should be doing in any case.

Opponents in Galatia

Paul's letter to the Galatians was an urgent, and apparently very passionate, epistle that he composed to counter the influence at Galatia of a group of rival leaders. These leaders were Jews, but they were more than this. In a critical fact often overlooked, a close reading of the letter suggests that they were also *messianic* Jews, which is to say that they were Jesus-followers like Paul, so they were, technically, part of the early church. Indeed, the letter's arguments show that they laid claim to a cosier relationship with Jesus's original friends, the Jerusalem apostles, than Paul himself enjoyed. And so they were present in Jerusalem, weighing in, when the church's leadership deliberated on important matters at a key conference (see 2:4—although Paul suggests that they were acting in a fundamentally deceitful manner when they did this). Irrespective of their motives—and we only have Paul's side of the story—the letter reveals that there is no love lost between this group and Paul. They are *opposed* to Paul. They clearly think Paul is a dangerous renegade who must have his teaching corrected in all his congregations. He is perilously close to being a heretic, if he isn't one entirely. So they are traveling around reconverting all his converts to a better gospel—to *their* gospel.

For his part, Paul thinks that this group of rivals has betrayed the heart of the gospel that he has been commissioned by God to preach to the pagans. *They* are the heretics! Obviously Paul is deeply upset by the teaching they have arrived with in Galatia, and so he urges his converts there, in all sorts of ways, to reject it utterly. It is a false "gospel," unworthy of that name (1:6–7). Only his teaching is the true gospel proclamation about God that comes, duly authorized, from God.

Some of the clearest evidence concerning this situation that gave rise to the letter to the Galatians is supplied at the very outset.

Paul usually begins his letters with an address followed by a prayer of thanksgiving for his converts' many virtues—although it is a slanted prayer that also reveals what he wants them to take on board as he writes to them. So we would expect that here in Galatians too Paul will begin with an address followed by a thanksgiving prayer. However, in Galatians, distinctively, Paul offers no thanks at all. The situation is both too serious and too negative for this. It is a crisis and at this point he can find absolutely nothing to thank God for when he thinks about his Galatian converts. Instead, in another striking departure from his usual practice, Paul breaks into his address with some strong assertions about the importance of his gospel, stating how he received it from God and so not from any figures who were apostles before him. (This is one place where we see especially clearly that his rivals in Galatia lay claim to a close relationship with the mother church in Jerusalem and its leadership, and so must be Jesus-followers as well.) And then, instead of a thanksgiving paragraph, Paul launches a scathing comparison, complete with curses.

> 1:6 I am astonished that you are so quickly deserting the one
> who called you to live in the grace of Christ
> and are turning to a different gospel—
> 7 which is really no gospel at all.

> Evidently some people are throwing you into confusion

and are trying to pervert the gospel of Christ.

8 But even if we or an angel from heaven should preach a gospel other than the one we preached to you,
let them be under God's curse!

9 As we have already said, so now I say again:
If anybody is preaching to you a gospel other than what you
accepted,
let them be under God's curse!
(NIV)

If we are still unsure about Paul's own posture vis-à-vis these figures we can note his advice to them later in the letter "to go the whole way and to emasculate themselves" (5:12 NIV). It is clear then that Paul regards these figures as profoundly inimical to his work and to the work of God through him. Having said this, we want to avoid Jewish stereotyping as much as we can, and the bitterness and anger of the Galatian situation is not necessarily reproduced helpfully today. So we will follow the lead of one of the most gracious modern interpreters of this entire sorry scenario, J. L. (Lou) Martyn, and call this opposing group in what follows "the teachers."

The key point to note moving forward is that Paul clearly wrote his letter to the Galatians to counteract the false gospel of the teachers who had apparently arrived in Galatia and started converting his followers to a "better" version of the gospel—to *their* version, but a version that Paul views as false through and through. And it follows from this that Paul engages this false gospel from various angles throughout his letter for his confused and possibly even disloyal converts. He will criticize it, undermine it, sideline it, and generally try to convince his converts that it is something not worth bothering with, even as he re-presents his own gospel to his wavering followers, all the while defending his position from the criticisms that the teachers have made of him. The result is a very interesting letter, even today—a complex debate. But the most useful point for our present concern is the new understanding of "Box A" that now comes into view.

The first time we encounter JT data in Galatians is in 2:15–16. And it is present within a text that lays out two systems in a binary way, alongside one another, which we have repeatedly called Box A and Box B. Now everyone agrees that a Box A and a Box B are in the text. They just disagree over their significance and relationship to one another. But we are not reading these boxes under the influence of JT. So we don't expect these boxes to lay out Paul's theology systematically. We don't even expect Box A to speak of Paul's gospel; it is something he clearly doesn't like. So what are *we* going to make of this data, viewing matters in context, historically, and specifically in Galatia in terms of a debate between two rival teachers and their teachings, and bearing in mind the overarching theological dynamics that we have spent so much time earlier in this book describing? Viewing things with a constant awareness of the profound differences between a covenant and a contract, and grasping, further, that a contract is in view in Box A, what do we now understand to be going on?

We hope it is not too obvious to suggest that the original Galatian recipients of the letter would have seen here straightaway a basic opposition between the false gospel of the teachers and the true gospel preached by the apostle Paul, from which it would follow that Box A refers in some way to the false (contractual) gospel of the teachers, and Box B refers to Paul's (covenantal) gospel framed in response.

Two gospels

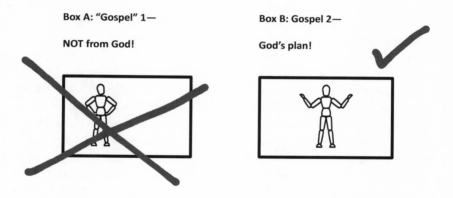

Box A: "Gospel" 1—

NOT from God!

Box B: Gospel 2—

God's plan!

Moreover, Box A is legalistic, and we know well by now that this makes it structurally quite distinct from the gospel Paul usually preaches. In fact, it is different "all the way down." Different understandings of God, of Christ's work, and of the entire direction of how we think about our situation, past and present, in relation to God are apparent *because it is a completely different gospel from Paul's, and this is why he doesn't like it.* And it might help to attempt a brief description of this false gospel here that we will fill out with more details later as we work through other key texts.

The teachers, probably with the best of intentions, were preaching a contractual, conditional gospel. They were preaching a Jewish version, but it was a gospel, laying claim in some highly inadequate way to the loyalty of Jesus-followers. In fact, it seems to have been a proclamation that the way to behave and ultimately to be saved and resurrected was by doing works of Torah. The teachers, sadly, were legalists, and they were capturing the good news about Jesus within their legalism.

This system would have involved any uncircumcised male converts in Galatia getting circumcised, and then everyone in the community taking on board all the instructions in the teachings of Moses. So the community would have undertaken distinctive Jewish practices in relation to eating kosher food, Sabbath-keeping, observing the Jewish calendar more generally, sending money to the temple in Jerusalem, and so on. Paul's pagan converts would, in short, have become Jews, and Jews of a certain distinctive sort: messianic, legalistic Jews. If they did so, however, following these sacred instructions perfectly—and they were not *that* hard, the teachers would have said—then on the great day of judgment they would receive a verdict from God of "fully righteous," and would enter into heaven. They would be saved. This at any rate is what the teachers promised. In Matthean terms, they would be one of the sheep instead of one of the goats.

It is a little hard to see what Jesus himself was contributing to this entire situation as the teachers seem to have laid it out, and the short answer from Paul's point of view would be "not enough." But it is not hard to imagine very early Jewish followers of Jesus underplaying Jesus's saving significance. This was something that Paul himself had great insight into but not necessarily everyone else. Perhaps the teachers accepted Jesus's resurrection and subsequent enthronement as Messiah, and were waiting patiently for his return in glory, but failed to detect how this changed any existing Jewish practices in relation to salvation and ethics. Perhaps Jesus was viewed as a great teacher as well, who added further insights to the Torah, but who did not displace it. Perhaps he had shown by his righteous life that perfect righteousness, following in his footsteps, was possible and would result in resurrection, or something like this. We don't know at this point, and we don't have to.

Whatever the precise view of the teachers, Jesus was not doing enough heavy lifting in it for Paul's liking, which is to say that he has a serious problem with this "gospel." In fact, he has all sorts of problems with it. First, it is, as later church tradition would say, "Pelagian."[7] It is far too optimistic about human nature and so about the possibility of salvation by works. For Paul, human nature is deeply corrupt. It cannot act rightly even if it wants to. (Paul is more "Augustinian.") Human nature needs to be transformed—to be *changed*. So

7. Pelagianism is defined briefly but accurately in the online *Britannica*: see https://www.britannica.com/topic/Pelagianism (consulted May 2, 2023). The relevant Wikipedia article is more detailed and also quite accurate: see https://en.wikipedia.org/wiki/Pelagianism (consulted May 2, 2023).

the teachers' gospel is, in its own terms, a one-way trip to hell. It proclaims salvation in terms that no corrupt person can actually achieve. "No one will be declared righteous on the day of judgment," Paul asserts, quoting a scripture that also seems to know this important truth (see Gal 2:15c quoting Ps 143:2).

Even more importantly, this "gospel" directly undermines the only thing that *can* transform human nature and save the person: the gospel that points toward our participation in Christ. We are transformed and saved as we enter into the death and resurrection of Christ, as enacted in baptism, and as we are filled and revivified by his Spirit. But we are getting a little ahead of ourselves.

The important thing to grasp at this moment is the simple yet very significant insight that Paul's JT antithesis, which contrasts Box A and Box B, is a contrast *in its original setting* between a *false* gospel and a *true* gospel—between a false gospel unworthy of that precious name and that is being taught by some hated rivals, the teachers, at Galatia, and Paul's gospel that is worthy of that name and that announces the good news of salvation through baptism into Jesus the Messiah. Hence, *Box A is nothing more or less than the false contractual gospel of the teachers*, and the reason why it clashes so deeply with so much of what Paul says elsewhere is now obvious; it does so *because it is not his theology at all!* Paul is bitterly opposed to this theology. Small wonder then that there are tensions.

Now this simple suggestion about how to read Box A in Paul's JT texts is, we suggest, a rather more compelling suggestion in exegetical terms than the opposing, more common suggestion that Paul is laying out the first phase of his theology in Box A, because we are reading his texts circumstantially, as an engagement with the practical concerns of his audience. This is always why Paul wrote his letters. He never wrote systematic theology *per se*, which is what JT advocates have to assume that he is doing uniquely when he starts into his JT arguments. So we expose here one of the most critical biases of JT advocates, which they have inherited unwittingly from church tradition. They read Paul's JT texts anachronistically, as if the apostle was writing his theology out abstractly for the later church to ponder and to benefit from. And he is imagined as writing that theology out, moreover, from a position that is insensitive to Jews, who are viewed as having long separated from the Christian church, which is another important anachronism. But we are simply doing what a good scholar of Paul should, which is reading his texts in the light of their original practical circumstances. And here these are very obviously generated at Galatia by the arrival of opposing teachers and teachings. From this point of view, Box A is "another gospel." It has *nothing to do with Paul's own theology*, and he is deeply and angrily opposed to its imposition on his converts.

If this reading of Box A is correct—and we know of no good reasons why it shouldn't be—then we have begun to resolve our many difficulties. The legalistic depiction of the Jew in Box A is actually a depiction of salvation by a small legalistic group of Jews within the church who are, like all Pelagians, wildly over-optimistic about their own ability to act consistently in a good way. It is true that *these* Jewish teachers and their followers are legalistic. But there is no need to suggest this is true of *all* Jews or of Jews at their best. All religious traditions seem to contain pockets of legalism, including the Christian tradition. But these are not necessarily representative of these religions at their best. Moreover, these legalistic claims are *not Paul's own* account of what Jews are. Legalism is the view of a small group of messianic Jews within the early church. For Paul's view of Jews we will need to read the more corporate, historical, and panoramic stories he tells about Israel elsewhere in places like Romans 9–11.

And if this is the case, it seems that Paul could be completely off the hook when it comes to Box A. Box A has nothing to do with his own theology, except to highlight that he is emphatically *not* a conditional, contractual, transactional thinker when it comes to salvation. He is implacably opposed to this approach to salvation. His God is kinder and gentler all the way down—a God, in short, of grace.

Sustaining our solution

We have clearly not yet made our case in relation to all of Paul's JT texts, and we will need to do so if our solution is ultimately to succeed. But it is clear now what we need to do. Two main tasks are before us.

First, we will need to sustain our reading of the "works of law" texts for the other passages in Paul where that phrase appears. Most are highly abbreviated, so it will not be too difficult to sustain our circumstantial reading there. But one long text will pose a much greater challenge, namely, Romans 1:18—3:20. We will have to spend some time offering a reading of this famous argument that is very different from its usual construal, although we are confident that we can do so.

Then, second, we will need to offer an appropriate reading of the Box B texts, texts that, like the Box A texts, speak of "justification" and "righteousness" but that, unlike the Box A texts, link those dynamics with "faith." Can we read Box B and its emphasis on faith as an announcement of Paul's gospel all by itself, separated from Box A? Because this is what we need to do if our solution is ultimately going to work.

We begin then with our first task, and at its most difficult point. The longest articulation of Box A in Paul, by far, is found in the opening argument of Romans which runs from 1:18 through to 3:20—a block of material longer than some of his other letters in their entirety. Can we read this argument as evocative directly of the false gospel of Paul's opponents as against of his own theological starting point? We are confident that we can do so—and that this even results in a more accurate reading of this material than JT can provide. There have always been wrinkles in the text that JT advocates have not quite known what to do with. But, reading from our new viewpoint, we do.

12

Understanding Romans
Chapters 1 through 2

Introduction

At the heart of our proposed solution to the challenges caused by JT is the realization that Paul's "works of law" texts refer to a false gospel being presented by a group of opponents, figures the apostle at one point calls his "enemies" (Phil 3:18). These figures are best viewed as a rival missionary team within the early church, so they are messianic Jews, and we suggest that they lie behind all three letters that Paul composed where justification terms and arguments appear, Romans, Galatians, and Philippians (and we infer partly on these grounds that these letters were all written around the same time, from the fall of 51 through the spring of 52 CE; it was a difficult winter season for Paul).[1] But someone might ask at this moment if this is really the case. It is very clear that the enemies, whom Martyn more respectfully calls "the teachers," are present in Galatia, and equally clear in Philippians 3 that they are about to arrive in the city of Philippi. But Romans is not usually presented as an engagement by Paul with a rival group of figures and their problematic theology. Nevertheless, we hold that some significant evidence in the letter points in just this direction.

Within the final instructions at the end of this great epistle we read:

> I urge you, brothers and sisters,
> *to keep an eye on those who create dissensions and hindrances,*

1. See Douglas's *Framing Paul*, 133–42; and *Paul an Apostle's Journey*, 131–44.

in opposition to the teaching that you have learned;
avoid them.
For such people do not serve our Lord Christ
but their own appetites,
and by smooth talk and flattery
they deceive the hearts of the simple-minded.
For your obedience is known to all;
therefore, I rejoice over you,
but I want you to be wise in what is good
and guileless in what is evil.
(Rom 16:17–19, emphasis added)

The language here is very similar to the language that Paul uses in Philippians to describe his enemies; they are driven by their "appetites" (literally "stomachs") and not by God. (This is an ancient philosophical slur suggesting that someone is in the grip of their base instincts and not guided by the elevated thoughts and morals of the mind.) And the agenda in the rest of Romans is the same as in Philippians 3 and Galatians. There is a repeated denial that salvation can be found by righteous works undertaken through circumcision and the Torah, rather than through participation in Jesus. So we infer that the same basic situation is in view. Unlike in Galatia, however, where the teachers have already arrived and stirred up trouble within the region's communities, this warning in Romans suggests that the teachers are on the way to Rome and have not yet arrived. The Jesus-followers at Rome are supposed to be on the lookout for their arrival (which is also what we see in Philippians 3, especially in verse 2).[2] Anyone who arrives and starts delivering a certain message, one laced with slick rhetoric, should not be listened to but rather "avoided." But it would be helpful, someone might say at this moment, if we actually knew what this gospel looked like so that the people peddling this false information could be recognized, and Paul seems to have thought just the same thing.

His letter to the Jesus-followers at Rome begins, we suggest, with an account of the opening position of the teachers, followed by Paul's first critical response. It is as if Paul is saying to the Romans, "If a guy walks through the door and starts talking like this, here's why you shouldn't listen to him." Moreover, Paul's initial response is quite brilliant. The first thing he does is to show how this "gospel" collapses in on itself in terms of its own assumptions. So his audience in Rome does not even have to agree with him to see that his rivals are offering nothing useful.

---

2. "Keep a sharp lookout for the dogs, keep a sharp lookout for the evil workers, keep a sharp watch for those who mutilate the flesh!" (NRSVue modified).

We see this technique being used constantly by one of the ancient world's most famous philosophers, namely, the figure of Socrates as he is presented in Plato's dialogues. Plato has Socrates often beginning his dialogues by questioning some unfortunate passer-by or arrogant opponent and showing how their confidently held beliefs collapse in upon themselves. This collapse can then function as a midwife so the underlying truth, which is more coherent, can emerge—something Socrates is usually happy to help with. But Plato's Socrates was not the only person who went around showing how people's positions caved in on themselves. Many other ancient philosophers and teachers did the same—along with not a few modern ones—and all of them knew this technique well. So it is nothing out of the ordinary to suggest that Paul is following much the same strategy in the first main phase of his letter to the Romans as he tackles the problem posed by the arrival of the false gospel of the teachers in Rome before he himself gets there.[3]

Few things are more effective at undermining an opponent's credibility before a neutral audience than showing how their own position, taken on its own terms, falls apart once one knows where to look. Why listen any further to someone who can't even present a coherent position? Such figures are laughable, not plausible. So it is a clever opening tactic on Paul's part as he crafts the first major section of his longest letter in these terms. He will undermine the credibility of his opponents, and thereby subtly establish his own. After seeing his perspicuity at work, the Jesus-followers at Rome will be all the more ready to hear what he has to say about the true gospel in the chapters that follow this initial engagement.

Section 1. Romans 1:18–32: the teacher's opening

In order to attack the teachers' gospel in its own terms Paul will first need to tell his Roman audience what it is, and like any good tactician, he chooses his ground carefully. He begins with the portion of the teachers' teaching that creates the most vulnerabilities—their opening preaching with its fiery rhetoric and harsh judgment of outsiders, who are pagan. And while verses 18 to 32 are a rather short summary, they provide Paul's Roman audience with just the right amount of information they need to recognize the teachers when they arrive. Note, in what follows in the letter Paul often concentrates his attention on a single figure who represents this group of enemies (see 2:1), a representative teacher, although he will sometimes address a group, so we will, like him, move between the singular and the plural in what follows.

3. He is in Corinth at time of writing, and he has to go to Jerusalem first, before he can head for Rome—exactly the wrong direction, and a very long journey.

Paul's synopsis of the teacher's preaching would have been clearly recognizable because of the way it differs significantly from the material preceding it, especially 1:16–17, which we will spend some time focusing on a few chapters hence. In those verses, as we will see, Paul talks about God's deliverance being revealed through the saving activity of a preeminently faithful figure, Jesus, who dies and rises again for us. We see here a God of compassion acting to save his people from an awful predicament within which they are distressed and helpless. And we see a powerful focus on Jesus as the expression of that compassion. These concerns are strongly signaled by verses 16 to 17. But in verse 18 an abrupt shift in tone and argumentation takes place that the original readers of the letter would have reproduced as they performed the text to gatherings of Jesus-followers at Rome, possibly accompanied by gestures. (So this would have been Phoebe, or perhaps one of her assistants, if she had some. These figures would also have been schooled by Paul at Corinth in just how to present the text of the letter, when they first received it to take it to Rome.) In 1:18 another "voice" barges in, although technically it is Paul's own writing depicting this new actor:

> [T]he wrath of God is revealed from heaven
> against all ungodliness and injustice of those
> who by their injustice suppress the truth . . . !

Here we have the opening of the teacher's preaching to pagans asserted with characteristic pomposity. The teacher is talking, like Paul, about the revelation of God's righteousness; however, he is doing so in a significantly different fashion from Paul himself. For the teacher, God is right insofar as God is just and executes that justice retributively. That is, God exercises his justice angrily by punishing people because of their sinfulness—"which includes you!" In the language of Karl Barth we could say that the teacher begins with God's "no" to humanity, after which he will try to speak a "yes." But the initial "no" on his part has trapped him. His basic beliefs about God, uncorrected by any insights as revealed by Jesus, will prove to be a massive problem for the rest of his program—for his "yes"—as we move through chapters 2 and 3 of Romans.

Following this opening in verses 19 to 23 Paul begins to explicate the teacher's initial points, which support the overarching claim just made that God punishes all godless pagan people justly for their transgressions. We are under God's "no" because we deserve to be. It will be helpful to walk through his chain of assertions in a little more detail.

Verses 19 to 20a state,

> For what can be known about God is plain to them,
> because God has made it plain to them.

Ever since the creation of the world God's eternal power and
divine nature,
invisible though they are,
have been seen and understood through the things God has
made. . . .

This is the basis of the teacher's overall argument: every person knows what God is like, which is why pagans are fundamentally culpable for their sinful behavior. This position is commonly known in theological circles as "natural theology" or "general revelation," because everyone in their natural state, wherever they are, can recognize the truth about God by observing the things around them, in general terms. (Later we will see that the teachers believe that they can learn the same things by turning and looking inward at their own moral reasoning as well.) Hence, while the reality of God is in some sense "hidden" or "invisible," God is nevertheless made known indirectly and so revealed clearly "through the things he has made," which has been the case "since the creation of the world." The whole created order speaks accurately about its invisible creator and his "eternal power and divine nature."

Verses 21 to 22, repeated by verse 28a, add the next step in the argument:

[F]or though they knew God,
they did not honor him as God or give thanks to him,
but they became futile in their thinking,
and their senseless hearts were darkened.
Claiming to be wise,
they became fools. . . .
[T]hey did not see fit to acknowledge God. . . .

People have, however, intentionally rejected and so turned away from God, refusing to thank him. Hence any claim to "wisdom" on humanity's part at this point is really just stupidity. The teacher proceeds to double down on humanity's guilt in verses 25 and 28. Humans make a wrong decision by suppressing the truth about God has made obvious to them, and this has happened "by means of their wickedness" (verse 18), so verses 23 and 25:

. . . [T]hey exchanged the glory of the immortal God
for images resembling a mortal human or birds or four-footed
animals or reptiles. . . .
They exchanged the truth about God for a lie
and worshiped and served the creature rather than the Creator,
who is blessed forever! Amen.

We learn here from the teacher something very Jewish, namely, that this intentional and sinful rejection of the truth about the invisible God results in *idolatry*. The teacher refers to this as an "exchange" of sorts—the worship of God the creator, which does not involve images, is exchanged for the worship of false gods, which does involve images, whether of human or human-like figures like the Greeks and Romans, or of animals and other creatures like the Egyptians (and the latter are in view here).

Verses 24 and 26 to 27 then point to a further significant decline:

> Therefore God gave them up in the desires of their hearts to
> impurity,
> to the dishonoring of their bodies among themselves. . . .
> For this reason God gave them over to dishonoring passions.
> Their females exchanged natural intercourse for unnatural,
> and in the same way also the males, giving up natural inter-
> course with women, were consumed with their passionate
> desires for one another.
> Males committed shameless acts with males
> and received in their own persons the due penalty for their
> error.

We learn here that another result of the pagans' rejection of God is their "surrender" to certain "unnatural" lusts, which the teacher defines in terms of the norms set up in Genesis chapter 1. According to the teacher, not honoring God leads to people to dishonoring their bodies sexually with members of their own gender, by adopting "homosexual" and/or "effeminate" behavior, which in the case of males leads to some further punishment—quite probably sterility.[4]

A litany of other transgressions then follows; the trickle of sins becomes a flood—so verses 28 to 31:

> And since they did not see fit to acknowledge God,
> God gave them up to an unfit mind and to things that should
> not be done.
> They were filled with every kind of injustice, evil, covetousness,
> malice.
> Full of envy, murder, strife, deceit, craftiness, they are gossips,
> slanderers, God-haters, insolent, haughty, boastful, inventors
> of evil, rebellious toward parents, foolish, faithless, heartless,
> ruthless.

---

4. This was Philo's view, and it may have influenced the teachers. See Rillera, "Paul's Philonic Opponent."

Here we see that in the teacher's view, humanity now possesses a "debased mind," which introduces a wave of resulting vices like envy, arrogance, and wicked speech. This lengthy list captures the teacher's aggressive, judgmental—and slightly bombastic—tone; the people in question, namely, all pagans, are "heartless" and "ruthless." Verse 32 summarizes their obstinacy pithily:

> They know God's decree,
> that those who practice such things deserve to die—
> yet they not only do them
> but even applaud others who practice them.

So here the guilt of the pagans is finally driven home by the teacher when he suggests that the problem is not only that pagans do these things but that they do them *knowing* that these things are wicked. And they apparently applaud other people who do the same. That is to say, they are *brazen* sinners, who sin themselves and encourage others to do so despite knowing that they are ultimately going to receive from God the justly deserved penalty of death. The teacher concludes triumphantly then with the perfect set-up for his solution: all of pagan humanity is contemptibly corrupt and justly deserving of the coming universal death penalty from God. The stage is set for *his* solution.

Section 2. A brief suggestion before proceeding

Having outlined the teacher's opening preaching, it would not be unfair to suggest that many Christians today actually agree with this theology. This kind of preaching tends to get deployed frequently against unbelievers and sometimes against other Christian groups as well. We tend to assume that this is, in fact, Paul's own position from start to finish because, well, he wrote it *and we like it*. Who are we modern readers to suggest otherwise? Will we not be guilty of inserting our own preferences into an ancient text if we question what is said here?

But perhaps this reading is guilty of inserting its own preferences into the text. Perhaps Paul himself, the victim on many occasions of "justice" from the Romans, and the follower of a Messiah who was grotesquely tortured to death in public, did not endorse the death penalty. Perhaps Paul had spent enough time in prison with those who were about to be executed to know that God loved even them, could forgive and restore them, and could offer them a wonderful plan for their lives. He had after all had to step back from the shameful aggression and violence of his youth, when he tried to arrest and punish Jesus-followers, and then learned that this was a horrible mistake.

So let us step back for just a moment and view these verses in a different light. More specifically, let us read these verses as Paul articulating his opponent's position and see what happens. Doing so not only allows us to gain different impressions from the text's assertions but will also help us arrive at a clearer understanding of a rather confusing subsequent chapter that has baffled generations of scholars.

How does a Socratic reading of the broader argument in Romans 2 work if this opening paragraph is not Paul's position but the teacher's?

Section 3. Romans 2:1–8: turning on the teacher

You might have noticed that the teacher left himself out of the orbit of indictment in his opening tirade in 1:18–32. The accusations about the retributive wrath of God being revealed against sinful people apply to *others* and not to the teacher himself or to people like him. And this is a common failing in arguments that a Socratic move will expose quite quickly. Because of the teacher's failure to include himself in the indictment of his opening progression, we can imagine Paul thinking, "Hmm. What if I take the argument that the teacher just presented in 1:18–32 to others and apply it to the teacher's followers, and ultimately to the teacher himself? What conclusions might follow from doing so?" I am sure that many of us have thought the same thing when trying to converse, perhaps on social media, with people who constantly judge others for their shortcomings but refuse to apply the same standards to themselves. People write screes of vitriolic prose attacking other people for being insensitive and intolerant, all the while speaking in a fashion that is deeply insensitive and intolerant. Or someone loudly pronounces that a politician or media figure should be condemned, exiled, and even incarcerated for sexual misconduct—until the sexual misconduct of one of their own leaders comes to light, at which moment everyone is urged to forgive, and to put the private misdeeds of the figure in question behind them and to move on. A Socratic move pushes a person's own commitments back onto themselves. And, most effectively, a group's judgmental claims concerning others can be applied to the group themselves as well. In this way any hypocrisy present in a judger is exposed.

Paul makes just this move in verses 1 to 5 of chapter 2:

> Therefore you are without excuse, whoever you are, when you
> judge others,
> for in passing judgment on another you condemn yourself,

because you, the judge, are doing the very same things.
We know that God's judgment on those who do such things is
in accordance with truth.
Do you imagine, whoever you are, that when you judge those
who do such things
and yet do them yourself,
you will escape the judgment of God?
Or do you despise the riches of his kindness and forbearance
and patience?
Do you not realize that God's kindness is meant to lead you to
repentance?
5 But by your hard and impenitent heart
you are storing up wrath for yourself on the day of wrath,
when God's righteous judgment will be revealed.

The "you" addressed here judges others for sinful behavior that brings about God's harsh judgment. But this "you" might do the very same things himself and will therefore be just as condemned.

Section 4. Pause for a moment and think about who this "you" sounds like

The "you" referenced in 2:1, who is also a "judger," is a dead ringer for the figure uttering the words of 1:18–32. That text *is* a judgment that condemns others who are "without excuse" because of their catalogue of sin and their supposedly intentional rejection of God and God's expectations. Those expectations contain, moreover, a recognizably Jewish but still quite harsh attack on idolatry and sexual immorality as many Jews understood those. Because of these activities, all the pagans deserve to die, and God will kill them all if they do not repent. It doesn't get more judgmental than this. It seems obvious then once we notice it that the judger addressed in 2:1–6 is the speaker of 1:18–32, and this judgmental figure will soon get described in more detail as a teacher. That is, the judger *is* the teacher who has just spoken from 1:18–32.

So it seems that from 2:1 Paul has turned on the teacher, asking him here to be consistent with his own preaching. And Paul will now hit the teacher's program from several different angles through the rest of Romans chapters 2 and 3. But before he does so, he needs to clarify the assumptions that the teacher has committed himself to in Romans chapter 1. It is the ruthless pressing of these assumptions within the teacher's own position that will ultimately hurt him and undermine his own position, so Paul's readers (and we) need to know exactly what they are.

Romans 1:18–32 makes it clear that the teacher believes in a God who will judge the pagans retributively for their sinful behavior. They know God but reject him, willfully turning to various unnatural activities. God responds to their sinfulness by executing retributive justice in the form of the death penalty (a retributive account of justice supposing that the right response to harm is the infliction of an equal amount of harm back on the perpetrator). And it follows from this, most importantly, that the teacher believes that damnation and salvation are based strictly on what someone *does*: disobedience leads to death, and obedience leads to life. So it is a gospel of *works*. Salvation is *earned* through *deeds*. Good deeds lead to the *reward* of eternal life while bad deeds lead to condemnation and death. And the teacher is an early version of Pelagian theology, as we have already noted (and God is a retributive God who measures out rewards and punishments exactly). Another way of talking about this is to say that this is a gospel based on *desert*. People get what they deserve—nothing more, and nothing less.

In 2:6–8, Paul states the teacher's central position explicitly:

> [God] will repay according to each one's deeds;
> to those who by patiently doing good seek for glory and honor
> and immortality,
> he will give eternal life;
> while for those who are self-seeking and who obey not the
> truth but injustice,
> there will be wrath and fury.

Paul is basically saying to the teacher here then, "According to what you just said in your judgmental opening, O teacher, we must affirm that every person is saved by their good deeds in accordance with God's will, or be damned in accordance with their bad deeds, right?" To do anything else would be unfair, and fairness is the whole basis of the argument—and the teacher will probably agree. But these commitments are going to have a devastating impact on the rest of the teacher's gospel, as he is forced to remain consistent with them.

Section 5. Romans 2:9–29: well that's embarrassing!

Paul now begins embarrassing the rest of the teacher's preaching in two related ways, which are threaded through the rest of chapter 2 and much of chapter 3. But we will only detect this if we hold in mind that the teacher is a Jew who is deeply committed, in his own way, to Jewish practices and to the importance of the Jewish Scriptures and the Jewish people. This is why he is traveling around trying to convert Paul's followers to his particular version of messianic Judaism. They aren't Jewish enough yet. We will learn more about the teacher's position as Paul's argument unfolds, although we already know that it involves a lot of *doing*. Here it suffices to note that Paul is going to hurt this position in what follows by pressing the teacher's opening assumptions in two directions.

First, it follows from the teacher's opening commitment to desert not only that wicked *pagans* will be condemned but that wicked *Jews* will be judged as well. Moreover, this group of sinful Jews might be much larger than the teacher initially concedes. This is embarrassing in and of itself. But the existence of this group causes a further problem for the teacher. It casts doubt on the positive proposals that the teacher is trying to introduce, namely, salvation through circumcision and Torah-observance. These are the practices that the teacher is urging on Paul's gentile converts. The existence of a category of sinful Jews proves, however, *that these practices do not necessarily work*. In short, the existence of wicked Jews casts doubt on the teacher's solution.

Second, it follows from the teacher's basic commitments as well that some pagans could exist who get saved by grasping God's righteous commands by way of natural theology, simply by gazing at the cosmos, who now do not need to convert to the teacher's Jewish program, getting circumcised and observing the teachings of Moses. They can be saved by attending simply to general revelation and through natural theology. So what the teacher is offering is redundant. Here then the existence of a group of good pagans—which are a necessary theoretical possibility for the teacher, Paul points out—casts doubt on the teacher's gospel as well, although in a different way.

In essence, the teacher who has preached Romans 1 is now necessarily committed to the existence of good pagans and of bad Jews, and the existence of both these groups undermines everything else that he wants to say about how someone can get saved by becoming Jewish in the manner he urges—a clever set of argumentative strikes it must be said. But first Paul just needs to set these groups up for his Roman listeners. So in the next verses he introduces the groups "Jew" and "Greek" (i.e., pagan), and shows how people within these ethnic groups could be present in both of the main categories set up through a judgment by desert, namely, the righteous saved and the wicked damned:

There will be affliction and distress for everyone who does evil,

both the Jew first and the Greek,
but glory and honor and peace for everyone who does good,
both the Jew first and the Greek.
For God shows no partiality.
All who have sinned apart from the law
will also perish apart from the law,
and all who have sinned under the law
will be judged in accordance with the law.
(Rom 2:9–12)

Paul continues:

For it is not the hearers of the law who are righteous in God's
sight
but the doers of the law who will be justified.
When gentiles, who do not possess the law, by nature do what
the law requires,
these, though not having the law, are a law to themselves.
They show that what the law requires is written on their hearts,
as their own conscience also bears witness;
and their conflicting thoughts will accuse or perhaps excuse
them
on the day when, according to my gospel, God through Christ
Jesus, judges the secret thoughts of all.
(Rom 2:13–16)

We might sense from the details Paul supplies here that his claim that righteous pagans saved by works exist is contentious. But it is completely consistent with what has already been said by the teacher himself. In 1:18–32, the teacher stated that pagans are without excuse because they know what is good but intentionally do the wrong things. So Paul points out here, quite fairly, that there is clearly sufficient information about God and what God expects of the pagans present for them to act correctly without the possession of the Jewish Torah if they choose to do so. According to the teacher's rhetorical opening then, pagans already possess a law innately, giving them accurate information concerning God's expectations. This general, internal law allows God to judge them fairly, just like the Jewish Torah allows the judgment of Jews. But what happens if pagans do not reject this guidance and instead carry it out? They would be righteous then, right? And God will judge them so at the end of the age and will go on to save them! This all seems fair, and some Jews in Paul's day even regularly conceded that very virtuous and impressive figures like Socrates and Plato were righteous in these terms.

But this realization is incredibly awkward for the teacher. Because pagans have an innate Torah they can do the necessary good things required by God on their own without any instruction from the written Jewish Torah and so still be declared righteous by God. And it follows from this that, strictly speaking, the teacher now has no reason to evangelize them! They do not need him. His mission to the pagans converting them to Jewish observances is pointless.

Section 6. Where is Jesus?

It is worth turning aside here from Paul's main argument quickly for just one moment to note that while Paul is primarily concerned to engage Socratically with the teacher through chapters 2 through 3, he will occasionally insert small anticipations of his own position which lies further ahead in the letter: it is as if he finds it difficult to refrain from including what he himself actually thinks, so little comments can slip into the text. One such comment is the statement we read here: this judgment according to deeds will take place when "according to *my* gospel, God through Christ Jesus judges the secret thoughts of all" (2:16).

As we noted quickly earlier on, one of the shocking features of the teacher's gospel articulated in 1:18–32, is that it does not mention Jesus. Jesus plays no clear role within its assumptions, and he has no real function for the teacher in relation either to the knowledge of God or God's nature. These all come from the Jewish Torah. And in fact Jesus *cannot* have a significant role within the teacher's gospel. His centrality has been closed out from the beginning. An approach to righteousness and damnation based on deeds which are potentially known and performed everywhere self-evidently necessarily overrides any contribution coming from any particular or special revelation, which is how all knowledge of Jesus comes. So the teacher's approach necessarily overrides the information we might get about God from the unconditionally liberative act effected through Christ, which occupies the very heart of Paul's own thinking. Those who operate in terms of general revelation do not need special revelation, and Jesus is the heart of special revelation. But the teacher cannot abandon his key position concerning the self-evident judgment of people on the basis of deeds or his whole argument would fall apart. This would be like removing the foundation of a house and expecting it to remain standing. So Jesus cannot play any significant role in the teacher's gospel, and Paul simply cannot resist noting this in verse 16 in passing.

For Paul, true judgment takes place before Jesus, as Romans chapter 14 will state later on quite clearly, and this is a very different sort of judgment from the harsh scenario he is sketching out in Romans chapter 2.[5] "*My gospel*," says Paul, "views things very differently, especially on judgment day, with the help of Jesus." In short, Christ's absence from the teacher's thinking is a massive shortcoming that Paul wants us to bear in mind here as he lays out the teacher's system and its internal problems.

Section 7. Romans 2:17–29: deepening the embarrassment

As we move into 2:17–29, Paul deepens his Socratic exposure of the teacher, pressing into the two embarrassing implications that he has already set up, namely, the presence of both sinful Jews and righteous pagans. Up to this point he has begun to talk about how the existence of righteous pagans is a developing problem. Now he sets up the existence of sinful Jews in more detail and considers the problems that they create for the teacher's position:

> But if you call yourself a Jew
> and rely on the law and boast of your relation to God
> and know his will and determine what really matters because
> you are instructed in the law,
> and if you are sure that you are a guide to the blind,
> a light to those who are in darkness,
> a corrector of the foolish,
> a teacher of children,
> having in the law the embodiment of knowledge and truth,
> you, then, who teach others, will you not teach yourself?
> You who preach against stealing, do you steal?
> You who forbid adultery, do you commit adultery?
> You who abhor idols, do you rob temples?
> You who boast in the law, do you dishonor God by your transgression of the law?
> For, as it is written,
> "The name of God is blasphemed among the gentiles because of you."
> (Rom 2:17–24)

5. A careful reading of Rom 14 reveals that while there is an important moment of accountability before Jesus's judgment throne, this is not a *salvific* examination but more like a *pedagogical*, parental evaluation. It is an *evaluative* judgment, and this is categorically different from the judgment being talked about in Rom 1–2.

Paul brings up a potential charge of hypocrisy directly against a generic teacher here in 2:21a, asking him if he has committed various offenses ranging from stealing (2:21b) to robbing temples (2:22b). While these particular transgressions do seem a bit extreme to apply to most people—the equivalent to challenging a congregation today if they have all committed armed robbery—they probably refer to a specific historical event that took place at Rome when certain rabbis proved to be outrageous, thieving charlatans.[6] The details of that infamous and highly traumatic event do not matter here as much as Paul's basic point, however, which is that this incident, or its general equivalent, proves decisively that the most outlandish sins can still happen. A Jew can still sin, and can do so egregiously, even when he possesses the Torah and is deeply learned in its details, that is, when someone is a rabbi. (And "rabbi," it is worth recalling, is the Aramaic for "teacher.")

The teacher is clearly convinced that the written law supplies a decisive moral advantage for its adherents as well as a resulting advantage in terms of salvation. The pagans who lack the Jewish Torah also, in the teacher's mind, lack the embodiment of knowledge and truth that it reveals. They are sinful to the core and need the saving presence of the Torah in their lives. The Torah's instructions will solve their basic pagan problems, creating in them the righteous activity that will secure for them a declaration of "righteous" from God on the last day. Recall 1:18–32. There, the gentiles reject accurate thinking about God (1:19–22), which results in "futile" discernment and the darkening of their minds. God sees this and proceeds to give them up to distorted desires (1:24–26), through which they engage in supposedly immoral and unnatural sexual behavior. From there, a list of sins follows. The teacher clearly believes that Torah-observance will help *reverse* this bad situation by *illuminating* the minds of pagans about God. Through the ongoing observance of Torah, they will regain and then maintain control over their sinful lusts. The spiral into disgusting sins will be reversed.

But Paul points out here that this just doesn't seem to be true in every case. Even outwardly law-observant rabbis can still be completely criminal.

And circumcision doesn't necessarily help either, as the teacher seems to have suggested.

> Circumcision indeed is of value if you obey the law;
> but if you are a transgressor of the law
> your circumcision has become uncircumcision.
> So, if the uncircumcised keep the requirements of the law,
> will not their uncircumcision be regarded as circumcision?

6. See Campbell, *Deliverance of God*, 561–62.

> Then the physically uncircumcised person who keeps the law
> will judge you who,
> though having the written code and circumcision,
> are a transgressor of the law.
> (Rom 2:25–27)

The teacher probably thought that circumcision of the especially lust-ful skin surrounding the head of the penis was very important preparation for the following observance of the teachings of Moses. (This is how Philo understood his anatomy, presumably along with various other Jews at the time as Rillera explains [2021].) Circumcision is commanded in the Torah. But it is also helpful, Philo and those who thought like him said, because it excises—literally cuts off—the desires that reside in the foreskin. Circumci-sion is thus a key commandment. It sets males up to obey the rest of the teachings of Moses.

But, again, the existence of sinful rabbis, who were obviously circum-cised, shows that this is not necessarily the case. So the teacher's positive suggestion to sinful pagans that they get circumcised—if they are males, obviously—and start vigilantly observing the Torah's instructions is not *nec-essarily* going to be any use. The existence of sinful rabbis proves this.

We can see by now that the teacher is in trouble on two fronts. He wants the sinful pagans to convert to Judaism. Male converts should be cir-cumcised, and they should start obeying Torah. This will lead to righteous lives beyond the idolatry and sexual immorality of their pagan past. But the way he sets up the self-evident sinfulness of pagans, under the wrath of God, actually leads to a different situation. Righteous pagans might exist who do not need to convert in response to the teacher's pleas. And sinful Jews clearly exist who show that the teacher's system won't necessarily work anyway. Indeed, circumcision and the diligent observation of other com-mandments won't necessarily work because clearly it doesn't always work, even for rabbis. Conversion to the teacher's Jewish gospel therefore seems doubly unnecessary.

Paul now draws both these embarrassing implications together in a clever anticipation of the day of judgment as that will play out if the teacher's assumptions are really true. It will be very different from what the teacher himself expects and has doubtless proclaimed will happen!

As we have just seen, the teacher's logic entails that when anyone pro-claims the importance of Torah-observance but does not actually follow it faithfully themselves they will not have any kind of advantage at the final judgment. At that moment even their circumcision will become pointless, which is to say, as if it had not happened. But alongside sinful law-observers, righteous pagans seem to exist as well. Pagans could perform the deeds of the Torah written on their hearts with no explicit need to adopt the Jewish Torah and so be saved. So it is now possible that these righteous pagans who keep the Torah written on their hearts will condemn an unfaithful Jewish person on judgment day, as verse 27 makes clear: "the physically uncircumcised person who keeps the law will judge you who, though having the written code and circumcision, are a transgressor of the law." And in fact, any righteous pagans will thereby positively humiliate any people who insist on full Torah-observance yet fail to follow its instructions obediently themselves. Groups of uncircumcised pagans condemning circumcised Jews on the day of judgment? The horror!

But Paul presses this point home remorselessly. As we press ever deeper into the assumptions driving the teacher's "gospel" the very definition of who a Jew is begins to fall apart.

> For a person is not a Jew who is one outwardly,
> nor is circumcision something external and physical.
> Rather, a person is a Jew who is one inwardly,
> and circumcision is a matter of the heart, by spirit,[7]
> not the written code.
> Such a person receives praise not from humans but from God.
> (Rom 2:28–29 NRSVue modified)

Paul is effectively saying to the teacher here, "According to what *you've* been saying about people deserving damnation or salvation depending on their deeds, the righteous are the ones who are truly Jewish, right? You're basically admitting that righteous gentiles are the true Jews! People who just look like Jews don't really count. After all, they are not always saved. And these righteous pagans are." He presses this point by way of a clever word-play. The word "Jew" comes from "Judah," which means, in Hebrew, "praise." So Paul is suggesting here that, *in terms of the teacher's system*, those who receive "praise from God" are really the true Jews, right? And they are not actually Jews . . . ! This is where your "gospel" has led us!

Paul has shown here then that the fiery opening to the teacher's instructions, summarized in 1:18–32, has painted him into a corner. The teacher has foolishly ended up defining Jewish identity in terms of anyone who has

7. Philo, who may have influenced the thinking of the teachers, held that circumcision of the heart, which was the seat of the person, could take place in a spiritual way, literally by way of the "breath" animating the body. This statement in Romans closely reproduces a statement in one of his writings. See Philo, *The Special Laws*, 1.6; and *Questions and Answers on Genesis*, 3.46, 52. See Rillera, "Paul's Philonic Opponent." The following point also draws on an insight from Wright in "The Letter to the Romans," 449.

access to God's expectations through nature and obeys them; such a person receives God's "praise" on the day of judgment, and so will effectively be called a "Jew" at that moment. So the teacher has unwittingly undermined the importance and distinct privilege of Jewish Torah-observance in general and circumcision in particular for gentiles. He has made himself and his people irrelevant. That has to hurt. If he is anything, he is a very proud Jew. But he is also a missionary, urging conversion to his Jewish ways, which now seem pointless.

By this point in the argument then, it is becoming clear that the teacher's argument, suitably scrutinized, has backfired, and the integrity of his gospel, as well as of his whole missionary program to the pagans, have begun to crumble. One can sense that the delighted Roman audience would have lapped up Paul's cheeky demolition job. Chuckles and smiles would have lit up the room as Paul landed another theological jab on his overconfident and overbearing opponent.

But Paul is not finished. He now starts a direct dialogue with the teacher that will set up his final deadly move. The two complementary arguments of chapter 2 have done a lot of damage. The pagans clearly do not need to convert to the teacher's particular Jewish program. They could just get saved on their own. And there is no guarantee that Jews are any better than they are. Even rabbis can be awful sinners! But the arguments of chapter 3 will pile on the pain.

13

Understanding Romans Chapter 3

Section 1. Romans 3:1–9: Paul sets his sights on the teacher himself

Chapter 3 in the letter begins with a short conversation between two figures and clearly some sort of debate is taking place. Some translations do not show this dialogue very clearly so we suggest the following layout:

> Person 1: Then what advantage has the Jew? Or what is the value of circumcision? (3:1)

> Person 2: Much, in every way. For in the first place the Jews were entrusted with the oracles of God. (3:2)

> Person 1: What if some were unfaithful? Will their faithlessness nullify the faithfulness of God? (3:3)

> Person 2: By no means! Although every human is a liar, let God be proved true, as it is written, "So that you may be justified in your words, and you will prevail when you go to trial." (3:4; quoting from Pss 116:11 and 51:4; see also Rom 2:3b–11, 16.)

> Person 1: But if our injustice serves to confirm the justice of God, what should we say? That God is unjust to inflict wrath on us? (I speak in a human way.) (3:5).

Person 2: By no means! For then how could God judge the world? (3:6).

Person 1: But if through my falsehood God's truthfulness abounds to his glory, why am I still being judged as a sinner? And why not say (as some people slander us by saying that we say), "Let us do evil so that good may come"? (3:7–8a).

Person 2: Their judgment is deserved! (3:8b)

Person 1: What then? Are we any better off? (3:9a)

Person 2: No, not at all. . . . (3:9a)

Most interpreters position Paul as "Person 2" in this conversation and some previously unknown Jewish objector as "Person 1." And this is consistent with the way most people understand the argument in Romans chapters 1 to 2 as unfolding. They think that Paul himself begins in Romans 1 with the stinging attack on pagans. This is his standard opening, such readers suppose. He then obviously endorses the corresponding judgment scenario in Romans 2 as well—a judgment strictly by desert, in terms of works—since this is presupposed by Romans chapter 1 and he has already committed to that argument. And the Jews then get crushed, on the assumption that Paul leaves his Judaism behind and wants us too as well. (He is a Christian now, we are told, which is different.)

Person 2 in this exchange continues this line of thinking. He is a judger who defends God's right to judge as well through thick and thin, even if that means throwing Jews under the bus. So this must be Paul. And it follows that Person 1 must be some previously unnamed Jewish questioner who is protesting, rather understandably, about any remaining Jewish advantage within Paul's thinking. Jewish privilege seems to have been eliminated, hence the protest. (And the previous argument has eliminated Jewish privilege.) Having said this, there isn't any left given the assumptions of Romans 1, as we have already seen, and Person 2 makes this quite clear in this paragraph, overruling the protests of the resistant, protesting Jew, who is Person 1.

These assumptions and the resulting reading of 3:1–9a have troubled various scholars in the past. One of the most serious difficulties they see is that the judgmental and marginalizing account of God's relationship with the Jews articulated here with such force, supposedly by Paul against a foolishly objecting Jew, seems to be very different from the much more covenantal and historical account of Israel that Paul spells out later in the letter in Romans chapter 9 and chapter 11. Paul's views seem to have changed mightily by this later point in the letter. Jews certainly do have a special role in history there, and before God. They have a lot of privileges that clearly do advantage them (see especially 9:4–5). And God is not going to let go of them. So almost everything that Paul as Speaker 2 *affirms* here in Romans 3 is *denied* by him later in the letter.

But Romans 9 and 11 are a long way away from Romans chapter 3 for most commentators, and interpreters have generally not known how to resolve the situation in any case. So they have learned to live with the tensions, and often end up attributing both sets of ideas to Paul himself. Perhaps he has shifted in this thinking between chapters 3 and 9. "It's a shame but there we are. Consistency is the sign of a small mind."

But we do not need to adopt this rather desperate solution, which is really no solution at all. And there is absolutely no need to posit a confused Paul. He is crystal-clear in what he is trying to achieve argumentatively here, and his position throughout Romans is entirely consistent. Our Socratic reading of Romans chapters 1 to 2 has not committed Paul himself to the assumptions deployed in Romans 1 which are then pressed so awkwardly against Jews through Romans chapter 2. Far from it! These are the assumptions undergirding the preaching of his enemies, and Paul attacks them skillfully throughout this material in terms of their own implications. So we have no need to position Paul in the role of Person 2. Rather, the maintenance of judgment by that figure suggests that this is the teacher, from which it follows that Paul is actually Person 1. And if we position Paul as Person 1, and the teacher who appeared in the preceding chapters as Person 2, then an entirely coherent picture comes into focus, both here and through the rest of the letter.[1] Paul is now situated in the role of the questioner, which is where the author of a dialogue is often operating. (Socrates is frequently—although not invariably—the figure asking the questions.) So the teacher learns something important here as he tries vainly to parry Paul's interrogation through 3:1–9a.

Here is what the conversation looks like with the two participants correctly identified:

> Paul: Then what advantage has the Jew? Or what is the value of circumcision? (3:1)

> The teacher: Much, in every way. For in the first place the Jews were entrusted with the oracles of God. (3:2. Incidentally, this is the wrong answer.)

---

1. For a fuller explanation of this, see Campbell, *Deliverance of God*, 574.

Paul: What if some were unfaithful? Will their faithlessness nullify the faithfulness of God? (3:3)

The teacher: By no means! Although every human is a liar, let God be proved true, as it is written, "So that you may be justified in your words, and you will prevail when you go to trial." (3:4)

Paul: But if our injustice serves to confirm the justice of God, what should we say? That God is unjust to inflict wrath on us? (I speak in a human way.) (3:5)

The teacher: By no means! For then how could God judge the world? (3:6)

Paul: But if through my falsehood God's truthfulness abounds to his glory, why am I still being judged as a sinner? And why not say (as some people slander us by saying that we say), "Let us do evil so that good may come"? (3:7–8a)

The teacher: Their judgment is deserved! (3:8b)

Paul: What then? Are we any better off? (3:9a)

The teacher: No, not at all. . . . (3:9a)

We need to grasp now just why Paul is doing this.

It is a setup for his final argumentative play.

Since 2:1 Paul has pressed the teacher's dependence on judgment through desert. And one of the embarrassing realizations flowing from this is that these premises have removed any advantage that the Torah and circumcision give to Jews, or to pagans who convert to Judaism. We need to emphasize here in passing that Paul is not targeting Jewish people *per se*; he is zeroing in on the teacher and his particular missionary project. It is the teacher's definition of what a Jew is—which he himself might not have grasped completely—that Paul is ripping up. The teacher's own *logic* rules out Jewish advantage and privilege in a way that he is clearly not yet aware of. But he needs to learn this.

God must judge fairly (the teacher says): Jews get saved by obeying their Torah and pagans get saved if they obey the moral revelations of the cosmos and their consciences. But it follows as well that sinful Jews will get judged and condemned on the day of judgment. And this final, rather threatening possibility needs to be very clear. So Paul asks the teacher a question directly in 3:1–9 that was implicit in 2:17–20: *Do Jews, according to the teacher's gospel, have any advantage at all when it matters?*

One would assume that by this point the teacher would have understood Paul's argument and so responded to the question of 3:1 by saying something like, "None! There really is no advantage for Jews in terms of ethics and salvation. Thanks for helping me see that, Paul." But of course he is never going to give in so easily. So Paul depicts the teacher as responding as if he has not been paying enough attention, which is often what opponents in a Socratic debate do. They are often slow learners—which allows those reading the dialogue to follow along. So the teacher misses the necessary inference present in Paul's question and asserts quite boldly the incorrect answer that Torah-observant Jews still enjoy an advantage in many respects (3:2). "They have been entrusted with God's very utterances!" The purpose of the next seven verses is to elicit the correct response from the teacher concerning Jewish advantage—that on the day of judgment they do *not* possess any significant advantage. It doesn't matter if they *possess* God's oracular instructions. They have to *obey* them. And if they don't, they will be judged and sentenced to death like everyone else—something the teacher does seem to have learned by verse 9.

Paul begins to draw this admission out from the teacher by asking another question:

> Paul: "What if some were unfaithful? Will not their faithlessness
> nullify the faithfulness of God?" (3:3)

This question returns the teacher to where he is most comfortable—thinking about who gets condemned. And he duly takes the bait. If said "faithless" Jewish person were to receive an advantage and thus to evade God's judgment, then God's justice and divine character would have to be abandoned altogether. In other words, God would not be retributively just if the severity of God's justice was selectively enforced, which cannot be the case. The teacher cares about God's punitive character more than almost anything else. So, faced with this question from Paul, the teacher responds with an emphatic, "By no means!" God will judge even those Jews who do not prove trustworthy. In this way he will be faithful *to himself*; he will, as the Greek suggests in verse 4, be faithful in the sense of being "*true.*"

Paul then presses the point. He asks the teacher whether sinful deeds will invalidate God's *justice*. The answer is, of course, "No": God's judgment will not waver in relation to sinful deeds any more than his truth does, and in fact those who even suggest that it does are themselves destined for a highly appropriate condemnation:

The teacher: "Let God be true and every person false. . . ." (3:4a, our translation)

Paul: ". . . Is it not unjust of God to pour out wrath on us?. . ." (3:5b, our translation)

The teacher: "For then how could God judge the world [if that is the case]?" (3:6)

Paul: "But if by means of my falsehood the truthfulness of God overflows to God's glory, why then am I still condemned as a sinner?" (3:7 our translation)

The teacher: ". . .[the] judgment [of those saying this] is deserved!" (3:8b)

The result of the conversation in general then, and this final back and forth between the two interlocutors in particular, is that the teacher ends up giving a different answer from the one he gave in response to Paul's initial question in verse 1. Paul places that question again in verse 9. And the teacher responds now as he should have answered in verse 2. Jews do *not* enjoy any advantages in the final judgment, and if they sin they will be sentenced to death like everyone else. This is where the teacher's own assumptions inexorably lead him. So the teacher has learned, and the basic dynamics within his position have been greatly clarified. He has admitted the implications of his own position.

3:1–2: Paul: "Then what advantage has the Jew? Or what is the value of circumcision? . . ."

Correct answer: *nothing.*

Actual answer: a great deal!, literally "Much, in every way . . ."

3:9: Paul: "What then? Are we any better off?"

The teacher: "No, not at all . . ."—the correct answer!

In short, in the light of the sort of God the teacher believes in and proclaims, he has been forced to admit in 3:1–9a that no advantage in terms of salvation actually exists for Jews if they sin. There is no valid ground within his system to suggest that God modifies his retributive character to go easy on Jews if they screw up. And the teacher has admitted this himself, at least here, as Paul depicts him in conversation. On the day of judgment his God

will inflict the death penalty on sinful Jews as well as on sinful pagans. This
· is now very clear.

But why has Paul take so much time to elicit this admission from the
teacher's own mouth?

He is now going to make a final crippling move.

Section 2. Romans 3:9–18: Paul lowers the boom

Paul's final argumentative play is introduced in 3:9b, with the claim that all
people—Jews and pagans—are gripped by sin:

> We publicly charge that *all*, both Jews and Greeks,
> are under the power of sin.
> (Our translation)

Now this is not necessarily an assumption that the teacher shares—he
doubtless thinks that he is righteous and obedient, along with the learned
and pious Jews with whom he associates—but Paul's claim is reinforced with
a massive display of scriptural support. There is no avoiding the way the
Bible seems to affirm this claim over and over again. The Scriptures, which
the teacher knows and swears by, "entrusted by God to his people," speak
repeatedly of the way that all humanity, obviously including Jews, sin, in
multiple ways and on every level. If the teacher is to deny this convincingly
before his Roman audience, he will have a hard time doing so.

> As it is written:
> "There is no one who is righteous, not even one;
>   there is no one who has understanding,
>   there is no one who seeks God."
> "All have turned aside; together they have become worthless;
>   there is no one who shows kindness,
>   there is not even one."
> "Their throats are opened graves;
>   they use their tongues to deceive."
> "The venom of vipers is under their lips."
>   "Their mouths are full of cursing and bitterness."
> "Their feet are swift to shed blood;
>   ruin and misery are in their paths,
>   and the way of peace they have not known."
> "There is no fear of God before their eyes."
> (Rom 3:10–18)

So in verses 9a to 18 we learn from a great mass of scriptural texts that *everyone sins*. There is no missing this point in the argument. But why does Paul do this?[2]

If it is the case that all have sinned, then it follows that in terms of the teacher's own account of salvation—his gospel—*no one will be saved*. And no one *can* be saved. Everyone, as Scripture says, is sinful. They sin and so will be judged inferior and inadequate on the day of judgment and condemned. They will be judged in terms of their works, and the Bible tells us how that is going to go. No one will have done enough; everyone will have sinned. So in terms of the teacher's preaching, everyone is going to be condemned.

We see at this moment just why Paul wanted to emphasize in the preceding dialogue in verses 1 through 9a the teacher's commitment in his version of the day of judgment to an implacable condemnation by God of sinners even if they are Jews. This closes off any special pleading as Paul's final argumentative move is made. "But we're Jewish," we can hear the teacher saying. "We get special treatment. We are God's people. He loves us. He won't sentence *us* to death, annihilation, or even to torment." But according to the logic of the teacher's own preaching God will, and God must, and the teacher has just admitted this. There is no escape from Paul's profoundly awkward inference.

Now it is pretty crippling to have to admit that a gospel offering a way to salvation with God in fact saves no one. It is literally a gospel that does not work. The good news is just bad news. But within this general concession, we need also to detect Paul's last barbed criticism.

Not even the teacher himself will be saved by this gospel. *He* must be sinful, at least in certain respects, and so he too will be condemned on the day of judgment. The teacher's gospel cannot even save the teacher himself!

---

2. It is also the case that our reading can explain why this major premise in the argument, affirming human *in*capacity, contradicts the major premise that the argument has presupposed up to this point, of human capacity. Romans chapter 1 explicitly affirmed the latter, as did Romans chapter 2; people are "without excuse" precisely because they *could* have done the right thing and chose not to, deliberately turning away. And it is a basic assumption of all fairness that people can only be asked to do and held responsible for actions that they can in fact undertake. But here the premise shifts to human inadequacy, which is *both* contradictory *and* undermines the fairness of what Paul has been saying in the previous two chapters. Those who view Paul as committed to the assumptions underlying Romans 1 and 2 have never been able to adequately square this circle. But fortunately there are now no difficulties here for us. Paul is himself committed to the more pessimistic position present in 3:9a–18, and this pessimism about how people are constructed—problematically!—is precisely why he is so unhappy about the teacher's gospel. Those following the teacher's suggestions will get nowhere.

We see at this moment then that Paul's final interrogation of the teacher's gospel, in its own terms, is an argumentative triumph. There are already multiple reasons for thinking that the teacher's offer of conversion to Paul's pagan converts is pointless—the story of Romans 2. On the teacher's own premises, Jews who get circumcised and observe the Torah are not necessarily saved. And pagans can be saved right where they are without converting to anything. But beyond this, we have learned in chapter 3 that the offer of salvation is just not going to work for *anyone*. Universal sinfulness, which the Scriptures attest to so clearly, entails that everyone will be condemned, including the teacher himself. So his gospel is not merely pointless as a missionary endeavor; it is a complete failure in salvific terms. There is no salvation on offer through its teachings at all!

Paul's opponent has now been reduced to an embarrassed silence. As verse 19 says,

> Now we know that whatever the law says,
> it says to those who are under the law [that is, those learned in
> the law, like teachers],
> so that every mouth may be silenced. . . .
> (Rom 3:19)

Those "in the Torah" are singled out here for special treatment—those who know it, are instructed in it, and can thereby instruct others (perhaps recalling here 2:17–20). And it follows that Paul's enemy, whom he has been targeting through Romans chapters 1 to 3, the teacher, has been silenced. The pompous, overconfident, harsh proclamation of Romans chapter 1 has been exposed and then ruined, to which the only appropriate response is a humiliated submission.

Paul's conclusion to this first argument in his letter now follows, and he has even found another verse from Scripture that states his point.

> ". . . no one will be declared righteous in God's sight
> by the works of the law" [Ps 143:2];
> rather, through the law we become conscious of sin.
> (Rom 3:20 our translation)

As Psalm 143:2 says, no one is going to get saved by undertaking deeds prescribed by the Torah and then showing up on judgment day and asking to be declared perfectly righteous by God and so worthy of salvation and resurrection. That is just not going to happen within the teacher's system. And while many of us have been taught that this is a possibility, the failure of which sets up salvation in another mode, by faith—i.e., we are witnessing here the right conclusions to draw within a "Box A" that will prompt us to make the jump to a "Box B"—we have learned enough from our theological investigations in early chapters along with our exegetical journey through Romans 1 to 3 to know that this statement by Paul is actually an *absolute* and not a *conditional* negation. This entire approach to salvation, in terms of works, is not just going to fail. It is just plain wrong all the way down. Its complete and universal failure indicates that this is not God's approach to salvation in the first place. It never has been and it never will be. Rather than offering us a way to salvation, this gospel collapses in on itself palpably and completely.

It might be worth noting in closing this particular part of our overall argument that the final line in this section of the letter is best interpreted as another hint by Paul of his own position that will be taken up in detail later on. In verse 20 Paul says, "for through the Torah the only thing that comes is the knowledge of sin." Pointing ahead especially to Romans 7, which uses the same Greek terms, Paul gives us a hint here of his own views. He has learned that, taken on its own terms, living by the Torah does open up into a dark journey—one that reproduces the garden of Eden and the manipulation of God's instructions there by the serpent to produce death. But a consideration of this dark journey is best undertaken after the illumination of the gospel has taken place, when our minds and hearts have been liberated and sanctified through baptism into Christ and renewal by the Holy Spirit. Romans 7 is sandwiched tightly between Romans 5 and 6, and Romans 8. It is only in *this* place that we learn that Torah-observance in the power of the flesh is never going to work to save, while behavior in the power of the Spirit gives us life and peace. So in that setting, this lesson becomes a warning not to step back from life in the Spirit into a life lived in the power of the flesh. This negative view of the Torah is not then the *basis* of Paul's theology, but one of its *consequences*—a realization that will draw the fangs from the apostle's anti-Jewish applications.[3]

Conclusion

With this last observation, our journey from Romans 1:18 through 3:20 is complete and we have ended up exactly where we need to be. Read sensitively and, we suggest, correctly, in broadly Socratic terms, Romans 1 through 3 strongly support the solution to the great puzzles of Pauline interpretation that we have been building toward throughout this book. We see here Paul,

---

3. In terms of Barth's language that we have been using to clarify these dynamics, this "No" effected through the Torah only becomes apparent after we have heard God's "Yes" and is effected in the light of that "Yes."

in a *tour de force*, driving his opponents' gospel in on its own assumptions, embarrassing it in successive realizations, ultimately reducing its advocates to an embarrassed silence. The teacher's proclamation that Paul's pagan converts should convert to Jewish practices is pointless and its ultimate offer of salvation is meaningless. And it follows from all this that the assumptions in Box A should be ignored, and if its representatives show up and attempt to peddle it to any Jesus-followers at Rome, they should be sent packing—advice that still holds for us today. (And if they hang around, there are a number of brutally effective arguments that can be made against their teaching.) That is, it also follows from all this, most importantly, that *none* of the assumptions about God and salvation introduced in Romans chapter 1 and developed by Box A should be attributed to Paul. Their retributive and conditional nature is advocated by his bitter rivals. And it follows from this in turn that Paul himself is *not* contradictory at a fundamental level in his understanding of the God revealed through Jesus Christ, of the basic direction that the gospel story flows, or in his understanding of how the truth about this gospel arrives, by way of revelation. Indeed, it is precisely his grasp of these truths that leads him to such a clear-sighted repudiation of the teacher's gospel, which is so unworthy of that name.

Moreover, in an equally positive result, the conditional, contractual and mercantile account of the Jews in terms of attempted justification by works that is generated by Romans chapter 1 and chapter 2 is not Paul's account of the Jews, and it is probably not even the teacher's. Paul drives the teacher here onto his opening assumptions. Those assumptions, pressed logically, eliminate the privileges of the Jews; a contractual account of Judaism that ultimately reduces it to irrelevance is present by implication within the opening stanzas of the teacher's preaching. But the teacher may not necessarily have been aware of this himself. It is hard to grasp embarrassing implications that flow from one's own rhetorical openings. He was most likely somewhat inconsistent in his view of the Jews, not unlike the author of the Wisdom of Solomon where Jews do receive special treatment. So even the teacher himself was possibly not an out-and-out legalist.

But too much is at stake for Paul to let the teacher entirely off the hook. The teacher's opening assumptions *do* undermine directly any claims to Jewish privilege within his own teaching, whether he likes those implications or not. And at least we are now freed from the need to attribute any of these assumptions to Paul. We can continue the solution we began in Galatians, attributing the model of attempted salvation through works of law to a small group of misguided messianic Jews. Our account of Paul's thinking, both about the gospel and about Jews, can be kinder, gentler, and more deeply coherent.

With our alternative reading of Box A in place, sustained through its most challenging—although ultimately most supportive—text, we turn to the following material in Romans to consider if our solution is sustainable through Box B. Can Paul's statements be read there in a way that unpacks directly into his transformational and resurrectional concerns that he speaks about so much elsewhere?

The way forward from this moment will run through a deeper understanding of the apostle's language of faith.

14

The Faith of Jesus

Finding Jesus in Box B

If our initial re-interpretative move is correct, namely, the realization that Box A is actually a direct attack on a rival and inferior "gospel" preached by Pauline opponents and not Paul's own theology at all, then we are well on the way to providing a solution to our difficulties. Certainly Box A has been well and truly taken care of. But for our solution to work completely we need to do something with Box B as well, and our reinterpretation of Box A has shifted the stakes here. We now have to show how Box B makes sense in its own right, self-sufficiently, detached from any assumptions or expectations carried over from Box A; *and* ideally our reading should unpack directly into the description of the gospel that Paul gives elsewhere, in the other 90 percent that he wrote, so that the tensions that are generated by JT at this interface are not simply reproduced in some other variation. Box B is not the second stage in Paul's gospel; it *is* Paul's gospel and so it needs to align with what Paul declares in his gospel everywhere else.

Two "gospels"

Box A:

Salvation through a contract?:

not the gospel!

Box B:

Salvation through Jesus!:

which connects with Paul's participation

and resurrection talk elsewhere.

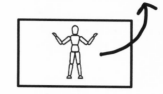

Now the key terms and phrases in Box B have not usually been read as unpacking directly into Paul's participatory gospel. But this is not surprising because they have been read in terms of JT, and JT reads Box B as if Box A is already in place. If Box A sets the terms of the argument, then readers expect Paul to continue to focus in Box B on the individual's journey out of an attempt to be saved by doing good works and into an embrace of salvation by faith alone. This is the only story they expect to find and so in these highly abbreviated texts this is what they do find.

But if we approach Box B without the interpretative lenses supplied by JT in place, and so without Box A in front of it, then we can detect that Paul might be saying something subtly different here from the way he is usually read. It is not that JT is entirely wrong. As we have had frequent cause to note in what precedes, JT exegetes are accurate readers. It is just that here their reading is too thin. Their reading of Box B focuses too strongly on the journey of an individual convert to faith—because this is all that it expects to find—and consequently overlooks the role that Jesus is playing. A little strangely then, JT has quite low expectations of the degree to which Jesus participates in Paul's argument. But it is the recovery of the centrality of Jesus to what is going on that opens up the possibility that this data is a special sort of announcement of what Paul says everywhere else in his writings—about how we are saved by participating in Christ.

So how do we find Jesus in Box B, and then develop this discovery in a way that lines up with Paul's transformational gospel? The way forward turns out to be all about faith. Which is to say that the recovery of the role that Jesus plays in Box B takes place when we realize that Paul's use of faith language in these texts is more nuanced and layered than many JT readers suppose. Paul's understanding of faith points toward the faith of people within the church *and* toward the all-important prior faith of Jesus himself.

And if our faith derives from our participation in his faith then Box B could indeed be announcing Paul's usual concern with salvation as we *participate* in the dying and rising Jesus.

The way forward then will turn out to revolve almost entirely around what Paul means by faith when he speaks of it in his JT texts, which he does so repeatedly. It is the central motif in Box B. But this question is so significant and contested that we will have to press into it in some detail. Somewhat paradoxically—but also entirely understandably—advocates of JT do not like what readers like us think Paul is saying when he speaks of "faith"—that he is focusing our attention on Jesus.

The meaning of faith in Paul

As we noted in chapter 11, scholars convinced by JT, like the translators of the latest NIV cited below, render Paul's original Greek in key JT texts like Galatians 2:15–16 roughly as follows:

> 15 We who are Jews by birth and not sinful Gentiles
> 16 know that a person is not justified by the works of the law,
> but by faith in Jesus Christ.
> So we, too, have put our faith in Christ Jesus
> that we may be justified by faith in Christ
> and not by the works of the law,
> because by the works of the law no one will be justified.

The word "justified," used here three times, is translating the Greek verb *dikaioō*, and we will make some observations about the suitability of this translation in due course. But this rendering will do for now. Clearly some process is involved that is saving, which Paul is referring to specifically here in terms of "justification" or "being justified." Moreover, the occupants of Box A who are "[doing] the works of the law" are *not* being justified. This seems to be very wrong. Over against this incorrect approach, Box B speaks of a process of justification that is successful and that takes place "by faith." And this motif too is repeated three times, at which moment the alert exegete might wonder if the JT reading does not result in Paul being somewhat heavy-handed; does he really need to repeat his key claim about the need for a person to believe in Christ in order to be saved three times in a single sentence? (Twice perhaps yes, but three times . . . ?)

> . . . by faith in Jesus Christ . . .
> . . . we, too, have put our faith in Christ Jesus . . .
> . . . justified by faith in Christ . . . .

If we are informed by JT, however, and so understand all this talk of faith and Jesus in the light of Box A, with the broad expectation that an individual is journeying from the horrors of attempted salvation through legalism to the generous relief of salvation by faith alone, then perhaps it is not out of the question to suggest that all these references denote the faith of the journeying individual. Faith in Jesus is the all-important step from Box A to Box B. It is arguably no surprise then that Paul is emphasizing it so strongly. But if we set these expectations from Box A to one side and think about how Box B, considered just by itself, could speak of Paul's participatory gospel, then something else emerges into view.

We noted earlier on that Tom Wright does not endorse the standard approach to the language of faith in Box B. Although he does speak of people joining the church as they wear "the badge of faith," and so retains a certain amount of the structure of JT, he adds another layer to this reading by speaking of Jesus as having faith too. Wright sees Jesus's faithfulness to the point of death in Box B as revealing the covenant faithfulness of the God of Israel because Wright attributes such a strong and pervasive role to the God of Israel in Paul's writings.[1] And if Wright is correct, even in basic terms, then a new perspective opens up on what Paul is saying in Box B that could sustain our new approach to this material as a whole.

So who is right, so to speak?

The all-important genitive

In order to resolve this question, we must grasp that Paul's faith language often appears in Box B in his JT texts in a grammatical form known technically as a genitive relation. Paul speaks here in the Greek about "(the) faith *of* Jesus," the "of" being the genitive connection. And this grammatical relation admits many meanings at first glance and so can be highly ambiguous and difficult to pin down.

We actually have numerous examples of just this sort of ambiguity in English genitives as well. The phrase the "love of my wife" is a genitive because it uses the word "of."

THE LOVE—OF—MY WIFE

But it is not clear what this phrase means exactly when we read it in isolation. This could mean the love that *I* have *for* my wife. I love her and so the love is something I direct toward her. Since I am the acting subject

---

1. See, for example, Wright, *Galatians*, 131–33 (discussing Gal 2:15), and the surrounding arguments.

of the love and she is its object we could call this "an objective genitive construction."[2] My wife here, connected to my love by the genitive "of," is being read as the object of my love. The acting subject of the love is only implicit, although it is me.

> THE LOVE—OF—MY WIFE
>
> =
>
> THE LOVE [*OF ME*]—FOR—MY WIFE

But this phrase could also refer to *my wife's* love. In this case she is the *subject* of the love and she is directing it toward something else—and hopefully at times toward me. Since she is the acting subject of the love we would call this "a subjective genitive." The word in the genitive, here "of my wife," consequently denotes the acting subject of the verb.

> THE LOVE—OF—MY WIFE
>
> =
>
> *MY WIFE'S* LOVE—FOR—X (hopefully ME)

Obviously we need clues from the context to judge what this genitive construction is actually trying to communicate then when it is used. (And there might even be other grammatical options, but we will not worry about those for now.) Am I gazing at my wife's photo while she is away on a long holiday? In which case, we must be speaking about my love for my wife? She is the object of my love so the genitive relationship denotes an object.[3] Or is my wife gazing into my eyes over a candlelit dinner, listening rapturously to every word I am saying, when we hear the words "the love of my wife"? In which case, it might well be referencing her love for me. She is the subject of the love, the one loving (although we might need more information to rule out my love for my wife again).

Just the same problems arise with Paul's use of the phrase "[the] faith of Christ" in Galatians 2:16 (which in Greek is *pistis Christou*), a phrase that occurs in this sentence twice.[4]

The most common translation, which you will find in the vast majority of English Bibles, is "faith *in* Christ." This is an objective understanding of

2. Some have argued that this exact classification and nomenclature is not quite right. See, e.g., Grasso, "A Linguistic Analysis of πίστις Χριστοῦ." However, it will do for our present purposes.

3. Thanks to Laura Robinson—New Testament scholar and my (Jon DePue's) wife—for this helpful illustration. If there are any concerned readers at this point, we should be clear that she is, indeed, a loving wife.

4. The third occurrence isn't quite the same—it uses the verb—but clearly its meaning is related.

the genitive because Christ is the object of a person's faith in this reading. We could call this an I-centered understanding of faith, as the emphasis is on the person who has faith in Christ, here "me" (or you).[5] Clearly the translators of the NIV think that this is what is going on. And if a translator is grounded in JT then this decision just looks obvious.

Of course faith here denotes the individual's faith in Christ, they will reason, because we have been following his journey out of the rigors of Box A as he tries to find salvation.[6] The entire logic of the situation, established by Box A, points toward this reading being correct. Moreover, there is very little room within the logic of JT for Jesus himself to have faith. He alone of all humanity does not need to journey from sinful legalism to salvation by faith alone. He is the one person who is saved by perfectly doing works, and the entire model relies on this, especially as someone like Piper develops it; we need Jesus's perfect righteousness to be imputed to us. So a subjective reading just makes no sense to a JT advocate whereas an objective reading seems to fit like a hand in a glove. We began with the individual searching for salvation in Box A and we are obviously continuing that journey here in Box B.

The word "faith," however, is in a genitive construction in Galatians 2:16, twice, and it is technically ambiguous when we first encounter it. And so it could be working subjectively. It might not be, so to speak, my love for my wife (an objective reading) but my wife's love for me (a subjective reading), which is to say, it might not be my faith in Jesus but Jesus's own faith that is in view here. We could call this a Christ-centered construal of the faith in question. And *there is absolutely nothing to stand against this reading once we have lost the prior influence of Box A* (which we have), while there is much to be said in favor of it in general terms when we start thinking about the centrality of Christ to what Paul says through the rest of his writings. Paul does spend most of his time everywhere else talking about Jesus. Indeed, if we simply start with his participatory and resurrectional material then the answer to our question will seem as obvious as it is to advocates of JT, *although in the other direction.*

---

5. An alternative reading would maintain the I-centered nature of the interpretation but claim that the content of the things in which the person's faith has been placed is specified by Christ. The genitive describes the content of the thing believed. However, although this is not an objective genitive, but more adjectival, the theological upshot is much the same—a continued endorsement of JT.

6. We say "his" here because the grammar of the text in the crucial extended passage underlying Box A in JT, Rom 1:18—3:20, uses singular male grammar (although it shifts at times into a plural). See especially 2:1.

Of course we get our faithfulness from participating in Jesus's prior faithfulness, just as we get every other virtue from our participation in Jesus's possession of those in a perfect form. No one objects to the suggestion that we get our love from Jesus, or our obedience from him, or our peace from his, and so on. So it really just seems to follow directly that we get our faith—which shades in meaning in Paul from our understanding of God and our believing in him, through our trust in him, to our ongoing steady faithfulness and loyalty to God through thick and thin—from Jesus. Indeed, it might be very comforting to think that God is lifting us up in all these areas into Jesus's perfectly faithful humanity by way of the Spirit. Faith is a gift, so we do not need to condemn ourselves if we cannot generate enough for ourselves—and who among us has perfect faith which they have created for themselves?

It seems then that this alternative understanding of Paul's "faith of Christ" genitives, in subjective terms, as a reference to the programmatic faith of Jesus, will take us straight from Box B into the other 90 percent of what Paul wrote, and our suggested solution to the overarching difficulties we have been grappling with in his writings will stay on track. Box B will focus on Jesus, and then will talk about us by way of our participation in him. But having said this, simply because the subjective and participatory reading is possible does not make it necessary. *Is* this what Paul was suggesting when he used this phrase so many years ago? Knowing this is a possibility is a much easier conclusion to reach than proving that this was the case (although both sides have to prove their case ultimately).

We think that we can do this. But in order to do so we will need to jump briefly from Galatians 2:16 to Romans 3:21–22.

Romans 3:21–22

Galatians 2:16 is not the only text in Paul that contains the critical genitive phrase "faith of Jesus" or its close equivalent. He uses it about half a dozen times: see, in addition to the two occurrences in Galatians 2:16, 2:20, and 3:22; Romans 3:22–26; Ephesians 3:12; and Philippians 3:9.[7] And some of the clearest and most concise evidence that Paul is speaking in all these texts of Jesus's own faithfulness, and then derivatively of the faith we get by

---

7. We say "about" because it is hard to pin the exact number of instances down. Some scholars think that an early manuscript suggests decisively that Gal 3:26 contains the form as well, while others do not, and some scholars do not think that Paul wrote Ephesians, while others do—and some of the latter think that 4:13 should be included here as well.

participating in him, can, we suggest, be found in Romans, Galatians's sibling text, in 3:22. The ESV translators, who are deeply convinced that JT is the gospel, render Paul's Greek, including the all-important context of 3:21 in the following way—and we need to read what these verses in Romans 3 are saying very carefully indeed:

> 21 But now
> the righteousness of God has been manifested
> apart from the law,
> although the Law and the Prophets bear witness to it—
> 22 the righteousness of God
> through faith in Jesus Christ
> for all who believe.

Now the ESV translators think that JT is in play so the genitive here in verse 22 must be objective; the text speaks of *our* faith as individuals *in* Jesus. But if we read this translation closely we will see that by making this decision the translators have left things dangling a little awkwardly. In fact, this rendering does not work very well.

In this translation the subject of verse 22, "the righteousness of God," does not connect very smoothly or coherently with the two prepositional phrases that follow it, one of which contains our key phrase. So if I type "the righteousness of God through faith in Jesus Christ for all who believe" into my computer and then try to finish this sequence with a period, suggesting it is a sentence, Word will flag this up as an ungrammatical sentence fragment. Technically, a verb is missing, and you almost certainly supplied one as you read these phrases without even realizing it so that the statement would make sense—a verb like "is." "The righteousness of God [is] through faith in Jesus Christ, for all who have faith," or some such (although even this doesn't make much sense). As things stand, in terms of what Paul actually composed and nothing more, we are not reading a complete sentence with a subject and a verb. So what verb should we supply to make a proper sentence since Paul clearly expected his original Greek-speaking audience to do this?

The answer is really quite obvious. The exact same noun phrase appears in the preceding verse where it has a verb and so we may immediately surmise that Paul, like any reasonable writer of ancient Greek, has omitted a clumsy repetition when he repeats material. Moreover, read in this way, with this verb supplied, verses 21 and 22 contrast a righteousness of God revealed *not* by the Torah *but* by faith, which is what Paul is always doing in his JT texts. He is writing about Box A and Box B stating that the former is wrong and the latter is correct. Verse 21 is a negation of Box A, although it also contains other crucial information, and verse 22 is Box B, which always revolves around faith. So what Paul meant in verse 22, and what his ancient listeners would have understood, is almost certainly this:[8]

> 21 But now the righteousness of God
> has been manifested
> apart from law,
> although the Law and the Prophets bear witness to it.
> 22 And that righteousness of God
> [has been manifested]
> through faith in Jesus Christ
> for all who believe.

And now comes the all-important realization. If "the righteousness of God" is "made manifest" through "faith" in some relation to "Jesus" then the ambiguous genitive construction "faith of Jesus" present in Paul's Greek really has to be Jesus's *own* faith and not the faith of converts, whose faith is mentioned here just after Jesus's in a derivative location when Paul writes "for all who believe." Why? Because of the little word "through." This denotes *instrumentality*. The faith of Jesus spoken of here is the instrument by means of which something is happening, and in these verses it is the instrument by means of which the righteousness of God is made manifest or revealed.

It is important to note at this moment, in passing, that the meaning of "God's righteousness," not unlike faith, is both important and much debated. Some even think that this was the phrase that launched the Reformation for Luther when he read its first occurrence in Romans in 1:17, back in the early 1500s, although he was reading in Latin. We will resolve the question of its exact meaning later on. For the moment it suffices to say that this phrase is referring to a dramatic act by God that will save humanity; almost everyone agrees that this is the case. All of humanity is being "justified" in some sense by this event as verses 23 to 24 go on to explain.[9] Something dramatic is happening, and God is doing it. And the answer to our current question concerning the faith of Jesus now emerges into plain sight.

It makes complete sense to suppose that *Jesus* reveals God's dramatic action that saves the cosmos from sin. Jesus *is* God's dramatic action that saves the cosmos from sin. Jesus's death and resurrection are obviously the focal point of everything Paul wants to say that God is doing on our behalf

---

8. An advocate of JT might argue that we should supply another verb, but that would be unconvincing in view of the close parallelism between verse 21 and verse 22, and the standard JT antithesis that is clearly present.

9. "23 . . .[S]ince all have sinned and fall short of the glory of God; 24 they are now justified by his grace as a gift, through the redemption that is in Christ Jesus."

in relation to a fallen and broken world. We are transformed as we participate by way of the Spirit in the critical Easter events Jesus experienced,
the journey that baptism enacts and Romans chapter 6 will spell out. This
is Paul's gospel, a gospel that speaks of a divine act accomplished through
Jesus that discloses to the world just what God is like and what God is doing
through Jesus. Jesus's faith—understanding this motif especially as Philippians 2:6–8 does, as his obedient faithfulness ultimately to a death by crucifixion—clearly *reveals* or *makes manifest* and so shows the world what God
the Father is doing through him. In short, Jesus is the *instrument* by means
of which God the Father's righteous plan and purposes are both effected
and disclosed. (We will discuss momentarily just why Paul speaks of this
disclosure through Jesus specifically in terms of faith.)

Conversely, it makes *no* sense to suppose that *our* faith functions *to
reveal* God's righteous action to save the cosmos, although this point needs
to be understood with complete clarity.

Recall that Paul's Greek asks us to understand faith here as an instrument by means of which something involving God happens. So it is functioning like a tool to get something done. Moreover, what is being done is
a divine manifestation. Something about God is being made known. So, as
we just saw, anything to do with Jesus clearly works well at this moment.
He tells us what God is like (which is really what all the creeds are saying).
But at this point we notice a problem for the JT reading in terms of the
individual's saving decision of faith. Our faith just doesn't really work this
way—as an instrument for making things known. It does not and cannot
operate as a kind of tool that takes things that are unknown and makes them
known because it just doesn't mean this or work in this way, and especially
when we are talking about God.

My faith responds with an affirmation of truth, believing, once something has been disclosed. So I believe in things that I already know and go
on to judge to be true. This is what the "believing" means. I believe them. I
believe them *because* I know them, and know them to be true. But I don't
know them *by* believing them! This is just confused if it isn't straight-up
nonsense. Think of something you don't know but would like to know, like
the question we sometimes ask ourselves—is there intelligent life on an M-
class planet in some part of the galaxy around Alpha Centauri? Now try to
use your beliefs or faith as a tool to figure out if this is true or not.

We are willing to surmise that you have quickly run out of steam. Your
beliefs are involved, and they might even be entertaining, not to mention,
in your opinion, deeply plausible. But you can't confirm or refute your conclusion just by further acts of believing. You can't make the truth manifest
by simply believing it. You need to prove or to disprove your beliefs and

this will involve a lot more than believing—perhaps constructing a new generation of spaceship that can enter and exit wormholes and so travel to Alpha Centauri and actually see if there is any intelligent life on any M-class planets there (and so on). Beliefs alone will not settle this. They are simply not a tool that takes things that are unknown and brings them into the light. Certainly we need them as a part of the process of knowing something, but we can't reduce that process to our beliefs.

A little closer to home: you might want to know what is inside the mysterious leather trunk in your mother's attic. This has been a closely guarded secret all your life. Now use your beliefs to figure out what is in there. Beliefs will again be involved. Indeed, you might have all sorts of beliefs about what is inside. But none of those will demonstrate or disclose what is really there. You need an instrument, in this case, an action. You will have to find the key, unlock the lock, and open the trunk. Then your beliefs will be confirmed or disconfirmed. It is the finding of the key and its introduction to the lock that is the instrument by means of which the contents of the trunk are known or, as Paul puts the point in 3:22, made manifest.

Just so, in Romans 3:22 Paul is speaking about something concerning God being made known by an instrument. God's righteous nature and plan are being revealed. And faith here is some sort of tool that makes that happen. (We are talking about the first instance of faith in this verse, through which something happens; the second instance of faith—our faith—denotes for whom it happens.) Moreover, we know this for certain because Paul goes on to speak in just a few lines of something that "proves" what God's righteousness is; he uses the Greek *endeixis* for "proof" or "demonstration" twice in verses 25 and 26. But how can your or my faith "prove" or "demonstrate" what God's righteousness is like as it is made manifest? It can't. God the Father is invisible. He is in heaven. You don't know what he is like unless he tells you. In fact, your faith can't make anything decisive about God known. Faith just doesn't work like that—although as we noted just above, *Jesus's* faithfulness can. He is the one who makes God the Father's purposes manifest, and who functions as the definitive proof or evidence of that loving, saving purpose. So a subjective genitive reading fits here perfectly. And it fits in with a revealing God. God is making himself understood and obvious through *Jesus*. The Father is revealed through his Son.[10]

10. It might be possible to rephrase this argument and speak of correct beliefs in our minds being a necessary condition for any action to take place. In this sense—a very modern one—we might understand them to be a tool. But if we grant this (anachronistic) rejoinder, it still remains the case that they are a necessary but not a sufficient condition in any of the examples mentioned.

In short, we suggest that a careful reading of what Paul wrote in Romans 3:21 to 22, even in the translation supplied by fervent advocates of JT, many of whom rendered the ESV, suggests that the ambiguous genitive construction "faith of Jesus" in Paul's Greek must really be understood subjectively, with Jesus as the one who is acting in faith. Only this reading can make sense of the rest of the sentence in context. Jesus is the instrument who discloses God's righteous nature and plan. He is the proof of that activity. Conversely, any claim that our faith is instrumentally disclosing God's righteousness does not really make sense, although that righteousness does want to reach out to include us within its cosmic purposes, and we are marked—at that point—by our believing. God wants us to believe *in* his righteous cosmic actions on our behalf that have been made manifest through the faith of Jesus!

We should re-translate this text accordingly.

21 But now the righteousness of God
has been manifested
apart from law,
although the Law and the Prophets bear witness to it;
22 [And t]he righteousness of God
[has been manifested]
through the faith of Jesus Christ
for all who believe.
(ESV suitably modified)

It is easy for these points to slip past an exegete in the grip of JT. Justification theory itself will fill in any blanks here quite quickly, and slide over the difficulties, which are subtle; it is not as if JT advocates are looking for Jesus's faith, or supplying the right ellipsed verbs in Paul's original Greek. Or the model's advocates might tacitly concede that this is a problem and offer something like the following solution.

Paul's gospel proclamation might be invoked as the instrument of revelation—as the tool that enters the lock and opens the lid on the trunk hidden in the attic. It is implicit in Paul's language and can be supplied by the reader as if it is there. And it is fair to suggest that the announcement of the gospel by Paul makes God's righteous activity through Jesus manifest or known. I should then respond to this by means of my faith. I should believe it. So this suggestion gets around the difficulty that my faith is not the "tool" or "instrument" whereby God's saving activities have been made known (thereby admitting that this is a problem).

But this is not what Paul actually wrote in Romans 3:21–22. Neither is it likely that he is presupposing "the gospel" in these verses. He last

mentioned his proclamation (Gk. *euangelion*) in passing in 2:16, and prior
to that, in 1:15, so more than two chapters previously. And he will not mention it again until . . . 10:16, which is *seven* chapters later, or a stretch of text
rather longer than most of his other letters in their entirety. So this appeal
won't work. Paul is clearly not presupposing the gospel here. Moreover, we
should resist solutions to problems of interpretation in the Scriptures that
rely on us supplying additional critical words *to* the Scriptures. Once we
notice the details of the text, we realize that Paul is talking about something
subtly different—something that revolves around Jesus and not around us.
And what can be problematic about suggesting this? Paul is always talking
about Jesus. Indeed, after 3:22, he doesn't really stop talking about Jesus until he is well into chapter 9, and even then Jesus is everywhere presupposed.

So far so good then. It seems decisively proven that Paul is talking
about the faith *of* Jesus in Romans 3:22, and so by implication in all the
debated "faith of Jesus" genitive constructions, at which moment we can
return to our initial focus on Galatians 2:15–16. This sentence should be
translated as the footnotes in the NIV recommend:

> 15 We who are Jews by birth and not sinful Gentiles
> 16 know that a person is not justified by the works of the law,
> but through the faithfulness of Jesus Christ.
> So we, too, have put our faith in Christ Jesus
> that we may be justified on the basis of the faithfulness of
> Christ
> and not by the works of the law,
> because by the works of the law no one will be justified.

But our alternative reading of Box B—at least in summary terms—is
not yet complete. Some further important questions now arise.

Why, someone might ask, does Paul speak here of the faith of Jesus?
Isn't this a little opaque? What does Jesus's faith actually do? Does Paul
talk about the faith of Jesus a lot in other places? (Answer: "no.") And what
broader argument is he making if this talk of Jesus's faith is not the second
part of JT but just a straightforward pointer to his gospel of resurrectional
transformation? The connections here are by no means obvious.

These are entirely legitimate questions. Having grasped that Paul is
talking about the faith of Jesus in these *phrases*, we need to explain how the
phrases fit into a coherent *argument*. And we also need to explain the *distinctiveness* of Paul's JT texts. Their language is different from the way Paul
usually writes (although, strictly speaking, this is an issue that JT advocates
need to solve as well, and in their case it's a tougher question). The Box B
texts do go on and on about faith.

Our answers to all these questions will lead us to a new dimension within our reading of the JT texts in their entirety. We need now to engage with Paul's use of Scripture—a subject large enough to warrant a chapter of further investigation in its own right.

15

The Presence of Scripture

A battle for the Bible

We focused in the previous chapter on the expression "the faith of Jesus," which comes up at least half a dozen times at strategic places in Paul's "Box B" texts, hence in locations like Galatians 2:16. Grasping that this expression referred to the faith of Jesus himself was the first step forward in understanding how Box B could unpack into what Paul talks about outside his JT texts, where he is usually talking about Jesus. This was such a controversial and critical insight we had to spend some time proving our case, drawing Romans 3:22 into the argument. And an important question then arose after we had reached this conclusion, namely, just *why* does Paul refer to Jesus's faith? We turn to answer this important question here.

There is, we suggest, quite a straightforward answer that Paul actually signals immediately before he speaks of the faith of Jesus in Romans 3:22, and this will ultimately explain the distinctive texture of all of Paul's JT texts.

> 21 But now the righteousness of God
> has been manifested
> apart from law,
> *although the Law and the Prophets bear witness to it.*
> 22 And that righteousness of God
> [has been manifested]
> through the faith of Jesus Christ
> for all who believe.
> (ESV modified, italics added)

Here Paul states that God's saving righteousness is made manifest apart from Torah and through the faith of Jesus *as attested to by the Scriptures,* which we sometimes need to remind ourselves were in his day the Jewish Scriptures or Tanakh, so our Old Testament. Paul refers to them here as "the Torah [or Law] and the Prophets." Galatians 2:15–16 make much the same point once we notice it:

> 15 We who are Jews by birth and not sinful Gentiles
> 16 know that a person is not justified by the works of the law,
> but through the faithfulness of Jesus Christ.
> So we, too, have put our faith in Christ Jesus
> that we may be justified on the basis of the faithfulness of
> Christ
> and not by the works of the law,
> because by the works of the law no one will be justified.
> (NIV footnote)

The phrase "by the works of the law no one will be justified" is a verbatim reproduction of Psalm 143:2 which Paul quotes again in Romans 3:20 just before he writes 3:21–22. Hence, it seems that Paul is quoting or alluding to Jewish Scripture in his JT discussions, and this should not surprise us.

Paul is arguing in all these texts, as we learned when we pressed into the circumstances that gave rise to Box A, with a set of rival missionaries who were Jewish Jesus-followers like him. But they were more than just Jewish rivals. Like Paul again, although more unusually, they were also learned Jewish *scholars.* It is useful to recall at this moment how Paul profiles them half-way through Romans chapter 2:

> 17 You call yourself a Jew and rely on the law
> and are proud of your relationship to God,
> 18 and you know his will and are able to distinguish between
> right and wrong
> because you have been instructed in the law,
> 19 and you are confident that you are a guide to the blind,
> a light for those in darkness,
> 20 an instructor of the foolish,
> and a teacher of the simple
> because in the law you have the embodiment of knowledge and
> truth.
> (Our translation)

"Instructed in the law . . . a guide . . . a light . . . an instructor . . . [and] a teacher . . . [from] the law." Clearly Paul's opponents were messianic Jewish teachers, and they taught from the Scriptures. So they were almost certainly quoting the Scriptures at Paul's converts like it was going out of fashion. And it follows that Paul must try to counter that learning, which is so shaking his converts, by presenting them with his own array of scriptural texts. He must show that the Scriptures are on *his* side. He must win this particular, very early, battle for the Bible.

Once we realize that scriptural quotation is in play throughout Paul's JT texts we begin to see how they receive almost all their distinctive texture from the way that the apostle is utilizing language within them that has been drawn from various useful Scripture verses. We can see Paul repeatedly either quoting or alluding to—in no particular order, and not even counting some of the secondary scriptural appeals—Psalm 98:2, Leviticus 18:5, Deuteronomy 27:26, Genesis 15:6, Psalm 143:2, Isaiah 28:16 and 52:7, Joel 2:32 (which in the Septuagint is 3:5), and Habakkuk 2:4.[1] Paul stitches all these verses together throughout his JT texts into a powerful refutation of his opponent's gospel and an affirmation of his own. "The Bible is on my side, affirming what I say in Box B, and condemning what you say, in Box A!"

We do not need to sort out all of the particular interpretative dynamics Paul sets in play with this complicated network of quotations for our present purpose, although his skill at recalling scriptural verses linked together by a shared keyword is impressive. (This was a standard expository technique that trained rabbis in his day used that we sometimes refer to as "pearl-stringing" or "catch-word linkage.")[2] We are focused for the moment on one specific question. Why does Box B, when it appears in texts like Galatians 2:15–16, revolve around faith, zeroing in at various critical points on the faith of Jesus?

At this moment our two previous lines of discussion helpfully link hands.

Habakkuk 2:4 as the key

When we read Paul's Box B texts carefully, especially in the original Greek, we can see that the phrase that he often uses to speak about faith, namely, "through faith," is a direct allusion to one of these Scripture texts. This phrase reproduces exactly the faith phrase that occurs in the middle of Habakkuk 2:4:

> The righteous one through faith will live. (Our translation)

---

1. Counting here only Scripture verses that Paul quotes or alludes to at least twice, usually in Romans and Galatians.

2. Explained by Richard N. Longenecker in *Biblical Exegesis in the Apostolic Period*.

And in fact, once we notice it, we can see that Habakkuk 2:4 was a very important scriptural text for Paul. He echoes its key faith phrase, "through faith," through Galatians and Romans, his two key JT letters, no less than twenty times. And these are the two letters where he quotes Habakkuk 2:4 explicitly as well.[3] So Habakkuk 2:4 is clearly grounding a lot of Paul's faith talk in his Box B texts. No other text receives this level of emphasis from him—not even Genesis 15:6 and Isaiah 28:16, which also use believing language.

But we need to link this realization now with the insight generated by the previous chapter, and at this moment, our two lines of inquiry helpfully connect. We learned in the previous chapter from Romans 3:22 that "the faith of Jesus" in Paul denotes *Jesus's* faith; only his faithfulness, ultimately to the point of death, could meaningfully disclose or make manifest to us the righteous activity of God. And now we can see that the Greek used to refer to the faith of Jesus, which usually speaks of something important happening "*through*" the faith of Jesus, is being drawn directly from Habakkuk chapter 2:4. So it follows from this in a fairly straightforward way that Paul must be reading Habakkuk 2:4 as a messianic prophecy that points toward Jesus.

The righteous one through faith will live.

This Jesus-centered reading of Habakkuk 2:4 by Paul becomes clearer for us modern readers when we realize that "The Righteous One" was a title that many early Jesus-followers used to refer to Christ, probably because of the influence of Isaiah 53, where that description comes up in verse 11. (Few texts were as important to the first Christians as Isaiah 53.)

> Out of his anguish he shall see;
>   he shall find satisfaction through his knowledge.
> The righteous one, my servant, shall make many righteous,
>   and he shall bear their iniquities.
> (Isa 53:11)

Most importantly for our current question, it follows that what Paul means by "the faithfulness of Jesus" will depend on what he thinks this text is saying as a whole. And in fact we now see at a glance that the "faith" that Habakkuk 2:4 speaks of is a prediction of Jesus's obedience and endurance as he journeyed from his exalted pre-human state and became a mere

---

3. A more detailed analysis of this data and its implications is provided by Chris Tilling, "Campbell's Faith: Advancing the *Pistis Christou* Debate," in Tilling (ed.), *Beyond Old and New Perspectives on Paul*, 234–50. And see also a summary by Douglas of one of his main arguments in "The Faithfulness of Jesus Christ in Romans 3:22."

human of flesh, and then submitted to a shameful death on the cross (and it might be helpful to recall Philippians 2:6–8 here where Jesus's "obedience," which amounts to the same thing as his "faithfulness," is spoken of). This long, hard walk by Jesus to and through death can now be both summarized and referred to as his "faith[fulness]." In like manner, when Habakkuk 2:4 says that the Righteous One "will live" it predicts—of course—Jesus's resurrection from the dead. And as a result of all this, Habakkuk 2:4 as a whole is read by Paul as a wonderfully compressed prediction by the prophet of Paul's gospel, as it announces the death and resurrection of Jesus: "The Righteous One [that is, Jesus, whom we also see predicted in Isaiah 53] through faith [that is, through his extraordinary journey of faithfulness to the cross] will live [that is, be resurrected, lifted up, and enthroned at God's right hand]." So when Paul quotes or alludes to Habakkuk 2:4, he is saying that his gospel proclamation has been foretold—"witnessed to"—by the Scriptures, here "the Prophets," which is just what he told us he was doing in Romans 3:21.

This is an important set of realizations. When we grasp that Paul is using the faith language of Habakkuk 2:4 to speak about Jesus, and to speak in particular about his faithful walk to the cross, we can see straightaway that Jesus can be right at the center of Paul's Box B texts, just as he is at the center of the transformational material that Paul develops directly in the 90 percent of material outside of the JT texts. Every time the language of Habakkuk 2:4 is either quoted or alluded to we must realize that Paul is talking about *Jesus*, so about twenty times in Romans and Galatians at least. Moreover, every time he uses the phrase "through faith" he evokes Habakkuk 2:4 *as a whole*, which speaks of the *entirety* of Jesus's activity on our behalf through *all* the events of Easter—his obedience, death, resurrection, and ascension, although we can probably detect a special emphasis here on the events leading up to the cross.[4] So there is a lot more Jesus present in Box B than some have hitherto suspected. In fact, the words "through faith" in all of Paul's Box B texts do nothing less than repeatedly evoke "the old rugged cross."

The way ahead then as we reread Paul's Box B texts seems to be getting clearer. We must be constantly attentive to the way that Paul's language of faith can open out directly into Jesus, and only within us as it passes through him—a thoroughly participatory claim.[5] Our faith is still important! More-

4. Strictly speaking, "faith" is a metonym or synecdoche in which a part stands in for a whole. So Paul will also allude to the entirety of Easter by speaking of Jesus's "obedience," "submission," "death," "cross," and "blood." Each one of these is, strictly speaking, a single element within the broader story, but each one *evokes* the entirety of that broader story.

5. The detailed, and very important, account of how Paul connects our faith to

over, Jesus's faith opens out to evoke all the events of Easter! In addition, to help us to find Paul's underlying position we must be constantly alert to the degree to which scriptural language is influencing the language in his JT texts as a whole, sifting their distinctive vocabulary and imagery. When we read in this way, connections with the transformational gospel that he speaks of everywhere else become apparent. Box B, properly understood, really does unpack into the other 90 percent of Pauline data. But in order to really make good on this claim, we now need to address how best to read some other key elements within the JT texts, and the situation is a little different for the next item to be considered here.

Box B tends to oppose "faith" to the teachers' emphasis on "works" informed by the Scriptures. So faith only occurs in Box B, and it was a critical step forward to grasp that this unpacks into Paul's Jesus-centered arguments elsewhere by way of his emphasis on the faith *of* Jesus. But both Box A and Box B hold some language in common. In particular, Paul talks about how a person is not "justified" (as it is usually rendered) by "works" but by "faith." That is, Paul uses a distinctive verb frequently in his JT texts, the usual translation of which even gives justification theory its name: "justification" (strictly speaking, rendering the verb here as a participle or verbal noun). Advocates of JT claim that this verb points directly toward the retributive God who underlies their model, and that this meaning needs to be held constant *from* Box A *to* Box B. So we will clearly need to address this claim if our alternative reading of Box B in terms of participation, transformation, and resurrection, is to hold.

Considering "justification"

There is no doubt that the verb "justify," rendering the underlying Greek *dikaioō*, is operating in both boxes. But we think that Paul is using this verb in slightly different ways *precisely because it is operating in very different boxes*. Unsurprisingly for us, the exact sense of the verb shifts a little because the stories it is framed by are so different. The gospel of the teachers is a very different thing from Paul's gospel.

The teachers expect their converts to be fully righteous in terms of what they do. God's all-important verdict on the day of judgment, as suggested by the verb *dikaioō*, will then simply recognize their goodness or lack of it. God will "pronounce [the teachers' converts] righteous" on the day of judgment because that is what they are (at least hopefully). So in fact, when it occurs

---

Jesus's faith takes place in relation to our discussion of Romans ch. 10, in chapter 18: see pp. 261–66.

in Box A, we suggest that the verb often translated "justify" is really more accurately translated "to pronounce righteous" or "to pronounce innocent of any wrongdoing," and we will translate accordingly. The view underlying this translation and use of the verb is of course retributive, because here, in this broader scenario, the teachers expect God to be retributive, measuring out the right proportion of either reward or punishment and "paying" it. And our suggestion has the advantage of being explicitly in view in Romans 2 (especially in verse 13). This meaning is clearly and we suggest unavoidably what Paul is evoking here. But this need not trouble us. We expect the language of the teachers to be conditional, contractual, and retributive. The key question is whether this meaning for the verb still holds in Box B. And we contend that Paul's viewpoint is subtly but significantly different here.

First, his frame: Paul believes that salvation takes place as we participate in the death and resurrection of Jesus, and this is enacted by baptism. So it follows that this salvation has already happened, and this is either past, or, strictly speaking, something that has begun in the past but has present effect. Paul does not want his converts frightened insecurely by the teachers into thinking that there is still something to do. Salvation is a fact, not a future event to be waited for uncertainly—and this even though the people who have been baptized into Jesus and raised through the power of the divine Spirit are still obviously, in certain respects, wicked, sinful, mortal creatures made of flesh like him. (And the Corinthians do spring to mind here straightaway.) We suggest then that Paul's use of the verb *dikaioō* in Box B suggests his own system, and maps onto his Christocentric narrative, evoking some of its key elements. In this way he is able to deny, once again, some of the teachers' key claims. But in order to grasp this subtle alternative we will need to take a couple of interpretative steps. How does Paul get from the teachers' claim concerning the need for converts to be pronounced innocent of all wrongdoing in the future to his own claim that this has already happened as we have participated in the death and resurrection of Jesus as symbolized by baptism?

We will need to consider the fact, first, that verdicts do not just make a statement about a situation, which we see in the teachers' scenario. They also *effect* something, namely, the entrance of the person pronounced righteous into "glory, immortality, and eternal life." A verdict is a *performative* utterance, in the language of the philosophers J. L. Austin and John Searle,[6] which is to say, it achieves something in the way that the pronouncement by a minister at a wedding, "I now pronounce you man and wife," makes a

---

6. See the classic analyses by these philosophers: Austin, *How to Do Things with Words* (1962); Searle, *Speech Acts: An Essay in the Philosophy of Language* (1969).

couple married. In this sense a verdict of "guilty" in a murder trial sentences a person to death, and effects this, sending them to death row, while a verdict of "acquittal" in a serious trial frees an accused person from jail and from execution, and effects this. A verdict enacts, performs, and achieves certain things. It does not just pronounce that certain states of affairs exist (which would be simply to recognize the presence of a piece of information). It is a "doing-word" in Luther's terminology—a command![7]

We suggest, in the light of this, that Paul's use of the verb *dikaioō* in his Box B texts evidences the difference that Christ makes, as we are baptized into him, dying with him, being buried, and being raised to new life. Under pressure from this story Paul de-emphasizes the descriptive part of a verdict of acquittal because it is simply not relevant as God in his grace saves evil and sinful people within Jesus; God is not literally pronouncing or declaring people innocent, because they are not. So its descriptive side is simply not in play. But Paul has retained the performative side of a verdict. There is still a sense in which a verdict by God has taken place when we die and rise with Jesus. God's gift of salvation through resurrection has set us free from the prison of our flesh and from the looming sentence of death! We have been released. And we have been released from the looming threat of death, at God's command. Moreover, when we take the countervailing position of the teachers into account, we can see just why Paul has done this.

As we noted earlier, the teachers are threatening Paul's converts with a fearful future judgment. At present his pagan converts are not observing the dictates of the law—and the males are not even circumcised—so according to the teachers they are destined for hell. They will experience a verdict of "wicked" on the day of judgment and thereby be sentenced to perdition. They will not be pronounced innocent of all wrongdoing but will be condemned. The teachers are consequently urging Paul's followers to convert to full law-observance and to seek a verdict of "fully righteous" that will save them. They are basically frightening Paul's converts into obedience with the prospect of this uncertain, future, retributive scenario (and this is what all "turn-or-burn" preachers do).

Paul's constant counterclaim to this suggestion by the teachers through his JT texts is that his own converts have *already* experienced this "verdict" from God since they have been baptized into Jesus and they already participate in him. This verdict is *past* and *it is positive.* (It is also not retributive.) To have died and risen with Christ *is* to have passed through the only "verdict" that counts. This was when the decisive step into salvation took

7. David C. Steinmetz explains the difference Luther argued for between a *Thettel-Wort* or deed-word and a *Heissel-Wort* or (just) a naming-word in *Luther in Context*, 132–35.

place, into the glories of the age to come. The sentence of death has been replaced by a judgment of life. Hence, it is the very pressure of this great event that has led to Paul's emphasis on the performative and liberational dimensions of God's "verdict" over us, and to a corresponding de-emphasis on its descriptive side. A verdict—when it goes well—is a saving event. God has pronounced us released from sin, the flesh, and death. We have been set free.

It might be a little hard for us to appreciate this because our imaginations are so strongly influenced by modern courtroom procedures, not to mention, by endless television dramas of the same. In these, descriptive dimensions are central to any verdicts that take place. Indeed, the TV drama is often generated as the innocent are accused unfairly of guilt, and perhaps even smeared and manipulated, but a courageous lawyer sees them through to a rightful declaration of innocence—or, conversely, an intrepid prosecutor, against the odds, takes down a wicked figure who has previously escaped their just conviction by nefarious means. But in Paul's day, courtrooms and "justice" were very different. There were overlaps, to be sure, but there were more differences than similarities. Hearings could last for a minute or less, and treatment depended very much on status, not to mention, on bribery. Low-status people could be treated in brutally summary and harsh terms, and frequently were. For them there was often little to no "justice" from the hands of powerful figures. Which is to say that our notions of fairness, innocence, guilt, and so on, would have had very little to do with most courtroom situations in ancient times, and especially if low-status and/or large status differentials were in play. In those desperately unfair settings a verdict of acquittal had little to do with innocence or guilt. It meant something much more practical, namely, release from squalid detainment in jail and from any associated starvation or interrogation as that had been arranged by powerful people. It meant freedom and life, not enslavement or execution. And this is how Paul is using the verb as he interprets it in dependence ultimately on what Christ has done for us.

In him, as we participate in him, we are released from the prison of our flesh. When we were in the flesh, as descendants of Adam, we were enslaved and imprisoned, guarded, and ultimately sentenced to death. But by being connected to Jesus we have passed through his death and entered into his resurrection and thereby into glorious, new, and incorruptible life. So any verdict has already taken place, and it has been positive; we have been "exonerated" and "acquitted," which is to say, set free. Moreover, we know what sort of God we are involved with because he has paradoxically "acquitted" the ungodly! He must be a God of overwhelming compassion. And this God will not suddenly turn on us and sentence us to death on the day of judgment. He has *released* us from our sin, liberating us from its grip and its consequences. As Elsa Tamez puts this: we have received an *amnesty*—an amnesty of grace![8]

We are confident that Paul really is using the verb *dikaioō* in this way when he speaks in Box B of his own gospel that announces our involvement with Jesus because this is the meaning that the word takes in Romans 6:7 in a statement that lies at the very heart of one of his most participatory discussions. There he writes, "the one who has died has been released from sin," supplying the preposition *apo* ("from") to make this liberational movement especially clear. (Note, even the pro-JT NIV effectively concedes the point here by rendering this verse "anyone who has died has been set free from sin.") This participation and liberation has, moreover, been explicated here in terms of baptism. So the moment of "acquittal" is explaining the way that a convert is raised out of the water, resurrected in Christ, and drinking the Spirit. It is, as we earlier said, *past*, and it is *positive*. But Paul's baptismal use of *dikaioō* is also seen very clearly in 1 Corinthians 6:11 and his liberational use in Galatians 3:24. So these texts allow us to supply this meaning wherever he is using the verb to explicate his own position. And, needless to say, that usage is always unpacking out of Box B to link hands with the transformational gospel articulated in the 90 percent of Paul's texts that lie outside his JT material.

If we grasp the two subtly different ways in which Paul uses the verb *dikaioō* in his JT texts, in terms of whether he is operating within Box A or Box B, things will clarify still further.[9] Ironically, it will no longer be necessary to use the translation "justification," which tends now to do far too much theological work. When *the teachers* speak of "justification" they really do mean that a retributive God judges someone to be righteous—literally, innocent of wrongdoing—and so worthy of salvation. However, when *Paul* speaks of "justification" he means that a compassionate God has set us free from the prison of our sin and from the sentence of death.

But how can we distinguish between these two usages?

As a rough rule of thumb, when Paul uses the verb within the system of his opponents, the teachers, it is future and it means "to declare righteous [or, innocent of all wrongdoing]." The underlying assumption is retributive because the gospel of his opponents, the teachers, assumes a retributive God. When Paul uses the verb to evoke his own gospel, however, it operates

8. Tamez, *The Amnesty of Grace: Justification by Faith from a Latin American Perspective*.

9. We ourselves will be set free from the need to make one translation ("justification") cover both these meanings when really it can't; and we will be released from the need to explain our translation with a theologically loaded sense that shifts away from common English usage and into a realm that needs a book to define it.

in the past, or in the present presupposing a past event, and denotes the transformation of the "ungodly" by the resurrected Jesus. The emphasis here is on a verdict that frees us from jail and from a death sentence, so "released," "set free," and "delivered" are accurate translations. And with these realizations, our second major obstacle to reading Paul's Box B texts constructively, in continuity with his thinking outside his JT texts, has been removed. Our solution remains on track.

Galatians 2:15–16 again

It might be helpful to see how these two major lexical realizations will allow us to grasp Paul's meaning in Galatians 2:15–16 rather more clearly than we possibly did before:

> 15 We who are Jews by birth and not "sinful pagans,"
> 16 who know that a person is not released by doing works
> prescribed by the law
> except also "through the faith" of Jesus Christ,
> even we believed concerning Christ Jesus
> that we are released "through the faith" of Christ
> and *not* by doing the works prescribed by the law—
> [and so we know also][10] that "by works of the law no one will
> be declared righteous."
> (Our translation)

Paul's compact argument now makes excellent sense. Jews like Paul, who were Torah-observant, have encountered Christ, been baptized, and so set free from their sin so that they can taste the presence of the resurrection at work now, even as they continue to shape their lives from the Torah's instructions. It follows from this, however, that the release that has just been experienced comes through Christ *and not* through any Torah-observance that they were undertaking prior to his arrival. In fact, salvation doesn't come about through anything else. It was Christ who made the difference! We are saved and resurrected through Christ and *not* through Torah. Moreover, in the light of this discovery, experienced through Jesus, we can see, as Scripture says, that no one is going to get declared righteous on a putative future day of judgment by undertaking Torah-observance. Again, we get saved through Christ and we have been saved through Christ. There's no need to wait, and there's no need to pursue some other way to salvation.

---

10. We are assuming another ellipse here of information just stated to avoid a clumsy redundancy in the Greek if it is written out in full again.

(That is, you could theoretically still try an alternative route to salvation and resurrection if you wanted to, but Paul would suggest that this is a very bad idea and ultimately won't work. One of the things he has learned as he has been drawn into Christ is just how sinful he is in and of himself.)

If things have clarified vis-à-vis the verb *dikaioō*, one last critical task remains. We will need to make a similar set of clarifications in relation to the cognate noun, "righteousness." This operates in both boxes as well, although in Box B within a distinctive and very famous phrase, "the righteousness of God." We will need to ask if this phrase can unpack into Paul's resurrectional gospel. If it does not, then we will have a problem on our hands. But if it does, then everything that Paul says that presupposes or explains this phrase in his Box B texts will lead us straight to his gospel as he expounds that elsewhere, and our overarching solution will be firmly in place.

The meaning of "the righteousness of God"

As Paul opens the body of his letter to the Romans in 1:16–17, he writes:

> For I am not ashamed of the gospel;
> it is the power of God for salvation to everyone who has faith,
> to the Jew first and also to the Greek.
> For in it the righteousness of God is revealed
> "through faith" for faith;
> as it is written,
> "The righteous one through faith will live."

It seems likely that Paul is again drawing on material from the Scriptures here, specifically the opening of Psalm 98:1b–3:

> [God's] right hand and his holy arm have worked salvation for
> him;
> The LORD has made his salvation known
>   and revealed his righteousness to the nations.
> He has remembered his love and his faithfulness to Israel.
> All the ends of the earth have seen the salvation of our God.
> (NIV)

In this psalm God is described as saving in relation to Jews and pagans (literally, the house of Israel and the nations), and this action is even said to be "revealing" his righteousness to them. There is so much overlap in vocabulary and thought evident here that we can be confident that the language of Psalm 98 is informing Paul's words in Romans 1:16–17. (Note the common use of "righteousness," "salvation," "revelation," "Jews/House of Israel," and

"Greeks/the nations.") And this basic connection helps us to grasp what Paul actually means when he uses the phrase "God's righteousness" or its close equivalent. We can turn to the psalm to mine a much richer vein of information about the special meaning of this distinctive phrase.

When we do so what we find is that his particular psalm, like the distinctive group of psalms to which it belongs, is telling a story about *divine kingship*. The God of Israel is being viewed in these texts as the king or monarch of Israel—a frequent motif in the Old Testament. Hence, the person writing the psalm rejoices as God arrives, in a royal fanfare, with his "right hand and his holy arm" (see verse 2), these being a symbol of a sovereign's power to rule. God is coming like a king in victory and in judgment. Most importantly for our current question, when "righteousness" language occurs in these specific contexts, it is referring to a saving or rescuing activity, and to an associated executive judgment, and so the Jewish Publication Society's translation of this verse in their edition of the Old Testament even renders "righteousness" here as "triumph."

We might ask why the texts are speaking of this act being "right," a connotation that some translators prefer to emphasize by translating the underlying Hebrew or Greek as "righteousness." But something "right" is happening.

Kings have responsibilities as kings in relation to their people, as do queens, and it is "right" when they act accordingly. They have certain specific duties that they need to perform—impartial judgment in court cases, wise rule and decision-making, and, in Israel, godly and pious behavior. But it is also right for a monarch to save their people when the people are in a difficult, and perhaps even in an especially oppressed, situation. In a conflict or a battle in which they are being beaten or oppressed, the monarch's people should be delivered, liberated, and rescued, while their oppressive enemies should be defeated and vanquished. This is the right thing for a monarch to do. And the same goes for the divine monarch. In situations where God's people are in some kind of difficulty or struggle or overwhelming battle, something "right" happens precisely when God rescues them and delivers them.

It might be helpful to note here that God's right activity resonates more clearly here with our contemporary understandings of *executive* as against judicial activity. In modern nation-states, we tend to think of the activities we are describing as being separate branches with distinct spheres of responsibility. Some of us might remember the lyrics from the old *School House Rock* song, "Three Ring Government": "Ring one, Executive, two is

Legislative, that's Congress. Ring three, Judiciary."[11] But in the world of the Bible, the functions of executive, legislative, and judiciary converged in the single figure of the king, because ultimately this person would make executive and judicial decisions. There was only one ring! And so God's righteousness in biblical terminology, by way of texts like Psalm 98, while it often referred to judicial actions, could also refer to the sorts of executive, kingly actions that we find in stories like that of the exodus (see Exod 12–15), the conquests (see Josh 1–12), and the saving of Jerusalem from the Assyrians (see Isa 36–37). These were the right delivering acts of Israel's divine King and here God's righteousness is revealed through God's activity of visiting executive judgment on his people's enemies and liberating his people. And this is the sense that is present in Psalm 98:1–2, which is being taken up again by Paul in Romans 1:17. So it makes the good sense to translate the Greek here as "the *deliverance* of God is being revealed through faith . . . ," the latter being a reference to Jesus's death and resurrection. What could be more plausible than to suggest that Paul is declaring here that God's greatest act of triumph and deliverance is both *accomplished by* and *seen in* the death and resurrection of Jesus?!

Another scriptural connection in Romans might help to solidify this liberational meaning of Paul's critical noun phrase.

We learn in a long passage from Romans 3:9–19, basically that "there is no one who is righteous, not even one" (this being verse 10), a claim that reinforces Paul's basic understanding of the deep problem facing humanity. Something enslaves people to such an extent that everyone has "turned aside; together they become worthless; there is no one who shows kindness; there is not even one" (verse 12). When we move to verse 20 in chapter 3, as Paul's argument draws to a close, he then cites another scriptural passage that we have already met, from Psalm 143. Verse 2 reads: "Do not enter into judgment with your servant, for no one living is righteous before you." This quotation is obvious, occurring both here and in Galatians 2:16, and we have already remarked on the way it confirms the extensive interaction with Jewish Scripture that is going on in Paul's JT texts. But less often noticed is the fact that this psalm also contains several references to God's righteousness. So in the original psalm, in the verse immediately preceding the verse Paul quotes, we read, "Hear my prayer, O LORD, give ear to my supplications in your faithfulness; answer me in your righteousness" (143:1). The psalmist is crying out for help, appealing to God's royal righteousness that rescues his people from some kind of plight. And we see this particular

---

11. Ahrens, "Three Ring Government," schoolhouserock.tv, 1979, http://www.school houserock.tv/ThreeRing.html.

righteous-but-saving dynamic spelled out clearly at the end of the psalm as well: "In your righteousness bring me out of trouble. In your steadfast love cut off my enemies, and destroy all my adversaries, for I am your servant" (98:11b–12).

In Romans 3:20 Paul quotes verse 2 of the psalm to sum up his contention at this point that no one is righteous and everyone is in the grip of sin—an insight that renders all of the teacher's suggestions about salvation by way of obedient law-observance useless. But this same psalm also suggests that some rescue of a trapped and sinful people by way of God's kingly righteousness or deliverance is necessary. And indeed, as we follow Paul immediately into 3:21–22, we read that "the righteousness of God *has* been disclosed," here definitively in Jesus. It is hard to avoid the conclusion that Paul sees Jesus as the physical embodiment of God's royal rescue operation, although this obvious focal point allows us to be even more specific.

God's "triumph" over a rebellious and enslaved cosmos—his kingly "righteousness" that saves and liberates—is for Paul definitively effected by, and revealed through, the events of Easter. In particular, when Jesus rises from the dead he triumphs over the hostile forces of sin and death. So the content of God's "righteousness" for Paul *is Jesus's resurrection*, which is of course just what Paul talks about everywhere else in his Box B texts. This is where and when and how God triumphs definitively over his enemies and sets his oppressed people free.

It seems then, in short, that our solution to the problems generated by JT remains firmly on course.[12] Paul really is continuing to speak in all his Box B texts, *in scripturally mediated language*, of the Easter events, effected by and through Jesus. The faith of Jesus is a reference, by way of Habakkuk 2:4, to his faithfulness to the cross, followed by his resurrection to new life; the verb *dikaioō* speaks of the "judgment" from God that takes place as we participate in this journey, through baptism, and are thereby liberated or released from the prison of our sin and the sentence of death; and "the righteousness of God" evokes the liberating intervention and victory of our divine King, as he delivers us. And with these judgments in place, it remains only to see if they can be sustained through the rest of Paul's key JT texts, to the most important of which we now turn.

What is Paul arguing with respect to the figure of Abraham, "the forefather of us all," in Romans chapter 4? If this argument too unpacks into Paul's resurrectional gospel, then our solution will be all but complete.

---

12. For a more extensive treatment of the "righteousness of God," see Campbell, *The Deliverance of God*, 677–711.

16

Abraham Is on My Side

New expectations[1]

There is a brief silence at Romans 3:20 after Paul's reduction of the teacher's gospel to absurdity, after which he goes on to signal in a compact paragraph (3:21–26) some of the major issues that will be tackled later in the letter—a paragraph we have just spent some time on. We have learned from 3:21–26 that Paul makes his claims vis-à-vis the teacher in scriptural language; moreover, controlling for this texture in his writing, one of his key assertions is that God's own righteous act is a great act of deliverance on our behalf effected through Jesus's "faith[fulness]," and apprehended by all those who have faith, which really means, it is effected through Jesus's obedience that culminated in his death on the cross, followed by his resurrection and ascension.[2] This event revealed God's "triumph" over a sinful cosmos, and his "deliverance" of his people. And it is this event that led to a "judgment" from God over us of release and liberation as we participate in Jesus through baptism and are thereby released from the captivity of our sin and liberated from a sentence of death.

After the programmatic claims of Romans 3:21–26, which resumed the brief but powerful anticipatory statements made 1:16–17, a more direct conversation with the teacher's false gospel takes place from Romans 3:27.

1. For a fuller treatment of Romans chapter 4, see Campbell, *Deliverance of God*, chapter 18.

2. The detailed, and very important, account of how Paul connects our faith to Jesus's faith takes place in relation to our discussion of Romans ch. 10, in chapter 18: see pp. 261–66.

(The last exchange was in 3:1–9a.) And this leads in turn into Paul's famous discussion of Abraham in chapter 4.

Now for JT advocates, Romans chapter 4 is where Paul uses an authoritative illustration from Scripture to explicate his central belief in justification by faith alone and not by works. Understood in these terms, this chapter has been viewed as a towering fortress for the theory's central claims. But we have a rather different understanding of what is going on in Paul's JT texts. So we will need to show in what follows how our non-JT approach can supply a fair reading of this famous section of the letter. Having said this, we would suggest that, freed from the expectations of JT, we can offer a very successful reading of the entire chapter.

As we will see in more detail shortly, while conventional JT readers make good sense of some of the verses in chapter 4, their expectations have marginalized other parts of Paul's argument. The important subsection that leads into Romans 4, namely, 3:27–31, tends to be neglected by JT readers (especially verses 29 to 31), as does the back third of chapter 4, verses 16 to 25, which is a big chunk of material. Liberated from JT's expectations, we will read 3:27—4:25 as a whole and show how the short subsection of 3:27–31 integrates neatly into Paul's ongoing critique of the teacher's gospel, which unfolds through the entirety of chapter 4. In short, we suggest that our non-JT reading of 3:27—4:25 is better than the JT approach; it is closer to Paul's text and makes excellent sense of all of it. Paul's basic claim throughout is, as we might expect, that "Abraham—properly read—supports *my* gospel and not yours." But he runs this thesis through several specific issues before finishing with a compact statement of his resurrectional gospel in verse 25.

Romans 3:27—4:3a: the debate continues

One advantage of being liberated from expectations shaped by JT is immediately apparent when we begin to read 3:27–31. We no longer have to find Paul focusing on one issue here, namely, how Abraham supports the claim that Christians are justified by faith and not by works. We are no longer constrained, that is, by the expectation that Paul must now speak of the transition from Box A to Box B and of nothing else. We are reading Paul's JT texts as a debate between an advocate of a false gospel in Box A, the teacher, and Paul's advocacy of a resurrectional gospel in Box B, by way of a heavy use of Scripture. So what we find from 3:27 onward is that more than one issue is in play, as is usually the case in debates between complex positions. Here several features of the teacher's gospel are compared with Paul's gospel in relation to the authoritative and decisive figure of Abraham, features we have already met before as we processed the unhealthy internal dynamics of the teacher's viewpoint. Paul effectively announces these issues that he is going to revisit now from a scriptural viewpoint rooted in the Torah in a jaunty dialogue that runs from 3:27 through 3:31.

In 3:27 Paul depicts the teacher breaking his silence to ask questions about Paul's gospel (as presented by Box B) that have begun to bother him (as Paul reconstructs the situation) since Paul's declaration in 3:21–26 that this is just how God has acted to save us through Jesus. In the first of three concerns the teacher begins by asking about the place of "boasting."

The teacher: "Then what becomes of boasting?" (3:27a)

Especially since the Reformation, boasting has widely been understood to be a bad thing. If you have heard sermons on Paul it is likely that you will have endured at least one address making sure that you are not being boastful about your salvation.[3] But if we remember that the teacher is a missionary preaching a gospel of works by which someone can glory in their accomplishments, anticipating a declaration of "righteous" on the future day of judgment—a declaration of "well done" by God!—then a concern with boasting by him makes sense. The teacher's entire approach is based on merit. So we can understand why the teacher would be worried that Paul's gospel of Box B has removed the boasting that results from doing good works. It is good to boast about one's accomplishments and to glory in their achievement, he would say. That is what motivates people to try to be good. Who doesn't rightly boast about winning a gold medal at the Olympics? You earned it right?! So the teacher's concern that Paul's approach cuts against this behavior is correct.

Paul: "It is excluded." (3:27a)

Obviously, Paul responds at this moment rather tersely. It simply is the case that Paul's gospel leaves no room for us to boast because from his point of view we have not accomplished anything in and of ourselves to glory in. As he said just a few verses earlier, God's saving activity as the world's righteous monarch has now been revealed through Jesus's faithfulness, quite apart from the Torah, to all who understand (3:22–23). And the offer of salvation made through this activity is a gift (3:24a). We are expected to *respond* to this reality, but we have nothing to brag about since we did nothing to earn it. God did it, not us. So boasting about this gift would be like a

---

3. Paul on occasion uses boasting in a positive sense himself in relation to his own resurrectional gospel; see 5:2–3. But this is very carefully framed.

group of hostages who have been rescued by skilled negotiators proceeding to take all credit for their release. They would have no basis for doing so.

But the teacher follows up quickly.

> The teacher: "Through what kind of teaching [*nomos*]?
> A teaching of works?" (3:27b NRSVue modified)

> Paul: "No, rather through a teaching [*nomos*] based on faith.
> For we hold that a person is released 'through faith'
> apart from works prescribed by the law." (3:27b–28 NRSVue
> modified)

This is another understandable query from the teacher and reveals where his challenge really lies. The teacher is bringing up the issue of Scripture here. A word about Paul's terminology will help us to grasp this issue clearly.

While we have often spoken in what precedes about two gospels, both the teacher and Paul would also have described their programs as "teachings," in Hebrew, *torah(s)*, rooted in the Jewish Scriptures. *Torah* was translated in Paul's day by the Greek word *nomos*, and most English translations of the New Testament go on to render *nomos* in English very unfortunately as "law." *Torah*, along with *nomos* in the right contexts, is really best translated as "teaching." It denotes the sacred teaching handed down to the Jewish people by God at Mount Sinai. So when we read "law" in our Bibles we often should really be reading "sacred teaching" and thinking of the discussion as focusing on the Bible and what it instructs.

Given this insight, we can now see that what the text is really talking about here are two different sets of "teachings" (not two laws). These teachings are of course supposed to be attested to by the Scriptures; we could say that they are Teachings with a capital "T." So doubtless, on the one hand, the teacher is saying that he derives his teaching of works from the Scriptures, and it allows him to boast about his good works, while, on the other hand, Paul claims to being doing just the same thing, although he is teaching about something centered on faith, and he is not supposed to boast. So basically the teacher is challenging Paul to prove how his gospel, which excludes boasting and is centered on faith, is a legitimate teaching from the Scriptures, and he is doubtless going to challenge him to get this teaching from the most important part of the Scriptures for Jews, namely, the first five books, which comprise the teachings of Moses—the *torah* proper! Nothing matched this part of the Tanakh for Jews in authority and centrality.

But in verse 29 the teacher now introduces another related but distinguishable issue. As we have discussed at length, the teacher's gospel summarized in Box A correlates salvation tightly with circumcised males, and this was the mark of being a Jew. So the teacher now expresses a worry that Paul's gospel revealed "apart from the law" and "through faith" has broadened out the boundaries of God's people much too far. For the teacher, God's people are defined by their observance of the Torah, and by their observance of one of its most crucial commandments, circumcision. So he asks:

> The teacher: "Or is [not] God the God of Jews only?!"
> (3:29a NRSVue modified)

Now we can be led astray here if we lapse into the expectations of JT. If we were to position Paul as the person posing this question, then the obvious answer would simply be "No." This would make the question that follows, "Is he not the God of gentiles also?" (3:29a), a repetition of the same basic point, and somewhat redundant. But having been liberated from the constraints of the theory, we can now see with improved clarity just what is going on here.

> The teacher: "Or is [not] God the God of Jews only?!" (3:29a)

> Paul: "Is he not the God of gentiles also?" (3:29a)

The second question here is not a repetition; it is Paul's own quick counter-assertion framed in terms drawn from the Scriptures that the teacher must accept. Paul's rejoinder will be filled out much more when we move into Romans chapter 4, but for now it elicits a concession from the teacher based on the important principle of a God who sovereignly rules over all his creatures.[4] The Bible is very clear that God is a universal God who presides over the cosmos as its creator. So the teacher responds, probably rather reluctantly, yet unavoidably:

> The teacher: "Yes, [he is God] of the gentiles also." (3:29b)

Paul now builds on this concession in verse 30, which we paraphrase here as follows.

> Paul: "If God is one, or unified
> —the God who will deliver the circumcised 'through faith'—
> then it follows that he will also deliver the uncircumcised
> 'through that same faith.'" (3:30)[5]

---

4. Paul picks up on and elaborates this principle more fully in Rom 9.

5. This is extremely tricky grammar in Greek. A complete conditional statement is possibly never supplied—although an unusual but possible meaning of *kai*, usually

The unity of God is as clearly attested by the Scriptures as his sovereign rule over all the cosmos. So Paul has now fashioned a quick rebuttal to the teacher's challenge. It is reasonable, he says, to expect God to be acting in a unified way in relation to both Jews and pagans since he is the cosmic ruler of both and he is a single, unitary God—a God who is One. Paul's point will be missed if we fail to catch the echo of Habakkuk 2:4 though. Read as a reference to the Messiah, Paul's point here using the language of this Scripture in particular is that both Jews and gentiles are delivered because of the faithful Christ's journey to death and his subsequent resurrection to new life.[6] It follows from this then that the verse as a whole is suggesting that the unified God has acted in a unified way over all of humanity, which he created and rules—so why restrict the boundaries of salvation to the circumcised?

Paul has now effectively rebuffed the teacher's commitment to the idea that salvation is limited to circumcised Jews. Jesus saves everyone and in some critical relation to faith. But the teacher now poses a third concern, and it is an entirely understandable charge. We come now to the heart of the matter:

> The teacher: "Do we then overthrow the Torah through this faith?" (3:31a NRSVue modified)

This makes sense if we grasp how the discussion of the Scriptures and their testimony is now focusing down here on Torah in the narrower sense. As we noted earlier on, the teacher, like all Jews, regarded the first five books of the Bible, handed down personally to Moses on Mount Sinai, as especially authoritative. So the issue being introduced here is the concern that Paul's emphasis on Christ's faithful death and resurrection decenters the Torah, meaning the Pentateuch, in a way that is inappropriate, and it is quite fair to ask this question. Indeed, many Jews continue to ask it. "What happens to the Torah?" "What happens to all the things that it tells us to do?" "Won't your teaching just gut it out almost entirely?" Paul's teaching about faith does not seem to represent what the Torah is talking about for most of the time. So the teacher is really just asking, are we eviscerating the teachings

---

translated "and," might be in play here: "the apodotic *kai*"—and Paul's wording trails off: "If indeed the one God, who will deliver the circumcision through fidelity, will also deliver the uncircumcision through that fidelity. . . ." But if an elided *estin* ("is") is supplied to the initial claim of God's unity ("If God [is] one . . .") then the entire sentence makes sense, as paraphrased above for the sake of clarity.

6. The use of an arthrous *pistis* ("faith"/"fidelity") phrase here accords with the function of the article back in 3:25 and resumes an earlier phrase using the same noun, which is itself anarthrous, because it is reproducing an anarthrous scriptural text (i.e., *ek pisteōs*) and applying it to Jesus.

of Moses if we follow your strange emphasis on the faithful One and those who have faith within him?

Paul will of course have several things to say about this in due course. But for now he simply responds vigorously, and rather boldly:

> Paul: "By no means! On the contrary, we uphold the Torah!"
> (3:31b NRSVue modified)

We will have to read on for a bit though to find out just how Paul makes his case in detail. And in fact, the text now moves into chapter 4, and reveals where this discussion has always been going.

The star witness: Abraham

The teacher now appeals to a key authority figure for both himself and Paul as Jews, namely, Abraham. Abraham is the father of the Jews, their great ancestral patriarch, and his life, and his journey with God, are recounted in the Torah in the book of Genesis. Clearly then what Abraham demonstrates there about the true nature of Judaism is authoritative. But it is also authoritative for any converts from paganism to Judaism, as Abraham was the first original convert who started it all off. Abraham began life as a pagan. God called him into relationship in "Ur of the Chaldees," and then presided over his generation of the children of Israel. So we learn now that the three issues we just mentioned will all be explored in relation to Abraham, and, unsurprisingly, Paul will deploy texts from his life as recounted in the Pentateuch to show how they support his gospel and not the teacher's. In this way he will make good on the claim that he made in 3:21–22.

> 21 But now,
> apart from Torah-observance,
> the righteousness of God has been disclosed,
> *being attested to by the Torah* and the Prophets—
> 22 a righteousness of God [disclosed]
> through the faith of Jesus Christ
> to all who believe.
> (Rom 3:21–22 NRSVue modified)

But how does Paul find Jesus and the resulting gospel that he preaches to the pagans in the Torah? It is not easy. Jesus is much easier to find predicted in the Prophets. But then Paul is a very skilled exegete, as we will see through the rest of Romans 4.

This chapter has three subsections that run through the three issues that the teacher has just introduced—the exclusion of boasting and works, the broadening of the circle of salvation beyond the circumcised to uncircumcised pagans, and an upholding as against a negating of the Torah—all of which are proved, in favor of Paul's position, by appealing to Abraham, the great forefather of the Jewish people. (A fourth issue, beginning in verse 16, then heads off an obvious but difficult objection to Paul's unfolding contentions; we will discuss this in due course.)

Romans 4:1–2: the teacher makes another foolish statement

In verse 1 of chapter 4, the teacher himself introduces Abraham as the star witness from the Torah to expand on the three challenges he has made in 3:27–31, although, characteristically, he is *again* shooting himself in the foot (at least as Paul portrays the argument).

> The teacher: "What then are we to say was gained by Abraham,
> our ancestor according to the flesh?
> For if Abraham was justified by works, he *has* something to
> boast about."
> (Rom 4:1–2a, emphasis added)

The teacher is obviously positioning Abraham on his own side straightaway, supporting his gospel's account of a future declaration from God of "righteous" based on merit and deeds. This sort of approach to salvation—as to anything else—justifies boasting when someone has accumulated or achieved merit successfully, so these two motifs are linked tightly together. And it is only fair to note that the teacher is appealing to a common reading of Abraham by Jews in Paul's day when he does this. Many if not all Jews venerated Abraham and held that he was a perfectly righteous figure. He was fully righteous, justified by his works, and so he could boast. Hence, the teacher makes a quite understandable appeal to Abraham as someone who was declared righteous by God because of his works.

But Paul is quick to step in and to counter this.

> Paul: "But not before God! For what does the scripture say . . . ?"
> (Rom 4:2b–3a)

It should be noted before we go any further that we basically agree with much of the conventional JT reading of verses 2 to 8 of this text at a literal level. Much like our analysis of Romans 1:18—3:20 showed, the conventional reading by JT advocates is highly accurate at the level of Paul's words and sentences; it just tends not to grasp the overarching arguments Paul is making (and occasionally it has to add a little too much information to the text to make JT fit what Paul wrote). But there is one detail in verse 3 (and again in verse 5) that does need to be sorted out for us to gain a more precise grasp on Paul's argument.

In verse 3b we read in the NRSVue,

> "Abraham believed God,
> and it was reckoned [Gk. *elogisthē*] to him
> as [Gk. *eis*] righteousness."[7]

The Greek word *elogisthē* translated here as "reckoned," or sometimes in other translations as "counted," might suggest some process of "viewing." And it can mean this. "I reckon you will be able to jump over that fence" we might say, meaning "I think or consider it probable that you will be able to jump over that fence." So JT readers will sometimes take this text as suggesting that God *views* or *considers* Abraham (and later us) as in some sense righteous. God *considers* Abraham *as* righteous. But it is better to read this word in context as "credited." (We will say why shortly.) In this more limited, concrete sense the verb denotes a financial arrangement, within which money is simply transferred to someone. Usually people have done something to get the money—to earn it—although not necessarily. There might be a promise to do something in the future that will earn it, or a generous patron might simply gift money to a client. We suggest that the verse is best translated utilizing this specific financial meaning and so like this:

> Abraham believed God,
> and this belief was credited to his benefit—
> with righteousness.
> (Rom 4:3b our translation)

Now usually we do think of "crediting" in relation to something that has been earned through work, perhaps in advance, and Paul knows this, but he makes it clear immediately that God is doing something very different with crediting here in this story.

> Now to the one who works,
> wages are not credited as a gift but as an obligation.
> However, to the one who does not work but trusts God who
> delivers the ungodly,

---

7. The expression here at the end of verse 3b, *eis dikaiosunēn*, is a Semitism that overlies a simple accusative, as the standard grammar BDAG notes—a construction that occurs in verse 6. Consequently, the NRSVue and NIV lead their readers astray by translating it ". . . *as* righteousness." It is rather difficult for the Greek *eis* to mean "as." Our reading, ". . . *with* deliverance," makes much more sense in relation to the underlying Semitism *and* Paul's crediting language that we will talk about shortly.

their faith is credited as deliverance.
(Rom 4:4–5 NRSVue modified)

Paul says here quite clearly that if someone works, he receives his wages as an obligation, and not out of sheer generosity or benevolence. A manager will credit them their wages. (Note, workers clearly do not have their wages "viewed" or "considered" to them in accordance with an obligation—this makes no sense—so concrete financial crediting is clearly what is being talked about here.) But for Paul and his gospel God does not behave in this way. An act of giving to those who do not strictly deserve it is in view here, and not an action of giving in relation to deserving and earning. This is just what the text says. Those who believe, and not those who "work" or "earn," receive deliverance. So it seems that in God's economy something is simply given to people as they trust in him without working or earning, and it is just as well because in this way God can gift important things to sinners who are undeserving. Thus, Paul points out fairly that the Torah here, in this verse, clearly disavows any notion of works as the basis of God's activity of gifting deliverance to Abraham.

The psalmist that Paul quotes after this in verses 7 to 8 provides him with further scriptural support that God's crediting of deliverance occurs apart from works and hence apart from any desert or merit. Paul's argument here depends on the Jewish exegetical principle that links two texts together because of their sharing of a word, here "credited." So the verse from Psalm 32 makes the same point as Genesis 15:6, although in the opposite direction. Abraham is given something positive undeservingly whereas in the psalm David speaks of someone *not* being given something negative despite deserving it. But the basic point is the same. God is not acting in relation to what someone has earned or deserved. A gifting is taking place that is not correlated with works.

> Blessed are those whose iniquities are forgiven
>   and whose sins are covered;
> blessed is the one against whom the Lord will not reckon sin.
> (Rom 4:7–8)

So it is first blood to Paul in the debate between him and the teacher over the nature of salvation as attested by Abraham. Abraham is *not* treated by God in accordance with works and desert in Genesis 15:6, and so works-based achievement and any boasting about this are excluded, as Paul earlier claimed in 3:27. Rather, we see here the importance of trust. God has written a divine check, as it were, to the patriarch, that was not worked for or earned, which is a devastating blow to the teacher's gospel in Box A.[8] God relates to us by *giving* to us, and not by *rewarding* us.

But now, as in 3:29–30, another question arises. The teacher thinks that even God's gifts will be given to a people who are marked out by circumcision. And this is, after all, what God eventually says to Abraham. So Paul turns to consider the practice of circumcision as that took place in the life of their illustrious forefather.

Do we have to get circumcised?

Throughout verses 9 through 12 Paul makes the simple argument that God's deliverance was promised to Abraham in relation to his trusting, as attested by Genesis 15:6, and this trust took place well in advance of circumcision, although a little knowledge of the Pentateuch will be needed for any understanding of what Paul is getting at here. Paul is obviously leaning heavily on Genesis 15:6 in his argument, where God appears to Abraham and makes a series of extravagant promises. The text then speaks of how Abraham responded with faith and was gifted with "righteousness." In Genesis 17, which obviously comes later than Genesis 15, God reappears to Abraham, making further promises, and instructs him to circumcise himself and the male members of his household. This ritual is then a sign of the covenant. He also renames Abram at this time as Abraham, "the father of many nations."

Now most Jews have understandably taken Genesis 17 as filling out the arrangement first made in Genesis 15 (and before that in Genesis 12). But there is a gap here in the story. So it is technically fair of Paul to point out that the promises were made to Abraham in advance of the covenant of circumcision, and were initially responded to simply by faith. A considerable amount of time actually elapsed in Abraham's life between the two events. In Genesis 16:16, some time after the giving of the promises in chapter 15, he is eighty-six. In 17:1, when the covenant of circumcision is given, he is ninety-nine (and in 21:5, when Isaac is born, he is one hundred).

---

8. We could also note at this point that Abraham does not recapitulate JT's expected journey from works, which fail and lead to the realization of sin, to faith in God/Jesus. For that theory to be correct Abraham would need to witness to just this journey from Box A to Box B, especially considering that this is a key text for JT. Abraham should learn that he is a sinner before he is justified. He should journey from anxiety and despair to hope and joy. But there is no journey from sin to faith in the text, and Paul never says that Abraham *himself* was ungodly, or that he first gazed upon his sinful life and despaired. (And later, we will see that this is exactly what did *not* happen.) So it is only when we recognize the debate between Paul and the teacher, freeing ourselves from the strictures of JT, that we can interpret exactly what the text says.

So he is faithful, without being circumcised, for at least fifteen years. Note, Paul's argument in these verses in Romans is that "righteousness" is given to Abraham in *both* the uncircumcised *and* the circumcised state, hence he can technically be the father of both types of later believers. So it is important to see that Paul does not exclude Jewish believers here, and he also makes room for circumcision as a sign of the covenant. But believing pagans do not carry this precious sign in their bodies. They believe and are gifted with deliverance, like Abram was in Genesis 15, while messianic Jews believe and are gifted with deliverance in their circumcised state, like Abraham was in Genesis 17. There is room for both groups and both groups can be said to be copying Abraham in some sense.

> Is this blessing, then, pronounced only on the circumcised
> or also on the uncircumcised?
> We say, "Faith was credited to Abraham with deliverance."
> When then was it credited to him?
> Was it before or after he had been circumcised?
> It was not after but before he was circumcised.
> He received the sign of circumcision as a seal of the deliverance
> that he had by faith while he was still uncircumcised.
> The purpose was to make him the ancestor of all who believe
> without being circumcised
> and who thus have deliverance credited to them,
> and likewise the ancestor of the circumcised
> who are not only circumcised but follow in the footsteps of the
> faith
> that our ancestor Abraham had before he was circumcised.
> (Rom 4:9–12 NRSVue modified)

This reading of Abraham gives Paul another technical victory over the teacher because it shows how their shared forefather prefigures both the uncircumcised and the circumcised Jesus-followers who have been gifted with God's deliverance in relation to their fidelity. However, it follows from this, more controversially, that pagans do not need to be circumcised in order to receive God's promised salvation, and that salvation does not need to be restricted to the circle of those who are circumcised. But Paul also does something a little strange here with the meaning of circumcision.

He redefines it in terms of a "seal." Circumcision would have been considered a "sign" of involvement within God's covenant people by most of the Jews in his day because this word is in the scriptural text, in Genesis 17; and in fact circumcision was *the* sign of the covenant made by God then with Abraham and his posterity. However, Paul qualifies this function by suggesting that circumcision is a seal or a stamp. "Seals" confirm something that is already established on other grounds. So ancient figures sealed or stamped goods that had been purchased, and Paul himself speaks repeatedly of the way that the Spirit seals Jesus-followers, marking them as God's possession before his return in glory and the final acquisition of his purchased property (so to speak). By using the word "seal" then Paul is saying that the prior, more fundamental state in Jesus-followers that the sign of circumcision "seals" is their *faith* (which is really another seal or stamp on their life within the faithful Jesus). So here Paul affirms the primary importance of the underlying state of being in Christ, which is denoted by the presence of faith—at which moment we see how the circumstantial arguments of Romans 4 continue to unpack into the participatory and resurrectional gospel.[9]

It is 2-0 to Paul—at least as he is setting things up! But what about the third challenge introduced in Romans 3:27–31? Paul addresses this in relation to Abraham from verse 13.

Does "faith" undermine or uphold the Torah?

In the light of Genesis 15:6, Paul is also able to counter the teacher's suggestion that his gospel eviscerates or negates the Torah, although, once again, it is important to appreciate how reasonable the teacher's concern is. Paul is a long way away from affirming most of the things that the Pentateuch seems to talk about. Where are all the instructions for holy living that run from Exodus 20 through the entirety of the book of Leviticus to Numbers 10? All the laws about blood and purity and food and communal behavior—the teachings that rabbis later expanded into the sixty-three volumes of the Talmud—seem to have been left to one side. Paul's gospel seems to be gutting most of the important things the Pentateuch says out of the picture entirely, and the teacher simply names this shocking fact.

But Paul rejects this suggestion and reverses it. Anyone who tries to detach the inheritance of the future world from faith is eviscerating the Torah, he asserts rather boldly. And this does follow from what he has already said, at least technically. If the terms of the later inheritance promised to Abraham and his descendants are changed, so that only those who are observing the Torah are heirs, then it is the original promise made to those who have faith that has been eviscerated, and this promise is a part of the Torah. Resisting this later switch in terms is therefore the only thing that

9. The detailed, and very important, account of how Paul connects our faith to Jesus's faith takes place in relation to our discussion of Romans ch. 10, in chapter 18: see pp. 261–66.

continues to uphold the Torah and what it says in this early verse. However paradoxically, to uphold the integrity of the Torah as prophetic Scripture, that speaks of an inheritance in the world to come which arrives in relation to faith, that inheritance must not be narrowed down and connected only to those who later observe the Torah as a teaching.

> For the promise that he would inherit the world
> did not come to Abraham or to his descendants through the
> Torah
> but through the deliverance of faith.
> For if it is the adherents of the Torah who are to be the heirs,
> faith is null and the promise is void. . . .
> For this reason the promise depends on faith, in order that it
> may rest on grace,
> so that it may be guaranteed to all his descendants.
> (Rom 4:13–16a NRSVue modified)

Now many Jews, and even many modern Bible interpreters *per se*, do not find Paul's claims here that convincing. Reducing what the Pentateuch says to one early verse is a risky business. But in terms of the way that Scripture was understood in his own time, Paul is not doing something unfair. Rabbis could place a huge amount of emphasis on one verse, and would take what it said with the utmost seriousness. And it might be helpful to recall at this moment, further, that Paul is not just making an argument on this basis alone. As we will see in more detail shortly, he is reading Scripture in this way because of the amazing reality that has burst in upon him—the risen Christ and the outpoured Spirit. Faith for Paul points toward Easter, speaking especially of Jesus's faithful walk to the cross. So Genesis 15:6 is a prefiguration of the way that God has sent his Son to die and to rise for us, and through that event, to resurrect us all. *That* is something that upholds the entire point of the Torah, and not a set of rules, irrespective of how helpful and inspired the latter might be. We need to hang on to this, Paul would have said (and this point of view will become still clearer later on when we read what he says in chapter 10).

Paul also makes a couple of short points here in 4:15 concerning the Torah working wrath (presumably the wrath of God), and we suggest that here Paul is again anticipating later arguments in Romans.

> For the Torah brings wrath.
> Only where there is no Torah is there no transgression.
> (Rom 4:15 NRSVue modified)

Paul discusses the Torah at great length in Romans 7:7—8:1, arguing there that Torah-observance *by itself* can create a situation that the power of Sin can exploit to introduce Death. This dynamic goes back to Adam in the garden of Eden (so see also Rom 5:12–14) and is endemic to human-kind. It is only when we have left this entire world behind, with all its flesh, rules, sins, curses, evil, powers, and death, that we no longer transgress. Obedience to God is only possible in the new reality inaugurated by Christ through his faithfulness and resurrection and entered by the Spirit. It is this new state then, somewhat counterintuitively, without Torah (because it is beyond Torah), that upholds the Torah and its larger promise of life, and allows humanity to fulfill God's expectations (see 1 Cor 7:19). But when we live out of the flesh that is rooted in the old world, instead of the new reality, which the teacher's gospel of works appears to recommend, then we eviscerate the Torah because we are then vulnerable to the manipulations of evil powers and our lusts, and we transgress and sin. God's anger is rightly elicited. There are lots of reasons then, once one presses into Paul's gospel, for claiming that "faith" upholds the Torah, while a primary dependence on works and rule-observance eviscerates it.

When we reach the end of 4:15, the three challenges put to Paul by the teacher in 3:27–31 have been rebutted in the light of the authoritative example of Abraham. By leaning into Genesis 15:6, Paul has shown his Roman audience that boasting of achievements on the basis of deeds or works is indeed excluded; God's deliverance is a generous gift correlated only with faith. Moreover, circumcision is not mandatory and the circle of God's deliverance is not limited to the Jewish people (although it is certainly meant to include them). Finally, maintaining the connection between God's promised deliverance and faith upholds the Torah in both a narrower and a broader sense. It respects this text and does not overrule it. And it affirms its all-important covenantal promises to the Jews of life by upholding the solution God ultimately offers to the problems of sin and death through the events of Easter.

But chapter 4 is not done yet. A powerful argument—essentially one sentence—runs to verse 22 that we now need to consider. This section of Paul's argument has long baffled JT and non-JT readers alike. Will we be able to make sense of it finally with our new angle of approach? It would certainly be a feather in our exegetical cap if we can do so.

17

Paul's Great Statement of Faith

The subsection of Romans 4 beginning in verse 16b and extending through verse 22 is often neglected by JT advocates. And with good reason. The account of trust in God that we see developed here by Paul in relation to Abraham is so extraordinary that it is simply not a realistic action for a sinful human to undertake in order to transfer from an unsaved to a saved state, which is to say, from Box A to Box B. If this is what Paul thinks faith is—and if faith is what we must generate for ourselves in order to be justified—then we are all doomed. No one can match Abraham's heroic faithfulness as it is described here. Much better then for JT advocates to brush this subsection of chapter 4 under the carpet and to move on.

But even if JT advocates do not really know what to do with Romans 4:16b–22, we still need to ask what Paul is getting at here. It is the longest account of faith that he ever gives us. So why does he write the following, strangely extended sentence with its dramatic portrayal of Abraham's faith?

> [Therefore the promises to Abraham are given] . . .
> not only to the adherents of the Torah
> but also to those who live by means of the faith of Abraham,
> who is the father of all of us,
> as it is written, "I have made you the father of many nations"
> [Gen 17:5]
> in the presence of which saying he trusted the God who gives
> life to the dead
> and calls into existence the things that do not exist.
> Hoping against hope, he trusted that he would become "the
> father of many nations,"

according to what was said, "So shall your descendants be"
[Gen 15:5].
He did not weaken in trust when he considered his own body,
which was already as good as dead (for he was about a hundred
years old),
and the barrenness of Sarah's womb.
No distrust made him waver concerning the promise of God,
but he grew strong in his trust as he gave glory to God,
being fully convinced that God was able to do what he had
promised.
Therefore "it was credited to his benefit with deliverance" [Gen
15:6].
(Rom 4:16b–22 our translation)

As always, we need to attend carefully to the subtle shifts in the discussion, and especially as Paul frequently gestures here toward different parts of Abraham's story as that is recounted in the book of Genesis. Paul has carefully intercalated elements together here from Genesis 15 and 17 even as he looks toward Genesis 21.

Every time that Paul mentions "faith" or something similar like "believing" he is referencing Abraham's behavior (strictly speaking, Abram's) as recounted in Genesis chapter 15, where Abraham believes in God. Faith—translated here often as "trust," as is appropriate in context—is mentioned five times in this paragraph, and in the negative once more, before Genesis 15:6 is quoted in verse 22—a total of seven references in one sentence. Paul also notes one of the promises that God made to Abraham in Genesis 15 in verse 18b ("So shall your descendants be"), generating eight allusions to the story in this early chapter in total. This saying points explicitly toward the way in which the biologically childless Abraham would nevertheless, according to God, ultimately father a great nation with descendants as numerous as the grains of sand on the shore and the stars in the sky.

[Therefore the promises to Abraham are given] . . .
not only to the adherents of the Torah
but also to those who live by means of the **faith** of Abraham,
who is the father of all of us,
as it is written, "I have made you the father of many nations"
[Gen 17:5]
in the presence of which saying **he trusted** the God who gives
life to the dead
and calls into existence the things that do not exist.
Hoping against hope, **he trusted** that he would become "the
father of many nations,"

according to what was said, **"So shall your descendants be"**
[Gen 15:5].
He did not weaken in **trust** when he considered his own body,
which was already as good as dead (for he was about a hundred
years old),
and the barrenness of Sarah's womb.
No **distrust** made him waver concerning the promise of God,
but he grew strong in his **trust** as he gave glory to God,
being fully convinced that God was able to do what he had
promised.
Therefore **"it was credited to his benefit with deliverance"**
[Gen 15:6].
(Rom 4:16b–22 our translation)

But the story told in Genesis 15 is woven tightly together by Paul here
with the very similar story told in Genesis 17 that we have already noted in
relation to issue two and circumcision. At that later time God reappeared to
Abram and reaffirmed the promises of numerous descendants. So emphatic
was this promise God renamed Abram *as* Abraham, which literally means
"father of many peoples." And this was also the moment when God asked
Abraham and all his male companions to be circumcised as a sign of this
special arrangement. Every time Paul speaks in Romans 4 then of Abraham
being the "father of many nations" or something similar he is referencing
the episode in Genesis 17; this motif comes up directly three times, and is
central to several other statements by direct implication.

[Therefore the promises to Abraham are given] . . .
not only to the adherents of the Torah
but also to those who live by means of the faith of Abraham,
who is **the father of all of us**,
as it is written, **"I have made you the father of many nations"**
[Gen 17:5]
in the presence of which saying he trusted the God who gives
life to the dead
and calls into existence the things that do not exist.
Hoping against hope, he trusted that he would become **"the
father of many nations,"** according to what was said, "So shall
your descendants be" [Gen 15:5].
He did not weaken in trust when he considered his own body,
which was already as good as dead (for he was about a hundred
years old),
and the barrenness of Sarah's womb.
No distrust made him waver concerning the promise of God,
but he grew strong in his trust as he gave glory to God,

being fully convinced that God was able to do what he had
promised.
Therefore "it was credited to his benefit with deliverance" [Gen
15:6].
(Rom 4:16b–22, our translation)

At the climax of the entire presentation, Paul then references Genesis
21, when the first miraculous fulfillment of the covenantal promises made
in chapters 15 and 17 took place—the birth of Isaac.

Throughout his long sentence Paul emphasizes that the promises made
in Genesis 15 and 17 could not be fulfilled without God performing this
great miracle. Two very old people well past the age of childbearing had to
conceive and to give birth to a healthy little boy, who then had to give birth
to surviving offspring in turn.[1] Paul portrays this event deliberately here
with resurrectional language. God had to call something that did not exist
into existence, and to bring life from the dead, in this case, the "death" of
Abraham's loins and of Sarah's womb. The Bible portrays this event as happening a short although indeterminate time after the promises of Genesis
17. But Paul then links this situation constantly with Abraham's response
of faith, which happened much earlier in time according to Genesis 15 and
16. He draws a detailed picture in one long sentence of Abraham receiving promises from God before the age of eighty-six, of trusting in those,
of receiving those promises again at the age of ninety-nine, of continuing
to trust, and of that unwavering and extraordinary belief continuing right
through to the miraculous birth of Isaac, by which time Abraham is one
hundred. So why does Paul introduce this dramatic tale and tell it so carefully in these terms?

We suggest that he does so to forestall an obvious objection to much of
his argument up to this point that could made by his opponent, the teacher.

In two of his earlier arguments—responding to challenges two and
three—Paul has used the early location of Genesis 15:6 to override any mandatory use of Genesis 17 against him by the teacher. Abraham received the
promises in Genesis 15 and trusted in them *before* he received the command
to circumcise, and so he can be the father of *both* those who believe and
are uncircumcised *and* those who believe and are circumcised. Similarly, if
Torah-observance, as Moses later laid that out at Sinai, is mandatory in order to receive the promises then this earlier arrangement is eviscerated; we
uphold the Torah by continuing to insist on the significance of Abraham's

1. Paul's view, like the Bible's at this moment, is patriarchal, with inheritance focused on male heirs. But the point we suggest remains exactly the same if we shift Paul's
language into a female modality and presuppose matriarchy, or simply move it into a
gender-neutral mode altogether.

first great act of faith and resisting any qualification of that by later instructions. Again, it is the earlier reception of the promises that makes the argument work.

But the teacher can now respond as follows: the *fulfillment* of all those earlier promises took place through the birth of Isaac. And this is recounted *later*, in Genesis 21, well after Genesis 15, with Genesis 17 coming in between these two events. So the teacher can say that God deliberately added in Genesis 17 and the covenant of circumcision before the first installment of the promises, which took place in Genesis 21, and those instructions are still therefore clearly mandatory. Abraham was justified by works and certainly circumcised well before God fulfilled his promise of uncountable offspring by way of the birth of Isaac.

Now this is a powerful objection. And it makes sense of what Paul is doing here in Romans 4:16b–22 (while nothing else really does). The teacher has made a really good argument here. How does Paul handle it?

Well, did you notice this problem as Paul covered the territory from Genesis 15 through Genesis 17 to Genesis 21 in this single, powerful sentence? Did you pick up as you worked your way through its serried clauses that circumcision as instructed in Genesis 17 was a key intermediate step? Of course not! Circumcision just slipped out of sight. And this is exactly what Paul wanted you to do. You were entirely focused on Abraham's extraordinary faith, which began in Genesis chapter 15, continued through Genesis 17, and was vindicated in Genesis 21. This faith was obviously what really mattered, even in the midst of Genesis 17. How incredibly impressive it was! And how foolish to suppose that anything else crucial was really involved—anything as trivial as circumcision, which was merely a seal on that faith!

Paul's contention here might at first glance seem a little forced and perhaps even unpersuasive. Once we notice what is going on we might be tempted to side with the teacher and to reintroduce the significance of circumcision as the Bible itself does. But Paul's story will make more sense as we consider the final three verses he writes in the chapter where we begin to see clearly just what underlies Paul's deep convictions about faith and the significance of Genesis 15:6—provided we resist the straitjacket that JT readers would try to wrap us in and grasp instead the layers in Paul's complex argument here accurately.

Romans 4:23–25:Paul's conclusion and transition

At first glance, verses 23 to 25 just pull the implications of Paul's arguments through to the present by way of an analogy between Jesus-followers and Abraham.

> Now the words, "it was credited to his benefit,"
> were written not for his sake alone
> but for ours also.
> It [i.e., deliverance] will be reckoned to us
> who trust in him who raised Jesus our Lord from the dead,
> who was handed over for our trespasses
> and was raised for our deliverance.
> (Our translation)

We have just been hearing for some time about how Abraham trusted God in relation to his son, Isaac, who was in effect raised to life from the dead—the death, that is, of Abraham's loins and of Sarah's womb. And so Paul simply seems to be saying here that in like manner we trust God in relation to God's Son, Jesus, who was delivered up to death and then raised to life. In this way we can still walk in the footsteps of "our forefather Abraham," essentially copying his pattern of believing as anticipated way back in the first book of the Bible, and ultimately receive a resurrectional deliverance like him as well.

Now Paul definitely wants to say this. He does want us walking by faith in the footsteps of Abraham, trusting steadfastly in God who one day will gift us with resurrectional life. But JT advocates might lead us to understand this analogy in an unhelpful way. Basically, they leave the analogy in this "thin" state, in just these terms. And this would suggest that we copy Abraham and that is the end of it. He believed and received life from the dead, in his case Isaac, and we, like him, believe in God and hopefully receive life from the dead eventually as well. He is an example to us and we just copy him. But some nasty problems will emerge if we leave things at this simple level, suggesting that there is more to this analogy than first meets the eye. The detection of one important problem will suffice to open this approach up to some expansion.

We have already spent a little time thinking about how extraordinary the depiction of Abraham's faith was in verses 17 to 21. It was unwavering, rock solid, and this in the face of biological impossibilities. There was not a moment of doubt but just a steadfast waxing in confidence—that God would make an impossibly old man a father by way of an impossibly old woman. And this steadfast faith continued, implacably, for over thirteen years and

possibly for rather longer. But who can maintain their faith in God in relation to something utterly impossible for over thirteen years without a single
moment of doubt? Most of us couldn't maintain that posture for thirteen
hours, assuming we were able to believe at this level at all. And yet this is
the picture of faith that Romans 4 supplies us with. The *strength* of this faith
is exceptional, and not something that sinners like us and you can conjure
up for ourselves. But there is a figure who did display this level of steadfast,
steely endurance—who did not waver in unbelief for a moment, despite the
suffering and death that lay before him, but gave glory to God. Jesus! And if
Jesus possessed this faith, we can grow into this faith as he gifts it to us and
we learn to walk in this way with the encouragement of the Holy Spirit. In
short, the extraordinary faith that Paul depicts in relation to Abraham suggests that Jesus lies behind his portrait as the only human being who could
possibly share this level of fidelity.

And all of this suggests broadening out Paul's analogy in the chapter's
final verses with one more set of relationships—the faith of Jesus himself in
his heavenly Father. When we supply this third story of faith, we head off
a nasty problem, and we take very seriously his final words in the chapter.[2]

Paul focuses in verses 24 and 25 on Jesus, and we can detect in the allusions he is making here to Isaiah 53 that he is pointing toward the way Jesus
offered himself up faithfully on our behalf and was resurrected in a stunning
act of deliverance that was foreshadowed in the miraculous conception of
Isaac.

> [Jesus] . . .was handed over for our trespasses
> and was raised for our deliverance." (Our translation)

And in the light of this we can now introduce an important clarification to
the way Paul is treating Scripture.

Paul has not been relying just on the exact wording and placement
of Genesis 15:6 in all the arguments that precede these verses, as well as
emphasizing the faith that the text speaks of once slightly inappropriately
as he pulls it through Genesis 17 as far as the birth of Isaac in Genesis 21.
He is hitting faith hard like this because he *already* knows that Jesus himself
walked faithfully to his death on the cross before being raised up to resurrection life and heavenly enthronement. The events of Easter have shown
Paul how God acts and he is now seeing that story in other parts of the
Bible—here right back at the inception of Israel in the story of the patriarch
Abraham. Putting things a little more technically we would say that Paul is

---

2. The detailed, and very important, account of how Paul connects our faith to Jesus's faith takes place in relation to our discussion of Romans ch. 10, in chapter 18: see
pp. 261–66.

reading Scripture here with a Christological hermeneutic. More prosaically we might say that he is wearing glasses with Jesus-colored lenses through which he is reading the Bible. They reveal the great truth that the Scriptures have always been pointing toward.

As we close out this discussion we should also emphasize how the resurrection of Jesus has re-emerged as a critical event within Paul's gospel with a powerful, saving function. It has an overtly saving function in 4:25, and so our reading now links up nicely with the transformational and resurrectional material that drives Paul's thinking elsewhere for 90 percent of the time. This eschatological event revealed in Christ delivers humanity, and it is anticipated within the life of Abraham at the inception of Israel. Small wonder then that for Paul it was *these* events that fulfilled the Torah. The precious promises conveyed by the Torah are certainly fulfilled through the dramatic events that unfolded—and still unfold—through Jesus. This is where all of God's promises are really fulfilled.

> For the Son of God, Jesus Christ,
> whom we proclaimed among you,
> Silvanus and Timothy and I,
> was not "Yes and No,"
> but in him it has always been "Yes."
> For in him every one of God's promises is a "Yes."
> (2 Cor 1:19–20a)

It is a critical shortcoming on the part of JT that it has no room for the saving significance of the resurrection. All that needs to be done for salvation is effected in this model through an exchange between the Father and Son on the cross, by way of penal substitution. The resurrection is either an apologetic moment that "proves" Christ was the Son of God, or it is a vindication that declares Christ "in the right" before God. But neither of these approaches make sense of 4:25, where Christ's resurrection is clearly liberating and saving humanity. This is a final critical insight into Paul's thinking that we very much need to hang on to. The resurrection of Jesus does critical saving and transformational work for Paul—and does so here, at the conclusion of the one of JT's key texts. It is a final sign that the JT model is not getting Paul right.

In sum then, we have now shown how our alternative reading of Paul's JT texts integrates smoothly into Paul's discussion of Abraham in Romans 4. Properly understood, every part of this chapter, whether its introductory exchanges in 3:27–31, or its final difficult account of Abraham's unwavering faith, from 4:16b onward, points toward Paul's transformational and resurrectional gospel. But our task of rereading Paul's principal JT texts in Romans is not quite complete. One more significant discussion of faith remains in Romans, namely, chapter 10. And it is here that we receive our clearest insights into how our faith connects with the all-important faith of Jesus. If we can prove our case there then we can be confident that our suggested solution works, and some very serious problems within the interpretation of Paul will have been solved. Our journey to a solution will be over.

18

Understanding Romans 10

At this point we have made our way through Paul's discussion of Abraham in Romans 4 and found it to be entirely consistent with the transformational and resurrectional gospel he speaks of elsewhere. Grasping these connections made Paul's entire discussion come to life; patches of argument that JT interpreters have previously not quite known what to do with, like the account of Abraham's extraordinary, unwavering faith in 4:17–22, became important and illuminating. But we need to ask now if this reading of faith in 3:27—4:25 is sustainable through the rest of Romans, and especially when Paul begins to discuss faith again at some length from the end of chapter 9 through chapter 10 (vv. 1–17). In fact, this later material presents our solution with three specific challenges: (1) there are two remarks that connect Israel as a whole with "works" (9:31–32), possibly suggesting that Paul and not just the teacher views Jews prior to the coming of Christ as defined by legalism and "works"; (2) one remark could state that Christ ends or terminates the Torah, which appears to dovetail with JT's forward-thinking and its erasure of Jews and law-observance in the church (10:4); and (3) a long account of faith through chapter 10 is often interpreted as Paul's further emphasis on the all-important condition for salvation that an individual needs to meet through their own efforts from within Box A to transfer to justification in Box B—the "decision" of faith! Verses 10:9–10 are much-quoted in supposed support of this part of JT. So there are some challenges here that need to be faced. Can this stretch of text be read accurately *and* in a way that resists reintroducing JT and disrupting the work we have accomplished thus far?

We think so.

Not only does this passage, read correctly, complement our earlier readings of Romans 1–4, but its arguments add some important emphases to our growing understanding of Paul's theology as he expresses that in Box B.

Romans 10:1–3: entering the discussion

As we begin to address the three challenges here to our rereading of Paul's JT material, it will be most helpful to enter into Paul's broader discussion through the first three verses of chapter 10.

> Brothers and sisters, my heart's desire and prayer to God for
> them is that they may be saved.
> For I can testify that they have a zeal for God,
> but it is not based on knowledge.
> Not knowing the righteousness of God and seeking to establish
> their own,
> they have not submitted to God's righteousness. . . .
> (Rom 10:1–3)

In verse 1, Paul speaks biographically (and see also 9:1–3; and 11:1). His heart's desire and prayer to God is that Israel will be saved, which means that from his point of view the vast majority currently are not. They have rejected Christ, along with the gospel announcement by Paul of Christ's arrival, importance, and work. Paul then notes in verse 2 that Israel's zeal lacks some kind of "recognition" or "acknowledgement," a notion that is taken up in verse 3 as well. As we read on it then becomes clear that when Paul looks at the state of present Israel he sees this rejection bringing two types of "righteousness" into view.

One type is the singular, saving act by God effected through Christ. God acted to save and to resurrect through this dramatic "right" act on his part. But Israel is rejecting this intervention and another type of righteousness becomes apparent at this moment. And it follows that, given that this is not God's righteousness, this must be a "righteous activity" that does not actually come from God. So it must be Israel's own idea. Two complementary mistakes are present here, although they are really two sides of the same coin. On the one side, Israel is rejecting what God has done for them through Jesus—and this was a very costly act on God's part, which involved the offering up of his beloved child to be rejected and executed. On the other side, Israel is pursuing their own alternative system of achieving righteousness and salvation that is necessarily—one would have thought—less effective. Hence, we see now very clearly that *when people reject the gospel as presented in Box B, they automatically end up in some form of Box A*, trapped in a system of their own manufacture. Box A is all about our own ideas about how we can get saved.

With these dynamics in view we can now turn to 9:30–32 where scholars have long struggled to make sense of the text's cryptic statements.

Romans 9:30–32a: Israel's righteous activity (continued) and the return of the teacher

> . . . Gentiles, who did not strive for [saving] righteousness,
> have attained it,
> that is, righteousness "through faith,"
> but Israel,
> who did pursue a teaching of righteousness,
> towards that teaching
> did not reach it.
> Why not?
> Because they did not pursue it "through faith"
> but as if it were through works.
> They have stumbled over the stumbling stone.
> (Rom 9:30–33a NRSVue modified)

This short section presupposes the two, antithetical approaches to righteousness we have already just observed at work in 10:1–3, although various pagans are now involved, *accepting* God's righteous act taking place through Christ, where many Jews have turned away from it and adopted their own. And it is reasonably easy to detect the voice of the teacher returning again here as he complains through 9:30–31 in response to what Paul has just been arguing through the opening verses of chapter 9. Having said this, we need to detect the seriousness of the charges that the teacher is currently leveling at Paul, and that Paul spends the best part of chapters 9–11 dealing with them. Think about the broader situation for a moment and consider it from a Jewish point of view.

Many pagans have accepted Paul's teaching, and yet many Jews have rejected it. Surely this is bizarrely anomalous? God's own people have turned their backs on their own God, yet those who are not God's people have embraced him, and done so in a way that effectively by-passes the great gift to God's people of the Torah? The basic absurdity of this situation calls Paul's entire program into question, the teacher is suggesting. *And he has a point.* What Paul is effectively endorsing does seem deeply counterintuitive. Think about how we would feel if a so-called apostle turned up today and proclaimed a Bible-lite "gospel" that the vast majority of Christians in the church rejected. Imagine further that a vast number of non-Christians accepted this "gospel" and proceeded to become Jesus-followers, yet had scant interest in the Bible, leaving it behind as "unnecessary." Many Christians would find such a situation immediately and completely unconvincing. So the teacher has a point as he places the equivalent scenario in his day for Jews in front of Paul.

But Paul is not going to give any ground in the face of these charges. And he immediately starts to have some fun at the teacher's expense.

> Paul: "What are we to say then [in view of all I have just said]?"
> The teacher: "Pagans not pursuing righteous activity have received righteousness?!" (v. 30a)
> Paul: "—the saving righteous act [of God] 'through faith.'" (v. 30b)
> The teacher: "But Israel, pursuing a torah of righteous activity, toward the Torah, have not?!" (v. 31)
> Paul: "Why? Because they did not strive for it 'through faith' but 'through works.'
> They have stumbled over the stumbling stone. . . ."
> (Rom 9:32 our translation)

To catch what Paul is doing here we need to press into the imagery he is using. The motif of "striving" and "pursuing" is prominent, and this operates within the broader context of Greco-Roman athletic imagery, which is focused here specifically by Paul on running a race. We should recall at this moment that Paul's Greco-Roman culture was as athletically obsessed as ours is. Appeals to imagery from the gymnasium, and from the Olympic games or their local equivalent, were very common. People loved this sort of language and its associations of sweat and struggle. As such, moreover, this imagery lends itself easily to the gospel of the teacher. For the teacher, the truly righteous need to be involved in constant practice, running, and effort, guided by the Torah, to receive the future prize of resurrection offered on the day of judgment. The athletic metaphors of training, striving, and ultimately being rewarded, communicate his gospel of works perfectly. It is highly likely then that he was using this imagery to make appeals to Paul's converts, potential and actual, couched in terms of athletic training and seriousness, and that these further highlight the apparent anomalies of Jewish rejection and pagan acceptance of Paul's views.

"God's athletes, the Jews, who train and work and compete, are, according to you Paul, not actually going to get the prize, but those who sit and watch, the pagans, who are not athletes, not trained, not involved—who are useless bystanders—*are* going to get the prize? This is completely stupid, as is your gospel and as are you!"

But Paul is never going to let these appeals stand. He accepts the basic frame of the athletic analogy but redirects the consequences of the situation. In his view, it is the Jewish rejection of Jesus that is absurd, and in several respects.

First, from verse 30, Paul accepts that the pagans are not actually running at all. They are not participating in a race, striving for the prize of righteousness through their own efforts like the teacher says that the Jews are. Nevertheless, true righteousness—which is God's saving act of deliverance through Christ's faithful walk to the cross—has come to them, as a gift, and they have responded. It simply is the case then that God has given the audience at the games the prize for the race. But far from being absurd, this makes the rejection by the Jews of this gift absurd.

Israel *is* intentionally competing in a race to attain a prize of righteousness, and Paul describes this pursuit of righteous activity in terms of the teacher's gospel—as in some sense being aimed toward the Torah, which would be functioning within this system as a law or a rule-book or even a training manual. It is as if Israel is being trained by the Torah and is striving after the Torah, with all its might and main. The Torah is the entire focus of the race. But Paul now points out, if this is the case, then the Jews are heading in the wrong direction, and this is a crucial assumption on his part. They are pursuing the Torah when they should be pursuing Christ because only Christ will award the ultimate prize of resurrection life (and we will see Paul confirm this assumption shortly when we consider 10:4). If you run in a race all the training in the world won't help you if you're heading along the wrong course toward the wrong finishing line!

Paul now layers on the pain. The Jews who have rejected Christ are not only running in the wrong direction, heading toward the wrong finishing line, but they have missed the real finishing line, which is right at their feet—and they have tripped over it, as Scripture foretold!

> They have stumbled over the stumbling stone, as it is written,
> "See, I am laying in Zion a stone that will make people stumble,
> a rock that will make them fall,
> and whoever trusts in him will not be put to shame."
> (Rom 9:32b-33)

According to Isaiah 8:14, which is quoted here,[1] Christ is a stone laid in Zion. This might seem odd at first glance, but the Hebrew for "stone" and

---

1. Along with Isa 28:16.

for "son" was so close (*eben* and *ben*) that Jews could pun on the similarities. And so many early Jesus-followers who knew their Scriptures well applied "stone" texts to Jesus because he was God's "son." Having said this, here the Son of God, Jesus, is the stone foretold in Isaiah, which is also a *stumbling* stone—a stone that trips people up. And so this stone trips up the teacher's followers. Israel is not just running vigorously in the wrong direction, pursuing the wrong goal; it has also, in a sense as a direct result of this, tripped over the correct goal of the race, which is right at its feet, and presumably fallen flat on its face.

These exchanges might all seem a little strange at first, and perhaps even rather petty. But it is worth reminding ourselves that Paul has good reasons for mocking the teacher's athletic imagery. Such an approach is fundamentally misconceived when it is applied too strongly to questions of salvation, partly because it ignores the way that God's salvation has been gifted to us, and partly because in the process of being gifted to us that salvation has illuminated the appalling sinfulness of our human nature. We *cannot* work our way to heaven, training and striving like athletes, because our moral nature is incapable of such training. We are too far gone. As the great philosopher Immanuel Kant once put this, we are made from crooked timber, and the teacher's gospel wants to build a house that needs huge beams of timber that are perfectly straight. So the teacher's "gospel" really asks people to help themselves when they cannot—a constant problem for the entitled. Such optimism is really thinly disguised cruelty.

It might also be worth noting here that by affirming this approach to salvation, the teacher anticipates the great problem of Pelagianism, while Paul's response anticipates the insights of Augustine.[2] Corrupt and depraved humans need liberation before they can be asked to act in the right way and to train hard in virtue.

But to return to the text at hand: we can now see that Paul's subversion of the athletic imagery that the teacher is using also explains the much-discussed statement made in 10:4. Indeed, this verse contains the basic claim that anchors the entire discussion.

> For Christ is the *telos* of the Torah
> so that there may be [saving] righteousness
> for everyone who trusts.
> (Rom 10:4 our translation)

2. We saw just this move on Paul's part earlier on in Romans as well, when he introduced the Scripture's witness to universal human depravity, in 3:9b–18, to overwhelm the teacher's foolish optimism there.

Paul's statement that Christ is the *telos* of the Torah here has led to much scholarly conversation about whether he means "end" or "goal," the Greek *telos* being capable of both meanings. Is Paul saying that Christ *terminates* the Torah? This would have very serious implications for the ongoing existence of Jews, especially messianic Jews. (This would be what JT advocates expect though.) Or is he saying that Christ is the *goal* of the Torah? The Torah can stay as long as it points toward Christ. Or is he saying both things? The Torah points toward Christ and is now redundant.

If we introduce the racing imagery from the context that we have just been discussing, however, it seems fair to suggest that he can be simply speaking of the "goal" of the Torah in the sense of the finishing line of a race toward which people are supposed to be running. The *telos* or goal of the Torah is Christ, as Paul also said in Romans 3:21, and has demonstrated with frequent citations throughout the letter.[3] So we see here the assumption on which the subversion of the athletic imagery from 9:30 onward is based. Everything turns on Christ being the center of God's activity and the goal of the Torah. He is the real finishing line, and he comes as a gift, at the behest of the electing God. If you miss this then you're running the wrong race in the wrong direction. And reading *telos* in this sense alone allows us to retain the space that Paul seems to keep open so carefully elsewhere for Torah-observant Jesus-followers in the early church. The Torah is not completely gone. It is just not an end in itself. And if it is a part of a discipleship aimed toward the Messiah, then it is a fine and good thing.

If these points are all becoming clear, we turn now to face our third and final challenge. We will hear very little more about "works" from this point onward in Romans—see only a brief, although telling, remark in 11:6. But there is an extensive discussion of "faith" running through chapter 10, which is resumed in fragments by chapter 11 and then still later in the letter. We need to read this passage carefully because it is appealed to so often by advocates of JT as decisive for their model. If Paul is not just laying out a key part of JT, what is going on?

Romans 10:6–13: the context in verses 4 and 5

As we read through Romans 10 from verse 6 it is important to keep in mind both the position in the broader context of Romans 9–11 that Paul is defending—which is really shaped by the charges from the teacher that he is rebutting—and the programmatic statement he has just made in 10:4.

---

3. Implicit here is a use of the Torah, and of the Tanakh as a whole, as *Scripture*. But see 2 Cor 1:20!

For Christ is the goal of the Torah
so that there may be deliverance for everyone who believes. . . .
(Rom 10:4 our translation)

Much of the argument that follows develops this statement, which makes at least two important claims. First, as we have just emphasized, the goal to which Torah points is somehow enacted through Jesus, not through the Torah itself (10:4a). And, second, ultimately those who believe are saved, so any pagans who believe are legitimately saved, and any Jews who don't are not (10:4b; see also 9:30–32). But Paul now gives us a clue immediately in verse 5 about why the first claim he makes here holds good, and his argument links hands neatly with much that he has said that we have already discussed in relation to Abraham and Romans 4. Why can he say so confidently that Christ is the goal of the Torah?

In verse 5 he states,

Moses writes concerning righteousness that comes through the
Torah that
"the person who does these things will live by them."
(Rom 10:5 NRSVue modified)

We need to recall now our earlier note that Leviticus 18:5 is speaking of someone who does something so that they "will *live.* . . ." Moreover, this is an exact parallel to Habakkuk 2:4, where "the Righteous One through faith(fulness) will *live.*" It follows that "live" in both these quotations denotes *eternal* life. So this sentence is addressing how we get saved, which for both Paul and the teacher revolves around the question of how we get resurrected and thereby enter into the age to come.[4] And in the light of this we confirm that Paul is suggesting in verse 4 that the *goal* of the Torah has always been to give its recipients *life.* It is focused on saving them and consequently on *resurrecting* them. And this suspicion is confirmed when we recall where the emphasis fell in Paul's earlier discussion of Abraham. Abraham received a foretaste of the coming age when the God who gives life to the dead gifted his dead loins and Sarah's dead womb with a living son and heir, Isaac. So

---

4. Paul is clearly suggesting that this approach to salvation is incorrect or will fail. It is hard to say whether he is himself quoting this statement by Moses and simply negating it, so Moses here is just wrong for Paul, offering "a ministry of death" or "service of condemnation" as Paul might be putting it in 2 Cor 4:6–11. Or perhaps Paul is quoting here a favorite text of the teacher, as also in Gal 3:12, and would say that here Moses is being read incorrectly, because he is not being read with reference to Christ. An example of the correct reading then follows from Rom 10:6. Our hunch is that this is a favorite verse of the teacher because it seems to be offering a different account of the "right activity" that is generated by the Torah to the Christocentric account suggested in verses 3–4 and then developed in verses 6–13.

there too the goal of the Torah is life. And that is why the resurrected Christ fulfills the Torah. God has given us resurrection life through him. The promises of an eternal inheritance made to Abraham and to all the other patriarchs and matriarchs are thereby fulfilled.

It is a simple point that can get lost in the weeds. But once we see this, we can see where the rest of Paul's discussion goes and why.

The "working your way to heaven" approach advocated by the teacher and stated in verse 5 is clearly wrong. The correct approach has something to do with faith. But it also has something to do with Scripture, and with the Torah, as Paul will go on to argue. Moreover, the Jewish people have to accept that they have *rejected* their God, who has reached out to them with outstretched arms. The reasons why so many of the Jews in Paul's day have not followed Jesus is . . . that, according to Paul, they have resisted and rejected the God who has come very close to them and so, to put matters bluntly, and somewhat sadly, it is on them.

Romans 10:6–13

First of all, it is not as surprising as it perhaps might have been that Paul now positions God in verse 6 as speaking the words recorded in the Torah and focusing those words on Christ.

> But the righteousness that comes "through faith" speaks in this
> way:
> "Do not say in your heart, 'Who will ascend into heaven?'
> (that is, to bring Christ down)
> or 'Who will descend into the abyss?'
> (that is, to bring Christ up from the dead)."
> (Rom 10:6 NRSVue modified)

Deuteronomy 30, which Paul quotes here, talks literally about the Torah itself. But the Torah also offers in this decisive moment a choice between life and death enjoining its listeners to embrace life, and for Paul life is evidenced concretely and dramatically in the resurrection of Jesus to the right hand of God where he now rules over all, one day to return in complete victory. So for Paul, of course God speaks here of the life offered to Israel, and ultimately to all humankind, by way of his Son, Jesus, who he has raised from the dead. The resurrected Christ—the Christ of life—must be the focal point of the Torah.

But Paul now presses on to the second part of his thesis as stated in 10:4b. How does this life reach others?

It is universally admitted that it reaches those who *believe*. It is they who will receive "deliverance" and "salvation." This is why the believing pagans are saved and the unbelieving Jews are not. We all should respond, at the least, by believing that Jesus really is the one sent to resurrect us. *But* the $64,000 question is *how* we all believe. What mechanism is in play linking the work of Christ, who was resurrected, with the promised resurrection of those who believe? These two things are, after all, cheek by jowl in this verse.

Now we suggest that JT offers us an account of this argument that is again too "thin." The model only knows of the faith of individuals, and, moreover, they generate this faith for themselves. So JT readers suppose that Paul is simply speaking of a basic saving contract here. Those who choose to believe will one day be rewarded by God with resurrection and salvation— and the logic underlying this easy saving contract that offers resurrection in response to faith alone is the prior collapse of the complete Jewish system, which was both legalistic and impossibly so. The individual who is working through the struggles of legalism in Box A is able to jump across into the relief of Box B by making the decision of faith. And it follows that Jesus is the end-point of the Torah and not just—or not even—its goal.

We, however, will again offer a "thick" reading of this data that is a little different. We hold that Christ plays a much more powerful and active role in Paul's argument, joining hands with the Spirit, ultimately to provide us with a much more persuasive account of how God saves and resurrects us. Moreover, it is also a more comforting and reliable account! We certainly still believe. But that believing is tightly connected with Christ and the Spirit.

As we press into the details of Paul's argument it will be useful to recall the key statement in 10:6a again as we do so.

> But the righteousness that comes "through faith" speaks in this
> way. . . .
> . . . But what does it say?
> "The Word is near you,
>   in your mouth and in your heart"
> (the Word about "faith" that we proclaim).
> That if you confess with your mouth that Jesus is Lord
> and believe in your heart that God raised him from the dead,
> you will be saved.
> For one believes with the heart, leading to righteousness,
> and one confesses with the mouth, leading to salvation.
> (Rom 10:6a, 8–10 NRSVue modified)

Things will begin to clarify considerably if we first grasp that the two instances of faith spoken of here initially refer to Christ himself.

The first instance contains the intertextual cue from Habakkuk 2:4 that we have encountered many times already in Romans (*ek pisteōs* or "through faith"), which we know is an allusion by way of that Scripture to Christ's faithfulness, death, and resurrection life.[5] And reading verse 6 Christo-centrically is supported by the two references to Christ in the Deuteronomy quotation in verses 6b and 7 that immediately follow. Paul is talking about Jesus's death and resurrection here. Once we have made these connections, we can then see that "faith" in the phrase "the word of faith" almost certainly refers to "that faith" that we have just been talking about, and hence to what Christ did for us at Easter again.

But believers like us enter the argument now (Paul using the verb here and not the noun). *We* believe and confess with the heart and the mouth and are thereby saved. And we suggest that as this happens we are encountering once more, although in a more expanded form, the faith progression that we have encountered in several other places earlier in Romans, from the series "through faith to faith" in 1:17, to the slightly expanded series in 3:22, to a broader analysis in much of chapter 4, which moved easily from the faith of Christ to the faith of others.[6] (And there are some similar texts in other places in Paul's letters, like Galatians 3:22.) There is a broad movement within the text through the faith of Christ, which really denotes his death and resurrection, to the salvation of those who believe in this. But what is Paul's argument? *How* is he connecting the faith of Christ and the faith of his followers, and *why?*

Paul's argument will not be fully understood until we recognize the presence and role of another important actor.

Someone divine *speaks* about the faithful Jesus from 10:6. And in 10:8 a *word* is proclaimed by way of Paul that is also spoken of in Deuteronomy 30—a word that reaches right down into the hearts and mouths of those who believe. Moreover, this "word" returns to Paul's argument in verse 17, where it elicits hearing and then believing.

The presence of this verbal phenomenon should not surprise careful readers of Paul's broader argument. The "word of God" was a key player as he began his all-important sketch of the origins of Israel in the patriarchs

5. This has been used already in context in 9:30 and 32.

6 Paul, that is, views our faith in participatory terms (of course!), and so holds that our faith derives from Jesus's faith, just as all our virtues derive ultimately from Jesus—our love from his love, our holiness from his holiness, and so on. This point is especially clear in Morna Hooker's well-known treatment of faith in Paul, "ΠΙΣΤΙΣ ΧΡΙΣΤΟΥ" (1989). So every now and again Paul speaks of faith twice in a series or progression, with the first reference pointing toward Jesus, and the second to us. His point is that our faith, which is important, derives from Jesus's. But Paul only spells out in full what he means by this in a few places, one of which is Romans 10.

and matriarchs in 9:6. The word is active again in verse 9, creating Isaac, and then in verse 12, calling Jacob and Esau into being. And in verse 24, after a suitable proof of its legitimacy, God "calls" followers, presumably using the "word" again, not only from among the Jews but also from among the pagans. But perhaps this is all just what we would expect after the way exactly the same thing happened in Romans 4:16b–22, where God's words accomplish what they say they will. There is then a key actor present here alongside Christ and his believers—a divine word. This word speaks the words of Scripture and reaches right down into the depths of people. And it works through Paul's words, eliciting both hearing and believing.

Paul's reliance on a divine word operating dynamically through his own words is also evident in some of his other letters. In 1 Thessalonians 2, for example, we read:

> We also constantly give thanks to God for this,
> that when you received the word of God that you heard from us
> you accepted it not as a human word but as what it really is,
> God's word, which is also at work in you believers.
> (1 Thess 2:13)

And in 1 Corinthians 2 he writes in a very similar vein:

> My speech and my proclamation were made
> not with persuasive words of wisdom
> but with a demonstration of the Spirit and of power,
> so that your faith might rest not on human wisdom
> but on the power of God.
> (1 Cor 2:4–5)

From which it follows that

> we speak . . . in words not taught by human wisdom
> but taught by the Spirit,
> interpreting spiritual things to those who are spiritual. . . .
> (1 Cor 2:13)

This word is the speech of the Spirit then, who is the creative and dynamic power and presence of God reaching into every corner of the cosmos. So the Spirit can reach right down into the depths of humanity, bearing its divine information and insights as it does. But the Spirit is also the Spirit of Christ for Paul, molding and shaping God's people into the image of God's Son, a son who was faithful and obedient to the point of death, and then raised from the dead and enthroned on high. As Paul said a little earlier in Romans, in chapter 8:

29 For those whom he [God] foreknew he also predestined
to be conformed to the image of his Son. . . .
(Rom 8:29)

Once we realize that the word in context is the word of God, which is
to say, the divine Spirit, spoken by the Father, and that the Spirit is also the
Spirit of Christ, the Son of God, shaping us in his image, Paul's argument
comes into sharp focus.

Jesus is the preeminent figure who has been faithful, has died, and
who has already been resurrected. He *is* alive. And the Spirit is now drawing those who are willing and responsive into him, drawing them into his
image or shape, so that they too now evidence the same faithfulness as he
did. Their faith is not just a copying then, or a pale imitation of Jesus's. It is
concretely connected to it. It *is* Jesus's faith as the Spirit takes from what is
Jesus's and imparts it to his followers. Our believing is a *sharing* in Jesus's
perfect believing. It shows that we are connected together.

And it is this connection that *guarantees* that the journey of faith will
result in life, which is to say, in life from the dead. Those who believe bear
the sign—and even the seal Paul might say—of their concrete connection
with the one person in human history who has already been raised from
the dead. So their own resurrection is guaranteed. (And the Spirit is indeed
the seal on God's possessions, denoting them as his, waiting for the future
day of complete redemption.) This is why Paul is so emphatic that those
who believe are destined for resurrection. Those who believe in the one who
raised Jesus from the dead and enthroned him as Lord are channeling Jesus
who believed pretty much the same things. This is a place where the character of Christ peeps through into our lives. But as we well know, he is now
in glory—and so that is where we are as well! Moreover, we can possibly
now better understand Paul's confidence that this is what the Torah was
always all about. The Torah points constantly away from death and sin and
toward life; it carries the all-important promises to Israel of eternal posterity
and inheritance with God. (It also gets tangled up in sin, but that is a story
for another day.) So its central concerns are emphatically fulfilled by the
risen Jesus and his introduction of his followers into the glories of the age
to come.

If we have grasped Paul's argument up to this point, it is now very important that we not slip back and allow JT advocates to *conditionalize* faith
on the basis of the grammar of verses 9–10. Paul has written there,

. . . if you confess with your mouth that Jesus is Lord
and believe in your heart that God raised him from the dead,
you will be saved.

For one believes with the heart, leading to righteousness,
and one confesses with the mouth, leading to salvation.
(Rom 10:9–10)

First, we know by now that Paul's use of faith is principally about Christ and his faithfulness, which has irrupted graciously and righteously into the cosmos, *and then* human faith as an *inclusion* within that person of fidelity effected by the Spirit. That is how the progression works. So 10:6–10 begins by focusing on Christ's story—his death, resurrection, and enthronement—recounted in verses 6–7 and 8b. The story then continues as Jesus's followers join his journey, believe in and confess his lordship, and wait for their resurrections.

Second, just because the structure of verse 9 is conditional at the grammatical level does not entail that it speaks of a conditional theology, although we can see this more clearly once we have left JT's expectations behind. These verses are simply saying that if A (belief and confession in this fashion) is present, then so is B (salvation), in just the way that if a bird with a flat yellow beak waddles, quacks, and swims, then it is a duck. The sentence is factual! The bird didn't *choose* a flat yellow beak, waddling legs, a quacking voice, and so on. What we *do* learn from the conditional grammar is that Paul is correlating belief and confession with salvation. If belief and confession occur, then one is saved. We can be completely confident of this. And that means that any pagans whom the teacher is trying to threaten can stand firm fully assured that they are on track for salvation. They do not need to be bullied into Torah-observance out of anxiety that they will not be saved on the day of judgment.

It is a powerful argument. And it is completely in line with the transformational and resurrectional material Paul usually speaks about more directly elsewhere. Moreover, Paul's inner trinitarian logic is starting to come into view, which should warm the hearts of the orthodox.

If this is all clear, then we are free to turn and to quickly consider the other side of the situation which takes us to the end of the chapter. Paul has thoroughly proved his claim made back in 9:30 that the believing pagans are saved, but this is not his main focus at present. Now he needs to consider the other side of the situation as stated in 9:31–33, namely, the unbelieving Jews.

Romans 10:14–21

Unsurprisingly, the teacher emerges into view here again to place the relevant questions on behalf of any rejected Jews. It is not their fault, he insists in various ways. Paul concedes that it is a tragic situation, but far from calling his gospel into question, he states that this scenario is actually anticipated in many parts of Scripture. Those Jews who do not believe have no one to blame but themselves—although God clearly knew that it was going to happen, and is able to turn even this situation ultimately to the good.

> The teacher: "But how are they to 'call' on one in whom they have not believed?
> And how are they to 'believe' in one whom they have never heard?
> And how are they to hear without someone to proclaim him?
> And how are they to proclaim him unless they are sent?"
> (vv. 14–15a NRSVue modified)

> Paul: "As it is written, 'How beautiful are the feet of those who bring good news!'" (v. 15b)

> The teacher: "But not all have obeyed the good news." (v. 16a)

> Paul: "[And] for this reason, Isaiah says, 'Lord who has believed our proclamation?'
> So then, belief comes from what is heard,
> and what is heard comes through the word of Christ."
> (vv. 16b–17 our translation)

> The teacher: "But I ask, surely they did not hear?" (v. 18a our translation)

> Paul: "Indeed they have:
> 'Their voice has gone out to all the earth,
> and their words to the ends of the empire.'" (v. 18b NRSVue modified)

> The teacher: "But I ask, surely Israel did not understand?"
> (v. 19a NRSVue modified)

> Paul: "First Moses says, 'I will use those who are not a nation to make you jealous;
> with a foolish nation I will provoke you.'
> Then Isaiah is so bold as to say,
> 'I have been found by those who did not seek me;
> I have shown myself to those who did not ask for me.'
> But of Israel he says,

'All day long I have held out my hands to a disobedient and
contrary people.'" (vv. 19b–21)

Paul's point here is to emphasize further, using Israel's Scriptures, con-
tra the teacher, that much of Israel has specifically and knowingly rejected
Christ. God's "Yes" has come near in Christ, but unbelieving Israel has said
"No" and has instead chosen to establish their own way of salvation. Mes-
sengers have been sent and have not been believed. Their message has been
heard and understood. But it has not been obeyed. Fortunately, this awful
situation is not the end of the matter.

> The teacher: "I ask, then, surely God has not abandoned his
> people?"
> (11:1 our translation)
>
> Paul: "Of course not! I am an Israelite. . . ."
> (11:1 our translation)

It is not surprising, given Paul's response, that the teacher would ask
if all of this means that God has simply given up on his people. But while
Paul does hold Israel accountable in the present for their lack of response
to Christ, Paul will not allow the issue to end here. Just as God's electing
purposes triumphed over pagan ignorance in 9:6–26 and 30, so too they
will ultimately triumph over Israel's rejection. *No one* gets the last word but
God in Christ.

All three problems solved

By this point, it should be clear that Paul's thinking in Romans 10 is perfectly in line with what we have discovered about his resurrectional and
transformational gospel and not with any reading in terms of JT. We have
shown that JT's expectation that "works of law" denote a Jewish, pre-
Christian phase that must collapse into salvation by faith alone—a Box A
to Box B progression—is not in Paul's text. Instead, the opposite is the case.
"Works of law" denote an alternative way of salvation that some within
Israel adopt *after* Christ has made himself known to them and they have
rejected him. And it follows from our reading that Paul does not necessarily envision Christ as obliterating the Torah on his arrival, which would
effectively erase the Jews and their practices. Christ is certainly the *telos* of
the Torah—its goal. This cannot be lost sight of or conceded because only
through Christ are life, resurrection, and the promised inheritance possible.
But further Jewish Torah-observance in itself, in the right spirit, so to speak,

does not need to undercut these basic truths. So Paul does not expect Jews to abandon their practices as they receive Christ, unless they are specifically called—like him—to do so for missionary purposes (see 1 Cor 7:17–24). But Paul is unhappy specifically about any rejection of Christ in the name of the Torah. Moreover, for Paul, such rejection necessarily involves a false understanding *of* Torah in terms of law and rules.

Finally, it is clear that human faith for Paul is never just a choice that an individual makes that creates access to salvation in a conditional or contractual way: "If you choose to believe then you are saved, and if not then you are not" or some such. Much as we saw in relation to Abraham in our previous chapter, there is a much deeper causality involved. Christ is the preeminently faithful One who believed steadfastly and was resurrected, and our believing is a participation, effected by the Spirit, within the first part of that journey. And it is this concrete connection that guarantees the arrival of the second part, which is life in the age to come. Our faith is *evidence* that we are in Christ through the work of the Spirit. To position faith then within the concerns of JT strips it of its powerful theological message, and detaches it from everything that makes it work, which is to say, from Christ and from the work of the Spirit. The comfort that Paul is providing is lost.

And with these realizations in place, we have basically completed our solution to the great conundrums generated by JT in relation to Paul's key text, his letter to the Romans. The fullest and most extensive letter he ever wrote, which contains the vast majority of his JT data in its most comprehensive form, has been shown to be smoothly consistent with the resurrectional and transformational gospel we have seen Paul talking about in the other 90 percent of what he wrote. Paul's "justification" texts have been reread in a way that is faithful to what he wrote—"tight to the text"—and yet also in a way that integrates smoothly with what he says almost everywhere else. Our problems seem to have been solved, and it remains only to draw all our arguments to a final conclusion.

Conclusion

We hope that by end of this interpretative journey you are breathing a great sigh of relief, as we did—although hopefully not so much because it is over, as because by now you will have in your hands a Paul who makes sense. He is possibly simpler than you have been taught, but also, more importantly, he is more deeply and profoundly in the grip of a God of love, and that is the point of our book. Paul attests with great power and clarity to a God who loves us so much that he offered up his only beloved Son for us. It is a wonderful message. But it has been obscured and overlaid in his name—hijacked—and it is long past time to set the hostages free. To state things in more biblical language: it is time for the exiles to be released from their Babylonian captivity to return home. Paul preached a God of liberation, but we cannot hear that message with complete clarity until we liberate Paul himself.

The liberation of Paul and his gospel began, as it had to, with a brief account in the first three chapters of the gospel that needed to be set free. Everything for Paul begins with God: the God who has disclosed himself to us through his Son, Jesus, and folded us into that disclosure with his very own Spirit. We emphasized that we learn through this process that we are being embraced by a God who has loved us from before the foundation of the world, and who will love us to the end, and even beyond it if necessary; we are involved with a God who never lets go. So it makes all the sense in the world that this God has personally reached into our current state, which is riven by sin, corruption, and ultimately by death, to carry that state to its end on the cross, so that he can rise again, beyond it, and thereby create a pathway to draw us into a new existence—one that is cleansed, renewed, and glorified. (Hallelujah, we murmur.) This is the Pauline gospel, attested by the creeds, and it really is good news.

Once we grasped this gospel clearly—which we dubbed participatory, resurrectional, and transformational—it was then immediately apparent that the gospel of justification—which we dubbed justification theory—was something different. Moreover, once we had that model clearly in view, it became apparent, in serried stages, that this competing theory was unleashing woe after woe within Paul's interpretation, and within any Christian activity based on that.

It generates confusion at the borders of its texts with the participatory approach Paul utilizes elsewhere. The clash played out in Romans especially as the text crossed over from the argumentation of the first four chapters to the rest of the letter, where participation, baptism, and the Spirit, took center stage. Melanchthon's solution here palpably failed leaving us with an incoherent apostle. And the tensions here ran deep, we learned further, in terms of the very knowledge of God, the overall direction of Paul's theological thinking and reflection, whether forward or backward, and the account of Christ's work on our behalf. Radically different views of the importance of his resurrection were in play. But with all these realizations, the model's problems—and the problems unleashed within Paul's interpretation—were far from done.

It turned out that it was the presence and dynamics of JT that underlay much of the teaching of contempt, insofar as that was conveyed through the interpretation of Paul. However unpleasant it was to face, we learned that JT is committed to the prior construction of "the Jew" in self-evidently immoral, irrational, and unstable terms; indeed, it depends on this construction and rises up out of it. Justification theory's life depends on the fact that the Jew ultimately has no right to exist—a shocking realization. And we then traced how the failure to detect this causality nevertheless hamstrung the ability of the new perspective, whether offered in the specific form of J. D. G. Dunn's proposals or those of N. T. Wright, to resolve all of our problems, including the Jewish conundrum. It was apparent by this point, that is, that only the complete elimination of JT from Paul's interpretation offered the hope of any genuine resolution—by now an obvious if somewhat intimidating realization.

So, summoning the requisite audacity, we turned to trace a solution out in the second half of the book that would fully displace JT, but assisted by the thought that JT might have found itself in Paul's texts too easily. (JT advocates are nothing if not zealous.) And our alternative viewpoint, grounded in Paul's participatory gospel, did reveal new ways of reading his key texts.

As we knew well by this point in the book, JT arranges itself in a sequence of two "boxes." Box A pivots around "works of law" and their inadequacies—which is where the problematic account of the Jew takes place—and then Box B is all about "faith," although Jesus is also clearly in play. But, now freed from the strictures of JT, we saw different things going

on. Instead of linking the boxes together in a sequence to describe the journey of a benighted individual to salvation—a point where the theological
influence of JT is especially significant, gluing these two "boxes" together in
a salvific sequence—we now saw a different argument that was, somewhat
ironically, also more responsible as a historical-critical reading. It turned
out that Paul's JT texts were, like the rest of his texts, contingent, composed
to address particular circumstances, here specifically the promotion of a
rival gospel—unworthy of that name, Paul says at one point—that he was
forced to oppose. Using Lou Martyn's respectful nomenclature, we called
Paul's rivals "the teachers." Moreover, it was apparent that Paul had to oppose the teachers with numerous appeals to key scriptural texts, since they
were learned Jewish exegetes like he was, and this generated the peculiar
linguistic texture of his JT texts. These were a patchwork of scriptural words,
phrases, and echoes. This underlying polemical circumstance was particularly evident in Galatians, although we held that it was demonstrable in
Romans as well.

It followed from this realization, quite quickly, that Paul's Box A texts
were a direct attack on the teachers' legalistic approach to salvation—and
these particular messianic Jews were legalists, although there is no need to
attribute their moralizing views to the rest of the Jewish people. So these
texts do not represent Paul's position at all, although they are certainly a
clear statement of what he was against. His rivals were an early anticipation
of Pelagius, and recapitulated the unintentional cruelties of the Pelagians by
exhorting people to undertake moral activity and be judged on that basis
when their sinful nature could not help but fail them—a position that ap-
palled the more Augustinian Paul.

Paul's emphasis on faith in Box B also came into clearer focus as we detected his clever use of Scripture. It became apparent here that he was claiming that his Christocentric teaching had been anticipated by numerous texts
in the Tanakh or OT. A sophisticated argument for assurance was apparent
as well, the faith of Jesus's followers attesting to their participation within the
faithfulness of Jesus himself. Moreover, in a further skillful move, Paul was
able to anticipate his gospel of faith followed by resurrection life in the situation of the patriarch Abraham before he was circumcised, but when he had
already been promised an heir, in Genesis chapter 15, thereby circumventing
a dominant role for circumcision and Torah-observance (which arrive, technically, from Genesis 17). Hence Box B and its associated claims turned out to
be a scriptural *tour de force*—one grounded in the risen Christ.

We sketched out these moves quickly in chapter 11 in relation to
Galatians 2:15–16. But then we had to enter in on the real battle. Could
this alternative approach be sustained through the key texts undergirding

JT, namely, the justification subsections in Romans? If so, then the other, briefer texts in Paul usually enlisted in support of JT would simply have to fall in line. So from chapter 12 onward we concentrated on the JT texts in Romans, knowing that this would be sufficient trouble for the day. A careful, but we hope not inaccessible or inaccurate, consideration of Romans 1:18—3:20, 3:21–26, 3:27—4:25, and ch. 10, then duly followed, after which we drew our detailed discussion to a close.

Our argument throughout, in essence, was that a careful reading of Paul's JT texts in their original contexts never mobilized a *theory* in terms of justification. Far from it. In what is surely one of the greatest ironies in the history of biblical interpretation, Paul, in Box A, *attacks* a legalistic and contractual approach to salvation, here in a Jewish variant, opposing against it, in Box B, a scripturally mediated statement of his usual gospel: we are saved and transformed as we participate in the risen Christ, although here, we see, as the Scriptures attest. Jesus's faith is our faith, and our faith comes from his. And his steadfast faith through death to resurrection life was anticipated by the great forefather of the Jews, Abraham, indicating that this was God's overarching plan for Israel all along. It is a powerful set of arguments, and it is hard not to be impressed by Paul's combination of theological insight and exegetical skill. And, most importantly, read in this way, his JT texts could now integrate smoothly into what he says for the other 90 percent of the time.

Hopefully it is not too audacious at this point then to suggest that it is, at least as far as these issues are concerned, case closed. We can turn the page on JT as a correct interpretative construct for understanding Paul, and move beyond its categories, as well as beyond all the disorders and issues generated within any proclamation or teaching in its terms that appeals to Paul. And this is a welcome thing. The confusion in the direction of Paul's thought, the saving role of the Easter events, and the very nature of God, can be released, as can the sinister definition of the Jew that lies at the heart of JT. Paul's gospel is free to move on to spread its fragrance, as he puts it once, now able to face the other challenges that reading Paul in a modern world still presents. So there is much still to reflect on, but also to celebrate. At least at this point we can know with complete confidence that Paul's gospel, properly understood, is a wondrous thing. Set free, it sets us free.

Appendix

Reviewing the Debate:
Romans 1:16—3:20

Paul's brilliant Socratic engagement with the teachers is much clearer to modern readers if its speeches and conversational exchanges are laid out more like the script of a modern play. On the left side of the page, we will place the words of the teacher, and on the right side of the page we will place Paul. We have chosen to use the widely available NRSVue as our base text. And, for the sake of clarity, we have not introduced all our suggested translation alternatives and modifications—only those that are strictly necessary.

> **Paul:** For I am not ashamed of the gospel; it is God's saving power for everyone who believes, for the Jew first and also for the Greek. For in it the deliverance of God is revealed through faith for faith, as it is written, "The Righteous One through faith will live."[1] (1:16–17)

---

1. As we have shown, Paul is quoting Hab 2:4 as a messianic prophecy attesting to Jesus. Jesus is the Righteous One, as Isa 53:11 also suggests, who is faithful unto death and then lives (i.e., is resurrected). Just prior to this—and as we have also previously shown—"deliverance" is also a more helpful translation of Paul's Greek *dikaiosunē* than "righteousness" in relation to God the Father's actions through Jesus. Jesus's death and resurrection on our behalf reveal not just God's rightness but God's "saving power" or "deliverance"!

The teacher: For the wrath of God is revealed from heaven against all the ungodliness and injustice of those who by their injustice suppress the truth. For what can be known about God is plain to them, because God has made it plain to them. Ever since the creation of the world God's eternal power and divine nature, invisible though they are, have been seen and understood through the things God has made. So they are without excuse, for though they knew God, they did not honor him as God or give thanks to him, but they became futile in their thinking, and their senseless hearts were darkened. Claiming to be wise, they became fools, and they exchanged the glory of the immortal God for images resembling a mortal human or birds or four-footed animals or reptiles.

Therefore God gave them over in the desires of their hearts to impurity, to the dishonoring of their bodies among themselves. They exchanged the truth about God for a lie and worshiped and served the creature rather than the Creator, who is blessed forever! Amen.

For this reason God gave them over to dishonorable passions. Their females exchanged natural intercourse for unnatural, and in the same way also the males, giving up natural intercourse with females, were consumed with their passionate desires for one another. Males committed shameless acts with males and received in their own persons the due penalty for their error.

And since they did not see fit to acknowledge God, God gave them over to an unfit mind and to do things that should not be done. They were filled with every kind of injustice, evil, covetousness, malice. Full of envy, murder, strife, deceit, craftiness, they are gossips, slanderers, God-haters, insolent, haughty, boastful, inventors of evil, rebellious toward parents, foolish, faithless, heartless, ruthless. They know God's decree, that those who practice such things deserve to die, yet they not only do them but even applaud others who practice them. (1:18–32)

Paul: Therefore, oh man, you, along with all who are judging,[2] are without excuse! For in passing judgment on one another you condemn yourself, because you, the judge, are doing the very same things. We know that God's judgment on those who do such things is in accordance with truth. Do you imagine, oh man, who judges those practicing such things and yet is doing the same,[3] that you will escape the judgment of God? Or do you despise the riches of his kindness and forbearance and patience? Do you not realize that God's kindness is meant to lead you to repentance? But by your hard and impenitent heart you are storing up wrath for yourself on the day of wrath, when God's righteous judgment will be revealed. He will repay according to each one's deeds: to those who by patiently doing good seek for glory and honor and immortality, he will give eternal life, while for those who are self-seeking and who obey not the truth but injustice, there will be wrath and fury. There will be affliction and distress for everyone who does evil, both the Jew first and the Greek, but glory and honor and peace for everyone who does good, both the Jew first and the Greek. For God does not respect mere appearance.[4]

2. The NRSVue reads "whoever you are," which is not accurate enough.

3. Same deficiency corrected as above.

4. This seems to be a better translation of such a well-known theological motif. See also Jas 2:1–7, 9.

All who have sinned apart from the law will also perish apart from the law, and all who have sinned under the law will be judged in accordance with the law.[5] For it is not the hearers of the law who are righteous in God's sight but the doers of the law who will be justified.[6] When gentiles, who do not possess the law, by nature do what the law requires, these, though not having the law, are a law to themselves. They show that what the law requires is written on their hearts, as their own conscience also bears witness, and their conflicting thoughts will accuse or perhaps excuse them on the day when God judges the secret thoughts of all (according to my gospel, through Christ Jesus).[7]

But if you call yourself a Jew and rely on the law and boast of your relation to God and know his will and determine what really matters because you are instructed in the law, and if you are sure that you are a guide to the blind, a light to those who are in darkness, a corrector of the foolish, a teacher of children, having in the law the embodiment of knowledge and truth, you, then, who teach others, will you not teach yourself? You who preach against stealing, do you steal? You who forbid adultery, do you commit adultery? You who abhor idols, do you rob temples? You who boast in the law, do you dishonor God by your transgression of the law? For, as it is written, "The name of God is blasphemed among the gentiles because of you."

5. We see even this sentence as a brief example of Paul subtly subverting the teacher's gospel by setting up existing elements in the teacher's thinking to eventually draw out their embarrassing conclusions through the rest of chapter 2.

6. This situation shows exactly how "justification" terminology works within the teacher's own system as against within Paul's participatory gospel. For the teacher, being "justified" is the result of doing the law—that is, people are *dikaioi* or "righteous" if they are faithful doers. So the best translation for "justified" here is "declared righteous" (because they are!). Contrary to this, Paul himself will use "justification" language in a way that is emphatically not based on human doing but on what God has done in Christ. It is unconditional, liberational, baptismal, and resurrectional! See, e.g., Rom. 6:7 and 1 Cor 6:11. In these texts "set free," "released," "liberated," and so on, are better translations.

7. We have re-sequenced the NRSVue's wording here to capture how Paul slips into a parenthesis or aside as a brief anticipation of his own position—that true judgment occurs through Jesus Christ and his love and mercy; see Rom 14:4.

Circumcision indeed is of value if you obey the law, but if you are a transgressor of the law your circumcision has become uncircumcision. So, if the uncircumcised keep the requirements of the law, will not their uncircumcision be regarded as circumcision? Then the physically uncircumcised person who keeps the law will judge you who, though having the written code and circumcision, are a transgressor of the law. For a person is not a Jew who is one outwardly, nor is circumcision something external and physical. Rather, a person is a Jew who is one inwardly, and circumcision is a matter of the heart, by the Spirit, not the written code. Such a person receives praise not from humans but from God. (Chapter 2)

Paul: Then what advantage has the Jew? Or what is the value of circumcision? (3:1)

The teacher: Much, in every way. For in the first place, the Jews were entrusted with the oracles of God. (3:2)

Paul: What if some were unfaithful? Will their faithlessness nullify the faithfulness of God? (3:3)

The teacher: By no means! Although every human is a liar, let God be proved true, as it is written, "So that you may be justified in your words and you will prevail when you go to trial." (3:4)

Paul: But if our injustice serves to confirm the justice of God, what should we say? That God is unjust to inflict wrath on us? (I speak in a human way.) (3:5)

The teacher: By no means! For then how could God judge the world? (3:6)

Paul: But if through my falsehood God's truthfulness abounds to his glory, why am I still being judged as a sinner? And why not say (as some people slander us by saying that we say), "Let us do evil so that good may come"? (3:7–8b)

The teacher: (3:8b) Their judgment is deserved!

Paul: What then? Are we any better off?
(3:9a)

The teacher: No, not in every respect . . .[8]
(3:9a)

Paul: [Moreover] we charge that all,[9] both
Jews and Greeks, are under the power of
sin, as it is written: "There is no one who is
righteous, not even one; there is no one who
has understanding; there is no one who seeks
God. All have turned aside; together they
have become worthless; there is no one who
shows kindness; there is not even one. Their
throats are opened graves; they use their
tongues to deceive. The venom of vipers is
under their lips. Their mouths are full of curs-
ing and bitterness. Their feet are swift to shed
blood; ruin and misery are in their paths, and
the way of peace they have not known. There
is no fear of God before their eyes."

Now we know that, whatever the law says,
it speaks to those who are under the law, so
that every mouth may be silenced and the
whole world may be held accountable to
God. For no human will be justified before
him by deeds prescribed by the law, for
through the law comes the knowledge of sin.
(3:9b–20)

8. We could also opt for, "No, not in everything," or some such. This captures the
meaning of Paul's *ou pantōs* more accurately than the translation, "No, not at all."

9. The NRSVue is reading the force of this Greek verb under the influence of JT;
without JT it can apply—as it should—to the charges of sin that *follow*, as amassed in
Scripture.

Bibliography

Austin, J. L. *How to Do Things with Words*. Cambridge: Harvard University Press, 1962.

Barr, James. *The Semantics of Biblical Language*. Oxford: Oxford University Press, 1961.

Barth, Karl. *Church Dogmatics*. Edited by T. F. Torrance and G. W. Bromiley. 4 vols in 13 parts. Edinburgh: T. & T. Clark, 1956–77.

———. *The Epistle to the Romans*. Translated by Edwyn C. Hoskyn. London: Oxford University Press, 1968.

Bauckham, Richard. *Jesus and the God of Israel: God Crucified and Other Studies on the New Testament's Christology of Divine Identity*. Milton Keynes, UK: Paternoster, 2008.

Boyarin, Daniel. *A Radical Jew: Paul and the Politics of Identity*. Berkeley: University of California Press, 1994.

Brettler, Marc Zvi, and Amy-Jill Levine, eds. *The Jewish Annotated New Testament*. 2nd ed. Oxford: Oxford University Press, 2017.

Briggs, Asa. *The Age of Improvement, 1783–1867*. 2nd ed. London: Routledge, 2000.

Bultmann, Rudolf. *Theology of the New Testament*. Translated by Kendrick Grobel. Baylor: Baylor University Press, 2007.

Byrne, Brendan. *Romans*. Sacra Pagina. Collegeville, MN: Liturgical, 2007.

Campbell, Douglas A. *The Deliverance of God: An Apocalyptic Rereading of Justification in Paul*. Grand Rapids: Eerdmans, 2009.

———. "The Faithfulness of Jesus Christ in Romans 3:22." In *The Faith of Jesus Christ: Exegetical, Biblical, and Theological Studies*, edited by Michael Bird and Preston Sprinkle, 57–71. Milton Keynes, UK: Paternoster, 2009.

———. *Framing Paul: An Epistolary Biography*. Grand Rapids: Eerdmans, 2014.

———. *Paul: An Apostle's Journey*. Grand Rapids: Eerdmans, 2018.

———. *Pauline Dogmatics: The Triumph of God's Love*. Grand Rapids: Eerdmans, 2020.

Carson, D. A., and Douglas J. Moo. *An Introduction to the New Testament*. Grand Rapids: Zondervan, 2005.

Cranfield, C. E. B. *A Critical and Exegetical Commentary on the Epistle to the Romans*. Vol. 1, *Introduction and Commentary on Romans I–VII*. International Critical Commentary. 2 vols. Edinburgh: T. & T. Clark, 2004.

———. *Romans: A Shorter Commentary*. Grand Rapids: Eerdmans, 1985.

Davies, W. D. *Paul and Rabbinic Judaism: Some Rabbinic Elements in Pauline Theology*. 4th ed. London: SCM, 1980.

Dunn, James D. G. *Romans 1–8*. Word Biblical Commentary 38A. Dallas, TX: Word, 1988.

Ehrman, Bart D. *The New Testament: A Historical Introduction to the Early Christian Writings*. 6th ed. Oxford: Oxford University Press, 2016.

Esler, Philip P. *Conflict and Identity in Romans: The Social Setting of Paul's Letter*. Minneapolis, MN: Fortress, 2003.

Fitzmyer, Joseph A. *Romans: A New Translation with Introduction and Commentary*. The Anchor Bible. New Haven, CT: Yale University Press, 2007.

Gadamer, Hans-Georg. *Hermeneutik*. Vol. 1, *Wahrheit und Methode: Grundzüge einer philosophischen Hermeneutik*. 6th ed. Tübingen: Mohr Siebeck, 1990.

———. *Truth and Method*. 2nd rev. ed. Translated by J. Weinsheimer and D. G. Marshall. London: Sheed & Ward, 1989.

Gathercole, Simon. *Defending Substitution: An Essay on Atonement in Paul*. Grand Rapids: Baker Academic, 2015.

Grasso, Kevin. "A Linguistic Analysis of πίστις Χριστοῦ: The Case for the Third View." *JSNT* 43 (2020) 108–44.

Grondin, Jean. *The Philosophy of Gadamer*. Translated by Kathryn Plant. London: Routledge, 2003.

Hauerwas, Stanley. "Seeing Darkness, Hearing Silence: Augustine's Account of Evil." In *Working with Words*, 8–32. Eugene, OR: Cascade, 2011.

Hays, Richard B. *The Faith of Jesus Christ: The Narrative Substructure of Galatians 3:1—4:11*. 2nd ed. Grand Rapids: Eerdmans, 2002.

Headlam, Arthur C., and William Sanday. *A Critical and Exegetical Commentary on the Epistle to the Romans*. International Critical Commentary. 2nd ed. Edinburgh: T. & T. Clark, 1902.

Holladay, Carl R. *A Critical Introduction to the New Testament*. Nashville, TN: Abingdon, 2005.

Hooker, Morna D. "ΠΙΣΤΙΣ ΧΡΙΣΤΟΥ." *New Testament Studies* 35 (1989) 321–42.

Hurtado, Larry W. *One God, One Lord: Early Christian Devotion and Ancient Jewish Monotheism*. 2nd ed. London: T. & T. Clark, 1998.

Jennings, Willie James. *The Christian Imagination: Theology and the Origins of Race*. New Haven, CT: Yale University Press, 2010.

Jewett, Robert, and Roy D. Kotansky. *Romans: A Commentary*. Hermeneia. Minneapolis, MN: Fortress, 2007.

Käsemann, Ernst. *Commentary on Romans*. Translated by Geoffrey W. Bromiley. Grand Rapids: Eerdmans, 1994.

Keck, Leander E. *Romans*. Abingdon New Testament Commentaries. Nashville, TN: Abingdon, 2005.

Keener, Craig S. *Romans: A New Covenant Commentary*. Eugene, OR: Cascade, 2009.

Lewis, C. S. *Mere Christianity*. The Complete C. S. Lewis Signature Classics. San Francisco, CA: HarperOne, 2002.

Longenecker, Richard N. *Biblical Exegesis in the Apostolic Period*. 2nd ed. Grand Rapids: Eerdmans, 1999.

———. *Paul, Apostle of Liberty*. 2nd ed. Grand Rapids: Eerdmans, 2015.

MacFarquhar, Larissa. "Living in Adoption's Emotional Aftermath." *New Yorker*, April 10, 2023. https://www.newyorker.com/magazine/2023/04/10/living-in-adoptions-emotional-aftermath.

MacIntyre, Alasdair. *Whose Justice? Which Rationality?* Notre Dame, IN: University of Notre Dame Press, 1989.

Martyn, J. Louis. *Galatians*. New Haven, CT: Yale University Press, 1997.

Matson, David Lertis. "Divine Forgiveness in Paul? Justification by Faith and the Logic of Pauline Soteriology." *Stone-Campbell Journal* 19 (2016) 59–83.

Moo, Douglas J. *The Epistle to the Romans*. New International Commentary on the New Testament. Grand Rapids: Eerdmans, 1996.

Moore, George Foot. "Christian Writers on Judaism." *Harvard Theological Review* 14 (1921) 197–254.

Novenson, Matthew V. *Christ among the Messiahs: Christ Language in Paul and Messiah Language in Ancient Judaism*. Oxford: Oxford University Press, 2012.

———. *The Grammar of Messianism: An Ancient Jewish Political Idiom and Its Users*. Oxford: Oxford University Press, 2017.

Piper, John. *The Future of Justification: A Response to N. T. Wright*. Wheaton, IL: Crossway, 2007.

Powell, Mark Allan. *Introducing The New Testament: A Historical, Literary, and Theological Survey*. 2nd ed. Grand Rapids: Baker Academic, 2018.

Ridderbos, Herman. *Paul: An Outline of His Theology*. Grand Rapids: Eerdmans, 1975.

Rillera, Andrew. *Lamb of the Free: Recovering the Varied Sacrificial Understandings of Jesus's Death as a Sacrifice*. Eugene, OR: Cascade, 2023.

———. "Paul's Philonic Opponent: Unveiling the One Who Calls Himself a Jew in Romans 2:17." PhD diss., Duke University, 2021. https://hdl.handle.net/10161/23818.

Ruether, Rosemary Radford. *Faith and Fratricide: The Theological Roots of Anti-Semitism*. 1974. Reprint, Eugene, OR: Wipf & Stock, 1997.

Sandel, Michael. *Justice: What's the Right Thing to Do?* New York: Farrar, Strauss and Giroux, 2009.

Sanders, E. P. *Judaism: Practice and Belief 63 BCE–66 CE*. London: SCM, 1992.

———. *Paul and Palestinian Judaism*. Philadelphia: Fortress, 1977.

———. *Paul, the Law, and the Jewish People*. Philadelphia: Fortress, 1983.

Schlatter, Adolf. *Romans: The Righteousness of God*. Translated by Siegfried S. Schatzmann. Peabody, MA: Hendrickson, 1991.

Schreiner, Thomas R. "Paul: A Reformed Reading." In *Four Views on the Apostle Paul*, edited by Stanley N. Gundry and Michael F. Bird, 19–47. Grand Rapids: Zondervan, 2012.

———. "Penal Substitution View." In *The Nature of the Atonement: Four Views*, edited by James Beilby and Paul R. Eddy, 67–116. Downers Grove, IL: IVP Academic, 2009.

———. *Romans*. Baker Exegetical Commentary on the New Testament. Grand Rapids: Baker, 1998.

Schweitzer, Albert. *The Mysticism of Paul the Apostle*. Translated by W. Montgomery. Reprint, Baltimore, MD: Johns Hopkins University Press, 1998.

Searle, John R. *Speech Acts: An Essay in the Philosophy of Language*. London: Cambridge University Press, 1969.

Seifrid, Mark A. *Christ, Our Righteousness: Paul's Theology of Justification*. New Studies in Biblical Theology. Downers Grove, IL: IVP Academic, 2001.

———. "Paul's Turn to Christ in Romans." *Concordia Journal* 44 (2018) 15–24.

Steinmetz, David C. *Luther in Context*. 2nd ed. Grand Rapids: Baker, 2002.

———. *Reformers in the Wings: From Geiler von Kaysersberg to Theodore Beza*. 2nd ed. Oxford: Oxford University Press, 2001.

Tamez, Elsa. *The Amnesty of Grace: Justification by Faith from a Latin American Perspective*. Translated by Sharon H. Ringe. Eugene, OR: Wipf & Stock, 2002.

Tilling, Chris, ed. *Beyond Old and New Perspectives on Paul*. Eugene, OR: Cascade, 2014.

———. *Paul's Divine Christology*. Grand Rapids: Eerdmans, 2015.

Torrance, James B. "The Contribution of Mcleod Campbell to Scottish Theology." *Scottish Journal of Theology* 26 (1973) 295–311.

———. "Covenant or Contract? A Study of the Theological Background of Worship in Seventeenth-Century Scotland." *Scottish Journal of Theology* 23 (1970) 51–76.

Torrance, T. F. *Space, Time, and Resurrection*. Edinburgh: Hansel, 1976.

van Driel, Edwin Chr. *Rethinking Paul: Protestant Theology and Pauline Exegesis*. Cambridge: Cambridge University Press, 2021.

Westerholm, Stephen. "Justification by Faith Is the Answer: What Is the Question?" *Concordia Theological Quarterly* 70 (2006) 197–217.

———. *Justification Reconsidered: A Pauline Theme*. Grand Rapids: Eerdmans, 2013.

———. "The 'New Perspective' at Twenty-Five." In *Justification and Variegated Nomism*, Vol. 2, *The Paradoxes of Paul*, edited by D. A. Carson et al., 1–38. Grand Rapids: Baker Academic, 2004.

Wilkens, Ulrich. *Der Brief an die Römer*. Vol. 1, *Römer 1 to 5*. 3 vols. Zürich: Bensiger & Neukirchener, 1978.

Williams, Jarvis J. "Violent Atonement in Romans: The Foundation of Paul's Soteriology." *Journal of the Evangelical Theological Society* 53 (2010) 579–99.

Witherington, Ben. *Paul's Letter to the Romans: A Socio-Rhetorical Commentary*. Grand Rapids: Eerdmans, 2004.

Witt, William G. "Anglican Reflections on Justification by Faith." *Anglican Theological Review* 95 (2013) 57–80.

Wright, N. T. "4QMMT and Paul: Justification, 'Works,' and Eschatology" (2006). In *Pauline Perspectives: Essays on Paul, 1978–2013*, 332–55. Minneapolis, MN: Fortress, 2013.

———. *The Climax of the Covenant: Christ and the Law in Pauline Theology*. Edinburgh: T. & T. Clark, 1991.

———. *Galatians*. Grand Rapids: Eerdmans, 2021.

———. "Jesus Christ Is Lord: Philippians 2.5–11." In *Climax of the Covenant*, 56–98. Minneapolis, MN: Fortress Augsburg, 1992.

———. *Justification: God's Plan and Paul's Vision*. Downers Grove, IL: IVP Academic, 2009.

———. "The Law in Romans 2" (1996). In *Pauline Perspectives: Essays on Paul, 1978–2013*, 134–51. Minneapolis, MN: Fortress, 2013.

———. "The Letter to the Romans. Introduction, Commentary, and Reflections." In *The New Interpreter's Bible*, vol. 10, edited by L. Keck, 393–770. Nashville, TN: Abingdon, 2002.

———. "The Messiah and the People of God: A Study in Pauline Theology with Particular Reference to the Argument of the Epistle to the Romans" DPhil diss., Oxford University, Oxford, 1980.

———. *The New Testament and the People of God*. Christian Origins and the Question of God, vol. 1. London: SPCK, 1992.

———. *Paul: In Fresh Perspective*. London: SPCK, 2005.

———. *Paul and His Recent Interpreters: Some Contemporary Debates*. Minneapolis, MN: Fortress, 2015.

————. *Paul and the Faithfulness of God*. 2 vols. Christian Origins and the Question of God, vol. 4. London: SPCK, 2013.

————. *Pauline Perspectives: Essays on Paul, 1978–2013*. Minneapolis, MN: Fortress, 2013.

————. *The Resurrection of the Son of God*. Christian Origins and the Question of God, vol 3. London: SPCK, 2003.

Author Index

Augustine, of Hippo, Saint, 256
Austin, J.L., 218

Barth, Karl, 3, 25, 30n12, 79–80, 171

Calvin, John, 56, 60
Campbell, Douglas A., 26n4, 182n6,
    188n1, 226n12, 227n1

Dunn, J. D. G., xxi, 114–29, 135, 139,
    141–43, 151, 269

Gadamer, Hans-Georg, 44, 156

Hauerwas, Stanley, 30n12
Hays, Richard, 146
Hegel, G. W. F., 127

Josephus, Flavius, 102

Kant, Immanuel, 256
Kingsbury, Jack, 114

Lewis, C. S., 34
Luther, Martin, 56, 59, 62, 206, 219

Martyn, J. L., 162, 270
Melanchthon, Philip, xx, xxi, 59–63, 70,
    136, 144

Novenson, Matthew, 145

Philo, 102, 183
Plato, 170, 179
Piper, John, xix, 45–58, 62, 67, 74, 77,
    83, 94, 95, 121, 131, 145–46,
    156, 203

Sanders, E. P., xx, 101–14, 120–22,
    127–29, 149–51
Schweitzer, Albert, 42, 111, 150
Searle, John, 218
Socrates, 170, 179

Tamez, Elsa, 221
Tolkien, J. R. R., 11
Torrance, J. B., 63n6
Torrance, T. F., 40n26

Wright, N. T., xxi, 46, 55, 114–15, 130–
    48, 151, 156, 201, 269

Subject Index

Scripture Index